THE STORY OF FILM

THE STORY OF FILM

Mark Cousins

THUNDER'S MOUTH PRESS
NEW YORK

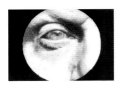

DIGITAL

1
Above: Steven Spielberg
(far right) directing the
Omaha Beach D-day
sequence in *Saving Private
Ryan*. USA, 1998.

INTRODUCTION

INTRODUCTION

The measure of an artist's originality, put in its simplest terms, is the extent to which his selective emphasis deviates from the conventional norm and establishes new standards of relevance. All great innovations which inaugurate a new era, movement or school, consist in sudden shifts of a previously neglected aspect of experience, some blacked out range of the existential spectrum. The decisive turning points in the history of every art form ... uncover what has already been there; they are "revolutionary", that is destructive and constructive, they compel us to revalue our values and impose new sets of rules on the eternal game.

Arthur Koestler[1]

The industry is shit, it's the medium that's great.

Lauren Bacall[2]

This book tells the story of the art of cinema. It narrates the history of a medium which began as a photographic, largely silent, shadowy novelty and became a digital, multi-billion-dollar global business.

Although the business elements of film are important, you will find few details in what follows of what films cost and how the industry organizes itself and markets its wares. I wanted to write a purer book than that, one more focused on the medium than the industry. As you read, therefore, you will come across works that you may not have seen and may never see. I make no apology for this because I do not want to tell a history of cinema that is distorted by the vagaries of the market-place. There are mainstream films described in what follows, but mostly I have focused on what I consider to be the most innovative films from any country at any period.

This could be seen as elitist or self-indulgent, but it isn't. Film is one of the most accessible art forms so even its most obscure productions can be understood by an intelligent non-specialist, which I assume you are. When I first read books about Orson Welles and François Truffaut, long before I saw their films, I experienced a real sense of discovery. I do not go into great detail about individual movies in *The Story of Film*, but I hope that what follows conjures similar pictures in your head, and creates a desire to see some of what is discussed.

You will almost certainly find that some of your favourite films are not featured in this story. Many of mine aren't. I have probably watched Billy Wilder's *The Apartment* (USA, 1960) more than any other film – the scene where Shirley Maclaine runs down the street at the end is one of the most beautiful things I have ever seen – but have not included it in this book. This is because, despite its exquisite tonality, it was less innovative than other films made in America at that time and before. Its adroit blend of irony and sexual comedy derives from Wilder's hero, the great director Ernst Lubitsch, for example. The movie's depiction of office life uses visual ideas from King Vidor's *The Crowd* (see page 88). And Wilder's admiration for the way Charlie Chaplin's films flicker between farce and rapture filters into his depiction of the characters. By focusing on the innovative rather than the merely beautiful, popular or commercially successful, I am trying to strip the world of movies down to its engine. Innovation drives art and I have tried in the chapters that follow to reveal key innovative moments in the history of world cinema. Without the mould-breakers, the fresh thinkers, the radicals and mavericks in cinema – without Lubitsch, Vidor and Chaplin – there would be no Billy Wilder directing Shirley Maclaine running down that street.

To pick up on the quotations at the beginning of this introduction, this book is, then, about *the greatness of the medium* of film and the *sudden shifts* that it has undergone. Take Steven Spielberg's *Saving Private Ryan* (USA, 1998) which was hugely popular, selling eighty million tickets around the world and finding larger audiences still on television, videotape or Digital Video Disk (DVD). Yet such popularity does not mean that it deviated from the conventional norm, as Koestler envisaged, or that it rose above Bacall's "shitty" industrial compromises. Instead, it warrants mention because of its shocking opening flashback sequence which showed what it was like to be a soldier landing on Omaha Beach (1) on one of the most important days of the Second World War. These events had been portrayed before in cinema but their impact here came from a shift in the language of film itself. Drills were mounted to cameras to give a juddering effect. The stock was exposed in new ways. The sound of bullets was more vividly recreated than ever before. Steven Spielberg sat at home or lay awake or drove through the desert, asking himself the question, how can I do this differently? The best filmmakers have always asked themselves this, on the set in the morning, at night when they can't sleep, in the bar with their friends, or at film festivals. It is a crucial question for the art of cinema and this book describes how directors have answered it.

The best composers, actors, writers, designers, producers, editors and cinematographers ask it too, but *The Story of Film* concentrates mostly on the central creative figure in filmmaking. This is not because directors should take credit for everything we see and hear on screen – many films are great because of their actors, writers, producers or editors – but because directors are the people who pull the creative bits together and who oversee that alchemy whereby the words of the screenplay come alive. The French term *realisateur* – realizer – describes this process well, and what follows is an account of how filmic ideas are realized.

Realizing is, I believe, the root of the medium's greatness. The ability of a shot to be about both what it objectively photographs – what is in front of the camera – and about the subjectivity of its maker explains the alluring dualism at the heart of cinema. Music, being less representational than film, is purer and more evocative; novels can more adroitly describe mental processes; painting is more directly expressive; poetry, far less unwieldy. Yet none of these are made quite so ambivalently as cinema. The Italian filmmaker Pier Paolo Pasolini tried to describe this personal-realistic dualism in his term "free indirect subjectivity" – *discorso libro indiretto*[3] – and a phrase in French philosophy – fourth person singular[4] – captures well the paradox of something which is personal but also objective and without consciousness.

The greatest directors – the ones described in this volume – are driven by this paradox, but the process by which, and the reasons why, they form ideas are diverse. Federico Fellini says that another man whom he doesn't know makes his films, and that that man tunes into Fellini's own dreams. David Lynch claims that ideas "pop from the ether". Neither of these are precise ways of describing things, but, as an example I will mention in the conclusion of this book shows (the one about the gorilla, if you want to flick forward) "nowhere" is where some of the best ideas originate. The creativity of other

2
Above: How directors learn from each other: Carol Reed has a visual idea (top), Jean-Luc Godard adapts it (middle) and Martin Scorsese modifies it still further (bottom).

filmmakers featured in the following chapters can be described in more conventional terms: Djibril Diop Mambety from Senegal was angry at colonialism and inspired by French cinema; Martin Scorsese's rich Italian-American childhood fuelled his imagination; Bernardo Bertolucci drew from his poet father, from the composer Verdi, and from great literature and cinema; Shohei Imamura in Japan was a kind of anarchist who hated the politeness of Japanese culture and movies; Billy Wilder in America did limbering-up writing exercises each morning by imagining more and more original ways in which a young couple could meet for the first time; the mental tensions of the early years of Polish director Roman Polanski were replicated in most of his film work; Spielberg wanted to do things differently because of his imaginative drive, because audiences will pay for something new, because he is bored with the norms of film-making, perhaps, and because he can see beyond them, because of new technical possibilities and because he wanted curiosity to teach young filmgoers how brave their grandfathers were.

Whatever their ways of dreaming up ideas, filmmakers seldom do so in isolation. They watch each other's work and learn how to tackle scenes from what has gone before, and from their collaborators, as the images on this page show (2). The first is from the 1946 British movie *Odd Man Out*. A character is undergoing a crisis and sees moments from his recent experiences reflected in the bubbles of a spilled drink. Director Carol Reed and his team asked how they could portray such a crisis in an imaginative new way and came up with this solution. The second image, made twenty years later, comes from the French film *Deux au trois choses que je sais d'elle/Two of Three Things I know About Her* (1967). Again a close-up of bubbles in a drink represents the point of view of the main character of the film, played by actress Marina Vlady. The film's director, Jean-Luc Godard, knew and admired Carol Reed's work, so it is likely that he was thinking of *Odd Man Out* when we filmed his version, though cinema had changed since Reed's day and Godard's use of the image is more intellectual than his predecessor's. Now consider the third image, from Martin Scorsese's American film *Taxi Driver* (1976). Again, a cup full of bubbles, again seen from the point of view of the main character. Scorsese knew Godard's film, saw how well the image worked and adapted it for his own purpose, to express his character's subjectivity and psychosis. This is cinematic influence, the passing of stylistic ideas from one filmmaker to the next.

The process is more complex than this simple example suggests. Thinkers and art historians have long discussed it. The American critic Harold Bloom wrote a book in 1973, *The Anxiety of Influence*, which touched on the negative feelings artists can have about their forebears. The German philosopher Georg Hegel argued that art is a kind of language, a dialogue between the artwork and its audience. Later, Heinrich Wofflin extended Hegel's thoughts to argue that the language of art is the result of the ideas and technologies of its time. John Ruskin shifted focus by saying that art has a moral obligation to society. More recently, scientist Richard Dawkins in his famous book *The Selfish Gene* changed the terms of the debate again, comparing art neither to a language which evolves through one artist influencing another nor to a moral system, but to genetics. Just as biological units are genes, so the units of art and culture are "memes", wrote Dawkins. Just as genes replicate and evolve, so do memes. Carol Reed's close-up of bubbles in a drink is a meme that replicated and evolved through Godard and Scorsese. Occasionally memes take off, as when everyone is suddenly singing a catchy pop song, or when many of the films made in the mid-1990s in the West seemed to be versions of American director Quentin Tarantino's *Reservoir Dogs* (1991) or *Pulp Fiction* (1993).

It is helpful to imagine cinema evolving as a language or replicating like genes because doing so illustrates that film has a grammar and that in some ways it grows and mutates. However, there are problems in applying the ideas of Hegel, Wofflin, Ruskin, Dawkins and others to the study of film. The first is that they seem to imply that art – and therefore cinema – is always advancing, getting more complex, building on the past. Good film historians know that this isn't true, and one of the arguments in this book will be that the frontal "technical thrill" of pre-industrial cinema, described in Chapter One, resurfaced in later years. It did not die out in favour of more complex filmic mutations.

The second reservation is more pragmatic. Film can be many things and shouldn't be reduced to an essence, whether that is moral – as Ruskin argued about painting – or linguistic – as Hegel argued about art in general. There were epochs when cinema did indeed reflect the great moral issues of its day, such as in Europe after the Second World War, but in France in the 1920s film's technical and formal qualities were to the fore; in Japan in the 1930s, spatial concerns were central to some directors; and in the works of the Russians Andrei Tarkovsky and Alexander Sokurov, the spiritual and religious aspects were what counted. These differences are not a matter of content – what was in front of the lens or what the story is about – but of what film actually is and what role it plays in human life.

A more useful model for understanding the nature of filmic influence can be found in the work of E.H. Gombrich who wrote in his introduction to *The Story of Art*, "There really is no such thing as Art, there are only artists." This single-volume account of the history of painting, architecture and sculpture asked the questions: What techniques were available to the artists of any period? How did they use and expand those techniques? How did art evolve as a result? This volume asks: What would happen if we did the same for movies? What if we consider that there is no such thing as Film, there are only filmmakers? Who are Griffith, Dovzhenko, Keaton, Ozu, Riefenstahl, Ford, Toland, Welles, Bergman, Truffaut, Ouedraogo, Cissé, Dulac, Chahine, Imamura, Fassbinder, Akerman, Scorsese, Almodóvar, Makhmalbaf, Spielberg, Tarr and Sokurov? What techniques did they have available to them? How did they use and expand those techniques? How did they change the medium of film?

Gombrich's argument was that artistic influence is a matter of "schema plus correction", but I would prefer the word "variation". His point is that for an art form to evolve, original images can't always be copied slavishly. They should be adjusted according to new technical possibilities, changing storytelling fashions, political ideas, emotional trends, etc. This is what I will have in mind when I trace the lines of influence throughout this book. If film A is very original, if it successfully varies the schema a great deal (as, say, David Lynch's *Blue Velvet* did in 1986) then films C, D, E and F will show the mark of that influence. I will write about A and mention the others. If, however, film E takes A's ideas and twists them again in yet another direction, influencing G, H, I and J, then I will write about A and E.

Some conventional historians will object that the model of schema plus variation is of limited use to the understanding of the art form of film which – unlike painting – is so driven by technological change. Why look at how directors have copied and varied each other's shots and visual ideas when the means of achieving such ideas have regularly been upgraded through the introduction of sound, widescreen, new film stock, camera craning methods and digitization? This is simply wrong. Look at Scorsese using schema from the 1900s in the 1990s (see page 448) or Von Trier in the same decade looking back to Dreyer in the 1920s and 1940s, or the resemblance between the "washing line" staging in CinemaScope of the 1950s and tableau films of the 1910s. Yes, technology has been a key element in the changing creative possibilities available to filmmakers, but deep down the questions of staging, point of view, pace, suspense, time and psychology faced by filmmakers as they walk onto the set in the morning have remained remarkably consistent. That's why schema plus variation works. It is for this reason that some of the most distinguished film scholars have suggested that it should be applied to film history[5].

Some circumstances are not covered by the Gombrich model, however. This book is about the films which were influential, but will also describe films which should have been influential. Famous works like *Citizen Kane* (1941) from America, *The Seven Samurai* (1954) from Japan, *Mother India* (1957) from India and *Battleship Potemkin* (1925) from the former Soviet Union fall into the former category. They were schema that other filmmakers varied. This can be proved. What, though, of the great, original films which seem not to have had an impact on successive filmmakers, because they were made in Africa, or poorly distributed, or flopped at the box office, or were directed by a woman, or were misunderstood or banned? Djibril Diop Mambety's Senegalese film *Touki Bouki* (1973) was the most innovative African movie of its time, but not widely distributed, even within its own continent. Dorota Kedzierzawska's Polish film *Wrony/Crows* (1995) is one of the most beautiful films about childhood, but was hardly seen. Kira Muratova made *Dolgie*

provody/Long Goodbye (Soviet Union), about a divorcé and his son, in 1971, but her brilliant and original work was not released in the Soviet Union until 1986. Are these films to be ignored because they failed to have impact? No. All good stories have ironies and these films add bitterness to our tale.

One should be cautious, too, about applying an individualistic notion of artistic creativity to places where it does not pertain. A Hindu director doesn't have the same conception of her or himself as an individual as Scorsese does. There isn't the same drive to articulate a distinctive point of view, so the factors that applied to Spielberg might not do so in South Asia. Also, Indian storytelling is more free-form than that in Western countries, and isn't so confined by space and time. Likewise, in African storytelling, the idea that an artist is an originator or a varier, is not strong. To vary is to wreck. A great story-teller builds and transmits. Nor was artistic originality an important motive in Japan, at least during the first half of the twentieth century. As in much of Africa, a great Japanese artist was one who subtly reworked tradition, recasting it in a new light.

Despite these qualifications, the intention has been to write an accessible, low-jargon movie history for general readers and those who are beginning to study film, the sort of book that I wanted to read when I was sixteen. As the title suggests, it is a narrative account, not a dictionary or encyclopaedia. Film theorists are suspicious of such attempts to see the history of the movies in story terms, as if doing so is trying to shoe-horn it into a formula. This is to under-estimate narrative, which can be as fluid, multi-layered and responsive to subject as a writer wants it to be. So *The Story of Film* intends to open a door to the world of cinema and describe a reliable path through it. If successful, the reader will advance to more detailed or learned volumes, such as Thompson and Bordwell's or Robert Sklar's.

In these writers' books they will find directors absent here: Catherine Breillat, Jonathan Demme, Abel Ferrara, Amos Gitai, Marcel L'Herbier, Neil Jordan, Ermanno Olmi, Bob Rafaelson, Jacques Rivette, Eric Rohmer, George A. Romero, Hans Jurgen Syberberg and others. Each has produced significant work but in a manuscript of this length, I could not find space for them. Many will dispute my emphases, suggesting perhaps that France's Rohmer deserves space over Ethiopa's Haile Gerima. It is crucial, however, to record East Africa's contribution to film ideas, and France, overall, gets its dues.

This raises two questions: how revisionist is *The Story of Film?* And what new points does it make? Revisionism for its own sake is not interesting – and presumptuous when it challenges primary research – so that has not been the impulse. However, it has been necessary to make several adjustments to received opinion:

Firstly – as the Ethiopian example has just demonstrated – this book is unashamably about world, not Western, cinema. Not in the spirit of tokenism, but to acknowledge that the Egyptian films of Youssef Chahine, for example, are unique because they engage with national and religious ideas, which have not been concerns of Western directors. Non-Western cinema is undervalued in film books, festivals, retrospectives, TV programmes, magazine polls, entertainment journalism and the like – a situation that damages the medium.

The second adjustment, in Chapter Three, is that the standard approach of mainstream Hollywood is essentially romantic rather than classical. Again and again in film books the phrase "classic American cinema" or "the classic period of American filmmaking" is used, as if "classical" means popular heyday or lucrative golden age, which it emphatically does not. Classicism in art describes a period when form and content are in harmony, when there is balance

5
Far right: A vivid example
of pre-cinema: *Leeds
Bridge* by Louis Le Prince.
UK, 1888.

between the style of a work and the emotions or ideas it is trying to express. American films are mostly given to excess rather than balance – their characters are emotional, their stories express yearning – so the lengthy but more precise phrase "closed romantic realism" is used to describe normative film style. This is new and the implications are considerable. In Chapter Four I propose that the films of Japanese master director Yasujiro Ozu are the true works of filmic classicism. This will cause some raised eyebrows, but my model is, I believe, more valuable than the previous one which used the word "classical" incorrectly.

Thirdly, it is proposed that far from being a fallow time for cinema, filmmaking from 1990s has undergone an unparalleled revival.

The structure of what follows is chronological and divided into three main epochs, Silent (1895–1928), Sound (1928–1990) and Digital (1990–present). While there have been many changes in the course of film history, those in 1928 and 1990 had the greatest impact. Within these epochs, chapters deal with various trends. American cinema will be discussed in all ten chapters in this book, because it has been active almost from the start. Native African cinema, by contrast, did not begin until the late 1950s, so will not become part of the story until then. If the work of a certain country or continent is not mentioned in a chapter, it is not being overlooked: either it was producing no films during the period covered or those that were being made were merely formulaic.

My Silent section looks at the thrill of early cinema, then how that thrill became narrative in the West and, finally, how movie factories dominated filmmaking after the First World War. Japanese film took another route through these years and this fundamental split is described. In the Sound epoch we look at the blossoming of Eastern cinema, Hollywood Romantic cinema, then the spread of realism. Two pairs of chapters follow: the first pair covers the great films of the East and the swelling and explosion of 1950s and 1960s cinema in the West. The second pair deals with the massive divergences in world film in the 1970s and 1980s. The last epoch, Digital, takes us up to the present day.

Finally, a confession: I have rewatched almost every film mentioned in this book. In some cases, however, that has not been possible. In these instances, I'm relying on memories of previous viewings. In addition, there are about forty films mentioned which I have never seen. Either prints of them no longer exist or

I have been unable to track them down. They are included because filmmakers or historians have made a case for their importance.

❋ ❋ ❋ ❋ ❋ ❋ ❋ ❋ ❋ ❋ ❋ ❋ ❋

The year is 1888. We are standing on a bridge in an industrial city in ... not France or America, where the first public screenings of projected films took place, but in Britain. The city is Leeds. A man is filming there ... his footage still exists. It was only ever shown in machines into which a single viewer looked, but predates the generally accepted birth of the movies in Paris in 1895 by seven years. To the right is what he shot:

1. Koestler, Arthur, *The Act of Creation*, London, Hutchinson, 1969.
2. Bacall, Lauren, *Scene by Scene*, BBC Television, 2000. Interview with the author.
3. Pasolini, Pier Paolo, *Heretical Empiricism*, Bloomington: IUP, 1988. Translated by Ben Lawton and Louise Barnett. It is Naomi Green in *Pier Paolo Pasolini: Cinema as Heresy*, Princeton: PUP, 1993 who provides this less literal but more precise translation of Pasolini's phrase.
4. Deleuze, Gilles, *The Logic of Sense*, London: Athlone, 1990. Translated by Mark Lester and Charles Stivale.
5. For example, Bordwell, David, *A Case for Cognitivism*, Iris Vol 9, Spring 1989, pp11–40.

SILENT

The short film, Leeds Bridge *(UK, 1888), was photographed by Louis Le Prince, a pioneering Frenchman in England. A horse-drawn tram moves slowly; we can just see two men, bottom right of the frame, looking down into the river* (5). *The first thing we notice is that it is silent. The majority of the films made in the first four decades had no recorded soundtrack. Why was this? The technology to record people talking was available, but the thrill of moving images excited the inventors and their audiences so much, that no-one said, "But these wonders are mute." As a result, "The Kingdom of Shadows" was more mysterious, fable-like and not of this earth. There were also practical implications. Absence of language barriers ensured that the birth of cinema was truly international and the films of the first decade were shown all over the world.*

6
Far right: Although silent, the first films had huge impact. *Battleship Potemkin,* Soviet Union, 1925.

7
Above: Stills of Fred Ott's
First Sneeze – a peep-show
Kinetoscope film, not yet
projectable, shot by W.K.L.
Dickson in Thomas
Edison's Black Maria
(overleaf).

TECHNICAL THRILL (1895—1903)
The sensations of the first movies

1

What was the world like in the late nineteenth century, just before the movies began? It was very different from today. The USA was still expanding. The Ottoman and Austro-Hungarian empires still existed. European empires governed three-quarters of the globe, with India as Britain's most important colony. The state of Israel did not exist, nor had Iraq gained independence. The creation of the Soviet Union was thirty years in the future.

The industrial revolution had transformed the way of life for Western city dwellers. Urban populations clustered together, yet people became more detached from what they consumed. Life became more kinetic. The steam train made travel faster. Rollercoasters, to which the cinema experience would be compared in the late twentieth century, had been around since 1884. Automobiles had just been invented and would evolve with cinema in fascinating tandem. While there was more visual stimulation in the West, its culture or human perception had not changed fundamentally, despite arguments to the latter. Photography had existed since 1827. People had painted for 150 centuries and would continue to do so. Scribes, poets and authors had written for at least fifty centuries.

Then, between them, a few French, British and American men took the lead in inventing what the Russian writer Leo Tolstoy called pointedly "the clicking machine … like a human hurricane".

This was a black box through which a ribbon moves, recording what it saw. Later, light was shone through this ribbon and the action was projected and repeated on a distant white wall, as if no time had passed. This repetition was possible because of a persistence of vision, via which the human brain perceives as continual motion a series of consecutive, rapidly projected, still images. The invention of this Western marvel was complicated, a kind of shambolic race. The runners were men with unfamiliar names: Thomas Edison, George Eastman, W.K.L. Dickson, Louis Le Prince, Louis and Auguste Lumière, R.W. Paul, George Méliès, Francis Doublier, G.A. Smith, William Friese Greene and Thomas Ince. As one edged forward, another took over and then a third sprinted past with a new invention. They worked in the sprawling state of New Jersey across the Hudson from Manhattan; in Lyons in western France; in sunny Le Ciotat on the Mediterranean; and in Brighton and Leeds in England. These locations were not flashy urban capitals, but glamourless working-class places.

Not one of these men solely invented cinema and there is no clear start date for its birth. In 1884, New York manufacturer George Eastman invented film on a roll rather than on individual slides. In the same decade, New Jersey inventor Thomas Edison, son of a timber merchant, and his assistant W.K.L. Dickson, discovered a way of spinning a series of still images in a box that gave the illusion of movement and invented the Kinetoscope.[1]

By the late 1880s, in England, Louis Le Prince, had patented a machine the size of a small refrigerator and filmed on Leeds Bridge and elsewhere. George Eastman came back into the race with a new idea: holes along the edge of the film roll that allowed it to be clawed accurately through the camera. The central problem tackled by these engineers, inventors and industrialists was that a strip

8
Above: Edison's Black Maria, the world's first studio designed to shoot moving images, which revolved to follow the light of the sun.

of film could not run continuously past an open lens in the camera. It had to stop, expose for a fraction of a second, then advance and repeat this staccato action: grab–expose–advance; grab–expose–advance. The Lumière brothers, who came from a family of photographers, noticed that sewing machines worked in a similar way and adapted the technology. They made the box smaller than Le Prince's huge camera, and reworked it, so that their Cinématographe could record and project images. A further problem was how to ensure that the whizzing jerkiness didn't snap the film. The simple solution was devised by the pioneering family of Woodville, Otway and Gray Latham in their otherwise unsuccessful Eidoloscope projector: a slack loop of film would be loaded into the camera and projector, allowing the film to act like a piece of elastic as it accelerated and stopped continuously without breaking. These details show that the invention of film wasn't a one-man effort. When it became clear that film was going to be a worldwide money-making phenomenon, many of these early pioneers tried to claim copyright for their contribution to the process. The rights battles were nasty and every bit of the process – even the sprocket holes and the loop – had legal claims made about them.

Of all the earliest films, it was those of the Lumière brothers which were the most widely seen. On 28 December 1895, a date many film historians consider the birth of cinema, they showed a short programme of their documentary films (and the fictional one *L'Arroseur arrosé*), to a paying audience in a room on the Boulevard des Capucines in Paris. These included a now famous single shot film called *L'Arrivée d'un train en gare de la Ciotat/ The Arrival of a Train at La Ciotat Station* (France) (9). The camera was placed near the track so the train gradually increased in size as it pulled in, until it seemed it would crash through the screen into the room itself. Audiences ducked, screamed or got up to leave. They were thrilled, as if on a roller-coaster ride.

The Lumière brothers dispatched films and projectionists to every continent with such speed that within one to two years audiences in most countries had seen the famous train in La Ciotat. Audiences in Italy (Turin) did so in 1886, as did those in Russia (St. Petersburg), Hungary (Budapest), Romania (Bucharest), Serbia (Belgrade), Denmark (Copenhagen), Canada (Montreal), India (Bombay), Czechoslovakia (Karlovy Vary), Uruguay (Montevideo), Argentina (Buenos Aires), Mexico (Mexico City),

Chile (Santiago), Guatemala (Guatemala City), Cuba (Havana), Japan (Osaka), Bulgaria (Russe), Thailand (Bangkok), and the Philippines (Manila). I repeat, these were all in 1886 and all Lumière films. British films were shown in 1896 in the USA and Germany alongside home-produced American and German films. By 1900 the Lumière films had reached audiences in Senegal (Dakar) and Iran, including the Shah in his mirrored Qajar Palace.

Films were considered a courtly novelty, a strutting peacock, rather than something for the masses.

A seventeen-year-old Lumière factory employee, Francis Doublier, was charged with taking films to Russia. Louis Lumière gave him a camera, but with stern instructions "to let neither kings nor beautiful women examine its mechanism".[2] Young Doublier presented the new Lumière films in Munich and Berlin, then travelled to Warsaw, St Petersburg and Moscow. On 18 May 1896, half a million Russians gathered just outside Moscow to see the newly crowned Tsar Nicholas II. The crowd became restive after waiting for some hours and stampeded when the rumour spread that the free beer being dispensed was about to run out. Doublier hand-cranked the camera, later saying, "We used up three [rolls] on the shrieking,

TECHNICAL THRILL (1895–1903): THE SENSATIONS OF THE FIRST MOVIES milling, dying mass around the Tsar's canopy."[3] Five thousand were rumoured to have died, but the Tsar later danced all night at the French Ambassador's ball.

The following month, Doublier and his colleagues showed Lumière footage in Moscow, but the tragic corona-tion film had been confiscated by the Russian authorities; censorship had begun. The train arrived at La Ciotat as it had done around the world and audiences were amazed. Writer Maxim Gorky was there. He called what he had seen "The kingdom of shadows".[4]

10
Above: In his film *The Kiss*, G.A. Smith filmed from the front of a moving train, an effect that became known as a "phantom ride".

English engineer Robert William Paul was a key figure in the formative years of cinema. He started making Edison and Lumière-style cameras in the mid-1890s. He sold the cameras rather than leasing them, which meant that British filmmakers felt freer to use the equipment. This may explain why the so-called Brighton School of early filmmakers was more innovative than their colleagues in France or America. The leading figure in the School was a portrait photographer called George Albert Smith, perhaps the most pioneering filmmaker of the earliest years. Mr Smith, as he became known, built his own camera while Doublier was heading eastward. In *The Corsican Brothers* (UK, 1898), Smith draped part of his set in black velvet, filmed a shot, rewound the film and then re-exposed the film to include the image of a ghost, which appeared to float through the original set.[5]

11
Above: How filmmakers like Smith achieved their phantom rides: cinematographer Billy Blitzer and his tripod-mounted camera on the front of a steam locomotive.

Smith was among the first to film action and then project it in reverse. In 1898, he shot what has since been called a "phantom ride" (10). This was a new visual experience for the audience achieved by putting the camera on the front of a moving train (11), as if it was a ghostly eye speeding through the air. In 1899 he combined this with a shot of a couple in a set modelled as a railway carriage. As they kissed the train went through a tunnel. Films with more than one shot started to emerge only in the late 1890s, and Smith's combination of interior and travelling shot was one of cinema's first attempts to say "Meanwhile".

12

Above: Alice Guy-Blaché (second from left), who directed 700 short films and established one of the first movie studios, Solax.

13

Below: Guy-Blaché's contemporary Georges Méliès combined painted theatrical imagery and trick effects to explore the magical and stylized possibilities of cinema. This still is dated 1897.

The phantom ride was more technically thrilling than the train arriving at La Ciotat. Imagery had never achieved this before, but it would become one of cinema's most effective ways of putting the audience in the place of a traveller. Its most commercial use to date has been in the "king of the world" sequence on the ship's bow in *Titanic* (USA, 1997) and its most profound use in the massive documentary, *Shoah* (France, 1985). In this account of the extermination of Jews in Nazi-occupied Europe the film's director, Claude Lanzmann, sometimes puts the camera on the front of the train as he travels along the same lines as the murdered Jews. The "ghost" on the train becomes all the dead of Treblinka and of the other concentration camps.

At the same time that R.W. Paul, G.A. Smith and others such as Cecil Hepworth and James A. Williamson were testing the creative boundaries of film in England, their near-contemporaries in France were Georges Méliès and the overlooked Alice Guy-Blaché (12).[6] Guy-Blaché started as a secretary to Léon Gaumont and directed perhaps the first ever scripted film, *The Cabbage Fairy/La Fée aux choux* (France, 1896), a comic fantasy about babies born in cabbage patches. Guy-Blaché experimented with sound, visual effects and even hand-painted directly onto film. Most of her subsequent films were biblical epics, and she created one of the first film studios, Solax, in New York State, where she had emigrated in 1907. In total she is thought to have directed as many as 700 short films, including Westerns and thrillers. [7]

Méliès' role in early cinema has not been overlooked. He started his career in illusionistic theatre, but became excited by the new medium, having seen the first public Lumière screening in December 1895. While filming in Paris, his camera jammed and,

a moment later, it started up again. When he viewed the printed result, he noticed that since no film was exposed during the jam, streetcars suddenly jumped forward and people disappeared. This discovery of another magical quality of film inspired him to make films like *The Moon at One Metre/la Lune à une metre* (France, 1896), in which we first see an observatory and then cut to a theatrical painting of the moon in close-up, as if we are looking through a telescope (13). Méliès was a great delver into cinema's magic box, turning the realist films of Lumière into theatrical fantasies.

Through accident and imagination, innovation and trial-and-error – our earliest example of Gombrich's schema plus variation – the potential of cinema was being discovered and pushed forward by risk-takers and inquisitive, visually talented people.

14
Above: Tally's Phonograph Parlour, a typical early cinema in Los Angeles, whose shop front nestled between a milliner and a hosiery store. The hoarding reads "See the great Corbett fight".

On the East coast of America, the now forgotten Enoch J. Rector extended film into another area: commerce, as the photograph of Tally's Phonograph Parlor (14) explains. Taken in Los Angeles in 1897, long before the city had become a centre for film production, it illustrates how cinema at this stage was a shop-front entertainment, vying with clothing stores on either side for the attention of

passers-by. The hoarding on the front of Tally's reads "See The Great Corbett Fight".[8] This boxing match was staged in Nevada, and filmed by Rector using a film format that would not become popular for nearly fifty years – widescreen. He invented a new camera for the process and named it a Veriscope. The film running through it was 63mm wide. Most other film of the time was 35mm.

This is the first example, to my knowledge, of filmmakers changing the shape of their canvas, as it were, to capture the visual spectacle of an event. There was very little editing at this stage, so Rector could not show his boxing match from multiple angles, as American director Martin Scorsese would do in his *Raging Bull* (USA, 1980). What makes *The Corbett-Fitzsimmons Fight* (USA, 1897) so interesting is that is helps reveal the changing social standing of cinema in America at that time. A local newspaper, *The Brooklyn Eye*, commented on its sheer spectacle, "The man who would have predicted ... that an event of the prior month would be reproduced before the eyes of a multitude in pictures that moved like life, and that lightning would move them and light them, would have been avoided as a lunatic or hanged as a wizard."[9] But film historian Terry Ramsaye's comments are even more interesting: the film brought "The odium of pugilism upon the screen ... all across Puritan America. Until that picture appeared, the social status of the screen had been uncertain. It now became definitively lowbrow, an entertainment of the great unwashed commonality."[10] French producers had identified the appeal of cinema to working-class audiences by this stage, but had also begun to make films for and market them to middle-class customers. One company, Film d'Art, would soon begin making highbrow theatre adaptations for the screen. In Scandinavia, Germany and India, film quickly took on literary and cultural ambitions. In the US, films like *The Corbett-Fitzsimmons Fight* (15) set off in a populist direction, which most follow to the present day. This explains the USA's eventual world domination of commercial cinema and its continuing reluctance to see film as art.

The end of the nineteenth century was a heady time for cinema. It was settling into the lives of people just as Tally's Phonographic Parlor nestled inbetween a milliner and a hosiery store. It was becoming a social ritual of the public but also the schema – the visual imagination – of budding filmmakers. Whether at Tally's or at the Shah's extravagant palace in Tehran, where the light of the projector beam must have scattered around those jewelled rooms like a glitter ball – cinema still had everything ahead of it. Socially, technically, politically, artistically, philosophically, transcendentally, nothing about it was yet pinned down. However, the storytellers and the industrialists would change this soon enough. The First World War would redefine the world and have a lasting impact on filmmaking, with the USA becoming the dominant force. But for now, filmmakers were still playing. They had discovered "shots" – a piece of visually recorded action extended roughly in real time. Today, the strangeness of a shot is muted by our familiarity with it.

And then, stranger still, cuts were introduced. What we are looking at suddenly disappears and is replaced by something different. Méliès realized the magic of this and by 1898 multi-shot – "edited" – films started to appear. The grammar, choreography, grace or poetry of cutting – what would or would not jar visually, giving meaning to this transition – was a little way ahead. The century would have to turn and another brainy, antsy character, Edwin S. Porter, would need to stumble through the possibilities of cutting and come out the other end with some rules or, rather, norms.

For now, though, the faltering steps and discoveries continued. In England, in 1899, R.W. Paul built the first of what would become the filmmaker's most sensuous tool, the camera dolly. This is a platform on wheels, on which a camera is mounted, so that it can move smoothly. In 1913 the Italians made *Cabiria* with dolly shots of such grace and frequency, that they prompted the expression "Cabiria movements", used to describe similar pieces of film in the US. The legendary American director David Wark Griffith bettered them in one of the most complex films of the silent period, *Intolerance* (USA, 1916). In 1924, Germany's master director, F.W. Murnau, would use a dolly shot to represent the flight of sound from a trumpet to the ear of a listener. Later still, in the expanding landscape of sound cinema, filmmakers like Max Ophüls, Stanley Donen, Orson Welles, Alfred Hitchcock, Kenji Mizoguchi, Guru Dutt, Andrei Tarkovsky, Miklós Jancsó, Bernardo Bertolucci, Chantal Akerman, Béla Tarr and Fred Kelemen would use dolly shots to express their story, their political, spiritual and philosophical ideas. Their sensual conception of film will be considered later. Together they created what Western art historians would call a "baroque" approach to shot construction: something elaborate and complete in itself.

The turn of the century ushered in more new things. Smith's *Let Me Dream Again* (UK, 1900) used what was perhaps the first example of a "focus pull" – a shot where a photographer twists the barrel of the lens to make the image go from sharp to soft focus. In it, Smith pulled a shot of a man kissing a beautiful woman out of focus, cut to another soft image, then pulled it into focus to reveal the same man kissing his less attractive wife. A cheap joke, perhaps, but such techniques would be used from then onwards to indicate a dream state or heightened desire. In the same year, Smith was first with yet another cinematic innovation. In 1894, W.K.L. Dickson had photographed Fred Ott sneezing in a head and shoulders shot (7), but one of the first true close-ups in cinema appeared in Smith's *Grandma's Reading Glasses* (UK, 1900) (16). We know of this film only from a catalogue listing which says that a grandson uses the lady's glasses to see objects "in enormously enlarged form". Would human beings ever have seen such huge images before? In ancient Greece, Egypt and Persia there were vast sculptures, and Italian religious art of the Renaissance some-times featured massive depictions of biblical figures, but it was not until the close-up was used that such enlargement becomes frequent.

Grandma's Reading Glasses does not provide a pure example of a close-up. As with images taken through keyholes and telescopes

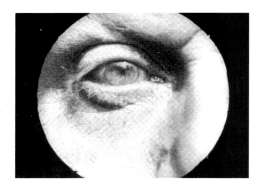

16
Above: The earliest close-ups in film tended to be motivated by onscreen characters looking through keyholes or spectacles, such as this one in G.A. Smith's *Grandma's Reading Glasses*. UK, 1900.

in early cinema, using reading glasses to explain why an image is so big is only a tentative first step in the selective enlargement of film imagery. The first close-up not involving characters looking through things, whose sole function was to show the audience an element of the story in more detail, was in the work of Mr Smith once again. In 1901 he made *The Little Doctor* (UK), which is now lost but which was remade two years later as *The Sick Kitten* (UK, 1903). In this we first see a room, two children and a cat (17), the master shot. Smith cuts to a close-up of the kitten as it is given a spoonful of medicine. No-one is looking through a telescope, yet Smith simply decided that it would be clearer and more enjoyable for the audience to see this action bigger and in more detail. Filmmakers at the time worried that cutting suddenly into a detail like this would jar an audience accustomed, in the theatre, to being at a constant distance from the action. Smith showed that this was not the case. Cinema was not theatre, the link between the two was broken, and the emphasis and intimacy of cinema was born. After this, many of international cinema's most memorable images were close-ups: the participants in the drama of *Battleship Potemkin* (Soviet Union, 1925) (18), Maria Falconetti in *The Passion of Joan of Arc* (France, 1928), Elizabeth Taylor and Montgomery Clift in *A Place in the Sun* (USA, 1951), Nargis in *Mother India* (India, 1957), Liv Ullmann and Bibi Andersson in *Persona* (Sweden, 1966) and the cowboys in *Once Upon a Time in the West* (Italy, 1969) (19). In each case, these contained close-up images of actors' faces. They became giants in the foreground. Out of such imagery grew movie stars and the devotional, psychological aspect of cinema.

17
Above: Only later did filmmakers use close-ups simply to show their audiences a dramatic incident in more detail, as in *The Sick Kitten* (1903), a remake of G.A. Smith's *The Little Doctor*. In the wide shot (top) the facial expression of the kitten could not be seen.

Soon movies began to feature at major international trade fairs, none more extravagant than the Paris Exhibition of 1900, which acted as cinema's coming-out ball. On a massive 82x49-foot screen in front of a huge audience, the Lumière brothers showed colour films, which would not become popular for more than fifty years, and widescreen films shot on film 75mm wide, which was bigger than that used for the American biblical epics of the 1950s. There were also sound films with recorded dialogue and a "Cinéorama", in which the audience sat on top of a circular projection box and watched film presented on a 330-foot 360° screen, comprising ten adjacent images. Its descendants are the IMAX screens in many modern cities. However, in its original form, Cinéorama only ran twice; the ten projectors created too much heat and the audience sitting above them was scorched.

Shots, cuts, close-ups and camera-moves – these were the technical elements providing the thrill of early filmmaking. Sneezes, trains, trips to the moon, babies in cabbage patches, boxing matches, children and kittens represented sentiment, fantasy, spectacle and moralizing. Cinema was still dealing in moments, fragments of real and imagined existence. One of the most striking things about these early short films is the "Hey, you out there in the audience" component, when their characters stare straight into the camera, sometimes taking a bow. Filmmakers had not grasped that audiences could forget that they were watching a film as they were drawn into it. This component was dropped once films started to tell stories, and later on, the American comedies of Laurel and Hardy broke the rules of narrative film when Oliver Hardy stared straight into the camera, disdaining his hopeless sidekick Stan Laurel (see pages 147–48).

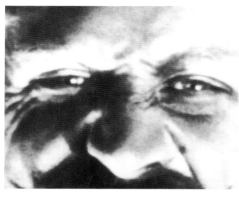

18
Above: Some Soviet directors used close-ups in much more polemical ways: *Battleship Potemkin*. Director: Sergei Eisenstein, Soviet Union, 1925.

Despite being shot in Western industrial locations like New Jersey, Leeds or Lyons, early movies were not yet made by a film industry. The medium was born non-narrative and non-industrial. It had more to do with action and novelty, it was more like a circus. However, in 1903, cinema started to abandon the thrills of the phantom ride. Direct address to the audience died out. Men like D.W. Griffith and Yevgeni Bauer came along. Movie stars were created. Italian and Russian filmmakers stole the thunder from the Americans, British and French. Film history started to get complicated. Chapters Two (1903–18) and Three (1918–28) respectively describe how story and industry came into the movies, but the films discussed in this, perhaps the most important chapter in the book, are thrilling, simple and inconsequential, as they have been, sporadically, ever since.

1. Edison's preoccupation with the Kinetoscope led him to underestimate the appeal for audiences of watching projected images communally and, as a result, to fall behind in the race to perfect cinema. The arrival of the home Digital Video Disk (DVD) in 1997 looked to some, who

admired its fine sound and image reproduction, like a moment in film history when audiences might finally abandon cinemas altogether and return to the more private experience afforded by the Kinetoscope. This has not proved to be the case.

2. Quoted in *Kino* by Jay Leyda.

3. Ibid.

Inventors from Germany, Belgium and Austria also contributed to the evolution of early cinema. In particular, Max and Emil Sklandonowsky trumped the Lumière brothers by selling tickets for a pioneering screening in Berlin on 1 November 1895. As the titles of the films screened are not known, as the conditions of the screening could not be characterized as a cinema, and as the Sklandonowskys did not continue to contribute to the evolution of cinema as did the Lumières, few film scholars accord them the founding role in movie history. Both set of brothers, as well as the other inventors, built on earlier entertainment forms including magic lantern slide shows, telescopic projections in camera obscuras and table-top spinning devices such as zoetropes. The work of Laurent Mannoni and David Robinson, amongst others, details this pre-history and is beyond the scope of the present volume.

4. In the review of the Nizhni-Novgorod fair in his local newspaper in 1896.

5. Barry Salt's *Film Style and Technology: History and Analysis* is an invaluable chronicle of the history of film style. While I do not agree with all Salt's generalizations, his accumulation of detail is unparalleled.

6. A third French figure in these early years, Ferdinand Zecca (1864-1947), is also worth mentioning. Directing between 1901 and 1914, he was, between 1905 and 1910, the head of production at Pathé. Zecca's early use of flashbacks was notable, as was his interest in social subjects, as the titles alone of *Histoire d'un crime/The Story of Crime* (1910) and *Les Victimes de l'alcoolisme/Victims of Alcoholism* (1902) suggest. Zecca pioneered elements of the chase sequence in movies, but his fantasy and trick films were not as distinctive as those of Méliès.

7. See Anthony Slide, editor, *The Memoirs of Alice Guy-Blaché*, Scarecrow Press, 1986.

8. John Kobal's photographs and Kevin Brownlow's annotations in *Hollywood: The Pioneers*, Book Club Associates, London 1979, collects this and many other important photographs of the time.

9. Quoted in Terry Ramsaye's *A Million and One Nights*, Simon and Schuster, New York, 1926.

10. Ibid. p286.

19
Above: Close-ups have remained among the most powerful devices available to directors. Few used them more dramatically than Sergio Leone in *Once Upon a Time in the West*. Italy, 1969.

20
Above: Sexuality and
eroticism in the screen
persona of Theda Bara.

THE EARLY POWER OF STORY (1903–1918): HOW THRILL BECAME NARRATIVE

THE EARLY POWER OF STORY (1903—18)
How thrill became narrative

2

The world's first aeroplane flight took place in 1903. Two years later, Albert Einstein published *The Special Theory Of Relativity* which argued that the speed of light, the flickering stuff of cinema, is the only constant in the universe. In Britain the suffragettes were agitating to obtain the vote for women. In his 1907 painting *Les Demoiselles d'Avignon*, the Spanish artist, Pablo Picasso, gave faces like African masks to two of his five naked women, and caused a scandal. In 1908, the Model T Ford went on sale for the first time in the US. Around 1910, a new music called jazz emerged in New Orleans and two years later, a massive ocean liner, the *Titanic,* sank off the coast of Newfoundland. In 1914, a gunshot in Sarajevo sparked a war in Europe that would cause millions of deaths. In 1917, two Russian revolutions deposed the Tsar and established the world's first workers' revolutionary state.

21
Below: Visitors to the St Louis Exhibition watched shots photographed from a real train while sitting in a static one.

With politics, science and art in turmoil, initially it might seem difficult to argue that film during this fifteen-year period deserves our attention, but it does. This was a time of far-reaching and enduring change in which Western cinema went from a predominantly thrilling, immediate novelty to a more absorbing psychological experience. Not until the mid-1970s would this balance in mainstream cinema revert to favour thrill.

In 1903 not a single film had been shot in the then tranquil Hollywood hills. Light was not being used expressively in films and there were no stars of the silver screen. Editing, close-ups and dolly shots – the techniques that had been discovered in the earliest years of cinema, had yet to be applied or explored self-consciously and systematically, and the first great directors who would articulate the medium were still to emerge. By 1918, cinema had its first artists: Yakov Protazanov and Yevgeny Bauer in Russia, Victor Sjöström and Mauritz Stiller in Sweden and David Wark Griffith and Charles Chaplin in America. This chapter looks at the careers of these men and charts the emergence of Hollywood, the star system, feature-length films and how Western movies discovered the power of stories. Japan had the most developed film culture in the East. However, it did not follow this path and the implications for the art of cinema were profound.

Audiences were becoming tired of the quick thrills of the earliest movies and new attractions had to be discovered. In response to this, the 1903 St Louis Exhibition featured Hales Tours, which included earlier footage of phantom ride shots projected inside a railway carriage, manipulated to simulate the movement of a real train. Directors became intrigued by which tricks worked and which did not, like the technique of having actors look off-screen and then cutting to another location, about which they were supposed to be thinking. Audiences did not understand this and it soon died out. On the other hand, chase sequences were later found to have a magnetic power as they consisted of pure

22
Above: *The Life of an American Fireman*. These four images feature the intercut version, between 1903 and 1905. Right: original version, 1903. Director: Edwin S. Porter. USA.

kinetic action. And filmmakers learnt to say "Once upon a time ...", and "then this happened ..." or "Meanwhile". How did they evolve the techniques of suspense and anticipation?

The beginning of the answer can be found in 1903, in the work of the dynamic, entrepreneurial Pennsylvanian, Edwin Stanton Porter. He was born in 1869 and in his twenties worked for a marketing company when he helped arrange one of the first public screenings of a film in New York's Koster and Bial's Music Hall, on 23 April 1896. Soon he was making pictures, such as *The Great Train Robbery* (USA, 1903). His *The Life of an American Fireman,* also made in 1903, is less written about than *The Great Train Robbery*, but is more revealing.

Its most celebrated sequence (22) is the arrival of a fireman outside a blazing house. The image cuts to a room inside the house where the fireman rescues a mother, then cuts to an exterior shot of the mother on the street. The camera then returns inside the house to show the rescue of the mother's child by the fireman and then re-establishes itself outside again. For many years, film historians claimed this was the first example of continuity editing. The image cuts from exterior to interior to exterior to interior and the audience follows this rescue narrative, despite the space of the street suddenly disappearing from the screen and being magically replaced by another space, the room. This would not have been possible in the theatre and, until Porter's apparent innovations in 1903, directors assumed that such spatial jumps would confuse audiences.

The truth about Porter's achievements in shooting and cutting this film is more complicated than it appears and reveals much about the evolution of storytelling technique in filmmaking.[1] Another print of the film exists in the archives, which shows all the street action in one continuous shot and then the interior action, similarly in one sequence. Film historians used to believe that this version was a "rough cut", which Porter had yet to fine-tune. However, it has recently become clear that this film was closer to the original release print. Only in later years, once intercutting was discovered, did Porter or someone else belatedly "improve" the more theatrical version by editing. The intercut version has a continuous time line – we see everything in the order in which it was done – but the space is fragmented. It doesn't jar because we understand that we are seeing what the fireman did next. The more theatrical version doesn't fragment the space, but repeats the time like an action replay. Cinema had learned to follow the flow of the action from one space to another. This made chase sequences possible, liberated movies and emphasized movement. Nearly every scene we look at in this book will, in some way, use this basic storytelling device. The continuity implied, "Then this happened". Within ten years of *The Life of an American Fireman*, Porter had experimented with sound, widescreen, colour and three-dimensional movies, long before they became popular. He was bankrupted by the 1929 Wall Street Crash and died, forgotten, in 1948.

23
Above: Actors turning their backs to the camera marked the beginning of the end of frontal, theatrical cinema. *The Assassination of the Duc de Guise*. Director: Charles le Bargy. France, 1908.

American Fireman was a landmark; schema plus variation. Theatrical cinema was giving way to action cinema and tableau imagery started to look dated. Out of this difference, D.W. Griffith evolved, as has every narrative filmmaker thereafter. Continuity editing led to longer movies. The first feature-length film was *The True Story of the Kelly Gang*, made in Australia by John Tait in 1906. In 1907, cinematic innovation went up a gear. Charles Pathé's *The Horse that Bolted* took the lessons of Porter's fireman film and advanced them. Here, a restless horse outside a house begins to wreck things around it, while inside the house, its rider dallies, unaware of the commotion outside. Pathé cut between outside and inside just as Porter had done. The action of the horse and its rider were separate, simultaneous events. Unlike Porter's continuity editing, this was parallel editing, the origin of "Meanwhile" in the cinema, the way in which filmmakers to this day contrast events, build tension or advance two storylines concurrently. The technique was brilliantly realized by director Alfred Hitchcock in *Strangers on a Train* (USA, 1951), by intercutting a character playing tennis with another trying to frame him by planting incriminating evidence at the scene of a crime. The suspense film *The Silence of the Lambs* (USA, 1990) played with the conventions of parallel editing by suggesting a congruence of plot at odds with the narrative.

1908 saw even more additions to the cinematic box of tricks. Shadows began to be used in film lighting to give more depth to the photographic image. In the American film *A Yiddisher Boy* (USA, 1908) a man in a street fight remembers an event from twenty-five years earlier. The shot of that memory is the first flashback acknowledged by film historians. In the same year, André Calmettes and Charles le Bargy directed *L'Assassinat du duc de Guise/The Assassination of the Duc de Guise* (23) for the French company, Film d'Art. Although not the first film company to look to adapt novels and plays for the screen, its self-consciously highbrow cinema, aimed at theatre-going audiences, was better marketed and more successful than most. The so-called heritage films made by Merchant Ivory in Britain in the 1980s and 1990s are the progeny of *The Assassination of the Duc de Guise*, often deriving from literature and emphasizing diction, set design and verbal nuance.

The social implications of films such as this and the one-hour film *Les Amours* (Henri Desfontaines and Louis Mercanton, France, 1919) which featured the theatre-star Sarah Bernhardt and which was imported to the US by Adolph Zukor, were considerable. Cinema had opened its doors to new, wealthier audiences, who would demand more comfortable and stylish cinemas than the nickelodeons, shop-front outfits and music hall auditoria which had hitherto been the sites for cinema. They wanted weightier subjects too, and the film world would accede to this. Within a generation, movie palaces or atmospherics would be built; places where ordinary people could feel like royalty for a night and where film became a medium of contemplation as well as sensation.

The Assassination of the Duc de Guise may seem static now, but at the time, its photography and staging broke new ground, as can be seen in image to the left. The camera is at waist height, at a time when shoulder height was the accepted norm in American and most of European cinema. Notice how some of the actors in the image have turned their backs to the camera. This was new. Most films until this date had been frontal, their action facing outward. The implications of this "inwardness" were extensive. If the audience wanted to see the faces of the actors' whose backs are turned, the camera had to be brought into the middle of the scene and turned toward the audience and the actors. It would be another four years before this technique, "reverse angle shooting", would start to be used. But this simple still from a starchy theatrical film seems to illustrate why it came about.

I say "seems to" because in Japan something very different was happening. The country's first projected films were, as in many other countries, the package of Lumière 1897 shorts. Home-grown production then developed swiftly, along Western lines, and by 1908 four production companies were making films. Shochiku established itself later, survives to this day and is the most famous company in Japan. It produced plays before it got into the film business, a precedent almost unheard of in the West.

That Japanese film grew out of theatre is profoundly important. The majority of that country's films made throughout the period covered in this chapter looked like filmed versions of the two dominant styles of popular theatre – *kabuki* and *shimpa*. The camera recorded the entire scene frontally. The actors wore traditional costume and make-up and male actors would portray women as well as men. The actors did not make contact during fight scenes and all movement would periodically freeze to emphasize a moment. When characters died, they performed a backward somersault. More significantly, a *benshi* would usually stand behind a lectern by the cinema's screen, explaining the events, commenting on the characters and sometimes making sound effects. By 1908, these *benshi* had begun to have some say in how films were produced, for example arguing for longer scenes which gave them more time to talk and

24
Below: Theatrical framing and acting styles in *A Tale of Loyal Retainers*. Director: Makio Shozo. Japan, c. 1910

THE EARLY POWER OF STORY (1903–1918): HOW THRILL BECAME NARRATIVE

describe. Some *benshi* became famous and many communities had their own favourites. They dominated Japanese film exhibition until the late 1930s and their presence meant that characters did not appear to be talking in early Japanese films, since this was the *benshi's* job. Critic Noël Burch has argued that their storylines were sometimes "outside" the flow of imagery and were an echo of a profoundly un-Western aspect of Japanese culture.[2] This separation of word and image is reflected in early traditional handscrolls in which sophisticated images were interspersed with a written storyline; there was no attempt to integrate the two.

So it was with cinema. While Porter, the *Duc de Guise* film and other Western directors were beginning to tell stories "from within", Japanese cinema was not. The still to the left (24) is from a film, but visually it is extremely similar to the theatre image we have just seen. To say that most Japanese films until the 1930s have to be understood in conjunction with a foreground narrator is not to suggest that they were made in a lazy fashion. Rather, they were derived from a visual tradition where space played a different role. Contemporary *kabuki* theatre stages tended to have flat backdrops, and their exquisitely painted handscrolls and screens, as well as prints, which proved to be so influential on Western painters, similarly emphasized shallow space and the surface of the paper, rather than illusionistic perspective. So while the *Duc de Guise* film seems to Westerners to be too "flat", this would not be a sensible response in Japan. Although Japanese audiences and filmmakers saw Western films and liked them, they did not feel the same need to put the audience visually at the centre of the story as Western directors did between 1908 and 1918. It was only after the Japanese defeat in the Second World War that Western-style storytelling becomes dominant in Japanese cinema.

INDUSTRIAL DEVELOPMENTS IN AMERICA

As filmmakers started to learn about depth and narrative in America, a fight over film copyright was brewing. The Patents War (1897–1908) began when Edison realized that ownership of the rights of this burgeoning medium was vital. Since he had not invented the film itself (that was Eastman) he patented the sprocket holes in the film by which it was clawed through the camera. Anyone who wanted to use film with sprocket holes, which was everyone, had to pay Edison.

Other film producers – all still on the East Coast of America – were furious at this and many of them refused to pay. This compelled Edison to join forces with an old enemy, American Mutoscope and Bioscope Company, to lend weight to his claim to ownership. The result was the aggressive Motion Picture Patents Company (MPPC), a very Anglo-Saxon group whose intention was to keep independent Jewish producers like Carl Laemmle out of the increasingly lucrative film business. The formation of the MPPC (also known as The Trust) in effect ended the Patents War, but not the disputes between competing vested interests. In 1910, Laemmle defied the MPPC and, following their example, banned the MPPC in the courts, thus igniting a second round of legal battles which became known as the Trust War. All hell broke loose and in 1912 a legal ruling was established against MPPC's claim to own sprocket holes. The Trust War finally ended in 1918 after a six-year court battle, when the courts declared the MPPC an illegal trust, but before that, the MPPC's counter-attack had a number of historic outcomes. The independent production companies went as far away from the East coast as possible in order to escape prosecution for using a loop in their cameras. Their destination was a sleepy Southern Californian town called Los Angeles, the City of the Angels, whose low taxation and lively theatres made it more appealing than other distant cities. Today's Hollywood evolved from these pioneers. Laemmle opened Universal Studios in 1915 and, twenty years later, he sold it for $5 million.

The MPPC emphasized itself as a brand with the on-screen slogan, "Come and see an MPPC film". The MPDSC realized that they had to do something equally distinctive, so they varied the schema. Instead of branding themselves, they branded the actors in their films. Previously, actors had seldom been named and audiences were not provided with information about them. In 1910, during the thick of the fight with the MPPC, Laemmle announced in the press that the Independent Motion Picture Girl of America or IMP Girl, the anonymous actress who had appeared in many of his films, had died. However, when she miraculously made an appearance to disprove this fact, Laemmle reported to the newspapers that the crowds were so hysterical that they tore off her clothes. This was equally untrue, but the ensuing furore burned her name, Florence Lawrence, into the public's consciousness. Lawrence became a huge star, earning $80,000 in 1912. Two years later she had a serious

25
Left: Two of the world's
most famous movie stars –
Mary Plckford and Douglas
Fairbanks (in the car) – are
swamped by fans in Paris
in 1920.

injury and her career declined rapidly. By the 1930s, she was reduced to playing extras in crowd scenes and in 1938, aged fifty-two, she committed suicide by eating ant poison.

The star system had been born in all its extravagant, tawdry glory and while we cringe at its contemporary excesses, the cynicism of the early star-making PR men still takes the breath away. Theodosia Goodman was a hardworking actress in summer-stock repertory theatre, but Hollywood rechristened her Theda Bara (see page 34, 20), an anagram of "Arab death". She started her life in Cincinnati, but the public was told that she was "born in the shadow of the Sphinx". She wore indigo make-up and gave interviews while stroking a snake. The growing publicity machine, awash with such racial, sexual and class clichés, has remained central to the continuing exotic, erotic imagination of Hollywood. Public obsession with movie actors rocketed. At the same time as the Lawrence US phenomenon, Mistinguett emerged in France, but the Danish actress Asta Nielsen became perhaps more internationally famous than either. Nielsen was as popular in Russia and Germany as in Denmark. When the film star Mary Pickford and her husband Douglas Fairbanks visited Moscow, 300,000 people came out to see her. Pickford became the highest-paid woman in the world, earning $350,000 a year. A young British man in Hollywood, Charles Chaplin, would soon become the highest-paid man, grossing $520,000 plus bonuses in 1916.

Every aspect of the industry was affected by the star system. As the adoring public became increasingly interested in stars such as Lawrence, Nielsen and Mistinguett, moviemakers had to learn what their idols were thinking and feeling. This meant seeing their faces more clearly. Despite their use in films like *Grandma's Reading Glasses* (UK, 1900), close-ups remained rare for some years. It was still the norm in 1908 to film the human body at full length (see the *Duc de Guise* still on page 38), but in 1909, as film historian Barry Salt has discussed, American films started to include closer framing, from the knees up (26). This was known in Europe as the "American shot".

It was not only the actors' faces, but also their thoughts that audiences were interested in. As cinema was still silent, actors could not be heard, but filmmakers and story writers began to understand that audiences would be drawn into the film if they could understand what the actors were supposed to be feeling and feel it with them. Action in early silent film was usually caused by external forces of nature or accident: for instance, the firemen in Porter's film rushed to the house because there was a fire. The actors trapped in the house were anonymous and the 1903 audience knew nothing about them.

26

Below: This still from *Daises* illustrates how American director's began to shoot from the knees up, gradually getting closer to the actors. 1910

Now jump forward eight or ten years. What if it was Florence Lawrence trapped in that house, the Florence Lawrence the public had read about in the papers? Her audience would want to know how she was feeling, if she was scared or safe. To express these things,

filmmakers had to move the camera closer and learn to use shots and cuts to reveal feelings. The star system ensured that psychology became the driving force of films, especially American ones.

If filmmakers were uncoupling themselves from the cheap technical thrills of their earlier films, if they were starting to tell longer, more psychological and convoluted stories, if they were producing more and more films every day, then new, respectable subject matter had to be found. They did this with their customary lack of guile. Between 1909 and 1912, eight versions of Charles Dickens' novel *Oliver Twist* were produced. In 1910, it is estimated that one third of all films were based on plays and a further quarter were adapted from novels. Shakespeare's *Hamlet* was filmed twenty times in Italy, France, Denmark, Britain and the US in the fifteen years covered in this chapter. In the same period there were more than fifty films about the British sleuth, Sherlock Holmes. Producers did not shy away from real-life figures, with scores of films on the lives of Napoleon Bonaparte, George Washington, Abraham Lincoln, Jesus Christ and Theodore Roosevelt.

The rise of the star system, the Patents War and the move to Hollywood make 1908–12 a fascinating period for American cinema. The elements of the power of Hollywood fell into place and it geared itself up for domination of the world's markets. But, until the First World War, other countries' film output still had more commercial and artistic impact than the United States'. The French industry had stopped being a cottage one, for example. By 1907, around 40 per cent of films showing in US nickelodeons were made by one studio, Pathé. The Gaumont company also made films, distributed them and screened them. A third company, Eclair, even opened a studio in the US, as Pathé had also done. A further sign of the industrialization of French cinema was Pathé's pioneering of serial films such as those starring André Deed. The success of these spawned many others, in particular the Italian Cretinetti series, again starring Deed after he had moved to Italy from France. The most significant of such series were those of performer Max Linder, perhaps the most famous international film comedian in the run up to the First World War. Linder's dapper loafer was developed and directed on screen between 1905 and 1910 by directors such as Ferdinand Zecca and Alberto Capelini; from 1911 onward he directed his films himself, establishing a precedent which Mack Sennett and Charles Chaplin would later follow.

Scandinavian cinema was also developing in the years before the First World War. In 1912, the most innovative use of film light was in the work of the Dane, Benjamin Christensen. Low-angle daylight contoured his imagery and sometimes the level of artificial light within a shot would be varied, to simulate a door closing or a lamp being switched on, as in *Night of Vengeance* (Denmark, 1915) (27). In the following year, the early films of Swedish directors such as Mauritz Stiller, Victor Sjöström and Georg af Klercker, though often based on literary source material, captured natural landscapes with a still, radiant grace, and themes of destiny and mortality were addressed with a maturity beyond that of contemporaneous filmmakers. Sjöström and Stiller became star directors and, as was

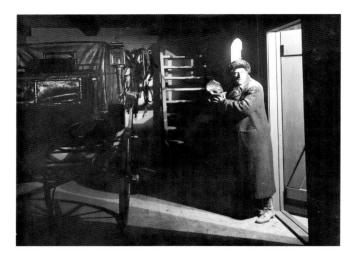

to be the pattern for European talent, they accepted contracts with the Hollywood studios in 1923 and 1925 respectively.

India made what some say was its first film, *Pundalik*, in 1912. Based on the life of the Hindu saint of the same name, it was shot on location in Bombay by P.R. Tipnis and N.G. Chitre. Early Indian filmmaking was dominated by the artistic son of a Sanskrit scholar, D.G. Phalke (28).

Having studied painting and architecture, the thirty-year-old Phalke went to London in 1910 and learnt film techniques from Cecil Hepworth at Walton Studios. Returning to Bombay in 1912 he set up Phalke Films and proceeded to make over forty silent feature films, often using innovative methods such as animated individual sequences, and one sound film, *Gangavataran* (1937). Inspired by seeing *The Life of Christ* in Bombay in 1911, Phalke took the ancient stories of Indian myth that form *The Mahabharata* (collected between 400BCE and 400CE), and adapted them for screen. He created a whole genre, the mythological, which has survived to this day. Phalke's first mythological film was *King Harishchandra* (1913), in which a respected King is drawn into a mystical world and his honesty is tested by, among other things, three inflamed spiritual manifestations. King Harishchandra's mythical suffering is curtailed when a god emerges to explain that the whole trial has been a test of his virtue.

Four types of film emerged in India in these early years, which would influence that country's massive film culture thereafter. These were devotionals about saints, such as *Pundalik*; mythologicals such as Phalke's *King Harishchandra*; historicals, derived from novels and melodramas; and socials, derived from reformist theatre. While the style and meaning of Indian film would evolve along very different lines from those of Western cinema, the mixture of piety and biography, emotional excess and myth of early Indian cinema was comparable to what was then emerging from the Hollywood hills.

Concurrently, cinema was playing an important role in Mexico's bloody civil war, which would claim over a million lives between 1911 and 1917. Cameramen in the north of Mexico, like the intrepid Lumière employee Francis Doublier outside Moscow in 1896, filmed the battles of the revolutionary Pancho Villa. *La vista de la revuetta/View of the Uprising* (Mexico 1911), was shown in Mexico City and Monterrey where free tickets were given to the poor to encourage them to support Villa's cause. Within a few years, Villa had become a star in his own right and, exhibiting some gall, the North American director, Raoul Walsh, paid him for the exclusive rights to film his campaigns. The revolutionary adjusted his battle plans and attack schedules to make them more appealing to Walsh's camera.[3] This, however, would not be the only time that the tail would wag the dog in this way, and a 1997 American film, *Wag the Dog*, showed how war could accommodate politics and cinema. The real and the cinematic would dance an uneasy *pas de deux* throughout the twentieth century. The first important Mexican fictional films were produced in the 1930s and their subject was Pancho Villa.

28
Above: D.G. Palke on set directing, *King Harishchandra*. India, 1913.

Italian cinema of this time draws attention to itself because of its symbolic and technical innovations. Salt credits the first-known symbol in a film to Mario Caserini's *La mala piñata/The Evil Plant*, whose opening shot features a slithering snake, a malign symbol from the Book of Genesis, or earlier. The thirty-year-old Giovanni Pastrone directed the far more innovative *Cabiria* in 1913. He had made a dozen or so films before he embarked on this tale of a Sicilian slave girl, Cabiria, who is constantly rescued by another slave, the muscular Maciste, but none was on the ambitious scale of *Cabiria*. Pastrone filmed Cabiria's near-sacrifice to Baal, Maciste's adventures in Carthage and Hannibal crossing the Alps with his elephants. He shot for six months, at a time when many films were still completed in a matter of days. "The technical innovations and spectacular sets revolutionized cinema", wrote film historian Georges Sadoul in 1965.[4]

Cabiria is a gigantic work whose scale, even viewed from the era of computer-generated imagery, is still surprising (29). Other epic films such as *The Life of Christ* (Pathé, France, 1910), *Quo Vadis?* (Enrico Guazzoni, Italy, 1912) and *King Harishchandra*, had used fixed tableau shots, which would establish a grand setting and then cut to smaller courtly or domestic scenes. Pastrone, however, would dolly into those closer scenes, either by moving the camera forward, or forward and sideways, on a diagonal. Cinema had discovered a way of moving seamlessly from a wide visual frieze to medium shots.

29
Above: *Cabiria*'s gigantic sets established a benchmark for epic filmmaking in the years to come. Director: Giovanni Pastrone. Italy, 1913.

On its release, *Cabiria* was a sensation in Japan, Europe and, in particular, the US, where, as mentioned in the previous chapter, its tracking shots came to be known as "Cabiria movements". R.W. Paul's simple dolly device found itself at the centre of the cinematic process.

However, it wasn't only Italy that had discovered the epic sensuality made possible by Paul's invention. In Russia, at the same time as Pastrone was filming, Tsar Nicholas II may have commented that cinema was an "empty, totally useless and even harmful form of entertainment ... no importance whatsoever should be attached to such stupidities",[5] but forty-eight-year-old former caricaturist and painter Yevgeny Bauer was making *Twilight of a Woman's Soul* (1913), which developed Paul's early tracking shot even further. Like many of the

one third of the film's shots.[6] Ince was an innovator and understood how to make people feel the story from the character's viewpoint by filming a character, his or her viewpoint, his or her reaction to this and then returning to his or her viewpoint. The increase in audience interest in stars encouraged directors to do this. Reverse angle editing (sometimes called "shot/reverse-shot pairs") had become one of the most important techniques in mainstream filmmaking by the 1920s. Since then, every popular film in the history of Western cinema has used it.

D.W. Griffith, mentioned several times in the story so far, now becomes central to it. Griffith was born in 1875 to a recently impoverished politician and war hero. He started his career as an actor, tried his hand at writing plays and attempted to sell stories to Edwin S. Porter. From 1908 to 1913 he made 400 short films, including *The Curtain Pole* (USA, 1909), one of his rare comedies which nonetheless established a crazy style that would dominate comic movies for the remainder of the silent period. So stimulating were his methods that he soon had a devoted stock of actors, including Lillian Gish, Blanche Sweet and Donald Crisp, and was working with one of the best cinematographers in the film industry, Billy Bitzer, who had made his reputation at The Productive Biograph Studio. Bitzer disliked the crispness of conventional film photography and made the edges of his own imagery slighter darker by placing a vignetting hood around the lens hood, "adding class to the picture" as Bitzer himself described it,[7] and influencing the look of dramatic film in America for a generation. Despite the claims of earlier film historians and his own publicist, D.W. Griffith did not invent any of the key elements of the language of cinema. He did, however, more than any other filmmaker, give films an interior human life. He applied greater emotional finesse to extant film techniques, collaborating brilliantly with actresses, minimizing their gestures and contrasting gentleness and ferocity. He understood

32
Above: Cinematographer Billy Blitzer used halo lighting on actors' hair to make them stand out visually from the sets.

the psychic intensity of a lens and allowed Bitzer to explore diffused photography and back lighting, which gave a halo to hair and made actors stand out against backgrounds (32).

Griffith made perhaps the most famous and certainly the most controversial film of the whole silent era, *The Birth of A Nation* (USA, 1915). Like most of his work, this film looks like it was shot in

his native Kentucky and glows with an affection inherited from his father for the Southern states. It was a history film, a state of the nation work designed to appeal not only to middle-class audiences in the tradition of Film d'Art, but to those who flocked to epic, exciting films too. It was also an inflammatory film about which serious newspapers could editorialize. It told the story of two families from the opposing sides in the American Civil War – the Camerons in the South and the Stonemans in the North – whose sons and daughters fall in love with each other. When the North wins, one of the Cameron sons becomes leader of the Ku Klux Klan. He and the clansmen triumphantly rescue Elsie Stoneman from an aggressive mixed-race suitor and the white couples marry.

The film's production was almost as big as *Cabiria*. It required an unprecedented six weeks of rehearsal, its budget was $110,000 and its running time was around three hours, depending on the version and speed of projection. It featured epic battle scenes (33); when they were shot the action was cued across their vast spaces with coloured flags. Such scenes alternated with others of brilliant emotional control. A Southern officer returns home to his once fine house, which is now burned and decrepit. His sister greets him and, as they embrace, he notices that the white tufts of ermine on her dress are cotton wool. As he goes to his mother in the door-way, he is enfolded within her arms and she is concealed by the frame. Her joy and sadness is all the more moving for being unseen. No-one in cinema to this date had better used the power of suggestion or understood how a schema becomes dated and needs to be renewed. A later American master filmmaker, John Ford, would copy this scene in *Pilgrimage* (USA, 1933) when a mother reaches her hand out of a train window. Such moments as these, combined with the

34
The visual influence of Pastrone's *Cabiria* (above) can be clearly seen on this production design for the Babylonian set of *Intolerance* (below). D.W. Griffith. USA 1916.

, 366

performance of Griffith's star Lillian Gish as Elsie Stoneman and the triumphant chase sequences, edited to the music of Wagner, prompted the then President of the United States, Woodrow Wilson, to say, "It's like writing history with lightning."

As the storyline suggests, *The Birth of a Nation* was

appallingly racist. Black senators were shown as drunk and unclean. Demonstrations for and against the film took place after some screenings; many protested the film's depictions of African Americans, others attacked black audience members. The KKK had been disbanded in 1877, but such was the power of this film that historian Kevin Brownlow wrote that "On Thanksgiving Night, 1915, in Stone Mountain,

35
Above: The composition, scale, placement of extras of frieze-like set design and costuming of this scene in Griffith's *Intolerance* all clearly derive from Edwin Long's 1875 painting *The Babylonian Marriage Market* (opposite).

Atlanta ... 2,500 former Clansmen marched down Peach Tree Avenue to celebrate the opening of the film".[8] By the mid-1920s, KKK membership was four million.

Griffith saw Pastrone's *Cabiria* the year after completing *The Birth of a Nation*. He was stunned by it, and in particular by its dolly shots. Inspired by this and by the novels of Charles Dickens, (he even said, "Dickens intercuts, so will I") he abandoned the Kentuckian mythology of his father and raised his sights to a three-and-a-half-hour film about "love's struggle through history". Illustrations 34 reveal the sources of Griffith's visual ideas for *Intolerance*, which became the film's title. The first (34 top) is from *Cabiria*, the second (34 bottom) is one of Griffith's colossal Babylon sets which stood near Hollywood Boulevard before demolition (it was partly rebuilt in 2001). Like many serious filmmakers, Griffith also used painting as a source of visual inspiration. Illustrations 35 (top left and right) show how direct such influences can be.

The film attempted to explore the theme of intolerance through history by intercutting Belshazzar's feast in Babylon (fifth century BCE), Christ's passion, the St Bartholomew's massacre (sixteenth-century France), modern-day gangsterism – all linked by

Lillian Gish rocking a cradle and finished by a premonition of Armageddon. Griffith filmed the Babylon sequence from hot-air balloons and rigged up a type of dolly shot in mid-air by placing the camera on a moving tower, which was a first. His story-telling was highly innovative: he would take storyline A so far, stop it, then go to storyline B, advance it a certain amount and return to storyline A and pick up where he had left off. This confused many of the audiences and the film did less well commercially then *A Birth of a Nation* for which, to some critics of the time, it seemed like an apology.

Intolerance appears stodgy today, but its relevance is twofold. First it took intercutting a stage further than Pathé's *The Horse that Bolted*. Griffith's intercutting is not saying "Meanwhile". He cut between different time periods, between events that were not happening simultaneously. He was not cutting for action (Porter) or temporally (Pathé), but was doing it thematically. He was saying, "Look, these very different events are examples of the same human trait" – intolerance, or the failure of love. *Intolerance*'s greatest contribution to the history of cinema was that it ambitiously showed that a cut between shots could be a thematic tool,

that it could be an intellectual signpost, asking the audience to notice, not something about the action or story, but about the meaning of the sequence. Secondly, it had a huge impact on other filmmakers. Soviets, such as Eisenstein, studied it and wrote about it. The Viennese-American director Erich Von Stroheim attempted to top its ambition. And in 1921 Minoru Murata made an atypical Japanese film that didn't follow the tradition of flattened imagery and heavy *benshi* narration, having been encouraged to do so after seeing *Intolerance*.

Murata was one of the modernizing pioneers of Japanese cinema and wanted to move beyond the historical dramas that had been the staple of that country's fledgeling film culture. *Rojo no Reikon/Souls on the Road* (Japan, 1921) (36) intertwined four storylines, including one about a penniless son returning home and another about two convicts who are greeted with kindness

by people they meet. The intercutting between time periods is handled with greater complexity than in *Intolerance*. At the end of the film, the stories come together when the two convicts find the impoverished son dead in the snow. The result is the first landmark film in Japanese history.

The influence of *Intolerance* was not reflected in its profitability. Griffith had risked his own money on its $2 million budget, which made it one of the most expensive films of all time, and as a result he was in debt for the rest of his life.

In the period from 1903 to 1918, many of the ingredients of Western storytelling cinema fell into place: continuity cutting, close-ups, parallel editing, expressive lighting, nuanced acting and reverse angle editing: an impressive array of techniques.[9] However, one is missing, perhaps the most important one. Its exact origin is difficult to trace, but it appeared at the very end of this period – "eye-line matching".

The two illustrations to the right show how eye-line matching works and why it so important (37). They are from a 1911 film, *The Loafer* (USA), and feature the very early use of rough reverse angle editing. A close inspection of these shows that something is wrong. In the first, the actor is looking slightly to the left of the camera (37 top). In the second (37 bottom), the man he addresses looks slightly to the right of the camera. The effect is disconcerting when cutting between the two of them. It appears as if they are talking to each other while looking away from each other. If the second man had looked to the left rather than to the right, it would still have disoriented the viewer because it would have appeared that both actors were looking at some unseen event to the left of camera while in conversation. Only if man one was looking right and man two was looking left would their conversation have been spatially clear and their eye-lines have matched. Western cinema had been striving for this absolute clarity and the majority of filmmakers mastered this last crucial element of narrative filmmaking by the mid-1920s. Only in Japan and, later, in modernist cinema, would eye-line matches not be the norm.

An estimated ten million men lost their lives in the First World War. The Armenians suffered almost mass genocide at the hands of the Turks and the German, Russian, Austro-Hungarian and Ottoman empires collapsed. Germany's borders had been closed to all foreign art, including films, since 1916, and Russia's borders had been similarly closed off from 1914. Russians fleeing the 1917 revolutions created a diaspora, settling in France and other countries.

During the period covered by this chapter, the medium of cinema had become adult and wildly ambitious. It had discovered the power of story and had evolved a complex set of devices for constructing narratives. In its haphazard creation of a star system, it had directed itself toward romance and the sublime. Movie palaces like Grauman's Million Dollar Theater in Los Angeles were constructed (38). These screens were the grand palaces of entertainment cinema, showing formulaic films, as well as those by significant directors such as Griffith. The movies of the other pioneering directors of this era – Protazanov, Sjöström, Stiller, Bauer, Phalke and Muratova – often found large audiences in their own countries too, but those of Bauer, Phalke and Muratova were less widely seen. Cinema already had a handful of mature talents.

37
Above: Eye-line matching had still not been perfected in 1911: These two men in the film *The Loafer* appear to be staring in opposite directions, yet they are supposed to be talking to, and looking at, each other.

This is only partly because of the cultural specifics of these filmmakers' concerns. Far more important was Hollywood's opportunism during the First World War. Importing few films between 1914 and 1918, it had a virtual monopoly on North American

38

Right: By the end of the
First World War, cinemas
had evolved from simple
shop-fronted buildings such
as Tally's Phonograph
Parlor (see page 27) and
had begun to look like
cathedrals. Grauman's
Million Dollar Theatre,
Los Angeles.

THE EARLY POWER OF STORY (1903–1918): HOW THRILL BECAME NARRATIVE

cinemagoers and visual entertainment. As the national industries of European countries such as France, which had been developing since the turn of the century, stalled under the exigencies of war, so Hollywood strengthened rapidly. And when the fog of war cleared in 1918, a powerful new North American entertainment oligarchy, ultimately controlled by the financial interests of Wall Street, came into view; one of its first actions was to flood European cinemas with its recent productions. The indigenous industries could not respond.

The next decade would witness a massive expansion of film style around the world. Audiences would flock to cinemas, stars would attract fanatical attention and every aspect of film form would be explored. The 1920s would be cinema's most lucrative and creative decade.

1. Earlier films by Méliès and Williamson perhaps solved the problem of how to get a character from one space to another, but these do not reveal as much as *The Life of an American Fireman*.
2. Burch, Noel, *To the Distant Observer: Form and Meaning in the Japanese Cinema*, Scolar Press, 1979.
3. This was not the first time that partially or fully staged scenes had been shown to audiences as documentary footage of real historical events. One of the most famous instances of this was J. Stuart Blackton and A.E. Smith's *Tearing Down the Spanish Flag* (USA, 1898) which was filmed in New York City and sold as an actual event in the US Spanish War. The unscrupulous Mr Blackton followed its success with *The Battle of Santiago Bay* (USA, 1900), in which cut-out boats were filmed in a large tub and naval smoke was provided by his wife puffing on a cigarette.
4. Sadoul, Georges, *Dictionary of Films*, University of California Press, English translation 1972.
5. Quoted in Leyda, Jay, *Kino*, op. cit.
6. Salt, op. cit., p95.
7. Quoted in Brown, Karl, *Adventures with D.W. Griffith*, Faber and Faber, 1973.
8. Brownlow, Kevin, in *Hollywood: The Pioneers*, op. cit.
9. Sound had still to make an impact on storytelling, of course, and will be dealt with in a later chapter. Transitional devices such as wipes between one image and the next had not yet become widespread but are less fundamental to film grammar than continuity editing, shot size and eyeline matching.

39
Below: The scale and
design of Fritz Lang's
Metropolis has influenced
directors and artists for
generations. Germany,
1927.

THE WORLD EXPANSION OF STYLE (1918—28)   **3**
Movie factories and personal vision

Cinema in 1918 was perhaps too young to engage fully with the complex realities of the First World War and the Russian Revolution. Films like *Intolerance* (USA, 1916) were ingressions into the world of ideas, and the warring powers in the turbulent mid-decade years were not above using film for propagandist purposes, but those works that maturely addressed the historical upheavals of the era were few and far between.[1] What cannot be discounted is Wall Street's reluctance to challenge federal and foreign policy, especially when both coincided with its own interests. Such conservatism from on high worked its way down the command structure of the film world and made it difficult for ambitious or radical filmmakers to pose tough historical questions in their work.

By the time of the collapse of the American economy in the 1929 Wall Street Crash, the cultural landscape would have changed. In just over a decade, cinema became both the most popular international form of entertainment and a serious chronicler of the human soul. The primitive filmmaking of the early 1910s with its simple shots, raw frontal acting and rapid action, unmoderated by the tastes and expectations of the middle classes, was disappearing. Like a humpback whale it went deep under water. There would be rumours of sightings in 1950s America in widescreen melodramas such as *Johnny Guitar* (1953) and in the films of Sam Fuller, but it would not be until the 1960s and the flickering emergence of African and Latin-American cinema, together with the extraordinary films of Pier Paolo Pasolini and the 1960s underground directors, that primal cinema would resurface. In the over-sophisticated film world of the 1980s and 1990s, films with some of the same elemental power began to emerge from Iran. The filmmaking of the 1910s had returned.

From 1918–28, filmmakers applied their techniques with increasing sophistication to every aspect of experience – the instinct to create laughter, questions of how we see and hear, the lives of people on the margins of communities, the dynamism of cities and how their residents behave, the unconscious and more abstract questions about life, science and the future. Once filmmakers around the world realized that their medium could do complex things, they stretched creativity to the limit and dazzled themselves and their colleagues with new discoveries. Not until the 1960s would there be so much stylistic innovation in the cinema, and the excitement of the 1920s is still palpable today.

This chapter starts in America as the components of its new film industry fall into place. The characteristics of the new industrially produced films, especially their most innovative examples – the comedies of Charles Chaplin, Harold Lloyd and Buster Keaton – will be looked at in detail. The various international challenges to the studio system will then be discussed: naturalism in Scandinavia, impressionism in France, expressionism in Germany, editing in the Soviet Union and the continuing frontal style of Japan. During this process, landmarks of film history and its seminal works will be encountered.

THE BEGINNING OF HOLLYWOOD'S GOLDEN ERA

During these years investment in cinema increased tenfold. In 1917, a court order dissolved the old Motion Picture Patents Company and Edison's old sparring partners, the independents, started to build movie empires. Film factories were established and movies were assembled in a production-line system rather like Model T Ford automobiles.

There was a free-for-all. People who had previously only produced films now invested in distribution, the business arm that sold their films to the cinemas. The next logical step was for them to buy the screens themselves to ensure a guaranteed outlet for their product. This was achieved with money from New York bankers and businessmen and the resulting system was, as in other industries, called "vertical integration" and guaranteed a continuous production line.

A series of uneducated working-class Jewish businessmen led the way. Adolph Zukor, for example, was a Hungarian immigrant who initially worked in the fur trade and then made a fortune copying *Duc de Guise*-type films in the US produced by his company, Famous Players. Joining forces with Jesse J. Lasky, a musical theatre producer, he formed the Famous Players-Lasky Corporation, which would later become Paramount Pictures, the most European of the Hollywood Studios. During the so-called "Golden Age of Hollywood", from the end of the First World War until 1945, its star actors and directors would be Marlene Dietrich, Joseph Von Sternberg, Gary Cooper, Ernst Lubitsch, Fredric March, Bob Hope, Bing Crosby, W.C. Fields and Mae West. In its later years, Billy Wilder, Burt Lancaster and Kirk Douglas would make their films for Paramount and, in the 1970s, after its purchase by Gulf and Western, the slimmed-down studio would make *The Godfather* films (USA, 1970, 1972) and *Grease* (USA, 1978). In the 1980s, box-office hits such as *Top Gun* (USA, 1982), *Beverly Hills Cop* (USA, 1984), *"Crocodile" Dundee* (Australia, 1986) and *Fatal Attraction* (USA, 1987) would carry the Paramount logo.

In 1923, four Polish-Canadian brothers who had made money in penny arcades and film distribution established the Warners studio, named after themselves. Their films were grittier, cheaper and less glossy than those of Paramount. Their subjects emanated from newspaper headlines and their contractees were Bette Davis, James Cagney, Errol Flynn, Humphrey Bogart and Olivia De Havilland, the last of whom would eventually sue them and help to bring down the studio system in the US. Warners was the first studio to invest properly in sound technology. Its long-term fortunes were typical of Hollywood in the decades to come: in 1989, they were bought by

40
Above: Large factory buildings like these at the MGM studios indicated how much Hollywood had industrialized.

publishing empire Time Inc. Time Warner would reconfigure again in the era of the Internet, becoming AOL-Time Warner.

A third studio, Metro-Goldwyn-Mayer, was established in 1924 and it became the biggest, eventually boasting that it had "more stars than there are in the heavens." MGM's driving force was a brash Russian émigré, Louis B. Mayer, who came from a family of scrap metal merchants. He made a fortune distributing *The Birth of a Nation* and became the highest paid individual in the US in his MGM years, earning $1.25 million plus bonuses. He steered the careers of Greta Garbo, Joan Crawford, James Stewart, Clark Gable and Elizabeth Taylor. The studio's signature roaring lion announced pictures such as *Greed* (1924), *The Crowd* (1928), *The Wizard of Oz* (1939), *Gone with the Wind* (1939), *An American in Paris* (1951) and *Singin' in the Rain* (1952), all landmarks in the history of cinema.

41
Above: This staged production still from *Flesh and the Devil* (1926), starring Greta Garbo, reveals how crowded was the filming of even intimate moments in industralized production.

Zukor, Warners, Mayer and their colleagues at the other Hollywood studios, 20th Century-Fox, Universal, Columbia and United Artists, shackled their rosters of talent with golden hand-cuffs. Actress Joan Crawford's contract was lucrative, but specified when she should go to bed. Former Olympic swimmer Johnny Weismuller's Tarzan contract fined him for every pound he weighed over 190lb. These absurd details illustrate how much the studios tried to control and standardize every part of their operation, attempting to assemble films according to a series of tried and tested blueprints, like the Ford production line. Technicians would become experts at their piece of the process and then hand the emerging film down the line. The standard division of labour in silent era preproduction and postproduction would involve the following: a production boss would pick a subject intended for key contract stars and assign a producer to it. In the major studios, subdivisions called production units grew up around certain producers with proven track records who liked to work with key technicians, such as David O. Selznick at RKO from 1931 onward. The producers would then attach a series of contract writers to the subject, who would produce a "photoplay" or script, detailing the action and the sparse dialogue that would be reproduced as intertitles in the final film. Using this the art department would design and build the sets necessary to film the written scenes or, as happened in most cases, modify existing large sets already constructed on the "back lot". Concurrently, a director would be assigned to the film. The best or most powerful directors, such as the ones who feature in this book, might have written the script themselves, as in Erich Von Stroheim's *Foolish Wives* (1921), King Vidor's *The Crowd* (1928) or Preston Sturges' *The Great McGinty* (1940). The chosen actors would have their costumes designed and fitted by the costume department, costume and make-up tests would be carried out to ensure that they photographed clearly and pleasingly within the sets and then the actors would learn their lines and rehearse with the director. This would be the end of the preproduction.

Production is the shooting process. The cinematographer would be assigned to the project and decide with the director the shot construction and the lighting. In the image below (42), from *Beau Sabreur* (1928), Gary Cooper is fencing in close-up as the camera dollies backward.

The cinematographer, C. Edgar Schoenbaum, is on the dolly, smoking a pipe. The cinematographer would usually have camera assistants who measured the distance between actors and camera (here, a wooden guide ensures Cooper stays in focus by keeping him a constant distance from the lens) and often a camera operator would film the shot as instructed by the cinematographer, although there is no operator in this posed still. A script/continuity girl noted down whether a "take" was good, which part of the script was being filmed and what aspects of the action should be repeated in further takes and scenes, so that the shots matched.

An electrician or "gaffer" set the lights according to the cinematographer's instructions. If the camera was to be moved, a "grip" (at left of image, wearing the white trilby) pushed or pulled the camera, on wheels or wheels on tracks. Special effects people might

42
Above: The cinematographer, Schoenbaum, films the action, while a grip (far left) pulls the camera dolly backward. A T-shaped stick keeps actor Gary Cooper at a constant distance from the lens. *Beau Sabreur*. USA, 1928.

43
Above: The production of
Ben-Hur closely followed
the Hollywood divison of
labour model. USA, 1925.

be on the set perhaps to blow smoke onto it or to arrange a miniature painting in front of the camera to simulate a location that would be too expensive to build or to travel to. Props people would be on hand to provide and arrange objects. Hair and make-up experts would be on standby to smooth a blemish or comb hair into place.

The shot footage would be given to an editor, often a woman, when the filming was completed or during the production, and this marked the beginning of postproduction. The editor cut the pictures together to tell the story in the liveliest or most engaging way. In the silent era, only the most prestigious films would have scores specially commissioned from composers; when completed, most films were sent silent to cinemas, which employed pianists or organists to provide music appropriate to the depicted action. With the advent of sound cinema, the composer would look through the "rough cut" and write a score, which could be recorded by an orchestra and whose sound layers would be added by a technician within the musical team. In the meantime, the editor got approval for the cut from the studio boss, producer and director and decided on the visual devices, such as dissolves and wipes, that would be used as transitions from one shot to the next. A laboratory then cut the negative according to the editor's directions and copied it hundreds of times to manufacture prints to travel round the world's cinemas.

Films such as *Way Down East* (D.W Griffith, 1919), *The Three Musketeers* (Fred Niblo, 1920), *The Four Horsemen of the*

THE WORLD EXPANSION OF STYLE (1918–28): MOVIE FACTORIES AND PERSONAL VISION

Apocalypse (Rex Ingram, 1921), *Robin Hood* (Allan Dwan, 1922), *The Ten Commandments* (Cecil B. De Mille, 1923), *The Hunchback of Notre Dame* (Wallace Worsley, 1923), *The Thief of Bagdad* (Raoul Walsh, 1924), *Ben-Hur* (Fred Niblo, 1925) (43), *Don Juan* (Alan Crosland, 1926), *Flesh and the Devil* (Clarence Brown, 1926) and *Wings* (William Wellman, 1927) were produced this way. These were the big adventure stories and romances of their day, intended to entertain. They attempted to be spatially and psychologically clear and were made to engage audiences emotionally and be more romantic than real life. Yet they also wanted to be accessible, about real people, perhaps more glamorous and exciting than the public, but still made of flesh and blood. The word "classical" has often been used to describe these characteristics, but that is too loose a term. Classicism in art refers to balance between form and content, a state of order where intellectual and emotional values are in harmony, but Hollywood studio films of the 1920s and 1930s almost never achieved this balance, this harmony. (There *was* a classical period in cinema, in Japan in the 1930s and 1940s.) Director John Ford is often described as Hollywood's key classicist, but his *My Darling Clementine* (1946) or *She Wore a Yellow Ribbon* (1949) are more romantic than classical.

Most Hollywood films have an emotional amplitude greater than that of everyday life. Dark clouds hang over them as they do in romantic poetry and painting, and their stories are drawn against the background of fate. Theirs is a phenomenally successful brand of emotional excess, against which other branches of world cinema would be defined. For the rest of this book their combined characteristics will be referred to as "closed romantic realism". I use "closed" because these films tend to create worlds that do not acknowledge that they are being watched and the actors behave as if the camera isn't there. Novice actors would be told not to look at the camera. (This is not always the case, examples being Japanese and Indian films.) They also try not to be open to uncertainty or alternative meanings. I use "realism" because they are seldom about gods, other planets or symbolic figures.

It was not only the tone and structure of closed romantic realism that was distinctive, but also the length of individual shots. Although these varied according to the film type, the Hollywood industrial approach led to shorter shots than in Europe. The average shot length in an American film in the period 1918–23 was 6.5

seconds, in Europe it was 30 per cent longer at 8.5 seconds. Industrial cinema, in Hollywood and elsewhere, also preferred its films to be photographed from many angles, which allowed their producers and editors to have more control of scene and story pacing.

The style of shots in closed romantic realism changed in the 1920s. Directors in America, in particular, put gauzes over their lenses to flatter the looks of their actresses, to soften the mood and to make the imagery more romantic. One of the first to do this, anticipating the trend by several years, was D.W. Griffith's cinematographer, Billy Bitzer, in *Broken Blossoms* (USA, 1918). The use of longer

44

Right: Greta Garbo and John Gilbert were shot with new 75mm or 100mm lenses in *Flesh and The Devil*. The resulting intimate and flattering imagery became the norm in romantic filmmaking. Director: Clarence Brown. USA, 1926.

lenses in the same period accentuated romantic detachment. In the American films of Swedish star, Greta Garbo, the close-ups were shot with these newer, 75mm or 100mm lenses rather than the normal 50mm. Giant, flattened, romantic images were created such as in *Flesh and the Devil* (USA, 1926) where her nose, lips and eyelashes are more clearly in focus than are her hair or the background (44).

This was before the onset of dialogue and sound, so hopeful, escapist, emotional Hollywood films, which could be understood in non-English speaking countries, took the world film market by storm. America was producing between 500–700 films annually, so over 6,000 flooded other film industry's markets during these years. Their gloss, high technical standards and utopian aims appealed to audiences in other countries more than local films. The Soviet Union was sealed off from much of this. In Britain, however, the local film industry took a "if you can't beat them, join them" approach, adopting the tenets of closed romantic realism, while the annual output of French films dropped considerably.

Novelist Henry Miller called this Hollywood production line "a dictatorship in which the artist is silenced".[2] The political writer Karl Marx said "Movies are made by blind people ... who seal, deal with and distribute them." Each of these commentators thought that an industrial approach to filmmaking is wrong and that movies are works of art, not Model T Fords. Throughout the course of film history, studio systems in America and in Japan, India, Mexico, Italy, Britain, China, Hong Kong, Korea and France undoubtedly produced cynical, repetitive fodder, but rigorously controlled production systems across the world and throughout cinema history were also flexible and sophisticated enough to make some of the great films of Marcel Carné (France, 1930s), John Ford (USA, 1930s and 1940s), King Hu (Hong Kong, 1960s), Buster Keaton (USA, 1920s), Vincente Minnelli (USA, 1960s) and Yasujiro Ozu (Japan, 1920s to 1950s). This not only occurred when the controlling studio heads and bosses had their backs turned, but also occurred in front of the bosses as a direct result of the way the factory system fostered expertise and taste. Some of these directors, such as Ford, navigated ways of controlling the system to their own ends. When Ford shot his Westerns, *Stagecoach* (USA, 1939) and *My Darling Clementine*, he would sit by the camera, and when it had recorded the precise piece of action he required, he would raise his fist in front of the lens. He did this to ruin the rest of the take and thereby prevent his producer bosses using anything in the final film except the moment he approved. The closed romantic realism of the studio system was the schema of international film style. It could not be rejected completely by studio directors, but the best varied and enhanced it, especially in the Hollywood comedies from 1918–28.

HOLLYWOOD COMEDIES

The freedom and technological expertise in Hollywood with which to explore the relationship between film and laughter was unmatched anywhere else in the world.

The English vaudevillian turned slapstick clown, Charles Chaplin, who was brought up in part in a London orphanage for destitute children, went to the US in 1910 aged twenty-one and was initially appalled at the crudity of the American slapstick in the Biograph and Keystone output. Inspired by the graceful French comedian Max Linder, who also wore a gentlemanly outfit and who directed his own films, Chaplin advanced film comedy in a way as profound as Griffith's contribution to film drama. He humanized it and gave it emotional and storytelling subtlety; he bent the studio system to his will with longer shooting schedules than other directors were permitted; and he wrote, produced, scored and acted in his films in addition to directing them.

Chaplin's career is a perfect example of schema plus variation. In his second film, *Kid Auto Races at Venice* (USA, 1914) he used a costume of bowler hat, scruffy baggy trousers, walking stick and oversized boots which became his trademark. Thereafter, as critic Walter Kerr wrote, "He had to find out by trial and error and sudden inspiration what was inside the outside."[3] His outfit was that of a penniless tramp, but also that of a gentleman and dilettante. This ambiguity would allow Chaplin, in his mature films, to explore with dazzling

45
Below: Chaplin's rapport with Coogan resulted in one of the best child performances in silent cinema.

THE WORLD EXPANSION OF STYLE (1918–28): MOVIE FACTORIES AND PERSONAL VISION

grace and timing the sadness of his childhood and also become as much of a sophisticate as his ambiguous beggar imagined himself to be. He would do twenty, thirty or forty takes of a routine to get it right and sometimes simply stop the production to think. Ideas came first.

A key to Chaplin's evolution, and to the role that visual ideas played in his work, is to be found in the Canadian producer-director-actor of Irish stock, Mary Sennett. A producer of more than 1,100 films, Sennett co-established the first film company devoted solely to comedy — Keystone — in 1912, and set the slapstick tone of its work which would be influential for generations to come. Sennett spotted Chaplin on stage and hired him in 1912. Within twenty-six months the latter had left Keystone, rebelling against the studio's manic house style. Even through the grace of his later work the following was clear, as historian Simon Louvish has argued: "Without Keystone's rickety sets, the pre-existing world of its eccentric characters, bums, ne'er-do-wells, violent philanderers, innocent young swains, rude women and social braggarts, however, Charlie the tramp would never have been born. For while Charlie brought the form of Karno pantomime to his new world, the content was Sennett's own America, contagious, nervous, always at high speed. All the little bits and pieces of business that made up The Tramp's many mannerisms, his cane-twirling, ear-picking attention to small details, were a realization in depth of Keystone's external chaos."[4]

In 1915, soon after leaving Keystone, Chaplin became a star. By 1916, he was earning $10,000 per week with massive bonuses and, crucially, had full creative control over the editing of the film, what is called "final cut". In 1919, Chaplin, with Mary Pickford, Douglas Fairbanks and D.W. Griffith, founded United Artists Corporation. Four of the most powerful people in world cinema banded together to establish a talent-led production and releasing company which, however, did not own a studio. In subsequent years it would release American films such as *The Night of the Hunter* (1955), *Some like it Hot* (1959) and *The Apartment* (1960) together with the James Bond films. Ironically, it was the extravagant and perfectionist director Michael Cimino, sharing many qualities with Chaplin, who prompted the demise of United Artists when he made one of the biggest box-office disasters in film history, the splendid Marxist epic Western, *Heaven's Gate* (1980).

Chaplin directed his first feature, *The Kid,* in 1921. It tells the story of an unmarried mother (played by Chaplin regular Edna Purviance) who is forced to abandon her baby son. Chaplin's tramp finds him and brings him up. The five-year-old boy (Jackie Coogan) works for his foster father, breaking windows so that Chaplin can reglaze them. Eventually the kid is taken away to an orphanage by the social services, Chaplin fights to get him back and the situation is resolved ambiguously. Coogan gave one of the freshest child performances in movies to this date.

46
Above: The locations and styling of *The Kid* derived in part from Chaplin's childhood memories. Director: Charlie Chaplin. USA, 1921.

It is possible to see *The Kid* and hardly laugh. Indeed, this is true of much of Chaplin, but it is impossible to ignore his deeply felt work. Some of the imagery of *The Kid*, for example, derives directly from Chaplin's own childhood. The street lamps are modelled on those in the London of his youth and the gas meter takes shillings rather than quarters. The room inhabited by father and son is based on one that Chaplin lived in as a boy. During the year of filming, Chaplin refined and deepened moments, weaving them together with innovative detail. The tramp father-figure wants to do well by the child and attempts to teach him to live in a civilized way. At one point he fashions a nightgown out of an old blanket and, so inventive is Chaplin as director and actor, we somehow see a cosy nightgown before our eyes. When finally released, *The Kid* was a huge hit, taking $2.5 million at the box office.

Chaplin's *The Gold Rush* (USA, 1925), *City Lights* (USA, 1931), *Modern Times* (USA, 1936) and *The Great Dictator* (USA, 1940), a satire on Adolf Hitler, made him one of the most influential filmmakers of the first four decades of movie history. George Bernard Shaw called him "the only genius developed in motion pictures". Chaplin changed not only the imagery of cinema, but also its sociology and grammar. In the Soviet Union they admired what they saw as his social criticism, which contributed to rumours that he was a communist. This resulted in his being denied re-entry into America in 1952, his adoptive home of forty years, after a trip to the English premiére of his film, *Limelight* (USA, 1952). Such was the mark left by Chaplin that many subsequent comedians adopted a uniform to express their comic persona. In France, from the late 1940s onward, Jacques Tati followed in Chaplin's footsteps, varying his schema as ugly. Very beautiful. Ostrich's eyes. Human eyes in the exact balance of melancholy."[7]

Born Joseph Frank Keaton in Kansas in 1895, he got his nickname Buster from world-famous escapologist Harry Houdini. At first he did not like movies, thinking they were all on a par with the boxing films shown at Tally's Phonograph Palace. However, in 1917 an event took place which changed his attitude. While visiting a film studio in Manhattan, he met Roscoe "Fatty" Arbuckle, a comic performer and director who became a lifelong influence. Arbuckle allowed Keaton to inspect a camera and so interested was he in its technology, that he nearly "climbed into it", according to his biographer.

After making fifteen short films with Arbuckle, Keaton, who still had a smiling persona in these early days, started directing his own short comedies. *One Week* (USA, 1920), about a week in the life of a newly-married couple, was a revelation. In a key sequence, their lopsided house is whirled around by a tornado, and Keaton is somehow catapulted through the building to its other side. In another, Keaton puts his hand in front of the camera to protect his wife's modesty as she takes a bath. *The Playhouse* (USA, 1921) is even more inventive. While at the theatre, Keaton discovers that it is entirely staffed and its pro-

duction performed by himself as stagehands, musicians, conductor, actors and an audience of mixed sexes (49) and ages. In order to achieve these effects, the film had to be shot, masked, rewound and re-exposed with unparalleled precision, constantly building up composite images on the negative.

In 1921, Buster's friend Arbuckle was accused and then twice acquitted of manslaughter after a woman he was said to have raped at a party — Virginia Rappe — died of a ruptured bladder. The story created headlines around the world; Arbuckle's career was finished and he died eleven years later. In response to this scandal, actor-director Wallace Reid's morphine addiction and the murder of

49
Above: Actor, director and writer Buster Keaton plays both characters in this theatre scene from *The Playhouse*. The precision required showed Keaton's mastery of the technicalities of the medium. USA, 1921.

director William Desmond Taylor, a terrified film industry set up, in 1922, a self-regulatory body headed by Postmaster-General Will H. Hays, whose remit was to censor sexual and violent imagery, stories and themes. Dubbed the Hays Office in the late 1920s, the organization drew up a strict line of prohibitions known as the Hays Code, which, together with religious pressure groups such as the Catholic Legion of Decency, inhibited Hollywood's realistic treatment of sexuality, race and social problems for nearly three decades. The otherworldly innocence of American closed romantic realism in the ensuing decades can be attributed, in part, to these no-go areas, as can the tone of moral denunciation in the work of directors such as Cecil B. De Mille, who would sometimes depict sexual and decadent scenes in his films, but who would punish his characters for indulging in such behaviour. The Hays Code was eroded in the 1950s, but remained intact until the mid-1960s.

Keaton's success in short films led to features, each extravagantly physical, exacting and architectural. The scenario alone of *Our Hospitality* (USA, 1923) is brilliant: Buster is in the home of a family intent on murdering him. However, their Southern hospitality forbids them to be anything other than kind to him while he remains their guest. So he is trapped in the strained embrace of his hosts.

A scene omitted from *The Navigator* (USA, 1924) illustrates Keaton's inventive discipline. While his character is welding the submerged hull of a ship, he notices that huge shoals of fish are colliding and so becomes an ocean floor traffic policeman as he directs one shoal to wait as the other swims by. In order to stage this visual gag, he had 1,500 rubber fish manufactured and mounted on a lattice that would make them appear to swim in front of the camera. The edited gag was shown in the film's trailer and had the audience in stitches of laughter, but when it was incorporated in the final film, raised not a single giggle. This was because, while Buster was doing his underwater point duty, the heroine was above, alone on the ship and being approached by cannibals. The audience was therefore too tense and cared too much about the girl to laugh at Keaton's surreal dalliance down below. When tension and laughter were part of the same scene, as in Lloyd's *Safety Last*, they worked in combination. However, when they were intercut in the sequence in *The Navigator*, they detracted from each other. Keaton's response was to cut the expensive joke.

Keaton learnt how to use comic anticipation to great effect in *The General* (USA, 1926), in which he plays a Southern train driver whose train and girl are stolen while he is still on board. For the first half of the film, he travels north to the thieves hideout and in the second, reunited with his girl, escapes south again on the locomotive. All the visual jokes and set-ups in the first section are repeated and amplified in reverse order in the second half. The audience realizes the pattern. The film's climax is, according to Walter Kerr, "the most stunning visual event ever arranged for a comedy, perhaps for any kind of film." Keaton has returned the train to his native South and as the Northern enemy armies advance, he sets fire to a strategically important bridge. He miscues the timing and as soldiers gather in the foreground (50), the burning bridge cracks under the weight of the engine, which rolls and topples into the river. No trick shots were used in this sequence and the train wreck was visible for years to come in Cottage Grove, Oregon. This scene is the best example of what could be called "the sublime" in 1920s cinema, that feeling of awe, verging on terror, engendered by the scale of the film's

production values. The sublime was attainable for several reasons. Labour in the US at this time was cheap, Wall Street had not crashed, imaginations were extravagant and sometimes uncapped, and studios had not yet become excessively wary of the scope of directors' dreams.

Unlike Lloyd, Keaton's box-office returns did not match the scale of his productions. He was sacked by MGM and eventually became an alcoholic and a gag writer for films such as *A Southern Yankee* (USA, 1948) and *Neptune's Daughter* (USA, 1949). By the 1950s prints of *Our Hospitality* and *The General* were lost, but in 1952 the British actor, James Mason, now owner of Keaton's house, found copies of each in a hidden cupboard. The films started to circulate and in 1965 Keaton attended a retrospective of his work at the Venice Film Festival, which was greeted with standing ovations. He died the next year.

51

Right: Buster Keaton's interest in machinery and how things are constructed was captured well in this Soviet poster for *The General*.

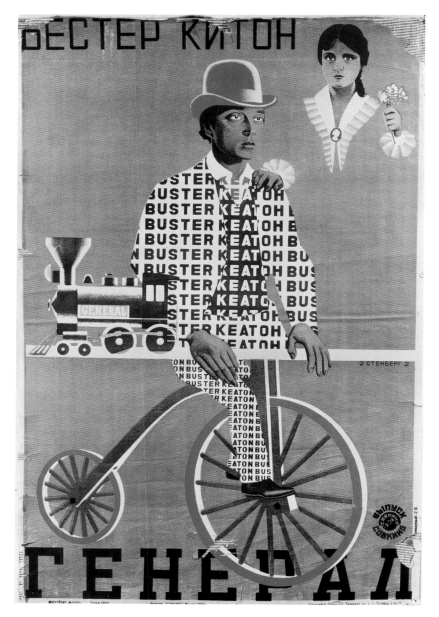

Like Chaplin, Keaton was popular in the Soviet Union (51), and the rigorous structure of his films, their feeling for space and land, was greatly admired. His influence can be seen in *Arsenal* (Soviet Union, 1929), one of the greatest Soviet works. More so even than Chaplin, Keaton's spatial humour anticipated the long takes of Jacques Tati in France. He succeeded in fusing entertainment values with cinematic invention, which edified the industrial approach

The camera cuts to the officer who has suddenly stopped the challenge. Perhaps the chancellor brandishes a more impressive weapon? No, he has pulled out a cheque book. The confrontation will be resolved in a more business-like fashion.

Middle-class salons, sophisticated clubs and great ballrooms became the places in which Lubitsch staged his stories of love triangles and extramarital relations. His films were, rather daringly, about the delights of desire – stark contrast to the coy Victorian portrayal of sexuality in American cinema as practised by D.W. Griffith. In Lubitsch's very successful *The Marriage Circle* (USA, 1924), a psychiatrist and his wife are at breakfast. A close-up of an egg, then of a coffee cup is revealed. The psychiatrist's hand cuts the top off the egg and his wife stirs the coffee. Suddenly his hand disappears, and then hers, and the breakfast is pushed aside. A more urgent desire than eating has overtaken them, and though Lubitsch does not film their lovemaking, his use of objects, of implication, is masterly.

The films of the undervalued Moscow-born Boris Barnet were similar in tone to those of Lubitsch. Barnet, a former boxer, was directing from 1926. Like Bauer and Protazanov a decade earlier, he contributed to the naturalization of acting in Russian and Soviet cinema. In contrast to their tragedies, his *The Girl with the Hat Box* (Soviet Union, 1927) is a jaunty and irreverent story about a country girl, Natasha, who makes hats and sells them to a Moscow milliner (52). She fakes marriage to a student in order that they can rent a room together. The scenes in the rented room portray the couple's flirtations with particular invention, especially when the landlady becomes suspicious of their marital status and removes everything from their living space, including the carpet. The hints that they are sleeping with one another could have been directed by Lubitsch or Chaplin, but Barnet raises the chutzpah further than either.

53
Above: Writer-director Lois Weber, pictured here at her typewriter, was one of the highest-paid film directors in the world. Her background in social work influenced the realism of her stories.

The last of our non-American comedy directors was the son of a Parisian soap-seller. Fascinated by poetry and theatre, René Clair made one of the most influential silent comedies, *Un Chapeau de paille d'Italie/An Italian Straw Hat* (France, 1927). In this, a gentleman is on his way to his wedding and en route his horse accidentally eats the straw hat of a married lady on an excursion with her lover.

Above: The documentary
Nanook of the North.
Director Robert Flaherty
used Eskimo drawings
(bottom) to help him
compose some scenes
(top). USA, 1921.

Fantastical incidents ensue as the fiancé tries to find an exact replacement for the hat to cover up the woman's dalliance. Clair would go on to be one of the screen's wittiest fantasists and much of his later visual skills, his interest in farce and parody, his enchantment, were introduced in *An Italian Straw Hat.*

In the 1920s, a disparate range of international filmmakers with diverse methods and subjects, who were dissatisfied with the escapism of mainstream filmmaking in America, Britain, India and France, and who wanted to make films about ignored aspects of human life, found themselves separately exploring the possibilities of cinematic naturalism. Lois Weber (53) was one of the most highly-paid directors in the world and certainly, in 1918, the highest-paid female director. A former social worker in deprived areas of Pittsburgh and New York, she acted in and then wrote, produced and directed films which she pronounced, "will have an influence for good in the public mind."[8] Despite her celebrity, from her earliest films she addressed themes beyond the conventional reach of closed romantic realism. *The Jew's Christmas* (USA, 1913) and *Hypocrites* (USA, 1914) attacked religious prejudice and *The People vs. Joe Doe* (USA, 1916) campaigned against capital punishment. Like Alice Guy-Blaché (see Chapter One), her role in film history is seldom acknowledged.

The American explorer and son of a mining prospector, Robert Flaherty, also challenged mainstream filmmaking from a campaigning standpoint, but with a profoundly different approach. Like Louis Le Prince, the Lumière agents and the cameramen who filmed the Mexican revolutionary war, he did not use actors. The result was his celebrated documentary, *Nanook of the North* (USA, 1921) which was the longest of its type to date. It centred on Nanook, famous hunter in the Itivinuit tribe of Alaskan Eskimos. Flaherty filmed as early as 1913 in the frozen landscapes of the arctic north, but discovered that without a storyline or themes, his footage lacked tension and drama. Returning in 1920, he took a more classical – in the true sense including the Dane Lars von Trier, particularly in his depiction of the Scottish island of Skye in *Breaking the Waves* (Denmark, 1998).

The 1920s work of American writer-director-producer Oscar Micheaux engaged with reality in ways that studio films did not. Micheaux was born in 1884, the black son of freed slaves. He raised money for the forty or so films he made between 1919–48 by selling shares in his work to communities and taking advance bookings from black specialist cinemas. His films were often bawdy and technically crude, but are said to have portrayed slavery and lynching themes, although few survive. *Within our Gates* (USA, 1920) shows the terrible results of a young black woman attempting to run a school for black children with the assistance of a northern, white patron. Its frank depiction of the racist backlash may have been Micheaux's response to *The Birth of a Nation* five years earlier. His *Body and Soul* (USA, 1924) features distinguished black actor and singer Paul Robeson in the role of a priest who exploits the piety of black churchgoers (57). One wonders how black American cinema would have developed if Micheaux had been admitted into and been trained by one of the studios, such as Warner Bros.

57
Above: One of pioneering black filmmaker Oscar Micheaux's few surviving films: Paul Robeson in *body and soul*. USA, 1924.

Indian cinema in the 1920s continued producing portraits of the lives of saints and developed what would later be called "All India Films", big fantasy movies, unmarked by specifics of creed or geography, intended to appeal to the diverse regions, religions, communities and castes of the continent. Much later, dissatisfied filmmakers would reverse this trend and, as early as 1924, socially committed directors were moving in that direction. Homi Master, one of the most successful Indian directors of the 1920s, went to Europe a few years earlier to market Phalke's earliest films (see page 46). In 1924, he made *Twentieth Century*, which created the genre of the reformist melodrama arguing for social change through the portrayal of gripping human problems. In the film, a street seller makes a fortune in Bombay, becomes an exploitative employer and cosies up to the colonial British.

58
Above: A scene from one of India's first social reform films – *Indian Schlock*. Director: Baburao Painter. India, 1925.

Former craftsman and painter Baburao Painter had more impact than Master on the themes of Indian cinema, especially in the central and western region of Maharashtra. Like Master, he was inspired by Phalke's *King Harishchandra* (India, 1913) and instigated the historical and social genres in Indian cinema. He used painted backdrops and coloured filters over the lens to control his film's tonal range of greys and blacks. India's first social genre film was *Indian Shylock* (India, 1925), which charts the story of a peasant (R.V. Shanataram) whose land is stolen by a moneylender and who is then forced to move to, and experience the harsh life of, the city. The film's performances were melodramatic but its reformist aim to draw attention to social problems places it outside the norms of conventional studio filmmaking of the time.

Back in America, a gigantic film with similar intentions had just been completed. Its title alone, *Greed* (1923–25), makes this plain. Its writer-director, Erich Von Stroheim, expressed a hope shared by every dissident Naturalist: "It is possible to tell a great story in motion pictures ... in such a way that the spectator ... will come to believe that what he is looking at is real."

Von Stroheim was a Prussian-Viennese former straw hat factory worker with aristocratic pretensions. Emigrating to the US in 1909, he became an actor and was rapidly typecast as a sadistic Prussian officer, particularly during the First World War. His first films as director reflected his fascination with providing authentic detail and exploring the decadence and moral corruption of rich and civilized people. Though Von Stroheim's style involved symbolism and expressionism as well as naturalism, he filmed every scene of American writer Frank Norris' naturalistic novel, *McTeague*, on which *Greed* is based, meticulously. The film's nine-month filming schedule was budgeted at $1.5 million and ran in its first cut for nearly ten hours. Its story was classic Von Stroheim in that it dealt with a bitter and loveless marriage. The wife of a dentist in San Francisco wins the lottery and, as she gets obsessively greedy, her husband becomes drunken and penniless. Eventually he murders her and, in an infamous climax filmed in Death Valley, also kills a rival who put him out of business, but is left handcuffed helplessly to the corpse. This was American cinema without hope; many commentators have compared Von Stroheim's vision to that of nineteenth-century Russian literature, with which *Greed* shares a determination to reveal the unvarnished truth about human beings. In one startling scene, shoot seven different optimistic endings. The one that was finally chosen shows John and his wife in a theatre, laughing at a clown dressed as an out-of-work, down-at-heel man. As they laugh at their own predicament being performed on stage, the camera pulls back to lose them in the multitude.

The Crowd encapsulates a lot about cinema between the two world wars. The theme of the emerging mass society, of everyman, was not only popular with Vidor and found in Mervyn LeRoy's depression musical *Gold Diggers of 1933* (USA, 1933), but was also explored in France in the films of René Clair, Jean Vigo and Marcel Carné. Likewise, the kinetic energy of cities themselves, their rhythms and compositions, seemed a perfect subject for this Western machine – the movie camera. Filmmakers such as Fritz Lang and Walter Ruttmann in Germany and Dziga Vertov in the Soviet Union[10] were at their most creative when taking cities as their subject matter in films such as *Metropolis* (Germany, 1927), *Berlin: Die Symphonie einer Grosstadt/Berlin: Symphony of a City* (Germany, 1928) and *Man with a Movie Camera* (Soviet Union, 1929) respectively.

The last in the line of naturalistic dissident films is only in part like the others – Florián Rey's *La Aldea maldita/The Accursed Village* (Spain, 1929). Like Painter's *Indian Shylock* it is about a family migrating to the city, celebrating the timelessness of rural values and so touching a national nerve since urbanization scared many people. Right-wing Spanish politicians had used this fear to attack modernity and what they perceived to be society's moral decline. The film's rural scenes are shot in a simple, painterly style, but the pace of its editing increases in the second half, which is set in the city. However, it is only in a few sequences that Rey stares at the real world with more intensity than was usually permitted by mainstream cinema.

The films of Weber, Flaherty, Sjöström, Micheaux, Master, Painter, Von Stroheim, Vidor and Rey are wildly different in form and content. But in their social awareness or anthropological ambitions, their meticulous commitment to naturalistic detail and their anxiety about capitalism and exclusion, these films indicate how incomplete was the view of the world reflected in closed romantic realism. Most of the directors of these films did not meet each other and they certainly did not represent any kind of cohesive social or intellectual movement, yet their work was sometimes used as a badge of prestige by the same studio whose very world view they challenged. By pushing at the boundaries of closed romantic realism they pointed to a space beyond what most people considered to be the appropriate one for movies. That space would be enlarged by 1930s British filmmakers, Italian filmmakers after 1945, and African and Middle-Eastern directors in the late 1960s and 1970s. To the extent that the work of this ragbag of formal and social naturalists outlasted more escapist films, they had the last laugh.

In 1920s France, industrial cinema was in crisis. Hollywood was flooding the market and in 1926 produced 725 films, Germany made over 200, but France produced only 55, many made by small companies. As would be the pattern throughout the course of film

61
Right: *The Smiling Madame Beudet* used camera manipulations and visual distortions to reflect the main character's emotions. Director: Germaine Dulac. France, 1921.

history, successful national films tended to be the smaller and more distinctive ones that attempted to challenge romantic cinema. However, in the case of 1920s France, naturalism was not the most important means of attack. Influenced by the impressionist painting of Claude Monet and Camille Pissarro and the writings of Charles Baudelaire, filmmakers such as Germaine Dulac, Abel Gance, Jean Epstein and Marcel L'Herbier tried to capture the complexity of people's perception of the real world and the way in which mental images repeat and flash before our eyes.

Dulac was an intellectual like Vidor. Born into a rich family, she became involved in films such as *Les Soeurs enemies/The Enemy*

Sisters (France, 1916) and, met her collaborator, the film theorist Louis Delluc in 1917. Together they evolved one of the first self-consciously innovative cinematic movements in the world, the first movie avant-garde. Louis was the first theorist to notice that psychoanalyst Sigmund Freud's ideas could influence film. After screening one of her movies Germaine said "I want to shout: 'Keep cinema to itself; movement without literature".[11] In Dulac's seminal Madame Bovary-like tale, *La Souriante Madame Beudet/The Smiling Madame Beudet* (France, 1921), the passionate Beudet lives in a provincial town and is married to a workaholic salesman. Dulac expresses her main character's erotic daydreams and bottled rage not only through acting and incident, but also by placing netting in front of the lens and by manipulating the camera (61). When Beudet is light-headed, a gauze makes her viewpoint look dreamy. This is very different from Griffith's use of gauzes, which were intended to make actresses look beautiful and ethereal to the audience. When Beudet spies a handsome man in a magazine, slow-motion photography pictures her reverie, as if the audience were looking at the world through Beudet's eyes. Visual distortions express her anger and the images are often speeded up.

La Roue/The Wheel (France, 1923), made the year after *The Smiling Madame Beudet*, extended Dulac's impressionism in certain sequences. It was written, directed and edited by the driven Parisian filmmaker Abel Gance, whose first significant work in cinema was for the company Film d'Art, responsible for *The Assassination of the Duc de Guise* (France, 1908). Gance had already directed a three-hour meditation on pacifism, *J'Accuse* (France, 1919), inspired by several months he had spent in the army during the First World War, but *La Roue* was more innovative. The film's story is a complex love triangle between a railway worker, Sisif, his son, Elie, and Sisif's adopted daughter, Norma. After a fight in the Alps between Elie and Norma's husband, Elie is left hanging over the edge of a cliff. To represent Elie's life flashing before his eyes, Gance edited together a series of single-frame images from earlier moments within his relationship with Norma. These single frames were just one twenty-fourth of a second in length. When viewed on the cinema screen in real time, they rush past in a disorienting blur. Gance knew that each could not be seen clearly by the audience, but wanted to give the impression of panic in his main character, the sense of perception and feeling accelerating intolerably. The scene was revolutionary and caused artist, poet and filmmaker Jean Cocteau to say "There is cinema before and after *La Roue*, just as there is painting before and after Picasso."

Nothing quite like this had been done before and *La Roue* became one of the most influential films of the silent era. Japanese director Akira Kurosawa, who was to work after the Second World War, said that it was the first important film he saw. The Soviet directors Vsevolod Pudovkin, Sergei Eisenstein and Alexander Dovzhenko

studied it in Moscow and D.W. Griffith considered its techniques to be exciting. During the following four years Gance would write, direct and edit a four-hour film about the early life of Napoleon Bonaparte, the French revolutionary, national leader and militarist, whose life straddled the eighteenth and nineteenth centuries, portraying its main character as a tragic hero. Gance rethought the camera's relationship to movement to capture the dynamism of the man, his fist fights and horse rides, grand society balls, battle charges and storms at sea. The camera did not merely witness the speeding, swinging, lunging events, but it rolled and lurched, swung and sped in the same way as Napoleon's life had. *The Los Angeles Times* described the results as "The measure for all other films, ever."

Napoleon (France, 1927) opens with a prologue showing Napoleon as a boy in a military academy. The sequence features boys punching right up to the screen; the actors were able to do this because Gance had ingeniously mounted a fur-covered sponge around the lens to absorb any blows hitting the camera. This is a clear advance on Gary Cooper fencing to the lens in the still from *Beau Sabreur* on page 65. Gance reused the technique from the climax of *La Roue* for the denouement of the sequence, as a single frame of Napoleon's boyish smiling face is edited into the action, six times

in a single second of twenty-four frames. Gance also attached a compressed-air-powered camera to the saddle of a horse (63) during an equestrian chase in the early Corsican scenes. One of the most famous sections in the film intercut Napoleon in a small boat during a raging storm, with shots of the assembled Revolutionary Convention. The shots of the storm were realized by flanking the boat with huge sluices in a studio tank, down which water was hurled. Gance's intercutting made the point that the Revolutionary Convention was also at sea, buffeted by huge political forces. In order to emphasize this fact visually, Gance had a platform suspended from a vast pendulum. The camera was attached to this platform and the apparatus swung through an arc. The film's climax was Napoleon's entry into Italy. In this sequence Gance surpassed the epic imagery of *Cabiria* and *Intolerance* by filming with three cameras mounted on

62
Above: Abel Gance combined images from three adjacent cameras to produce the famous panoramic scenes in *Napoleon*. The overlaps between each image are just visible. France, 1927.

top of each other (the black box to the right is a motor). Each camera pointed in a slightly different direction and filmed adjacent parts of a battle scene which, when projected together, combined in one vast horizontal panorama (62). Nothing like it, since the aborted panorama at the 1900 Paris Exhibition, had been seen in the cinema and audiences had to turn their heads to take in the whole spectacle. The three-screen technique was later to inspire Cinerama, an ultra widescreen multi-projector process, whose first fiction feature was *How the West Was Won* (USA, 1962).

   Napoleon was shown infrequently to great acclaim in its original format, but the film's enormous budget undermined Gance's independence. Despite being the leader of the vanguard of French filmmaking, he ended up working for French studios and modifying his style like others in the impressionist film movement. Various versions of *Napoleon* appeared in the 1950s but it wasn't until the results of a major restoration of the negative by British historian and filmmaker Kevin Brownlow were screened at the 1979 Telluride Film Festival in Colorado that it was seen in something like its former glory. Gance, aged eighty-nine, travelled to the festival; many who saw it in Telluride or at its subsequent premières in London and New York felt that it was among the greatest films ever made. Gance died aged ninety-two, two weeks after *Napoleon*'s New York première, which was sponsored by Francis Coppola. Coppola's *Apocalypse Now* (USA, 1979) was as a similar study in power on the scale of and in the manner of *Napoleon*.

   Two years before *Napoleon*, a Franco-German film critic turned director, E.A. Dupont, made a movie in Germany which, despite its country of origin, has many of the qualities of French impressionism. *Variety* (Germany, 1925) begins and ends in a prison in which an acrobat, played by the powerful German actor Emil Jannings, recalls events from his life. He eloped with a trapeze artiste, watched her fall in love with a younger man, killed that man, then surrendered himself to the police. The film was photographed by Karl Freund, an Austrian cinematographer who shot some of the most significant films of the 1920s, directed the extraordinary, expressionist *The Mummy* (USA, 1930) and ended his career shooting 1950s American television comedy. He uses the camera almost as subjectively as Gance. When Jannings looks jealously at his girl with another man, a close-up of Jannings' eyes is shown as the lighting changes. Then the camera cuts to her with an out-of-focus background. Within the same shot, the focus shifts to

63
Above: Techniques, such as attaching the camera to the back of a horse, created the ground-breaking cinematography in *Napoleon*. Director: Abel Gance. France, 1927.

reveal her suitor beside her. This is one of many sequences that illustrate this kind of intricate geometry of looking and longing. The camera is later mounted on a trapeze as it swings over the audience in a way that echoes the pendulum movement in *Napoleon*'s convention scene. The spectators below do not stare or gasp, but look on casually, chat and smile: the effect is brilliantly modern. The trapeze artists swing luminously through the air high above as if they are clothed in reflective material, an almost abstract effect (64). *Variety* was seen more widely in the US than other impressionist films and, as a result, influenced cinematographers there to move their cameras more.

64
Above: Cinematographer Karl Freund's semi-abstract imagery in E.A. Dupont's *Variety*. Germany, 1925.

The 1920s naturalists introduced lasting aspects of realism to the cinema, whereas the innovations of the French impressionists had died out by 1928. Why was this the case? Perhaps because the phenomena the latter explored — the rapidity of perception, the film image as it approximates human vision — were fleeting experiences. Their most important influence — mainly through the work of Gance — was on the work of Soviet directors such as Eisenstein, and it could be argued that their fast cutting (*The Smiling Madame Beudet*'s average shot duration was just five seconds, shorter than the average American film of the time) anticipated the music-video-influenced style of 1980s American cinema, where momentary slow motion and whip panning were popular again.

Across the border, their German colleagues were attempting to use film for deeper purposes. Dulac and Gance may have tried to capture fleeting and hidden feelings in their work, but Robert Wiene, Fritz Lang and F.W. Murnau were interested in still more repressed and primitive aspects of human beings. Influenced by so-called Expressionist painters and theatre designers, whose jagged and shard-like work was the antithesis of delicacy, they began making expressionist films. Less than thirty were produced, but these were among the most influential films of the decade 1918–28, exported widely and seen all over the world. Germany had just been defeated in an appalling war, its economy was in freefall and yet, unlike that of France, the German film industry was expanding. At the start of the war, there had been about twenty five production companies but this had increased to 130 by 1918. Germany had closed its borders to foreign films in 1916 and this ban wasn't lifted until 1920, so in the interim there was a protected market for indigenous filmmakers, which stimulated production considerably. The rampant inflation of the crippled post-war economy and its weakened currency meant that German films were very cheap to buy to show abroad, although it was expensive for Germany to import goods, and this encouraged film exports over import. The German film industry was also bolstered by the government, who despite the hard times, prioritized film and supported it.[12]

This is the background against which a film, which not only launched the German expressionist film movement, but was also one of the first landmark films in the West to challenge closed romantic realism, was made. *Das Kabinett des Dr. Caligari/The Cabinet of Dr. Caligari* (Germany, 1919), directed by Robert Wiene, was produced before Chaplin's first feature, before the world had heard of Mickey Mouse, before the discovery of Tutankhamun's tomb, before the death of Lenin or the accession of Japan's emperor, Hirohito. Image 65 shows how controversial *Caligari* was. While studio filmmakers in America, Britain and France took a black box approach, excluding all daylight, and Scandinavians did the opposite, Wiene and his designers Hermann Warm, Walter Reiman and Walter Rohrig found a third way. They flooded their set with flat light and then painted shadows directly onto the walls and floor. The effect was to stylize the look of naturalistic film lighting, almost to ridicule it.

The story was structured like Chinese boxes. A student, Francis, tells of a sleepwalker, Cesare, who is on

65
Below: Shadows and light beams painted directly onto the set in Robert Wiene's influential *The Cabinet of Dr. Caligari*. Germany, 1919.

show at a fairground and who, at night, murders the enemies of his master, Dr. Caligari, including one of Francis' friends, Alan. In the process of abducting a beautiful young woman, Cesare dies and Francis goes to a local mental hospital whose director, he discovers, is Caligari. The film's writers, Carl Mayer and Hans Janowitz, had considered their story in political terms. Caligari represented the malign and controlling German state, Cesare represented ordinary people manipulated by it. The thirty-eight-year-old Wiene and his producer, Erich Pommer, removed the film's political edge by adding not only an opening sequence, but a coda in which Francis completes his tale but on returning to the asylum discovers that Cesare is not, in fact, dead after all. This revelation terrifies Francis, who is then strait-jacketed and whom Dr. Caligari — now, apparently, a benign physician — insists he can help. The whole film becomes the dream of the deranged Francis. Wiene's own father, a famous German actor, had become mentally unbalanced toward the end of his life, and perhaps as a result of this, his son showed more interest in this aspect of *Caligari* than its social bite.

This low-budget film took less than three weeks to shoot. Most of the sets were constructed from painted canvas and the costumes were cheaply made. The extreme expressionism of the imagery raised one of the most fundamental questions in cinema. Whose point of view does the imagery of a film represent? If it is that of the audience, the behaviour of the characters may continue to be dreamlike or insane, but the settings will be naturalistic, because the audience is not insane. If it represents some kind of objective, all-seeing storyteller, similar to the narrator in nineteenth-century novels, then this storyteller will not see the whole world as distorted. Perhaps the director is showing how he himself sees circuses and somnambulists, but Wiene was not mentally ill and not until the explosion of cinematic style in the late 1950s would the audience see the world explicitly as the director saw it. The answer to this question seems to lie in Pommer and Wiene's new beginning and ending, which show that the film is told by the madman, Francis. *Caligari*'s imagery, sliced spaces, jagged lighting, twisted lines, emphatic movements and heavy pauses are the expression of Francis' extreme mental state. However, in the last scenes, when the audience has withdrawn from Francis' distorted view of the world and he is observed from the perspective of normal life, the imagery remains expressionist. The idea that a film solely reflects its characters' mental states is not enough to explain such ambiguities; the suggestion is that the film itself, and the shattered society that produced it, are what are really deranged.

Seen in its recent tinted print, *Caligari* remains among the most beautiful of all silent films. It had a sensational première in Berlin, but also had a huge impact in France and later in the US. Although Wiene was the only famous German director who did not go to Hollywood, it is impossible to imagine the later dark Hollywood thrillers made by European directors such as Lang, Wilder, Curtiz and Siodmak without *Caligari*'s formative lesson: that the viewpoint of film imagery can be ambiguous, both outside looking into its characters' neuroses, and inside them. Movies were becoming more complex as their form and content danced around each other.

The expressionist movement in Europe, to which Caligari was the most striking cinematic addition, would colour the films of Fritz Lang and F.W. Murnau and beyond. Alfred Hitchcock, who had been working in Germany in 1924 and 1925, made his first distinctive film, *The Lodger* (UK, 1926, 66) under its influence. Japanese cinema, which continued to use un-Western flattened visuals and *benshi* narrators throughout the 1920s, felt its strong influence. Teinosuke Kinugasa began his film career in 1918, in the traditional Japanese manner – as a female impersonator. By 1922, he was one of the few Japanese directors who wanted to adopt Western filmmaking and express himself, in Gombrichian terms, individually. This was something that even Murata had not achieved in his *Intolerance*-influenced *Souls on The Road*. The historian of Japanese cinema, Noël Burch, underlines this point, "Although the Japanese cinema has known ... independent artists who correspond to the Western image of the original creative temperament, Kinugasa was undoubtedly the first of these."[13]

After having seen both *The Cabinet of Dr. Caligari* and *La Roue*, Kinugasa made *A Page of Madness* (Japan, 1926),[14] about an old man who takes a job in an asylum which houses his wife, who has drowned their baby and attempted suicide. He thinks he can help her by working there, but his own mental state deteriorates. As the image

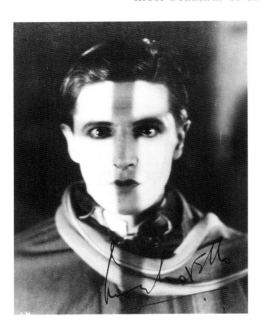

66
Above: Alfred Hitchcock imported some of the shadowplay he saw in Germany for *The Lodger*. UK, 1926.

THE WORLD EXPANSION OF STYLE (1918–28): MOVIE FACTORIES AND PERSONAL VISION

to the right shows, the film was not as formally designed as *Caligari*. What links the two films is Kinugasa's jumbled imagery of the asylum, its visual overlays, flashbacks and symbols, which cannot be ascribed solely to the husband's deteriorating mental state. When he sees events through windows, they are as likely to be flashbacks to his former life, as they are to be what occur outside, but the film as a whole, not just its characters, becomes disorientated and ambiguous. *The Cabinet of Dr. Caligari* and *A Page of Madness* challenge the clarity of mainstream studio filmmaking by telling their stories from the outside and the inside concurrently. This film was for many years considered lost, until Kinugasa discovered a print of it in his garden shed in 1971. When he struck a new print, commissioned a new score and re-released the film around the world, many considered it the most personal Japanese film of the 1920s.

The theme of madness was rife in innovative 1920s cinema. Back in Germany, the son of a Viennese architect, Fritz Lang, created another doctor in the mode of Dr. Caligari, Lang's own doctor, Dr. Mabuse. Lang's wildly exotic and successful adventure-drama *Die Spinnen/The Spiders* (Germany, 1919/1920), now on video, led producer Pommer to ask him to direct *Caligari*, on which he could only

manage some preparatory work. *Dr. Mabuse der Spieler/Dr. Mabuse the Gambler* reached the screen in 1921 and depicts a character who starts the film sane, but criminal. He abducts a countess and bankrupts her millionaire husband through gambling. He then hypnotizes the prosecutor who charges him and convinces him that he must kill himself. Finally, the forces of law close around Dr. Mabuse and he goes insane. Like *Caligari*, *Mabuse* was intended as a critique of the lawlessness and moral decline of 1920s Germany, although its visuals were less stylized than in the former film. Instead, as had been suggested in *The Spiders*, it was the details of Lang's narrative that were expressionist. Mabuse's instincts are excessive and underneath the rich and decadent surface of the characters' lives lie primitive urges. Lang emphasized the tension in society's structure rather than the false ease of its surface, as he would later do in the American films produced after he left his home country, partly in retreat from the Nazis, having declined a key post in the new German industry.[15]

Many saw something architectural in these films, but *Metropolis* (Germany, 1927) was more literally about the structure of complex societies and became the most iconic film of the silent era. Set in the year 2000, it tells the story of clashes between workers and an authoritarian industrialist in a giant city. The workers' anger is regularly quelled by the strange influence of a saintly young woman, Maria. The industrialist, a Mabuse-like figure, hopes to spark revolt among the workers by building a robot that resembles Maria (see page 60, 39). The robot does fool the populace and incites anarchy, but eventually Maria and the industrialist's son save the city, and the workers and owners are united. *Metropolis* took almost eighteen months to shoot, used two million (650,000 metres) feet of film and 36,000 extras. It was photographed by Karl Freund, who had also shot Dupont's *Variety*. Its special effects technician, Eugen Schufftan, invented a mirror process, the "Schufftan process", where a miniature set is reflected into the lens at the same time as characters in its foreground are filmed. He later became a cinematographer and shot key films such as *Quai des brumes/Port of Shadows* (France, 1938) and *The Hustler* (USA, 1961).

68
Above: Futurism meets Art Deco in a poster for Fritz Lang's *Metropolis*. The success of the film popularized linear design and cityscape imagery. Germany, 1927.

The themes of control and descent into madness are central to German film of this period. Its cityscapes and robotics, its iconography of the underworld, its interest in exploitation and in urban paradise, had a profound influence on subsequent science fiction films. Vidor was impressed by *Metropolis*, whose expressionist echoes can be seen in *The Crowd*. The film has been restored and re-released several times in recent decades, once with high energy dance music on its soundtrack. The explosion of American pop culture, which started in the late 1970s, drew on it as a source. The robot, C3PO in *Star Wars* (George Lucas, USA, 1976) and the look of the futuristic cities in *Blade Runner* (Ridley Scott, USA, 1976) and *Batman* (Tim Burton, USA, 1989) derived from *Metropolis*, as did 1990s American director David Fincher's video for Madonna's song, *Express Yourself*. Adolf Hitler also liked *Metropolis* and its epic set design appealed to his architect, Albert Speer. In 1943, when inmates of the Matthausen Nazi concentration camp were forced by their captors to build a gigantic ramp, they compared it to *Metropolis*.[16]

The last great movie of German silent cinema, voted the best film of all time by French film critics,[17] was made in America. *Sunrise* (USA, 1927) was directed by Friedrich Wilhelm Murnau, perhaps the most talented director of the whole silent period, who studied art and literature and then established himself with a dreamy vampire film, *Nosferatu* (Germany, 1922) and an ironic drama about a doorman, *Der Letzte Mann/The Last Laugh* (Germany, 1924). *Sunrise*, was like many 1920s films, including those by Master, Vidor and Rey, already considered, about the contrasting values of country and the city. Its love triangle storyline was also typical of the decade that produced Gance's *La Roue* and Dupont's *Variety*. A country man, happily married, is seduced by a city woman who convinces him to drown his wife. He cannot bring himself to do this and instead travels with his wife across a lake to the city, where they have a joyful day together. Returning to the country she seems to drown during a storm. Grief-stricken, he tries to strangle the city woman.

This skeletal outline describes the elemental nature of *Sunrise*, but does not capture its poetic force (69). Murnau planned the production in Germany and, almost uniquely, Hollywood promised him a free rein, allowing him gigantic city sets and complex lighting set-ups. In keeping with *Caligari*'s expressionism, the interiors were built with slanted walls and sloping ceilings to reflect the characters' distorted perspectives. In fact, it is difficult to categorize Murnau's filmmaking ethos: he was soon collaborating with Robert Flaherty on the quasi-documentary *Tabu* (USA, 1931), and the 1930s French poetic realists considered him their master. *Sunrise* also helped prepare the way for some expressionist American films in subsequent years, including *Foursome* (USA, 1928) and *The Informer* (USA, 1935), by director John Ford.

69
Right: The contrast with *Metropolis* could hardly be more pronounced. Naturalistic sets and romantic lighting in *Sunrise*. Director: F.W. Murnau. USA, 1927.

Continuing our move eastward through the 1920s, we reach the last great national film movement of the decade, and the one most clearly opposed to closed romantic realism – that of Soviet Russia. In 1924–30 a group of young Marxist filmmakers became fascinated by the power of editing to create intellectual responses in viewers. Rejecting the continuity and angle/reverse-angle cutting methods evolved in the first two decades of industrial cinema, they began to juxtapose shots that had little to do with each other in the conventional terms of story or flow of action. Their theory was that viewers would be jolted by such apparently unrelated images and forced, instead, to search for another connection between them, perhaps at a political or metaphorical level. This connection would activate audiences' thought processes and thereby make cinema an ideal way of enlightening the working classes about the nature of their subjection.

We have already encountered three Russian directors, Yevgeni Bauer, Yakov Protazanov and Boris Barnet (see pages 48–49 and 81). Bauer died in 1917 while scouting locations for a new film. Protazanov's first instinct after the 1917 revolutions was to flee the country and, like many other such exiles, find work in France. However, he was persuaded to return and, from 1924–43, made a series of accomplished melodramas such as *Besprid'annitsa/Without a Dowry* (Soviet Union, 1936) and comedies such as *Zakroishchikiz Torzhka/The Tailor from Torzhuk* (Soviet Union, 1926) which are rarely seen today, but which are highly regarded. Barnet didn't enter the industry until the time of the revolutions and *The Girl with the Hat*

Box, already discussed in the 1920s comedy section, would be his best film of this decade. In the 1950s and 1960s he failed to make movies that satisfied the regime, the critics or himself. In 1965, he committed suicide.

The Bolsheviks attempted to reorder the life of a whole country, establishing the "dictatorship of the Proletariat". Cinema did not become a state industry under the new regime immediately, but its leader, Lenin, famously declared in 1922 that "Of all the Arts, for us cinema is the most important." Not even in Germany, where it was state-assisted, was cinema promised such a formative role in society. In the ensuing years, and especially after 1924, the Soviet film world took on the experimental and cohesive elements of a think tank. Its base was a Moscow film school headed by a former fashion designer, Lev Kuleshov, whose aim was to undertake film-making experiments to match the new social order. Kuleshov talked about "engineering" new film techniques and the central metaphor was the machine. Filmmakers from other states such as the Ukraine humanized some of this mechanized philosophy, but world cinema's greatest innovations occurred when this group of filmmakers coalesced under one roof and attempted not only to vary the schemata, but to smash them to pieces.

70
Above: Soviet agitprop trains – movie theatres in train carriages.

The speed of events is exciting to consider. In 1919, one year after the ending of the First World War, agitprop (agitation and propaganda) trains, with theatres and cinemas in their carriages, departed from Moscow (70). They distributed leaflets, performed theatre shows and projected films to promote Leninist reforms, the new governmental programmes, which included literacy, hygiene information and anti-alcoholism initiatives. Their film section was headed by a wiry, twenty-one-year-old Swedish cameraman, Edward Tissé, who would go on to photograph the most famous film of the Soviet montage era. One of the remits of agitprop trains was to shoot documentary footage as well as show it, and in charge of the editing of Tissé's work was a twenty-year-old poet and musician, Denis Kaufman, who extravagantly changed his name to Dziga Vertov, which, combining both Ukrainian and Russian, translates as "spinning top". The following year, a key international influence came to bear on the evolution of Vertov and the others' methodology. A print of *Intolerance* found its way through the blockade of foreign goods. When Lenin saw it, he cabled D.W. Griffith immediately, asking him to head up the new Soviet film industry, which was nationalized in August of that year. Film historian Jay Leyda wrote: "No Soviet film of importance made within the following ten years was to be completely outside *Intolerance*'s sphere of influence." In 1920, the twenty-two-year-old Latvian, Sergei Eisenstein, who was studying engineering, switched to theatre and became a student of Kuleshov. In 1923, Kuleshov edited together scenes of Moscow and Washington which suggested that a famous Moscow monument to Gogol was sited in front of the White House. Continuing in this experimental vein, he filmed the face of an actor first instructed to imagine that, having been imprisoned and starving, he is brought a bowl of soup. The actor's face attempted to register hunger and anticipation. After this, Kuleshov filmed the same actor's face, asked to imagine he has been released from prison and is looking at birds and clouds. He asked people to look at the two faces and no-one could distinguish between them. This opacity, this inability of acting alone to distinguish between bread and freedom, led directly to the idea that if the actor cannot show a thought, editing must.

71
Above: Editing as metaphor: intercutting police charges with the slaughter of an ox in Sergei Eisenstein's *Strike*. Soviet Union, 1925.

Lenin died in 1924 and, in the same year, the whirling Vertov and his brother started making Kino-Eye newsreel, by filming life on the streets, often with hidden cameras mounted in police vehicles, the forerunner of many twenty-first-century American television shows. Eisenstein began filming *Strike* (Soviet Union, 1925), which starts with a worker's suicide. A strike follows and, in the climactic attack at the end of the film, police brutality is intercut with the bloody slaughter of an ox, whose tongue is pulled through the gash in its throat. *Strike* was the first notable film to demonstrate the think tank's radical new ideas. D.W. Griffith's thesis in *Intolerance* that intercuts could suggest thoughts, combined with Kuleshov's bread-and-freedom editing

but for just sixteen frames. While Vera Baranovskaya delivers a great, stoical performance in the lead role of the mother, the film's moments of humanity are undercut by its brutal literalness. When the mother is filmed from a high viewpoint, Pudovkin signals her pathos, and when she is filmed from below, she appears noble (73 bottom). This ideological smugness, which also taints much of 1920s Soviet cinema, weakens Pudovkin's work.

The same criticism cannot be applied to the Ukrainian Alexander Dovzhenko, the son of an illiterate peasant, whose lyrical films did not have the immediate dramatic impact of the work of Eisenstein or Pudovkin, but which influenced Russian cinema in the 1970s, 1980s and 1990s. Dovzhenko was not part of Kuleshov's think-tank and had not even seen many films before he started directing. Eisenstein and Pudovkin were at the première of his first significant film, *Zvenigora* (Soviet Union, 1928), and Eisenstein wrote of the occasion: "Onto the [screen] *Zvenigora* leaps! Mama! What goes on here?!" No other filmmaker at the time was producing such dreamlike images. In comparison to Dovzhenko's free play of tone and association, much of Soviet cinema in the 1920s seems intellectually strait-jacketed.

Dovzhenko's next film, *Arsenal* (Soviet Union, 1930), answers the questions of why he was so good. The complex plot follows the emergence of a Ukrainian political movement after the First World War up to a disastrous strike in Kiev in

January 1918. The film starts with captions printed onto shot footage, "There was a mother", "There was a war". Timeless scenes of Ukrainian women standing motionless in the sunshine in lifeless villages are intercut with bombings and the chaos of killing. A title card for a horse speaks after he has been flogged by a man: "You're wasting blows on me, old man, I'm not what you need to strike." At the site of the bombing, as a German soldier reels with the effects of laughing gas, another title card reads: "This gas is so gay". There follows an astonishing image of a dead soldier, half-buried, but with a fixed smile (74 third image). Later in the film, a factory owner confused

74
Above: *Arsenal*. Director: Alexander Dovzhenko. Soviet Union, 1930.

by the strike looks indecisively at the camera, and there are nine jump cuts to that same face, a moment later (74 bottom). He looks left, right, then straight on, then a closer shot and another closer still. This is three decades before the acclaimed jump cuts in Jean Luc Godard's *A Bout de souffle/Breathless* (France, 1959). Toward the end of the film, a soldier is magically rushed through the snow on horses in fulfilment of his desire to be buried at home. (One almost expects the horses to take off into the sky as the boys' bikes do in *ET* [Spielberg, USA, 1982].) His mother stands waiting at an empty grave. Dovzhenko described *Arsenal* as "100 per cent political".[50] It is also about travelling on a train, about speed, about landscapes and about sunlight.

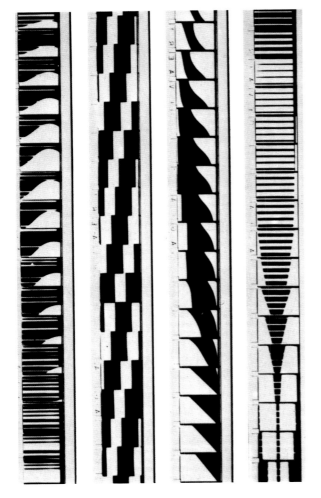

Cinema became intellectually fashionable in this period and artists and thinkers were drawn to it. Painters and sculptors started to see it as equal, if not superior, to their own media and it was all the rage in art schools. The result of all this intense interest was the final category of dissident 1920s cinema, experimental films.

The painter Walter Ruttmann was influenced by expressionist painters like Wassily Kandinsky. Ruttmann painted directly onto glass and would film the result; he would then wipe the still-wet paint, adding more pigment, and then re-film it, to make *Opus 1, Die Sieger* (Germany, 1923), perhaps the first abstract animation (75). Ruttmann would soon work with a former dancer, Lotte Reiniger, whose *The Adventures of Prince Achmed* (Germany, 1927) was one of the first animated feature films. Her painstaking technique involved adapting the methods of Victorian silhouette portraiture. She hand-cut each frame and the process took nearly three years.

The animator Wladyslaw Starewicz was born in Wilno, Poland (then Russia, now Lithuania) in 1892 and from 1910 onward started making bizarre children's films, using stop-frame animation technique for the first time in cinema, which involved manipulating the puppets slightly for each filmed or re-filmed frame. Starewicz moved to France in 1920 and made films such as *Frogland* (France, 1922) based on one of Aesop's *Fables*, about a group of frogs who ask their god, Jupiter, for a king. At first he sends them a wooden one, then a stork, which is a bird that eats frogs. Finally, when they insist, they get the monarch of their dreams, but soon regret having done so.

The anarchistic art movement, Dada, entered cinema in 1924. One of its key members, Francis Picabia, was staging a disruptive ballet, *Relâche*, and hired René Clair, who would later make *An Italian Straw Hat*, to direct a short film for it. This would be shown in the ballet's interval and as such was called *Entr'acte/Interval* (France, 1927). It was the first significant Dadaist film. It featured Picabia and a roster of other Dadaists including Man Ray, Georges Auric and Marcel Duchamp. It was a wild abstract farce involving, among other things, a camel, a cannon and dolls with ballooning heads (76), and was influenced by the chase comedies of Mack Sennett. Picabia said of the result, "It believes in the pleasure of inventing, it respects nothing except the desire to burst out laughing." One of the film's actors, Man Ray, would also photograph *Le Ballet mécanique/The Mechanical Ballet* (France, 1924), influenced by Gance's *La Roue* and directed by the French artist, Fernand Léger. *The Mechanical Ballet* features a series of metal objects and machines photographed abstractly, moving around in a sometimes random, sometimes choreographed way.

76
Above: Dolls with ballooning heads in *Entr'acte*.
Director: René Clair.
France, 1927.

Several years after his painted glass abstract animations, Ruttmann hired cinematographer Karl Freund (his third appearance in this chapter) to help him make a film about the pulse of a big city. *Berlin, Die Symphonie einer Grosstadt/Berlin, Symphony of a City* (Germany, 1927) found its structure in music like *Entr'acte* and *The*

Mechanical Ballet and was not only one of the most influential experimental films of the period, but also one of the longest. It tells the story of the movements, rhythms and repetitions of Berlin during one spring day, from dawn to dusk. Ruttman's highly influential film is almost devoid of people, and uses some of the editing techniques of Eisenstein. The Brazilian filmmaker, Alberto Cavalcanti, was to direct *Rien que les heures/Only The Hours* (France, 1926) about Paris a year later, and the result was strikingly similar.

Perhaps the most notorious experimental film of the 1920s was the astonishing *Un Chien andalou/An Andalusian Dog* (France, 1928) which still remains as shocking as *Entr'acte*. This was the first significant film influenced by the Surrealist art movement, which emphasized dreams and the irrational mind. It was directed by Luis Buñuel, the son of Spanish landowners, who had established one of the world's first cinema clubs in Madrid in 1920, aged twenty. Around this time he met Salvador Dalí, later a leading Surrealist painter. Sometime after 1926, Dalí and Buñuel spent three days talking about their dreams and unconscious desires and they then wrote a script loosely about a couple's split and reconciliation. Buñuel directed and edited the film and the result was the seventeen-minute *Un Chien Andalou*. The film begins with an image of Buñuel smoking. A woman's eye is then slit with a razor (77) as a thin knife-like cloud

77
Right: Shock and metaphor in *Un Chien Andalou*. Director: Luis Buñuel. France, 1928.

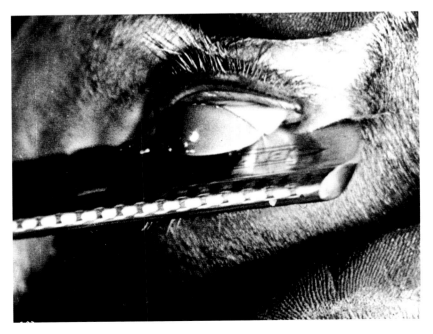

passes across the moon. Later a man's hand crawls with ants, a severed hand appears followed by naked breasts and buttocks, and two pianos surmounted by dead donkeys. A caption reads "Sixteen Years Earlier", but the action continues as before. The man with the ants on his hand discovers that his mouth is covered with hair, which is contrasted with the woman's shaved armpit.

Finally, the man and the woman are buried in sand. This absurd film was a direct influence on several subsequent movies, including David Lynch's *Blue Velvet* (USA, 1986, see pages 394–396), especially in the strangely erotic discovery of an ant-covered ear (78). Buñuel would go on to have one of the most international careers of the major art cinema directors, working in Spain, France, America and Mexico. There would be important experimental film movements in nearly every subsequent decade, but the 1920s work of Ruttmann, Clair, Léger and Buñuel was a foundation on which they all built.

78
Above: Recent American cinema's most notable surrealist, David Lynch. Jeffrey (Kyle MacLachlan) finds a Dalí-esque ear complete with crawling ants in *Blue Velvet*. USA, 1986.

The period of 1918–28 was a tumultuous one for world cinema. It became an established industry and its great studios evolved their house styles. These styles were extended, challenged and rejected by a series of unprecedented film movements, which constituted a worldwide expansion in film aesthetics. Cities, love triangles, hubris, machinery and descent into madness were the great obsessions of this expansion.

The image overleaf from *La Passion de Jean d'Arc/The Passion of Joan of Arc* (France, 1927) (79) amalgamates the internationalism, the technical brilliance and the human ambition of 1920s cinema. It is taken from the second part of the film which depicts the historic story of a fifteenth-century French girl, who is the saviour of her country and is then tried for witchcraft, sentenced and burnt at the stake. It was directed by Carl Theodor Dreyer, a Dane who had a strict Protestant upbringing. Maria (also called Renée) Falconetti (Joan of Arc) had not acted in a movie before, nor would she again. Her face has almost no make-up and on a big screen her freckles are visible.

In the film, her eyelids quiver like butterfly wings, but in other ways her face is immobile, almost expressionless. There is almost no depth to the image, nothing in the background. Although this was a black-and-white film, the walls of the set were painted pink to remove their glare and not to detract from Falconetti's face. This image was shot by a Krakow cinematographer, Rudolph Maté, who was brought up in Hungary. He worked with Fritz Lang and René Clair before collaborating with many of the great Hollywood directors discussed in the next chapter. The film's set designer was the German Hermann Warm, who painted the shadows in *Caligari*. Falconetti had her hair cropped just before this image was made. It was done in silence and such was the atmosphere on the set that some of the electricians cried. In some shots she is framed at the edge of the image, almost trying to escape it. Not many intertitles explain what is being said, but Falconetti and the other actors move their lips throughout the film, speaking the precise words recorded at Joan of Arc's trial. This was a premonition of a kind, because in the year of *The Passion of Joan of Arc*'s production, Warner

79
Above: The purity and piety of the imagery of *The Passion of Joan of Arc*. Director: Carl Theodor Dreyer. France, 1927.

Bros. released a film, *The Jazz Singer* (USA, 1927), which had a sound-track. It did not contain much more than a song and a few dialogue sequences but, as a result of it, silent cinema came to an end.

Cinema's subsequent rebirth is the subject of the next chapter. One major director, John Ford, called it "A time of near panic in Hollywood." So momentous were the changes for the industry that other landmarks of these great transitional years are sometimes overlooked – for example, Mickey Mouse débuted in 1928 in the animated short, *Steamboat Willie* (USA). However, on the other side of the world from Warner Bros. and *The Jazz Singer*, in a place where *benshis* still held sway over film's narrative and where movies were filmed from the front as if they were stage plays, cinema's true classicism was about to emerge.

1. Among those that did use the war as a subject were Chaplin's *Shoulder Arms* and Griffith's *Hearts of the World*. Of the few that tackled the political themes, Gance's *J'Accuse* was the most powerful.

2. Miller, Henry. *The Cosmopolitan Eye*, New Directions Publishing Corporation, 1939.

3. Kerr, Walter. *The Silent Clowns*. Da Capo, 1980, p98.

4. Louvish, Simon, *Keystone: The Life and Clowns of Mark Sennett*, Faber and Faber, pp.100-1

5. Mention should be made here of the influence producer-director Hal Roach had on Lloyd's career. Roach formed the Rolin Film Company and hired Lloyd, who was by then working for Mack Sennett at Keystone. Roach helped Lloyd experiment with his screen persona, removing some of Sennett's trade-mark slapstick elements from it and moulding it more in his − Roach's − own taste, emphasizing characterization and strengthening the storylines of Lloyd's vehicles. Roach was the survivor and chameleon of silent comedy, effortlessly adapting Laurel and Hardy's slow burn techniques to the requirements of the sound era, diversifying to Westerns and other genres, then having some success in television. He died in 1992, aged 100.

6. Though Ozu doesn't seem to have mentioned Lloyd in interviews, his films are clearly influenced by the American. Ozu's earliest films, *nansensu* ("nonsense") comedies in the *gendai-geki* ("contemporary life") genre, used prop jokes in the Lloyd manner. The latter's *The Freshman* (1925) was the model for Ozu's early college comedies and, as David Bordwell has noted, a poster for *Speedy* (1928) (Lloyd's nickname in *The Freshman*) adorns one wall in *I Graduated, But . . .* (Ozu, 1929). Bordwell also argues persuasively that Lloyd's films' recurrent scenes of embarrassment are echoed in the moments of humiliation in Ozu's *Tokyo Chorus*, *Equinox Flower*, *Early Summer* and *I Was Born, But... .*

7. Lorca, Federico Garcia, *Buster Keaton Takes a Walk*

8. Weber, Lois. *Lecture to the Women's City Club of Los Angeles*, 1913.

9. Quoted in Sadoul, Georges, *Dictionary of Films*, Editions du Seuil, 1965.

10. Though Lang, Ruttmann and Vertov each saw affinities between cities and the medium of film, they did so in very different ways. Lang's *Metropolis* used the production designs of Otte Hunde, Erich Kettlehut and Karl Volbrecht, for example, to imagine the futuristic precipitousness of city architecture and the etiolation of human life therein. Ruttman in *Berlin, Die Symphonie einer Grossstadt/Berlin, Symphony of a City* (Germany, 1927) attempted to capture the mood and time of day of the German capital through montages of observed details. Vertov's *Man with a Movie Camera* (Soviet Union, 1922) is more distinctively edited than the other two, as would be expected from its provenance, but its theme is not city spaces but the nature of filming such spaces.

11. A talk given to The Friends of Cinema, Paris 1924. Quoted in Flitterman-Lewis, Sandy, *To Desire Differently. Feminism and the French Cinema*, University of Illinois Press, 1990, p56

12. The main instrument of the German government's involvement with the film industry was the film company Universum Film Aktien Gesellschaft (UFA) which was established in 1917, as a merger of several existing companies, with public funds. At the end of the war, Deutsche Bank bought into it but, despite the taste and vision of production chief Erich Pommer, the company failed to hold its own against the flooding of the German market with Hollywood product. In 1927, the beleaguered company was bolstered by investment from a Nazi sympathizer, but lost its way artistically after 1933 when Jewish producers such as Pommer fled the country.

13. Burch, Noel, op. cit., p 127.

14. Burch notes that Kinugasa cannot remember having done so but that most Japanese film historians are convinced that he did.

15. The irony is, that despite Dr Mabuse's criticisms of contemporary Germany, its co-writer Theo Von Harbou − whom Lang married in 1924 and whom he divorced in 1934 − became an ultra conservative, taking Nazi party membership. A former novelist, Von Harbou also co-wrote *Metropolis* and worked with F.W. Murnau and Carl Theodor Dreyer.

16. See Sadoul, Georges, op. cit., p218.

17. Writers for *Cahiers du Cinéma*.

18. Mikhail Koltzov in *Pravda*.

19. Eisenstein, Sergei. *Notes of a Film Director*. Moscow, 1958.

20. Western governments' wariness of the propaganda function of Potemkin meant that its screenings in those countries often took place in cine-clubs or at trades union events.

SOUND

We do not hear the sound of the horse-drawn carriage crossing the Leeds Bridge, the Klan galloping in The Birth of a Nation, Cesare's madness in The Cabinet of Dr. Caligari, the distant traffic as Harold Lloyd climbs his building in Safety Last, the ocean the eponymous hero crosses in Napoleon, the pram bumping down the Odessa steps in Battleship Potemkin or Falconetti's breathing in The Passion of Joan of Arc. The energy or tenderness of these images have a power to impress, but not as things in the real world do.

The otherworldliness of cinema started to decline after 1927 as the next great epoch in film history began. Movies across the world began to speak over the next eight years. At first, sound films were stagy because the equipment was cumbersome and audiences heard starchy conversations, people singing, doors slamming and dogs barking. Films largely moved indoors because filmmakers needed silence to record voices. Then something else happened: filmmakers discovered that sound could make their films more intimate by letting characters voice their thoughts. They used sound as a magnet to draw people into their films, into scenes and into emotional exchanges. Audiences started to feel that they could be with movie stars not only in their fantasies, but also in their ordinary lives

Sound was "the discovery that halted cinema on its royal road". Suddenly the image was not primary. However, it would be forty-five years before a

mainstream movie would take the effect of sound as a philosophical subject in itself, in Francis Coppola's The Conversation (USA, 1974), a film about a man's obsession with what two people say to each other, which leads to his eventual breakdown.

81

Below: Choreographer
Busby Berkeley's interest
in regimented movement
and eroticism led him
toward semi-abstract
imagery such as this one,
an overhead shot of
twenty-five chorus girls
playing violins. *Gold
Diggers of 1933*. Director:
Mervyn Leroy. USA, 1933.

JAPANESE CLASSICISM AND HOLLYWOOD ROMANCE (1928—45)
Cinema enters a golden age

4

Cinema started to sing in the years 1928–45. Five times as many people flocked to the movies each week as do now – they became an international obsession. Popular music and the tabloid press fostered escapism too, but cinema had more impact. One writer commented on how the "abundance, energy, transparency, community" of the entertainment films appealed to audiences because it was the opposite of the "scarcity, exhaustion, dreariness, fragmentation", of their real lives[1]. Surely, this is how entertainment works. It finds form for feelings that are missing. It is "what Utopia might feel like rather than how it would be organized."[2]

This chapter is about cinema's attempts to describe this utopian[3] feeling. Countries such as Egypt, China, Brazil and Poland start, for the first time, to make significant films and, stylistically, film-makers learnt to use sound creatively. Japanese masters Ozu, Naruse and Mizoguchi, among others, tell stories in a rigorous way which partly qualifies them as film history's classicists. The biggest formal shift in this period is that, after years of flattening and romanticizing its imagery, Western mainstream cinema begins to explore space in more visual depth. In the last chapter, each stylistic group was discussed separately, but this one navigates the period chronologically, criss-crossing the globe to examine cinematic events and landmarks.

THE CREATIVE USE OF SOUND IN AMERICA AND FRANCE

There had been previous attempts at sound cinema before *The Jazz Singer*'s release at the end of 1927, but this film was well-funded and widely released.[4] It was successful and, as a result, American cinemas, followed by those of other countries, started to install speaker systems behind their screens; ten million more cinema tickets were sold in the US immediately after the introduction of this new technology. Many silent-filmmakers, such as Chaplin, thought that the onset of sound destroyed the mystique of film and delayed using it for as long as possible. Some highly-developed national film industries, including Japan's, did not invest in sound technology until the mid- to late 1930s. From the filmmakers' point of view, shooting sound was a whole new ball game. Real locations were now difficult to use because as soon as the director shouted "Action!", someone nearby was bound to start digging a road or hammering metal. No one wanted to hear these sounds while the actors were speaking; so directors and producers were forced to return to filming in "black box" studios, which were now called "sound stages".

The image to the right (82) illustrates how problematic this new system was. The scene is a simple one, a couple talk on a park bench. They are placed on the far right of the frame and in front of them are three large wardrobe-shaped boxes. At the beginning of the sound period, cameras had to be housed in such boxes, or "blimps" as they were called, so that their whirring would not be picked up by the microphone. Each container is further muffled by large blankets and, behind the third of these, the "boom operator" stands in a trilby hat. He holds a long pole, a "boom", at the end of which the microphone records the actors' dialogue. He moves this left and right according to which actor is speaking and must at all times keep it out of shot. Surprisingly, an orchestra to his left performs as the actors speak. It was not until 1933 that music could be added separately to a film's soundtrack after the editing had taken place. Until then, astonishingly, it had to be recorded simultaneously. Quite a pressing reason for not filming on real streets.

In the silent period, multi-camera shooting was used only for big action stunts that could not easily be repeated, so why were these three cameras used to cover this intimate park bench conversation? The answer again relates to sound recording problems. If this scene was first filmed in a wide shot followed by close-ups of the man and the woman, it would be very difficult to edit or match the sound from each shot together. The orchestra and dialogue would have to pace each other to precise fractions of a second – if they failed to do this and the editor cut from a wide shot to a close-up, the sound would jar. The solution was to run three cameras, one filming the wide shot (in this case the centre camera) and further cameras photographing the actors' close-ups (here one on the right and one on the left in front of the boom operator). The actors would then perform the whole scene in

82
Below: This photograph, taken during the making of a Warner Bros. film, shows the coordination involved in early sound recording. Three large draped boxes house the cameras (bottom), a man holds a long boom over the actors' heads (far right) and a small orchestra plays.

a continuous take to ensure that the sound on each camera would match seamlessly.

Actors' performances were affected by this new technology. The director could no longer talk to them during a take, as was the norm in silent cinema, and in the first years of sound actors had to talk with unnatural precision to be recorded successfully by the crude sound recording technology. It was not until 1932 in America, and later in other countries, that directional microphones were introduced which could record specifics rather than picking up every sound. Notice, finally, that the couple on the bench are illuminated by just two big studio lights, one on each side of the trio of cameras. In late silent films, close-ups were lit separately and with great care to create attractive facial shadows and moody or romantic backgrounds. But here there is no chance of doing this, because the lighting stands for such set-ups would have to be behind or beside the actors, in the place of the bushes. They would then be clearly visible in the wide shot, which is filmed simultaneously with the close-ups.

Creative directors were immediately frustrated by these obstacles to their artistic freedom and the best devised ways of obviating them. The Russian director, Rouben Mamoulian, went to the West as a student of the great acting guru, Stanislavski. At first Mamoulian directed opera in Paris, London and New York, which quickly confirmed that he had no feel for naturalism. Hired by Paramount on the strength of his inventive theatrical productions, his first film, *Applause* (USA, 1929) pushed the creative boundaries of sound films. The film's storyline was not innovative – an ageing stage entertainer sacrifices her career for her daughter – but some key scenes made the industry sit up and pay attention. One example contrasts the hushed atmosphere of the convent, which has housed the daughter, with the hubbub of traffic and the street sounds of bustling New York as she visits her mother. Mamoulian used sonic contrast to reflect the feelings of the disorientated daughter. In a later example, there is a more daring technical innovation. A wide shot, which encompasses most of the bedroom, shows the mother trying to calm her child's frayed nerves in a night-time scene. The camera dollies into a two-shot, which frames the mother and child and remains there for a minute of dialogue, before moving into a closer two-shot, followed by two medium close-ups and then into a single close-up of the praying daughter as her mother sings a lullaby. Finally, the camera tracks out again and the father's shadow falls across the scene.

Mamoulian's sound crew told him the prayer and the lullaby could not be done simultaneously; we could hear one or the other or a combination of the two, but not both clearly. Mamoulian suggested that they use two microphones, one for each actress, run separate wires from them and then combine them in the printing process. The sound men said this would not work. Mamoulian was furious and stormed off the set. The studio boss, Adolph Zukor, ordered the technicians to try Mamoulian's way, and it worked. A single scene in *Applause* proved simultaneous sound possible in cinema. New schemas were opened up and directors now had to decide whether they wanted audiences to hear one thing or more and if other sounds should derive from the action within the image or from elsewhere. The ideas of background noise, sonic landscape, threatening or warning sounds, were born in this advance.[5]

Three years later, Mamoulian would direct a musical so explosively innovative that it makes the majority of contemporaneous films look hopelessly dated. *Love Me Tonight* (USA, 1932) tells the story of a bored princess (Jeanette MacDonald) living in a French château, falling in love with a plucky Parisian tailor (Maurice Chevalier). The boredom of château life is brilliantly satirized as Mamoulian cuts from real time to slow motion within a single piece of action in order to joke about the dullness. Little details like this are great fun, but their inventiveness is dwarfed by Mamoulian's major coup: to have the musical and percussive score recorded before the shoot started. Although it was commonplace in opera to have the entire score written before the staging began, this was unprecedented in cinema. This then allowed Mamoulian to choreograph Chevalier's movements during his first visit to the château in time to the music, which was played during the takes. Though walking, Chevalier seems to dance and dart around the huge rooms (83).

83
Above: Maurice Chevalier's actions are perfectly timed to music in *Love Me Tonight*. Director, R. Mamoulian played the recorded score while the shot was being taken. USA, 1932.

The director not only wanted to create visual rhythm and grace with his new approach to sound, but also biting satire. Not relying on the witty script alone, he at one point adds the sound of yapping dogs to a shot of old ladies playing bridge. Mamoulian also links the city and countryside as the tailor in Paris says, "Isn't it romantic", and this is overheard by a pass-

84
Above: Jeannette Macdonald bored on her balcony in an innovative early musical *Love Me Tonight*. Director: Rouben Mamoulian. USA, 1932

er-by who heads out of town, only to have his musical rendition of this successively picked up by others until the stranded princess hears it (84). Sound was unifying a sequence as a metaphor for travel. *Love Me Tonight* was called Mamoulian's "first flawless masterpiece"[6].

While the saucy romanticism of *Love Me Tonight* seems to have been influenced by Ernst Lubitsch who had been working in Hollywood for nearly a decade by 1932, it was also indebted to René Clair, who carried his penchant for mockery into sound films like *Le Million/The Million* (France 1931) and *A Nous la liberté/Freedom is Ours* (France, 1931). *The Million* is the story of a man who wins a million francs on the lottery, but who loses the ticket with which he can claim his winnings. Clair ensured that all the actors in the film sing except the lottery winner, which makes it a clear forerunner of *Love Me Tonight*'s musicality. In *Freedom is Ours*, a close-up shot of a quivering bell-shaped flower is combined with the sound of singing voice, as if the flower is literally in song. Such metaphorical use of sound freed directors from sonic literalness and clearly led to Mamoulian's yapping dogs.

In the Soviet Union in 1928, Vsevolod Pudovkin, Sergei Eisenstein and his associate Grigori Alexandrov had issued a statement of principle, which was very similar to Clair's approach. "Only the contrapuntal use of sound will open up new possibilities for the development and perfection of montage.... It cannot fail to provide new and enormously powerful means of expressing and resolving the most complex problems." The Soviets were not technically advanced enough to pursue this potential, but they realized, like Mamoulian and Clair, that sound could do far more than merely reproduce a conversation or a song.

INDIA'S APPROACH TO SOUND

Indian films in the silent days, as we have seen in Chapter Four, divide into categories similar to the Hollywood genres: historicals, socials, mythologicals and melodramas. In the 1920s social concerns about caste, exploitation and the poverty of burgeoning city life also influenced filmmakers. In 1930, the pacifist protest leader Mahatma Gandhi ended a 300-mile march against the British re-imposition of salt taxes, and an important national debate about the acceptability of British colonial rule was gripping the country. However, seventeen years would pass before the British finally withdrew and, in the meantime, Indian cinema crossed the most important threshold of its history – it, too, wired for sound.

India was producing over 200 films per year by the early 1930s, but until the introduction of sound recording, it was missing one of its cultural heritage's key elements, song and dance. This was to change in 1931 when a talkie, *Alam Ara* (Ardeshir Irani, 1931) was filmed. It contained seven songs recorded simultaneously with the photography, in the same way as the park bench conversation which began this chapter. It was a massive commercial success and, astonishing though it seems to Westerners, only two of the many thousands of films made in India between then and the beginning of the 1950s would not have musical interludes. The whole of Indian cinema became one big musical genre. The most popular of these, the so-called "All India" films, were made in the federal language, Hindi, and mostly shot in Bombay (Mumbai).

The live method of shooting musical numbers was so cumbersome that, like Mamoulian, Indian directors and producers looked for ways to liberate their camera work. A solution was found in the playback system introduced in 1935, wherein a song would be recorded in advance by singers such as Lata Mangeshkar, then played during the actual filming and mimed by the actors. The camera could now dolly and dart, filming could stop and start, various angles could be used and yet the musical recording would remain constant.

The first classic of the playback-influenced Indian cinema would be *Devdas* (1935), which is still one of the most influential South Asian films. It was directed by Pramathesh Chandra Barua, an aristocratic Assamese who started directing in 1934, aged thirty-one, and who died just sixteen years later. He had studied the films of

Lubitsch and Clair and started his own company in 1929. His most resonant work is set in the aristocratic circles familiar to him, but they are viewed with a Lubitsch-esque irony and sometimes are actually bleak. His expressive camera style and restrained direction of actors, counterbalanced each other in a way similar to Mizoguchi. "The static stories and mask-like actorial postures are counterpointed by

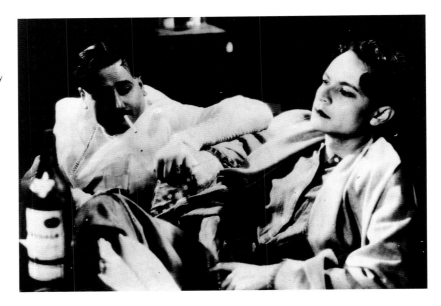

85
Right: One of India's most celebrated films, *Devdas*, told the story of a young man driven to alcohol. Cinematographer Bimal Roy shot the lead actor with green filters in order to emphasize his immoral character. Director: P.C. Barua. India, 1935.

the most mobile subjective camera in the Indian cinema of his time, the visual excess of his sweeping pans announcing the landscapes of later Bengal School painting."[7] The tension between the acting style and the camerawork noted by Rajadhyaksha and Willemen would later be echoed in Japanese cinema.

Devdas was based on Saratchandra Chattopadhyay's well-known novel about a young man driven to alcohol over his impossible love for a childhood sweetheart (85) and would be much remade in the course of film history, and widely seen around the world by the growing Indian diaspora. The film's daring cinematographer, Bimal Roy, used green filters to make Devdas seem unsympathetic and morally wrong. He would go on to become a major director, who combined 1930s extravagance with an Italian-inspired neo-realism. Together with Raj Kapoor and Mehboob, Roy combined two filmmaking counter-tendencies in Indian cinema – visual gloss and realism – rarely achieved elsewhere.

JAPAN REMAINS SILENT

At the time of the sound revolution in America, the dazzle of Mamoulian and Clair, the intellectual rigour of Eisenstein and the musical extravagance of Barua, it is surprising that Japan was initially indifferent to the possibilities. It was producing more than 400 films per year and had an industrial film system in the late 1920s and 1930s similar to the US. However, it was director rather than producer-led and *benshis* still commentated in cinemas. This apparent refusal to embrace the modern way of making movies was echoed in Japan's broader political conservatism at the time. Nationalism was becoming more popular and the belief that Asian culture was superior to the Occident held sway. Japan retreated psychologically from the advances of the twentieth century. This resulted in Eastern fascism, and it invaded Manchuria in 1931 in an attempt to fend off Western influence in the East and spread its new chauvinistic ideas. Over thirty million lives would be lost in the subsequent years of the Sino–Japanese war.

Although it is a very uncomfortable fact, Japanese cinema soared artistically during this ignoble episode in its history, despite taking a slower route to technological change. Some of its most significant films were produced within this period of political, technical and artistic isolation. The era of aggression in Japan was also a golden age for Japanese film, producing the most balanced and internally directed body of work that the cinema has witnessed to date.

Yasujiro Ozu did not marry, had no experience of factory life, did not attend university and yet for more than thirty years made films about the calm everyday lives of married people, factory workers and students. Contemporaneous Japanese culture did not generally value pure self-expression, and filmmakers have often told stories about subjects of which they have no personal experience, but perhaps it was Ozu's particular rejection of autobiography that gave his films such additional equilibrium.

Ozu was born in Tokyo in 1903, the son of a fertilizer merchant, and from the age of ten, he lived in the countryside with his mother. At school he was a rebel and was expelled. In the 1920s he defiantly watched hundreds of American films, which did not conform to Japanese notions of restraint, and when he started directing in 1927, his early efforts show their influence. By 1932, one year after Clair's *The Million* and *Freedom is Ours*, he had shed Western cinema's influence and evolved a style and a recognizable world that remain distinctive today. Ozu's first box office hit, *I Was Born, But …* (1932) is a good introduction to this fascinating world. It is a funny, wise and fresh film about two brothers who go to a new school, and are bullied, and realize that power in life comes from how strong you are and how many pigeon eggs you can eat. Following this ethos, they themselves become bullies, and when they discover that their father, Mr Yoshii, is subservient to his boss, they are ashamed and go on hunger strike. Gradually they start to understand an important lesson of the adult world: that it is money and social standing that gain respect. Most of Ozu's films are about the relationship between ordinary parents and their children. In this example, typical of his work from this period onward, the sons come to a deeper understanding of the pressures on their father. Ozu's themes are the opposite of much of Western individualistic cinema, in which young people are forces for change and their energies are directed away from the family home. Instead, Ozu, the master of reconciliation, quells the sons' rebellion. His first sound film, *The Only Son* (1936) ends with a mother saying, "My son's really made good. And he's found a good wife. Now I can die in peace." In the finale of a much later work, *Early Summer* (1951), a wife says, "We were really happy", and her husband mumbles "Hmmm". These might sound slight, downbeat or even reactionary moments, but provide beautifully calming alternatives both to Hollywood's happy endings and Russian cinema's tragic closures. Ozu's films derive from what the Japanese call "Momo no aware", this sense that life is essentially static and sad. He saw human nature as not only balanced between parent and child, but also poised between hope and despair and public and private life. Remarkably few filmmakers share this vision. Their medium is called the "movies" and they see life as something that moves. One writer wrote that, "Eliciting sorrow and happiness through drama was easy," and he felt that it "smothered the basic truth of character and life."[8] Closed romantic realism strived for the emotions and Ozu wanted to avoid them.

Ozu not only pared down feeling, but the plot itself was reduced in his system. Most of our story so far has been about the way filmmakers used tools to tell stories and now we come across a director who was "not only bored by plot. He actively disliked it."[9] Ozu's films provide plenty of incidents in homes, offices, tearooms and other locations, in masterpieces such as *I Was Born But...*, *Late Spring* (1949), *Early Summer* and his most famous film, *Tokyo Story* (1953), but despite the fact that his characters often learn something about life by the end of his films, they do not undergo a driven "journey", in the sense used by American actors and directors of a psychological process of life changing discovery.

Then to feeling and story, add style. From the late 1920s onward, "Ozu honed, pared down, refined his form to a spare essence allied with the devastatingly simple, everyday problems his characters face."[10] By 1932 and *I Was Born, But...* he had started rejecting dissolves from one image to the next as well as fades to black, and dolly shots were reduced in number. What remained were shots and cuts and, famously, he even made these his own. The shots in *I was Born, But...* are exquisitely beautiful and unlike almost any sequences in Western cinema. They are filmed from a different height from most Western films and the legs of the tripod used by his cinematographer and editor, Hideo Shigehara, are purposefully set much shorter than those of Griffith, Vidor, Lubitsch or any of the directors discussed in previous chapters. This would continue during most of Ozu's career.[11] When the camera is pointing at Mr Yoshii or his sons, they look above it. This is remark-

able. For a few years around 1907, Pathé filmed with the camera at waist height (86), but adult shoulder or eye level had otherwise become the norm in film's evolution. This height approximated the perspective of an adult onlooker standing at the edge of the set watching the action unfold. Ozu's continuous use of low angles cannot be read in this way and some critics have tried to find a simple explanation for this, claiming that the director might be approximating a child's point of view. However, this argument is not convincing, because many of his films without children are also shot from a low level, while in the still overleaf (87), the children are looking above the camera, which is below their height. Other critics have argued that the low camera position and the frequently seated characters in Ozu's

scenes reflect the Japanese
cultural tradition in which
people sit on the floor.
However, low-level shots also
occur in his exteriors, in which
people are not sitting and if
this visual level is so ingrained
in Japanese culture, why don't
other Japanese directors use
this viewpoint consistently?

Ozu's lowered horizon has a
threefold spatial effect. First,
it sets the human being's
centre of gravity (the naval, as
Leonardo da Vinci had shown in his 1492 drawing [88]) at the centre of
the movie frame. The result of this is that no images in world cinema
are more at rest or less likely to topple or twist, than those of Ozu and
Shigehara. Secondly, the camera tends to look up slightly in order to
frame its characters and, consequently, the ground features much less
in medium and even wide standing shots. Repeated throughout a film
and throughout a career, this gives Ozu's characters a weightlessness
that is absent from more grounded cinema traditions. Thirdly, a new
area of space above the camera is opened up; ceilings are shown in interiors and Ozu was one of the first directors in the world to insist that his
interior sets were built with them. Critics have long argued that as well
as responding to the narrative and psychological aspects of films, we
also intuit them as complicated spaces: Westerns are geographic
spaces, road movies are ribbon-like linear ones, the films of Eisenstein
and Pudovkin and fragmented spaces like cubist paintings, and so on.
If this is true, and I believe it is, then Ozu's films are some of the most
spatially original and distinctive in the history of the medium.

Tokyo Story will be considered in a later chapter but despite
its failure to be shown in the West, the spatial, stylistic and human
equilibria of *I Was Born, But...* can now be seen to herald the mature
phase of a career with profound implications for those who consider
the spectrum of world filmmakers. No one before had found a way
of centring the human body as Ozu did; no one had found a more
satisfying balance between movement and stasis than he would in the
coming years; no one was more interested in 90-and 180-degree
angles and rejected 45-degree ones to the same extent; few

shunned heightened human activity to the same degree; few attempted as often as Ozu to photograph the human face in the calm consideration of life's problems.

It is difficult not to see, in this vision of Ozu's, the values of the classical tradition in Western art. Greek and Roman sculpture and architecture prized order and repose over action and rejected emphasis or exaggeration. Fundamentally, they required style to be rigorous. Their buildings were constructed to create maximum visual balance and not to dwarf human beings. Exactly the same could be said of Ozu's visual system. With this in mind, it is revealing to consider the aesthetic map of world cinema. If Ozu's films have profound elements of classicism, where should he be situated on that map? One starting point is clear: while America has dominated world cinema economically and technically since around 1918, and much of the world has been entranced by its entertainment values, it has never been the axis around which other film styles can be understood. Hollywood in all its glory and attendant, intermittent barbarity cannot be judged the norm. Perhaps Ozu's aesthetic is closer to this idea of a conceptual centre of film aesthetics, with closed romantic realism on one expressive flank and a range of austere filmmakers and minimalists, such as Robert Bresson, Andy Warhol, Chantal Ackerman and Béla Tarr, on the other. If Ozu's people are most clearly at the spatial centre of his films than they are in any other filmmaker's work, and if his world view – his sense of the possibility of social and psychological change – is so measured, then in this sense at least, his body of work, more than any other, is the centre of the map.

Not all film historians will be comfortable with this idea, and it certainly does not mean that Ozu was the most influential director in film history. On the contrary, his films were not much seen outside his own country until the 1950s and even then, their un-showiness meant that they didn't attract attention. Also, even if Ozu is the most classical of world filmmakers – in the specific sense set out above – this does not explain his cultural roots in Japan. Although fascinated

88
Below: A famous Western precedent for Ozu's technique of putting the human body at the centre of his composition: Leonardo da Vinci's *Study of Proportions*. Pen and ink, Accademia, Venice.

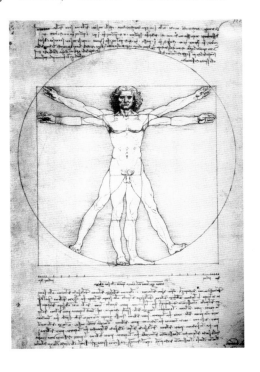

by Western cinema, he did not derive his balance of form and content from ancient Greece, and there is one most distinctive aspect of his filmmaking that is profoundly unclassical.

In Western filmmaking, a new scene, especially if set in a new location, is usually introduced by an establishing shot, which can be a wide general view of a city, street or building, in which the subsequent action occurs. Often one of the characters, whose story has been followed, walks through such a scene, after which the shot will cut to a more important piece of action. However, Ozu approaches things differently and from *I Was Born, But...* onward, he moved from one scene to another in increasingly interesting ways. In one scene Mr Yoshii and the boys walk past a lamppost and in the next shot we see a long angle shot of a similar lamppost, with no indication of how it relates to the previous image (89). The subsequent image shows Mr Yoshii stretching between washing lines of shirts which are strung between poles. Then, Ozu and his editor cut to another shot of the father exercising in the foreground. The poles from the last shot are visible in the background, but no washing can be seen. This transition does not take you progressively into the next coherent situation as does a Western establishing sequence. There are visual connections between the four shots of poles, but they have no clear purpose, either for the point of view or the story. They do not represent the viewpoint of one of the characters, nor are they an objective general view to give the audience its bearings.

89
Above: One of Ozu's first "intermediate spaces" – shots that neither clearly establish a location nor introduce a new scene.

The significance of Ozu's use of "intermediate space" or "pillow shots", as such images have been variously termed, has been much debated. The American film critic and director Paul Schrader, who would subsequently write *Taxi Driver* (USA, 1976) and *Raging Bull* (USA, 1980) wrote that they are similar to the Zen philosophical idea represented by *Mu*, "... the concept of negation, emptiness, void ... *Mu* is the character used to refer to the spaces between the branches of a flower arrangement."[12] He claims that to try to understand Ozu's imagery as either the point of view of an individual person or as the story's objective overview is to categorize a non-divisible Eastern approach in a Western way. What is seen on screen is not the character looking, nor is it Ozu looking, but it is the world looking. The story stops flowing; there is a moment of graceful abstraction.

For many years the West remained oblivious to Ozu's Zen classicism. Japanese films began to be seen internationally only after Kurosawa's *Rashomon* won the top prize at the Venice Film Festival in 1951. By the 1970s, however, Wim Wenders, the key figure in Germany's filmmaking revival, claimed that Ozu was the greatest director the cinema had witnessed. The Belgian director Chantal Akerman filmed her most famous work, *Jeanne Dielman 23 Quai du Commerce 1080 Bruxelles* (Belgium, 1975), with cameras placed on low tripods, as in Ozu films (90). Yet, even his native Japan rejected Ozu in the late 1950s. One of his apprentices, a rebellious doctor's son called Shohei Imamura, repudiated Ozu's traditional qualities. When Imamura started making movies in 1958, they were as earthy, sexual and impolite as Ozu's films were serene. Distancing himself at every opportunity, Imamura and others such as Seijun Suzuki rejected the Zen qualities that Schrader was to write about. These filmmakers appear later in this story, when cinema exploded in the 1950s, Imamura becoming one of the greatest filmmakers of his generation.

Ozu was not the only significant Japanese director of the 1930s and two in partic-ular expanded his ideas of cin-ematic balance. Mikio Naruse was the director of the first Japanese sound film to be shown in the West, which was the strikingly entitled *Wife! Be Like a Rose!* (1935). Naruse had one of the poorest starts in life of any filmmaker in the history of cinema. His family was impoverished, he had to leave school at fifteen to work, and when he finally entered the film industry he was intensely lonely. His best films, unlike those of Ozu, are marked by his experiences. He said, "From the youngest age, I have felt that the world we live in betrays us ... This thought remains with me."[13] Despite its exclamation marks, *Wife! Be Like a Rose!* reflected his bleak view of life. In the film, a daughter, Kimiko,

90
Above: Decades after Ozu's example, Chantal Ackerman filmed *Jeanne Dielmann 23 Quai du Commerce 1080 Bruxelles* at waist level. Belgium, 1975.

tries to assert herself and marry the man of her choice. Her father, Yamamoto, involves himself in the plans. His mistress is helpful behind the scenes, and his former wife, Kimiko's mother, is his intellectual superior (91).

The situation is pure Naruse: A ring of self-aware women surrounding a weak man who, nonetheless, holds sway because of how society operates. Not all his films are as good as *Wife! Be Like a Rose!* or those made in the 1950s, but his best share with

Ozu's an ironing out of life's peaks and troughs. They are bleak and beautifully controlled.

This could also be an apt description of the films of Naruse's more famous contemporary, Kenji Mizoguchi's. His work also centred around women,[14] but unlike the work of Naruse or Ozu, they were often set in the past, usually the end of the previous century, when social norms limited women's choices even further. Mizoguchi is said to have loved and hated women in equal measure and his work enacts a similar tug of war. This began with *Osaka Elegy* (1936) and *Sisters of Gion* (1936), of which he said, "It is only since I made [them] that I have been able to portray humanity lucidly." His method in so doing set form against content brilliantly. Associated with leftist filmmaking in the late 1920s, Mizoguchi introduced rare elements of realism into Japanese film at the time. *The Sisters of Gion* of the title are Kyoto geishas. One is traditional, the other is more modern, but both are dealt with in a psychologically penetrating way. In *Osaka Elegy*, Mizoguchi started to use the long, flowing shots, that would become his trademark. They are striking because they frequently pull in the opposite direction to the human feeling they elicit. In scenes where his female characters are undergoing intense emotional pain, the actresses often turn their backs to the camera, or move away from it, or Mizoguchi moves the camera away from them (92). As in the films of Ozu, the effect is one of balance.

CHINESE CINEMA IN THE 1930s

The unsettling coincidence of Japan's brutality abroad and domestic creativity in the 1930s becomes more galling when viewed from the Chinese perspective in these same years. There had been very little Chinese filmmaking before the fall of the last Manchu emperor in 1911 and the earliest available film is probably *Loves' Labours*, made by Zhang Shi-chuan in 1922. At least 400 films were made between 1928 and 1931, mostly film versions of famous Peking operas, which would be influential subsequently, and folk tales. China's first significant entry into the story of film occurs in 1931, the year of the Japanese invasion of Manchuria, and in the next six years over 500 films would be produced. They were mostly silent, like their Japanese counterparts, and were broadly in the closed romantic realist mode. The best of these were by filmmakers who were opposed not merely to the invasion but also to the emergent Chinese nationalists led by Chiang Kai Chek. Their work anticipates the great Italian neo-realists of more than a decade later.[15]

The Peach Girl (1931) is a tentative example of this. It was directed by Bu Wancang in Shanghai, one of the most cosmopolitan cities in the world. Its story is a parallel one, of a girl and a peach tree, each being a metaphor for the other. The film is chiefly remembered today because of its astonishing lead actress, Ruan Lingyu (93), often called the Chinese Greta Garbo, whose dramatic life eclipsed her Swedish counterpart's. Ruan was one of the first Chinese movie stars, and in films like *The Peach Girl* and *Small Toys* (China, 1933) she

played characters whose stories debated women's roles in society and, more broadly, in modern Chinese life.[16] Naruse and Mizoguchi were focusing almost exclusively on Japanese women during the same period, the German director Douglas Sirk would do the same in his 1950s American films, and 1960s French directors would explore how life was changing through actress-muses like

93
Above: Ruan Lingyu, the Chinese Greta Garbo, in *The Peach Girl.* China, 1931.

Jeanne Moreau and Anna Karina.

Ruan Lingyu served this function for Chinese filmmakers. In *New Women* (1935) she played a real-life actress and screenwriter who committed suicide after being hounded by the press. The prurient Shanghai tabloids of the time attacked the film and the leftist Ruan because they felt threatened by *New Women.* Ruan's response was tragic – she took an overdose of pills and died. Her funeral procession was three miles long, during which three women committed suicide, nine years after similar events at Rudolph Valentino's Hollywood funeral. *The New York Times*' front page described it as "the most spectacular funeral of the century".

In 1937, Japan invaded China proper. In the same year, China's most significant director of the time, Yuan Muzhi, released *Street Angel*, often voted one of the best Chinese films ever made. Its opening title sets the scene: "Autumn 1935. In the world of Shanghai's underclass." A young trumpet player falls for a Manchurian tavern singer, and a story unfolds about the way that the Shanghai underclass suffer under the Japanese occupation. Yuan intended the film to be a critique of the nationalist government, which was threatened by his film's success. He fled the Japanese invasion and worked for the communist leader, Mao Zedong, in Yen'an in 1937, where the Chinese communists had regrouped after their "Long March" to escape the nationalists. Shanghai remained the centre of conventional, state-approved filmmaking but by 1938–39, a small island off the southern coast of the mainland, Hong Kong, became the focus for Cantonese filmic innovation.

THE NEW AMERICAN SOUND GENRES

Back in America in 1931, the nine studios established during the 1920s – Universal, Paramount, United Artists, Warner Bros., Disney, Columbia, MGM, RKO and Fox (which would become 20th Century-Fox in 1935) – formed an oligarchy which controlled the industry. Hollywood had not only transformed itself physically, from a sleepy location of orange groves and mountain cats to a boomtown of Deco cinemas and hi-tech studios (94), but had also accrued myths. Destinies were manipulated, it was the home to the world's best jazz music, its grand cinemas were sometimes modelled on Egyptian palaces and Grauman's Chinese theatre, a Shanghai-esque extravaganza, started to perpetuate the hand and foot imprints of movie stars on its sidewalk. The Hollywood Hills were dotted with swimming pools and its graveyards received the first shocking reminders that stars were not immortal. Fading Hollywood actors and exalted stars started to feel the agony of this existential fall-out. A bookish bisexual Italian, Alfonzo Guglielmi, had been carried shoulder-high by the town for just five short years, from 1921–25. He conspired with Hollywood's heady, cheap and erotic image of him, and when he died at the age of thirty-one, his gravestone had on it a more familiar name, that of Rudolph Valentino.

The oligarchy eroticized and idealized all the beautiful, immature, expendable stars and starlets that it seduced in Southern California. They had palaces built for them, which were then razed within a generation. They wore platinum dresses and drank martinis at a set time (usually 5.50pm), clustered together around their azure pools, which emptied Mojave desert lakes, while intermarrying and displaying their smiles and biceps, flushed by the glory reflected off each other. They tried to transform the Hollywood Hills into a vision of Tuscany.[17] And the things they made, the reasons why

94
Before: By the early 1930s, Hollywood had become a sprawling oligarchy: This aerial shot shows Paramount studios.

they pushed back the Southern Californian desert in the first place were, indeed, sometimes splendid works of cinema. We have seen how musicals grew out of the potential of sound technology, but other genres and branches of filmmaking blossomed during this period: gangster pictures, Westerns, screwball comedies, horror films, war films, animations and serious dramas. The first four of these were the most distinctively American. Nine major companies were now producing eight types of film, which encompassed the matrix of Western entertainment until the 1950s.

Horror movies had already been made in the 1920s. The most striking, *The Cabinet of Dr. Caligari* (Wiene, 1919), *The Golem* (Wegener and Boese, 1920) and *Nosferatu* (Murnau, 1921), were German. Hollywood's Universal Studios followed in this tradition with Lon Chaney's haunting performance as *The Phantom of the Opera*, directed by Rupert Julian in 1925, but it was not until after two massive box-office successes in 1931 that the same studio launched horror as a genre, a type of pleasurable film that audiences recognized and enjoyed and which had its own actors and style.

These two films were James Whale's *Frankenstein* and Tod Browning's *Dracula*. Browning's film, full of silent, almost static appearances by Bela Lugosi as the vampire, is cinema literally holding its breath. It shocked audiences on its first release, but today has little of the unsettling power of *Nosferatu* of a decade earlier. Like *Dracula*, *Frankenstein*'s design was based on theatrical dramatizations of the story rather than Mary Shelley's original novel. The film's English director, Whale, a gay former actor, cartoonist and set designer realized, unlike Browning, that German expressionism would lend a striking style and mood to popular Hollywood horror. Whale and his writers combined elements of *The Golem* and *Caligari* with the theatrical imagery and elevated the story of a scientist creating a monster out of body parts into a mature tale of a mute outsider, shunned by society because he is visually repulsive. Boris Karloff's tender performance added depth to this theme of ostracism. *Frankenstein* (95) is early cinema's greatest essay in prejudice and illustrates how apparently commercial studio genre material could be meaningful. It is also a bold and surprising reversal of the normal methods of novelistic adaptation. In Shelley's novel, the monster speaks frequently and articulately. Moreover, when novels are used as source material for films, their characters' internal thoughts are usually externalized and given

95
Left: Boris Karloff as the monster in James Whale's *Frankenstein*. This publicity still captures the persecuted quality of Karloff's performance as well as the influence of German expressionist shadows on Whale's film. USA, 1931.

dialogue. However, Whale and his screenwriters ensured that the monster was practically mute.

In many other ways *Frankenstein* was hugely influential. Karloff became a star and for the next forty years was Western cinema's most famous horror actor. German and American cinematic horror continued to intersect when Karloff played the title role in *The Mummy* (Universal, 1932), directed by Karl Freund who had shot *The Golem*, *Variety* and *Metropolis* in Germany. Horror became Universal Studios' trademark and to this day its back-lot tours display Frankenstein sets which are still standing. The success of *Frankenstein* and *Dracula* established the thrill of fear as commercial cinema's newest attraction. Films like *King Kong* (Merian C. Cooper and Ernest Schoedsack, USA, 1933), *Eyes Without a Face* (Georges Franju, France, 1959), *Psycho* (Alfred Hitchcock, USA, 1960), *Onibaba* (Kaneto Shindo, Japan, 1964), *The Exorcist* (William Friedkin, USA, 1973) and *The Blair Witch Project* (Daniel Myrick, Eduardo Sanchez, USA, 1998) not only tested the audience's appetite for horror, but also became aesthetic and technical landmarks in film history. Although the Frankenstein cycle would soon degenerate into cheap laughs, its artistic legacy was ensured by the original tenderness of the Whale–Karloff vision. Forty years after the release of the original *Frankenstein*, Victor Erice made *The Spirit of the Beehive* (Spain, 1973) about a little Spanish girl who sees *Frankenstein* and then imagines that the monster comes to her village. Set soon after Franco's victory, Erice uses the monster as a symbol for the sort of outsiders who were denounced by the country's new right-wing political regime. *Gods and Monsters* (USA, 1998) explored Whale's complex feelings of love for his actors.

The gangster picture also shocked and fascinated audiences and, unlike horror films, had no European roots. It too became a recognizable genre in 1930–31 with its own stars, plots, imagery and themes. It is easy to see why, at first, it was a purely American genre: the manufacture and sale of alcohol were illegal in the US between 1920 and 1933, and gangs of entrepreneurial lawbreakers, or gangsters, ran alcohol between country still and city speakeasy. Often of Italian or Irish descent, they structured their empires like families and became famous figures in cities such as Chicago and New York. This mixture of fame, crime, family drama and ethnicity proved to be irresistible to Hollywood. The first film that integrated these elements fully was *Little Caesar* (Mervyn Le Roy, 1930), in which

Edward G. Robinson plays an Italian mob leader, who wages war on his rivals[18] and is brought down by his moll (96 top). The story is violent and Robinson plays his role unsentimentally, as would the other gangster icon of these years, James Cagney. In the following year, Cagney took on the role of a middle-class lad who becomes a mobster through the liquor racket. *Public Enemy* (William Wellman, 1931) is more violent than *Little Caesar* and, controversially for the time, less damning of its main character. Cagney, an ex-dancer, moves gracefully throughout the film and spits out his lines with relish. He had charm, and many organizations in America

denounced the film for indulging his seductive qualities. This was to be the start of the moral debate about gangster films that continues to this day. Robinson's Rico and Cagney's Powers were Italian and Irish respectively. Catholicism and the familial and deferential aspects of this type of Christianity have remained central to gangster pictures ever since. Forty years later, and the most famous and morally and visually darkest gangster films in cinema's history continued this tradition. Francis Coppola's[19] *Godfather* trilogy continually contrasted the piety of their Italian Catholic characters with their murderous brutality. This made for potent cinema but there were objections, as in the early 1930s, that Hollywood cinema had acquired a fascist taint in its ongoing love affair with gangsters.

The Russian-Jewish New York journalist Ben Hecht wrote two of the earliest gangster pictures and established the genre's themes as much as any director. *Underworld* (Joseph Von Sternberg, 1927) was a precursor about a gangster and his moll on a moral trajectory, which became the genre's staple in subsequent years. *Scarface: Shame of a Nation* (Howard Hawks, 1932), was the most significant gangster film of its era. It was stylistically more daring than others, using expressionist lighting and symbols. It was more interested in detail, recreating real-life incidents such as the St. Valentine's Day Massacre in journalistic detail. It emphasized the sexual inadequacy of its main character, Catholic Tony Camonte. Hecht, who would become one of the most successful screenwriters in Hollywood history, wrote a highly cynical script which disregarded civilized feelings and the niceties of life, and the censor forced its director, Howard Hawks, to add scenes

96
Above: The first film to portray the social and psychological aspects of 1920s gansterism. Edward G. Robinson in *LIttle Caesar*. Director: M. Le Roy. USA, 1930. Below: Lead character Tony Camonte's sexual inade-quacy was highllighted in *Scarface: Shame of a Nation*. Director: Howard Hawks. USA, 1932.

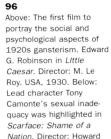

denouncing Camonte. *Scarface* was remade and updated, with cold brilliance, by Brian De Palma in 1983. He augmented the violence, having characters fight with chainsaws at one point. Camonte's character had metamorphosed into a Cuban thug who goes to Florida and becomes a drug lord, dealing in cocaine. The ethos that greed is good was only too appropriate in the consumerist 1980s. De Palma took Camonte's demise in the Hawks–Hecht picture (he dies under a tourist sign which says "The World is Yours" [97 top]) and transformed it into an extraordinary shot in the middle of this remake, which centres on a giant balloon in the sky, emblazoned with "The World is Yours" (97 bottom two) and then cranes down to an artificial coastline and Al Pacino who stares up at it blankly.

Hollywood made at least seventy gangster films in the first three years of the genre, 1930–32. They captivated audiences and worried commentators, and their themes and style influenced filmmaking in France in the 1940s, 1950s and 1960s, in Britain in the 1950s and 1970s, in Japan from the 1940s onward, in Hong Kong from the 1960s onward and then in India and the Middle East from the 1970s onward. Back in the US, the complex setting of Abraham Polonsky's *Force of Evil* (USA, 1948) was a number gambling racket and its characters spoke some of the most poetic dialogue in cinema. *On the Waterfront* (Elia Kazan, USA, 1954) turned a former boxer, who breaks the mob's control of a labour union, into a Christ-like martyr. In that same year, *The Seven Samurai* (Akira Kurosawa, Japan, 1954) combined gangster and Western themes with a traditional Japanese story of swordsmen and villagers and became a hugely influential film. *Le samouraï/The Samurai* (Jean-Pierre Melville, France, 1967) took Kurosawa's style and fused it with American gangster and Western movie motifs. In the same year,

Bonnie and Clyde (Arthur Penn, USA, 1967) made two bank robbers appealing to the emerging counterculture. *Performance* (Nicolas Roeg and Donald Cammell, UK, 1970) used the gangster milieu for their piercing exploration of identity. *The Godfather* (Francis Ford Coppola, USA, 1972) shrouded its characters in darkness, as if in a portrait by the Dutch painter Rembrandt. A new master of the genre, Martin Scorsese debuted with *Mean Streets* (USA, 1973) and emphasized the Catholicism of gangsters by using religious quotations from James Joyce. *Once Upon a Time in America* (Sergio Leone, Italy, 1984) was the most stylistically complex gangster film since *Force of Evil*. *Reservoir Dogs* (Quentin Tarantino, USA, 1992) was a highly influential, talky drama with elements of classical theatre (98).

As audience's fear of evil became a new theme for filmmakers to play with after the success of *Frankenstein*, so the lawless lust for power became a fascination for international filmmakers after the early gangster cycle. International filmmakers saw gangsters as existential heroes, fascists, social victims, enigmatic, hubristic and tragic. Gangsterism's later social and aesthetic richness found its roots in the schema of early 1930s America.

Musicals, horror films and gangster pictures multiplied in the 1930s, but the other genres within American closed romantic realism cannot be placed so easily. Many Westerns were made between 1928 and 1945, but they were better explored in their later 1940s heyday. However, it should be noted how richly

they compare to gangster pictures. The majority of films about the mob are concerned with decaying societies and an exploration of the consequences of lawbreaking. A large proportion of Westerns are about emerging societies and an exploration of lawlessness and the consequences of creating laws. Westerns tend to be set in the period 1860–1900, years that overlap with the beginning of filmmaking. Former cowboys were often extras or stuntmen in early movies. William F. Cody, also known as Buffalo Bill, became friendly with filmmakers, who transformed his life story into myth.

98
Above: Six decades after *Scarface*, filmmakers and audiences remained fascinated by gangsters. *Reservoir Dogs*. Director: Quentin Tarantino. USA, 1992.

Several epic Westerns such as *The Covered Wagon* (James Cruze, 1923) and *The Iron Horse* (John Ford, 1924) were made in the 1920s and in 1935 a new, small film studio, Republic Pictures, started producing B-westerns and serials, or oaters, to play before the main feature. It was this cheap and cheerful world of low-budget production and audiences' avid responses to it that led the American film industry to make more movies of this genre than any other. Few of these films' actors transferred to major studio A-Westerns. But one did, and he would become not only the most famous of all Western stars, but also an icon of American masculinity and idealism. His breakthrough film will be discussed later in this Chapter. His name was John Wayne.

99
Above: One of the great closed romantic realist directors, Howard Hawks (left), used a camera unobtrusively, had a distinctive view of the relationship between men and women and handled the movie genres more adroitly than most.

Silent American cinema's greatest genre, comedy, had changed course at the beginning of the sound era and the fates of its director–stars were varied. Chaplin continued to make significant films such as *City Lights* (1931) and *Modern Times* (1936), but the careers of Lloyd and Keaton petered out. The most unexpected change was the feminization of comedy. Under the influence of Lubitsch and partly as a result of early feminism's advances, women became important, not only as performers (such as Mae West, Katharine Hepburn and Carole Lombard) but also as the subject of and inspiration for 1930s comedy.[20] However, the studios' only high-ranking woman director, Dorothy Arzner, who had previously been a respected editor in the 1920s, contributed little to this shift. There might be feminist touches in her films, for example *Christopher Strong* (1933) in which Katharine Hepburn plays an aviatrix, but Arzner ends the film in a moral manner – Hepburn commits suicide on discovering her pregnancy.

The battle of the sexes became a wellspring for writers and directors. The reason (or unreason) of the comediennes disrupted the story (and male characters) with delightful results. The most distinctive of these films were farcical in tone and performed at a very fast pace, legacies of the madcap style of 1910s chase movies and the dizzying pace of some vaudeville and burlesque routines. The first of these new comedies was *Twentieth Century* (USA, 1934) and the best – the funniest and fastest – was *Bringing Up Baby* (USA, 1938). Both were directed by the casual chameleon of American cinema, Howard Hawks, who was perhaps the most important 1930s studio director (99). He was born in Indiana in 1896, his family moved to California around 1906, he studied engineering and, at the age of sixteen, became a professional car and airplane racer. He got into the film business by taking a summer job at Famous Players-Lasky around 1912 and worked his way up through the editing and story departments. Aged twenty-six, he directed a few short films with his own money and then started working on features at the end of the silent era. Having teamed up with Hecht, he made *Scarface*; the screwball comedy, *Twentieth Century*; the first and best of the dark films of the Humphrey Bogart–Lauren Bacall pairing, *To Have and Have Not* (1944) and *The Big Sleep* (1946); two of the most significant Westerns, *Red River* (1948) and *Rio Bravo* (1959) and one of cinema's most playful musicals, *Gentlemen Prefer Blondes* (1953). He was also a brilliant talent spotter, discovering Lauren Bacall and Montgomery Clift.

It is hard to believe that these diverse movies were overseen by one man. Hawks directed forty films in forty-three years, often producing and writing them as well, contributing to other projects, and switching between genres. How could someone capture Chicago gangsters' cynical lust for power, invent screwball comedy's breathless near-madness, pare the Western down by removing much of its action and focusing on its friendships and camaraderie or make the sisterly tenderness of Jane Russell and Marilyn Monroe so engaging? His own dismissive answer to these questions in interviews was that his formula was "make a few good scenes and don't annoy the audience". Film writers have attempted to answer these questions by searching for a deep, unifying view of life and people deep in films. Companionship and professionalism are undoubtedly important elements in many of them, from *Gentlemen Prefer Blondes* to *Rio Bravo*. Hawks' women are often tough; his men are sometimes humiliated during the course of his films; he repeats almost identical sparring dialogue in several. His work with Humphrey Bogart reveal a broader inclination toward men who are unexcitable and slow to react.

This might be a settled view of life, but there is little agreement over what that "view" constitutes. One distinguished critic describes Hawks as "the greatest optimist the cinema has produced."[21] Another refers to his "distinctively bitter view of life",[22] and such ambiguities carry over into his private life. Lauren Bacall (100), whom he cast aged eighteen in *To Have and Have Not*, points to his casual anti-Semitic remarks made in a studio system run by Jewish executives. Others suggest that this great womanizer might have been bisexual. Whatever the complexities, they never ripple the surface of his style. Hawks was a closed romantic realist of the purest kind, its poster boy and patron saint. His films take place in a parallel universe in which people are psychologically real, but history has been suspended. Despite making movies throughout America's Great Depression in the 1930s, his characters mostly have jobs. He almost never used a flashback in his films, only used dolly shots where necessary and seldom filmed from other than shoulder height. There is nothing of Mizoguchi's elaborate tracking in his work, nor of Griffith's intercutting, nor of expressionism or impressionism. He added nothing to the language of cinema and did not vary the schemata in any way whatsoever. "The old grey fox" (as he was nick-named because of his silver hair), with a slow, throaty laugh, was a

100
Above: Hawks discovered Lauren Bacall and honed Humphrey Bogart's screen persona.

canny producer of his own work, a great judge of public taste and a reluctant interviewee, who dismissed penetrating questions. He encouraged the perception that he was nothing more than a "good-all rounder", but French critics admired him from *Scarface* onward. Future director, Jacques Rivette, wrote a seminal *Cahiers du Cinéma* article on him in 1953, "The Genius of Howard Hawks", and thereafter his reputation in Europe grew. The enigma of his greatness, which was plain to see, but difficult to define, fuelled critics' theoretical enquiries into the nature of creativity within the studio factory system.

I have written that Hawks added nothing to the language of cinema, but a closer look at the films of the 1930s reveals this to be not wholly true. *Twentieth Century* starred distinguished dramatic actor John Barrymore as a theatre producer who follows an actress (Carole Lombard) onto a train (the Twentieth Century of the title) to convince her to return to Broadway (101 top). Hawks wanted to use a new way of natural, but fast comedy acting, which he adapted from Chaplin and Keaton. His instructions to Carole Lombard on *Twentieth Century* were as follows: "I told her if she acted, I'd fire her ... she would just throw lines at him so fast that he didn't know what to do sometimes. It was so fast, I didn't know what to do sometimes."[23] In an interview with Joseph McBride, Hawks said, "I don't think John Barrymore had made a complete idiot out of himself until he did *Twentieth Century*."[24]

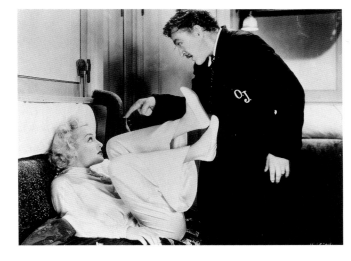

Bringing Up Baby, based on a Hager Wilde story, developed this further. A scientist who is to be married, hears that a dinosaur bone has been discovered. A millionairess will help him purchase it for his museum if he accompanies her to Connecticut to deliver her pet leopard, Baby (101 bottom). She falls for the scientist, but the distinctly dangerous leopard makes the path of true love far from smooth. Eventually, back at the museum, the wedding is called off and the millionairess arrives with the bone. Nothing is demure in this mayhem, but Hawks' ignoble universe, which brought down Barrymore, similarly humiliates Cary Grant's apparently stuffy scientist. Hawks' plain words describe the

101
Above: *Twentieth Century*'s new, faster acting style was influenced by Chaplin and Keaton.
Below: *Bringing up Baby* continued their accelerated style and added elements of surrealism.

situation. "You take a professor, and you use the girl's part to knock the dignity down."[25]What was innovative here was not only Hawks ensuring that "the woman had the dominant part",[26] but that throughout the film Cary Grant and Katherine Hepburn overlapped each other's dialogue. This had not been done so emphatically before and it added to the realism of film acting in comedy and drama

thereafter. *Bringing up Baby* is singled out by its kinetic energy, and its insane touches fuelled the 1950s American comedy of director Frank Tashlin and actors Jerry Lewis and Dean Martin.[27] Its spirit was revived by director and film historian Peter Bogdanovich for *What's Up Doc* (USA, 1972) (102).

War movies and serious dramas were the other Hollywood genres of the mid-1930s, but will be dealt with later, in the light of the Second World War. The next surprising fact in this story, coming as it does after a discussion of closed romantic realism's master filmmaker, is that although US studio filmmaking throughout this period more or less conformed to the Hays Code and the political, religious and corporate forces of the day, there were times in the 1930s when closed romantic realism broke some of its own rules. Momentarily, it shattered the illusion of a sealed-off parallel universe, like ours but more enjoyable and emphatic. Three examples illustrate this: the comedies of Laurel and Hardy, the musicals of Busby Berkeley and the melodramas of Joseph Von Sternberg.

Laurel and Hardy did not start working together until 1927. Their first significant pairing was *Putting Pants on Philip* (USA, 1927), in which Laurel plays a Scotsman who must swap a kilt for trousers. As the tailor approaches, he goes all weepy and a scrum ensues. Hardy thinks of himself as a courtly, genteel Southerner, an aspiring sophisticate (103) who insists that a man in a skirt is indecent. He has Chaplin's delusions of grandeur, but combined with the grace of a bull in a china shop. He eases Laurel aside and says "Let me do it", and the world collapses. Laurel piles in on top and looks bewildered.

Laurel and Hardy were two little boys, they were afraid of their wives and they had no foresight, insight or hindsight. There was no surprise in this comedy, just the pleasure of anticipation. It was obvious that they would fall down the manhole, but they were too busy greeting people on the street and raising their bowler hats to avoid this. They fell down the hole and then down another hole and the more expected it became, the more the laughter grew. In the short *Big Business* (USA, 1929), for example, the comic duo are trying to sell Christmas trees to a resistant home-owner (James Finlayson). He will not buy the tree and so Laurel and Hardy decide to trash his house. Their childish "That'll-teach-him-Stanley", "Too-right-it-will-Ollie" spite is infectiously joyous. At one point, Laurel throws vases for Hardy to bat. Finlayson reciprocates by bashing their car to bits. The 1920s had three master comedians, but only as I write about Laurel and Hardy, their successors, do I laugh.

Laurel was the innovator of the two. He had, like Chaplin, worked with the famous comedy troupe of Fred Karno in the UK and for a while was Chaplin's understudy. Stand on the ordinary street where Laurel was born in a small house in Lancashire and then in a small Santa Monica apartment in California, overlooking the glittering Pacific Ocean, where he ended his days, and you will know everything about the Hollywood dream. Visit the Laurel and Hardy Museum in Ulverston and you will discover old men and young girls giggling over reruns of their films. Amid the gales of laughter, at the end of mishap after mishap, amid the chaos, Hardy looks at the camera, straight down the lens for 10–15–20 seconds (104). The stare implies, Can you believe that it's come to this? Why am I always the fall guy? This is not closed romantic realism. Hardy's look (sometimes mirrored by Laurel) bridges the gap between the audience in the auditorium and the screen on which the mayhem unfolds. In the 1940s and 1950s, comedian Bob Hope would also look into the lens, make wisecracks to the audience and even comment on the absurdity of the storyline. Since comedy such as this is anarchic in spirit, it could be argued that it is more likely to break rules, even stylistic ones. The case of Laurel and Hardy illustrates how complex this point is, however, because while their adventures usually result in mayhem and destruction, there is nothing in their comic personas that is in itself anarchic. By comparison, mainstream film drama seldom addressed the audience directly, since the whole logic of Western storytelling was to draw the audience into the action, making them forget that they were outside it, watching a movie. In 1903,

103
Above: Screwball was fast but Laurel and Hardy's slow and signposted approach to comedy was equally popular. *Putting Pants on Philip*. USA, 1927.

104
Above: Actors did not look at the camera in conventional cinema because it was believed that to do so broke the dramatic spell for the audience. In certain modes of comedy, however, such looks became the norm. Few performers looked down the lens more regularly than Oliver Hardy.

one of the gunslingers in Porter's *The Great Train Robbery* looked directly into the camera and shot at the audience, but this was long before the screen became a closed parallel world of narrative. A rare example of a 1930s film that did have its actors look straight at the audience, was *Kühle Wampe/Whither Germany?* (Germany, 1932) written by playwright Berthold Brecht. After a character's death an actress turns to the camera and says "One fewer unemployed". Later, director Jonathan Demme would use the same technique in *The Silence of the Lambs* (USA, 1991), Jodie Foster (105) and Anthony Hopkins looking straight at the camera. Scorsese would reprise Porter's gunshot in *GoodFellas* (USA, 1990).

Comedy was not the only genre that broke the rules of closed romantic realism. The innate artifice of the musical genre gave it leeway in the area of audience address and, indeed, at the end of a dance routine, the performers would sometimes look straight at the lens, as if the audience was directly watching them put on a show. The film's grammar would then segue into traditional closure and they would continue to act as if no one was watching. However, some musicals did something even more surprising, borrowing from Richter's abstract films or Clair's surreal *Entr'acte* (France, 1927). The ones in question are *42nd Street* (USA, 1933) and *Gold Diggers of 1933* (USA, 1933) both choreographed by Busby Berkeley. The illustration of the Shadow Waltz musical number from the latter (81, see page 116) looks like a flower or an artichoke. In fact, it is a group of violin players photographed from a sound stage's roof, looking directly downward. Although E.A. Dupont had swung the camera from a trapeze in *Variety* (Germany, 1925) and Gance had moved and thrust it ubiquitously in *Napoleon* (France, 1927), it had rarely been placed directly overhead the action and never to such abstract effect. The innovator here was Berkeley, a successful Los Angeles-born choreographer. Like Mamoulian he had worked in the New York theatre and, again like his predecessor, seemed liberated by the infinite number of angles from which a camera could photograph. Berkeley was inspired by two different sources. Firstly, as a US soldier he was stationed in France during the First World War One and was struck by the drama, discipline and theatricality of the military drills and marching patterns. Many of his later sequences were simple military routines, eroticized, abstracted, utopianized in the manner to which Dyer refers at the beginning of this chapter. Secondly, he took a thirty-minute hot bath every morning in which he dreamt. So distinctive were the results of the military memories, together with the bath-time doodlings, that the industry started calling the results "Berkeley top shots". *Gold Diggers of 1933* was Hollywood's greatest Depression musical and one of the strangest works of art of the first half of the twentieth century. Its marriage of social concern and abstract pattern-making with human bodies is captured in Berkeley's military, geometric, erotic and horticultural images.

Joseph Von Sternberg's films reflected another type of visual excess in Hollywood. Born in 1894 into a poor, Viennese Jewish family, he became famous for devising the sultry, veiled eroticism of German star Marlene Dietrich. Director and star collaborated on such films as *The Blue Angel* (Germany, 1930), *The Scarlet Empress* (USA, 1933) and *The Devil is a Woman* (USA, 1935) together with filters, furs, veils, props, wigs, outfits and visually extravagant lighting, as shown in the image overleaf (106) from *The Scarlet Empress*. Hollywood's lighting and design departments had a tendency to decorate films beyond credibility and to seduce the audience through design, but in *The Scarlet Empress* the instinct shades into lunacy. The whole of the middle-ground is laid out in a freeze of actors and sculptures. There is almost no perspective in the image; people are stacked as in a mediaeval painting. Larger than life candleholders look like gargoyles on the façade of Notre Dame. Marlene Dietrich (centre) is haloed in

105
Above: In later years, filmmaker Jonathan Demme regularly had his cinematographer place the camera square on the actors' faces. In this moment from *The Silence of the Lambs*, Jodie Foster looks directly towards the audience, but the effect is far from comic. USA, 1990.

Above: *The Scarlet
Empress*. The imagery of
the film was so stylized
that it bordered on
surrealism. Director:
Joseph Von Sternberg.
USA, 1933

feathers whose textural softness is doubled by the misty effect of lens gauzes. Surrealists would say that the confusing space in such a scene, its seductive lighting and over emphasis on texture and display, indicate the erotic and unstable impulses behind certain aspects of Hollywood cinema.

Oliver Hardy staring at the audience, the abstractions of Berkeley and the excesses of Von Sternberg were cracks in the gleaming, sealed orb of Hollywood, whose system of genres was mastered by Hawks.

EUROPEAN AVANT-GARDE

While Hollywood was flirting with abstract and experimental cinema, the real avant-garde was emerging elsewhere. Although this was not as experimental a period as the 1920s, key films were produced. Buñuel and Dalí had followed up *Un Chien Andalou* (France, 1928) with the equally subversive *L'Age d'Or/The Golden Age* (France, 1930) and two years later, as the Spanish Civil War drew closer, Buñuel would make *Las Hurdes/Land Without Bread* (Spain, 1932), an intense documentary about the crippling poverty of those living on the Spanish–Portuguese border. Returning to France in 1930, the Duc de Noailles, Buñuel's benefactor on *L'Age d'Or* also funded the poet and artist Jean Cocteau to make *Le Sang d'un poète/The Blood of a Poet* (1930) as he would his later films, *La Belle et la bête/Beauty and the Beast* (France, 1945) and *Orphée/Orpheus* (France, 1950). *Le sang d'un poète* treated film as if it was a bunch of magic tricks, in the spirit of Méliès. Using reversed motion, upended sets, overlays of imagery and mythological references, it told its story of a poet who is inspired by a personified statue to go through a mirror into the underworld. The scene in which this happens is particularly effective. The shirtless poet stands over the mirror which, in a single cut, turns into a rectangular pool of water into which he splashes as a chorus of men roar.

Still in France, we find creative energy as brilliant as Cocteau's in the films of Parisian Jean Vigo. The son of an anarchist, Vigo made his first experimental film, *A Propos de Nice/About Nice* (France, 1930) in the south of France, where the weather benefited his tuberculosis. His third film, *Zéro de conduite/Zero for Conduct* (France, 1933) was a forty-five minute work about a revolt in a boys' boarding school. It starts with a schoolboy prank about hiding marbles and develops into a riot in the spirit of the surrealists, but with more clearly political intent. Shot by the brother of the Soviet director Dziga Vertov, Boris Kaufman, its most striking sequences are a dormitory

107
Right: Boris Kaufman's striking cinematography: the pillow-fight scene from Jean Vigo's *Zéro de conduite*. Director: Jean Vigo. France, 1933.

pillow fight and the slow-motion procession of the boys (107). The mystical and physical qualities of the former scene – it looks as if it is snowing inside – are enhanced by the musical accompaniment which was composed and transcribed backward by Maurice Jaubert and then performed. The film was interpreted as a political attack on French schools and – for this reason as well as its general spirit of rebellion – banned in France until the mid-1940s; It inspired the British film *If...* (Lindsay Anderson, 1968). Vigo was to make the poetic romance *L'Atalante* (France) in 1934, before dying of leukaemia in the same year, aged twenty-nine. He was the most

talented figure in French cinema during this period.

Elsewhere in the world, underdeveloped film industries found that low-budget avant-garde films were the most productive way to impact on international film culture. For example, in 1930 a Brazilian director made not only that country's first avant-garde film but also one of the first significant films made in Latin America. Movies had been distributed there from the mid-1890s and the first Brazilian feature was made in 1906, but none of the 100 or so full-length films produced seems to have been distinctive. This changed with Mario Peixoto's *Limite* (1930). Made when the director was just nineteen, its portrait of two men's and a woman's

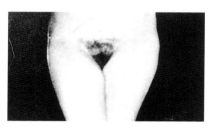

vision while lost at sea was described as "very beautiful" by Sergei Eisenstein. Peixoto was not only influenced by Eisenstein, but by the subjective camera work of Abel Gance. Three years later, a diminutive Portuguese actress, Carmen Miranda, would make her first films in Brazil before heading to Hollywood where she worked with Busby Berkeley. It was not until the early 1950s that Brazil would again begin to make stylistically innovative films, but when they did they would be splendid.

The pattern was repeated in Poland where an avant-garde film, *Europa* (1932), by Franciszka and Stefan Themerson, was the country's first significant production. There had been some filmmaking before this and the country's first studio was established in Warsaw in 1920, but the Themersons were the first filmmakers to gain attention. *Europa* (109) was a vivid collage of film styles and a bold and

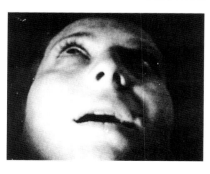

successful adaptation of a poem by Anatol Stern. Its directors were the core members of SAF, one of the world's first filmmaking co-operatives. They developed Richter's abstract ideas of painting and scratching film, which they applied to *Europa*. Poland's next significant modernist film was Eugeniusz Cekalski and Stanislaw Wohl's *Three*

Chopin Studies (Poland, 1937) and it would not be until the mid-1950s that this country would again come to the fore cinematically[28]. Its most celebrated director, Roman Polanski, is said to have been influenced by the Themersons.

Within two years of *Three Chopin Studies*' release, Poland would be invaded by its neighbour, Germany. In 1933 Adolf Hitler became Germany's chancellor and his party, the National Socialists (Nazis), enacted restrictive laws that banned Jews from working in the film industry. Twenty thousand books with Jewish or modern themes were burned publicly and curtailment of Jews' civil rights increased throughout the 1930s. Most filmmakers and artists fled to France, the UK or straight to the US. Among those who left Germany were some discussed in this story: cinematographers Karl Freund and Eugene Schüfftan, and director E.A. Dupont. There were also filmmakers who will play important roles in subsequent chapters: Max Ophüls, Billy Wilder and Robert Siodmark. Fritz Lang went to Hollywood in 1934 and Ernst Lubitsch had gone eleven years before that.

The Nazis took complete control of the German film industry in 1934 and in the mid-1930s the most prodigiously gifted filmmaker associated with them, Leni Riefenstahl, made two astounding films, which were as important and troubling as *The Birth of a Nation* had

108
Top left: Mario Peixoto's
Limite. Brazil, 1930.

109
Bottom left: *Europa* by
Franciszka and Stefan
Themerson. Poland, 1932.

110
Left: Elements of Busby
Berkeley's regimented,
overhead aesthetic in
Leni Riefenstahl's
Olympia. Germany, 1936.

been two decades earlier. *Triumph des Willens/Triumph of the Will* (1935) and *Olympische Spiele/Olympia* (1936) (110) were both quasi-documentaries. The former was a bombastic record of a 1934 Nazi party rally, the latter an account of the 1936 Berlin Olympics, in which she was assisted by former avant-garde filmmaker, Walter Ruttmann. Riefenstahl was a thirty-four-year-old former dancer and actress who directed her first film only three years earlier (*Das Blaue Licht/The Blue Light*) in 1931, yet on these two films she was provided with resources similar to those available to Griffith on *Intolerance* or Gance on *Napoleon*. The result was a film technique with all the bravura of Gance or Berkeley. Cameras were attached to balloons, dug into the earth or tracked alongside the action (111). Zoom lenses, which simulated a move toward or away from a distant point as their focal lengths were changed, became available from 1932 and Riefenstahl used them to pick out details in crowds. For *Olympia*'s striking high diving sequence, she photographed an athlete soaring and arcing through the air, then, before he hit the water, cut to an endless succession of divers. These were human beings in flight, a dream only previously dreamt of in musicals.

111
Below: Like Abel Gance, Riefenstahl (centre) devised elaborate ways of creating camera moves and visual compositions.

Riefenstahl used symmetry, scale, slow-motion, low-angle shooting, suspense and mystery to aggrandize her subjects. These films worshipped the physical perfection of athletes and soldiers alike, picturing each as the other. Like Berkeley, she explored the discipline of military manoeuvre, its absence of individuality or doubt, and eroticized it. She filmed her subjects as if they were Greek gods, apparently approving of, or oblivious to, the politics of her paymasters. Next to Orson Welles and Alfred Hitchcock, Riefenstahl was the most technically talented Western filmmaker considered in this section, yet her inflexibility, her inability to doubt her aesthetic, damns her. She was commissioned to film the invasion of Poland and, although she disputed this to the end of her life, she seems to have used people from a concentration camp as extras in her film, *Tiefland* (1954). In life she seemed indestructible, surviving car accidents, trekking through Africa to photograph the Nuba and scuba-diving well into her nineties. She died in 2003, a few weeks after her 101st birthday.

Other, less talented German directors emerged. Their films, such as *Jew Süss* (1940) by Veit Harlan, were vile slurs and devoid of human content, although such outright propaganda was rare at the time. The Nazis behaved with uncharacteristic modesty about the most extreme product of their imagination – the homicidal gas chambers at Treblinka and Auschwitz-Birkenau – not a single foot of exposed film captured their methodical killing.

Filmmaking had gone somewhat quiet in 1920s Britain. Pioneers such as R.W. Paul and G.A. Smith were still alive (they died in 1943 and 1959 respectively), but they witnessed, the overtaking of their innovations by other countries' advances. Only five per cent of films shown in the UK in the mid-1920s were indigenously produced and in an attempt to reverse this decline the British government passed the Quota Act, which stipulated a minimum amount of screen time to be devoted to native product. Production quadrupled, and a country with one-seventh of the US population attempted, as it would do several times in later decades, to emulate the American studio system. The majority of its output was very low-budget, but eventually the 1930s became the most creative period in the UK's cinema history. The careers of three major figures are at the core of this achievement: director Alfred Hitchcock, producer Alexander Korda and documentary maker John Grierson.

Hitchcock's formative experiences in the film world were in Germany and, as discussed in Chapter Three, his silent film *The Lodger* (UK, 1926) bears the marks of 1920s German expressionism. From the start of his career, this precisely-spoken, rotund son of a London fruit and poultry dealer was exceptionally talented. Few, however, would have guessed that by the 1960s he would be a visual artist to rank with the painter Pablo Picasso. Those who have never seen an Alfred Hitchcock film should close this book now and watch *The Man who Knew too Much* (UK, 1934), *The 39 Steps* (UK, 1935), *Rebecca* (USA, 1940), *Notorious* (USA, 1946), *Strangers on a Train* (USA, 1951), *Vertigo* (USA, 1958), *North by Northwest* (USA, 1959), *Psycho* (USA, 1960) and *Marnie* (USA, 1964). In these nine films you will find everything you need to know about Western sound movies. They speak the technical language of cinema more gracefully than any other body of work of this period, have more erotic precision, are lessons in cinema's pleasure and dread of looking and are metaphysical. Hitchcock is as great as Ozu, but his films begin where the Japanese director's end. Ozu's are about the essential repose of ordinary life, whereas in Hitchcock's, Western society may have acquired the appearance of such order, but this only fuels their characters' sex and death drives.

Hitchcock's British films established the combination of suspense, sexuality and comedy that would become known as Hitchcockian, but did not have the psychological depth of his American work. *The Man who Knew Too Much* (UK, 1934) concerns an ordinary couple who accidentally hear about a plot to murder a diplomat and whose daughter is kidnapped to buy their silence. The film starts in the Swiss Alps and moves location to London.

The visual contrast is very Hitchcockian, as is the climax: the assassination is to take place during a grand concert. Hitchcock had seen a magazine cartoon in which a man gets up, goes to work, takes his seat in an orchestra, plays a single note and then goes home. What, thought Hitchcock, if the shooting of the ambassador was timed to take place at the moment of such a single note, such as the crashing of cymbals? This was what he staged. The kidnapped child's mother is present at the concert, and gradually realizing the scenario, lets out a piercing scream just before the crash of the cymbals, which interrupts the carefully planned assassination attempt and saves the ambassador (112).

112
Above: The famous concert scene in *The Man Who Knew Too Much* where the mother of a kidnapped child realizes that an ambassador is about to be shot, so stands up and screams. Director: Alfred Hitchcock. UK, 1934.

Hitchcock remade the film in America in 1954, and what is striking about both versions is how carefully he spells out the exact sequence of events leading up to the shooting. He repeats the piece of music so that the audience will know its structure and have their expectations heightened, as Keaton had done similarly for comic purposes in *The General*. When discussing the scene, Hitchcock said, "The reason why the cantata record is played twice is to prevent any confusion in the viewer's mind about the events that are to follow."[29] *The Man who Knew Too Much* was a huge success in the UK and America. Hitchcock's next film, *The 39 Steps* (UK, 1935), took his cinematic ideas further by turning each scene into a self-contained short narrative. Rigorously planned as a series of set pieces, it is the story of a Canadian, Richard Hannay, travelling to Scotland to track down those who killed a woman in his London flat. A Murnau-like scene in a Scottish crofter's cottage was based, for example, on a story about a South African man with a young, sexually starved wife. In the famous finale of the film, a character based on an old music hall figure blurts out the secret of the spy ring, the Thirty-Nine Steps, and just as he does so is shot by one of its members. Each set piece is crafted with the same clarity as the cantata climax of *The Man Who Knew Too Much*, but Hitchcock was so eager to segue into the next dramatically and tonally rich self-contained section that he made the transitions between them as brief as possible. At one point Hannay is captive, but his method of escape is uninteresting, so he holds a match up to a heat-sensitive device and Hitchcock rapidly cuts to his exit. He would continue to remove the undramatic events from his scenarios, distilling them over the years until every moment, object and shot was part of his system of desire and anxiety. He went to work in the US at the end of the 1930s and he became the most famous director in the world; his American films will be discussed in subsequent chapters.

Alexander Korda was one of Western cinema's nomadic talents. Born in Hungary in 1893, he was directing by the age of eighteen, helped nationalize Hungary's film industry, and worked in Hollywood and France before settling in Britain and establishing London Film Productions in 1932. The next year he produced and directed *The Private Life of Henry VIII* (UK, 1933), Britain's first internationally successful film. It, together with London Film's *Rembrandt* (Alexander Korda, UK, 1936), are still remembered for actor Charles Laughton's performances in the title roles, the first of which won him an Oscar for best actor. Both films influenced a

113
Above: Charles Laughton as the title character in *The Private Life of Henry VIII*. This scene so impressed American Method actor Rod Steiger that in the late 1990s he cited it as one of the greatest pieces of acting he had ever seen. Director: Alexander Korda. UK, 1933.

generation of 1950s actors, including the significant US figure Rod Steiger, who said later that Laughton eating a chicken leg (113) was the best piece of acting he had ever seen. Korda built the UK's biggest studio, Denham, in 1936 and his success encouraged J. Arthur Rank, who had set up British National Film in 1934 and built Pinewood Studios, which were to be home to many of the 1960s and 1970s James Bond movies. Korda went on to produce films by British directors Carol Reed and David Lean and was executive producer on *The Third Man* (Carol Reed, UK, 1949). His productions established the international perception that British cinema was prestigious, which remains to the present day.

114
Above: Dramatic compositions such as this one, together with a poetic sound-track and a vivid portrayal of a mail train's journey from London to Scotland made *Night Mail* a hugely influential documentary. Directors: Basil Wright and Harry Watt. UK, 1936.

The producer and some-time director John Grierson brought a very different kind of film to the fore. Grierson studied philosophy in Scotland and communication in America, before returning to Britain in 1927 where he won government support for films in the mould of Flaherty's *Nanook of the North* (USA, 1922). He named these films, "documentaries", and produced them at the Empire Marketing Board from 1928 and at the General Post Office from 1933. As well as directing some of these himself, he also fostered the careers of a raft of socially conscious, poetically inclined young men, including Basil Wright and Paul Rotha. Wright and Harry Watt made *Night Mail* (UK, 1936), an impressionistic account of the journey of a postal train from London to Scotland (114), with major artistic collaborators. The music was by the celebrated composer Benjamin Britten, the commentary was by the poet W.H. Auden and the evocative sound was designed by Brazilian Alberto Cavalcanti.

Wright and Watt were influenced by the Soviet editor-compiler, Esfir Shub, whereas documentary directors Arthur Elton and Edgar Anstey were inspired by the new realism to be seen in socially committed still photography. *Housing Problems* (UK, 1935) was one of the first films in which real working-class people were interviewed on camera. Although simply photographed, the scenes of Londoners describing their living conditions had great impact on leftism and reformist filmmaking thereafter and helped launch the tradition of interview-based documentary, which has sporadically dominated documentary filmmaking at the expense of *Night Mail*'s more poetic techniques. Ten years later, director John Huston would film interviews with soldiers traumatized by the Second World War. The rawness of the result, *Let There be Light* (US, 1946), so disturbed the American military that they banned the film until the 1970s.

Humphrey Jennings, born in England in 1907, and a former surrealist painter, was the most gifted filmmaker in Grierson's group. His poetic short- and medium-length documentaries were more in the tradition of *Night Mail* than *Housing Problems*. *Listen to Britain* (UK, 1941), *Fires were Started* (UK, 1943) and *A Diary for Timothy* (UK, 1945) intercut scenes of British people of different classes and ways of life, in cities and in the countryside, coping with the realities of war. His use of sound was as poetic as Cavalcanti's in *Night Mail* and he succeeded in capturing the timeless, civilized qualities of Britain. Jennings' interest in small over grand gestures and the lack of panic or bombast in his films lends his work an enduring dignity. Those of 1939–45 portrayed the quiet nobility of the British people just as those of Leni Riefenstahl essayed the epic nobility of the Germans.

In the Soviet Union in the early and mid-1930s, musicals and comedies were being made, but realism was the subject of debate. Josef Stalin had succeeded Lenin as head of state in 1924 and soon his collectivization of farms was causing millions of deaths. In the world of art, experiment fell out of favour. Significant musical and comedy films were made in this period by directors such as Yakov Protazanov, who had directed *Queen of Spades* in 1916, but Stalin wanted cinema to be heroic and optimistic, charting the happy lives of model working citizens. Eisenstein felt uncomfortable working within such clichéd confines and when Stalin started interfering with his work, in 1930 he took up an offer of four years earlier from Douglas Fairbanks and Mary Pickford to go to the US. Dovzhenko followed *Arsenal* (Soviet Union, 1930) with another more poetic masterpiece, *Earth* (Soviet Union, 1930), which was attacked by the cultural authorities. Eisenstein soon became disappointed with the creative limitations of the Hollywood studios, but was inspired by meeting Chaplin and documentary filmmaker Flaherty. He would later travel to Mexico in

1930 to shoot the eventually unfinished film *Que Viva Mexico!* and returned to Moscow in 1932. In 1934, the First Congress of Soviet Writers proclaimed "Socialist Realism" as the only appropriate style for revolutionary art. Heroic model behaviour, an idealistic view of

115
Right: Strange-edge composition and close-to-the-camera placement of actors characterize the stills that are available from Sergei Eisenstein's *Bezhin Meadow.* Soviet Union, 1935–37.

life, work and the state became the norm and policy. Within months Eisenstein's more experimental and poetic techniques were criticized at the All-Union Conference of Cinematographic Workers. The transcript of this meeting reflects the slide into conformity, and still makes depressing reading today.

Although curtailed, Eisenstein made inventive films like *Alexander Nevsky* (Soviet Union, 1938) and the long-lost *Bezhin Meadow* (Soviet Union, 1935–37), whose remaining stills (115) are a tantalizing reminder of the film. Despite Alexander Medvedkin's *Happiness* (Soviet Union, 1935) being rich and funny, its pro-Stalinist sensibility and pro-collectivization lends a bitterness to its enjoyment. The same is true of Vertov's *Three Songs For Lenin* (Soviet Union, 1934) – literally three songs for the former state leader. The first is "My Face was in a Dark Prison", showing exquisitely photographed Islamic women in the Eastern soviets who, after "liberation and enlightenment", no longer had to shroud their heads in burkhas. The second, "We Loved Him", about Lenin's death: one banner reads "Lenin is our Immortality". The third, "In a Big City of Stone", is about construction, dams and people flocking to see Lenin's body in Red Square. But Vertov's real interest is in people and his sense of space and drama jar with the political slogans. The triumphant boast of progress contained in the refrain, repeated no less than five times, "If Lenin could only see our country now", sounds deeply ironic.

The forced optimism of the Soviet films contrasts with those made in France at this time. The decade there had started with the sonic wit of Clair and the disruptive magic of Cocteau and Vigo, but soon major directors such as Jean Renoir began to explore other genres. Renoir was the son of the famous artist, Pierre Auguste-Renoir, whose legacy funded his son's first forays into cinema. As a young man Renoir began his career in the silent era after studying mathematics and philosophy and described his films as "half way between a certain realism – not exterior – and a certain poetry."[30] His first notable work was *La Chienne/The Dog* (1931), a realist story set in an artists' district of Paris. Both this and *Boudu Sauvé des eaux/Boudu saved from Drowning* (1932) featured the extraordinary actor Michel Simon in leading roles. Simon was a big, working-class, untheatrical actor and Renoir understood how to capture his gruff personality. Renoir said, "the idea of artificially attracting the audiences' attention to certain elements, to a star, for example, is a purely romantic idea. Classicism contains an idea of evenness that no longer exists in romanticism."[31] He could have been talking about Ozu, but he was referring to his own, even, unshowy style in which stars are not given special emphasis.

116
Above: Jean Renoir's *Toni* used non-professional actors, real locations and naturalistic lighting to challenge what the director saw as the romanticism of more mainstream filmmaking. France, 1935.

Toni (France, 1935) (116), a story about immigrant Italian quarry workers extended the realistic elements in Renoir's work. It used non-professional actors and no sets or make-up and was one of the most important films of fictional naturalism in cinema since Von Stroheim's *Greed* (1923). It was not seen widely so didn't exert a major influence on the realist Italian directors of the 1940s, but Renoir's *La Grande illusion/Grand Illusion* (1937), by contrast, was an international success. It starred Von Stroheim – who had turned more to acting than directing by this period – as the First World War German commandant of a prison camp to which three French soldiers are sent. The screenplay was based on stories Renoir had heard from friends, it avoided grand gestures and weaved a fine tapestry from the men's nuanced interactions. Each character's humanity is explored and at one point the film appears to stop as the men discuss the meaning of Jewish generosity. Generosity was, indeed, at the core of Renoir's approach to human beings on screen. His now-celebrated film, *La Règle du jeu/The Rules of the Game* (1939), jeered at its première and a tremendous financial flop, will be discussed in greater detail when we come to that year (see pages 170–71).

Few other mid-1930s French films attempted such dramatic even-handedness and the best shared a pessimism attributable to their times. By the middle of the decade, stars like Jean Gabin and Michèle Morgan were playing the leads in stories about forgotten people aimlessly encountering each other in the bleak morning or evening light, momentarily enlivened in each other's company, but then retreating into themselves and their pessimism. There are several parts reasons for this prevalent mood. There was much fear of a resurgent Germany in a country still weak from the bloodletting of 1914–18. Unemployment stood at nearly half a million in 1935 France, where the Depression began later but lasted longer than elsewhere, and there was political instability. The right wing was dominant in the first part of the century and then an uneasy alliance of left-wing parties – the Popular Front – held power for a short period. And the industry itself was unstable; the personae of Gabin and Morgan capturing the subtle hopelessness of the decade. Both actors had melancholic faces which were slow to register feeling, in the manner of Humphrey Bogart.

The image to the right (117) is from *Quai des Brumes/Port of Shadows* (1938), a key work of 1930s French poetic realism and one of the first pairings of Gabin and Morgan. He plays a Foreign Legion deserter and she an orphaned young woman with a violent guardian. Set mostly in a café in the port of Le Havre in 1936, it reaches its climax when Gabin shoots the guardian, only to be killed by a local crook just as his ship is leaving the harbour. The film was written and directed by the poet-director team of Jacques Prévert and Marcel Carné, who almost single-handedly defined the romantic pessimism of their time. They would on to make *Le Jour se lève/Daybreak*

(1939) and *Les Enfants du paradis/The Children of Paradise* (1945), a memorable epic set in the world of nineteenth-century Parisian theatre. Carné's meticulous studio style became unfashionable in the late 1950s, but he lived well into his eighties, long enough to see *Les Enfants du paradis* revived as one of the most enjoyable of French films, and *Quai des Brumes* rediscovered as an outstanding mood piece. The latter's misty visuals were photographed by Eugen Schüfftan who had been visual effects designer on *Metropolis* (Germany, 1927) and, having fled the Nazis, was now in France en route to America. The film's significance to French culture of the period is best summed up by the words of a French Vichy government spokesman: "If we have lost the war it is because of *Quai des Brumes*." Carné retorted that you can't blame a storm on the barometer.

Quai des Brumes was not the first time that Gabin had played an isolated man who is killed before he can escape on a boat with his lover. In *Pépé le Moko* (Julien Duvivier, France, 1937), the town was Algiers and the girl was played by Mireille Balin. Director Duvivier derived many visual ideas from Hawks' *Scarface* and, in an example of film style crossing the Atlantic, *Pépé le Moko* was remade first as *Algiers* (John Cromwell, USA, 1938), then as *Casbah* (John Berry, USA, 1948).

A small but telling coincidence in film history now enters this story. In the same period that these French and American filmmakers were trying to recreate the densely constructed spaces of North African casbahs in Western studios, so the first studio opened in the Arab world. The founding of Misr in Cairo in 1935, which was also the first production facility on the African continent, helped establish Egypt as the filmmaking centre for the whole of the Middle East. The first films shown here had been by the Lumière brothers in 1897 but no features were made by Egyptian filmmakers until Misr was established. Thereafter, production numbered about twenty per year, increasing to fifty from the mid-1940s to the 1980s. *El-azima/The Will* (Kamil Selim, Egypt,

117
Above: Jean Gabin as the deserter and Michèle Morgan as an orphaned young woman: This famous image captures the haunting pessimism of Marcel Carné's *Quai des Brumes*. France, 1938.

1939) is the most distinctive of the early Misr films. Its story of Mohamed, the son of a barber in a run-down part of Cairo, was rooted more in the realities of North African life than in atmospheric exoticism, but its acting was more stagy than *Pépé le Moko*. Gabin lives above the city of Algiers in *Pépé le Moko*, but is oppressed by it visually, whereas Mohamed (Hussein Sidsky) battles against Cairo's economic conditions. *The Will*'s director, Kamal Selim, died aged thirty-two, but his first steps toward North African cinematic realism influenced the great Egyptian director Salah Abu Seif.

The very different French and Egyptian approaches to realism were not mirrored elsewhere in the world. By the second half of the 1930s, the biggest box-office star in America and around the world was a doll-like Californian girl, Shirley Temple, who became a star at Fox in 1934, aged six, and who danced and sang, most famously, "On the Good Ship Lollipop". She was a licence to print money but, in 1937 the American company Disney made a film that would eclipse even Temple's box-office appeal. *Snow White and the Seven Dwarfs* (David Hand – supervising director, USA, 1937) was so successful that it established the company's reputation for generations. In the subsequent four decades, Disney was responsible for nine of the top grossing American films. *Pinocchio* (1940), *Bambi* (1942), *Peter Pan* (1953), *One Hundred and One Dalmatians* (1961) and *Mary Poppins* (USA, 1964) outperformed others in their year of production and they often doubled, tripled or even quadrupled the takings of the top ranking films in adjacent years.

Walt Disney was born in Chicago in 1901 and died in 1966. He was not the first to make films by photographing drawings. These had been projected as early as 1896 but the technique remained undeveloped until J. Stuart Blackton's *Humorous Phases of Funny Faces* (1906) and Winsor McCay's *Gertie the Dinosaur* in 1909. The first animated feature, which no longer survives, is claimed to have been *El Apostol* (Frederico Valle,

118
Below: A year before *Quai des Brumes*, Gabin starred in *Pepe Le Moko*, set in Algiers. Just before it was made Misr, the first film studio in the Arab world was opened in Cairo.

seventeenth-century English writer John Bunyan, but with a MGM makeover. Dorothy's quest, taking her from black-and-white Kansas to the Technicolor magic garden of Oz, contains the pure elements of heightened 1930s Hollywood escapism. Yet the land of song and dance and sleepy meadows and the towering green city of Oz is a false dream. Its distractions do not solve the human problems encountered there and she realizes that "There's no place like home". The film questions the very 1930s idea of escapism, gently weighing it up against humbler and more traditional values. In doing so it is reminiscent of contemporaneous Hindi cinema.

Gone with the Wind, based on Margaret Mitchell's widely read book of the same name, took more at the box office than any one of the Disney films or the 1950s epics such as *The Robe* (USA, 1953) and *Ben Hur* (USA, 1959) and was not superseded financially until the blockbuster horror movie, *The Exorcist* (USA, 1973). It tells the story of Scarlett O'Hara (122 bottom), a spoiled and selfish young woman who loses everything, including the man she eventually loves, Rhett Butler, during the American Civil War. Like *The Wizard of Oz* and *Ninotchka*, it charts the development of a young woman as she explores the relationship between an escapist view of life and a more truthful understanding. Whereas the first two films benignly allow their heroines to make mistakes and discover the realities of worlds around them, *Gone with the Wind* ruthlessly punishes Scarlett for her egotism and denial both of the brutalities of war and that her grand lifestyle is over. It is difficult today not to see this story as an extravagant wake-up call to America. It would be two years before the Japanese bombing of Pearl Harbor would force America into the Second World War, but the film makes plain the consequences of a lack of realism about war and, although it was considered one of the most escapist films ever made, its content explicitly attacks escapism.

122
Far left: The themes of home and escape were explored in three of Hollywood's most distinctive characters in 1939: Ninotchka, played by Greta Garbo (top), Dorothy, played by Judy Garland (middle) and Scarlett O' Hara, played by Vivien Leigh (bottom).

123
Above: The moment where Dorothy leaves the sepia world of her Kansas home and enters the Technicolor dreamscape of Oz.

The form of *Gone with the Wind* is another matter. It invented no new film techniques, but created such a vivid, emotional universe and lush, sonic and visual experience that the film's bitter message was somehow smothered. Entire books have been written about why a film that punishes its heroine should have been so enduringly popular with women. The answer to this does not stem from the film's content, but lies in its form, or production values. Although the majority of the film was directed by Victor Fleming, a former garage worker who had started in films under D.W. Griffith, its scale, look and feel were controlled by its powerful producer David O. Selznick. One of its most famous images was an idealized one painted on glass showing O'Hara's house, Tara, in the distance. The dramatic sunset, which occurs at the end of the golden age portrayed in the film, was a second painting above it. In the foreground, there was yet another painted image of Scarlett, surveying their world as people do in eighteenth-century European landscape art. Finally, a fourth separate painted image of a huge tree created a sense of age and timelessness (124). Composite storybook images such as these are the crux of *Gone With the Wind* because they root the film in the romance and artifice of their symbols of home and love. The film's opening title reads that the story is set at a time that "is no more than a dream remembered", in "a civilization gone with the wind". Selznick, designer William Cameron Menzies, art director Lyle Wheeler and cameramen Ernest Haller and Ray Rennahan created this remembered dream so successfully that audiences could suffer with Scarlett and emote with this detached, overwhelmingly intense, narrative experience, without having to deal with the real consequences of the tragedy of war. Every one of these crew members got Oscars as a result.

The film's premiere was in Atlanta, Georgia, on 15 December 1939. The state's governor declared a three-day public holiday prior to its opening night and all schools and public buildings were closed. Over 250,000 people queued for hours to catch a glimpse of actors Clark Gable and Vivien Leigh. Gable arrived in a plane emblazoned with the words "MGM's Gone With The Wind". The Mayor asked for applause at one of the civic events for the "Negro members of the cast", who were not allowed access to all the festivities. Ironically, it later emerged that Leigh was part Indian.

The most critically acclaimed film of 1939 was made not in Hollywood, but in France. Jean Renoir directed *La Règle du jeu/The Rules of the Game* two years after *La Grande Illusion*. Although it had a similar theme to *Gone With the Wind*, its tale of rich people's lives and loves in a grand house on the eve of war was radically different from the Fleming–Selznick film. It was black and white, satirical, left much unsaid and was acted in a fast, heightened style. Its charac-

Left: This composite image of Scarlett O'Hara surveying her beloved Tara at sunset works at emotional and allegorical levels. Its dreamlike, storybook qualities, its depiction of longing, its sense that an era is coming to an end, are all key elements in Hollywood's romantic aesthetic.

ters are morally empty pleasure seekers, immersed in overlapping love triangles. The film's tone is difficult to define, frivolous one minute, vicious the next, as in an early scene in the downstairs kitchen, in which the servants are openly anti-Semitic. Renoir devised new ways of extending space in his imagery (see pages 175 for more on this), but then put gauzes over the lens to soften the harsh edges. Jocular and vicious, romantic and classic, the film's fame derives from these complex internal seesaws. Renoir himself played a failed artist in the film who delivers its often-quoted line, "It's another sign of the times – everyone lies – everyone has his motives." The film's portrayal of them — and perhaps its even-handedness — infuriated its upper-and middle-class audiences, and seats were torn up at the première, which was literally inflammatory, since one man threw lighted papers around the auditorium. Its portrayal of anti-Semitism was timely and it captured the prevalent mood of pessimism in France which derived from the fall of the Popular Front and the threat from Germany. It was a telling portrait of "these days", the last words spoken in the picture.

The reputation of *La Règle du jeu* has increased over the years and critic Raymond Durgnat spoke elegantly for many when he called it "An interrogation of spontaneity, convention and self-deception".[33] Renoir was the favourite director of Orson Welles (whose work is discussed on pages 176–180) and he was the patron saint of the new wave of French filmmakers of the late 1950s and 1960s.

Our last film of 1939 is *Stagecoach* (USA, 1939). It was directed by the Irish-American John Ford, who made over 100 films and won more Oscars than any other director. His name was Sean Aloysius O'Feeney, but changed it to the simpler John Ford. He was from the East coast of America, but went to Hollywood in 1913 where he was given his first job by Carl Laemmle, the founder of Universal and the man responsible for the Florence Lawrence publicity stunt. From the outset it was clear that he had an eye for composition and an Irishman's romantic feel for the American dream and, like Griffith, he took epic stories and brought their foregrounds alive with convincing human characters, combining what one critic called, "The twitches of life and the silhouettes of legend." He developed the shock effect of the Lumière brothers' 1895 train in the Western *The Iron Horse* (USA, 1924) by digging a pit under a railway line to photograph a locomotive running straight over the camera. However, such shots were not typical of Ford. He preferred the simplest of camera angles and little movement and, if it had not been for his films' Irish sentiment, this simplicity would have qualified him as a classicist, like Ozu. His longtime screenplay collaborator, Dudley Nichols, called the static style "studied symbolism".

Stagecoach, written by Nichols and based on a Guy de Maupassant story, is about a group of misfits travelling by coach. They are joined by a horseless cowboy known as the Ringo Kid before being ambushed by Indians. One of the travellers, a saloon girl and prostitute, is shunned by others of higher social standing, but Ringo and she leave at the end to start a life together in Ford's mythical, meritocratic West.

125
Above: Unlike *Gone with the Wind*, Jean Renoir's *La Règle du jeu* found a rare balance between romantic and classical elements. France, 1939.

Ringo was one of the many flawed righteous men in the Ford–Nichols collaborations. He was played by John Wayne, who had already been in films for twelve years, but it was *Stagecoach* that made him a star. Eventually Ford and Wayne would emphasize the loneliness of men like Ringo more than their decency in films such as *The Searchers* (USA, 1956), which has become among the most influential ever made.

In the seven years after *Stagecoach*, Ford would make no fewer than seven extraordinary films: *Young Mr Lincoln* (USA, 1939); *The Grapes of Wrath* (USA, 1940); *The Long Voyage Home* (USA, 1940); *The Battle of Midway* (USA 1942), a documentary filmed when he was in the Navy; *They Were Expendable* (USA, 1945), which the director Lindsay Anderson called "Ford's most personal film, perhaps his masterpiece";[34] and *My Darling Clementine* (USA, 1946), which is an almost mythic film about civilizing the wild western frontier.

During the production of *Stagecoach*, Ford filmed for the first time in the startling Monument Valley, Arizona (126), which became as iconic in his films as John Wayne. He would shoot eight other films there. Cities and towns had been photographed in every conceivable way by filmmakers, but there had been few, until Ford, who found open space central to their work. Not since the Swedish masters of the late teens and early 1920s had any filmmaker shown so strong a feeling for landscape. Ironically, Ford's pastoralism would be cited as influencing key Western filmmakers but, more surprisingly, directors far beyond the reaches of Western cinema, such as

126
Above: The buttes of Monument Valley in Arizona became a timeless backdrop to John Ford's movies of cowboys and frontiers. The director used it for the first time in *Stagecoach*. USA 1939.

Kurosawa in the 1950s, the Brazilian Glauber Rocha (127) in the 1960s and Ousmane Sembene and Dani Kouyaté from Senegal in the 1990s.

The rise of the star, the growing role of psychology in story-telling, the shortening of shots, the increasing use of close-ups and of panchromatic film stock, which was sensitive to all colours in the spectrum, had all reduced the role that single wide shots played in the earliest years of filmmaking. But Ford understood the power of such imagery and knew that the emotion felt by each character could be expressed dramatically by using deep space: a scene in the middle of *Stagecoach* shows Ringo watching the saloon girl, Dallas, go outside. A moment later, he will follow her and, in a daring exchange, propose that they spend the rest of their lives together. Not only is the lighting similar to that of a 1920s Expressionist film, but Ringo in the foreground and Dallas in the background are far apart. Ford staged the sequence in a single image rather than following a close-up of Ringo with a separate shot of Dallas walking away. Whole sequences within the film were handled in this way, making *Stagecoach* one of the most visually distinctive films of the year. This exploration of visual depth was seminal. Early filmmakers had tended to photograph scenes in a wide shot, as if they were happening on a stage; in *The Assassination of the Duc de Guise* (France, 1908) (see page 38–9) actors performed around the set at various distances from the camera. However, in the late 1910s and 1920s, there was a trend in Western mainstream cinematography for flatter, softer and more romantic imagery. The picture of Garbo in *Flesh and the Devil* (USA, 1926) (see page 68) is a good example of this.

Stagecoach radically reversed the visual flattening of cinematic imagery of the 1920s and 1930s, but Ford was not the first director to do so. As early as 1929, Eisenstein had suggested, as an alternative to his famous editing theories, staging and filming an event in depth, so that if the viewer looks at the foreground, then the background, then

127
Above: Although deeply American, Ford's Westerns – and in particular the ways in which he had his landscapes photographed – influenced international directors such as Brazil's Glauber Rocha in films such as *Black God, White Devil*. 1964.

the foreground again, a kind of mental editing occurs. His *The General Line* (Soviet Union, 1929) illustrates this theory. As the viewer's eyes flick between images of a farmer in the background and his tractor in the foreground, it is difficult to look at both concurrently. Six years later, Eisenstein was to use similar deep-space composition in his uncompleted film, *Bezhin Meadow* (Soviet Union, 1935–37). In France, Renoir was sometimes using a similar technique, as shown in image 129 from

128
Above: Mizoguchi going further than most directors of the time in having action take place very close to the camera and very far away from it. *Naniwa Elejî*. Japan, 1936.

Le Crime de M Lang/The Crime of Mr Lang (France, 1935) and in *La Règle du jeu*. In certain scenes in these two films the action takes place close to and far away from the lens, although Renoir seldom felt the need to have both in crisp focus. The rare image (128) from Mizoguchi's *Naniwa Elejî* (Japan, 1936) brings the foreground action radically closer to the camera than do either Ford or Eisenstein.

While Eisenstein, Mizoguchi, Renoir and Ford were the key directors in 1930s depth staging, the key cinematographer in American cinema working in this field was Gregg Toland. Toland entered the industry in 1919, the year that Eisenstein started describing his "editing within the shot" ideas. In 1938, Eastman Kodak and Agfa produced new film stocks, rated between 64 and 120 ASA, three to eight times faster than normal studio stocks. Toland quickly realized that if the stock was more sensitive to light, he could use the same amount of illumination in a scene, but close down the lens's aperture without it resulting in a darker image. The cinematographer and director could also stage action near the lens and far from it, without losing focus on either, because the more the aperture decreases on any camera, the sharper the focus across a range of distances. This made the measuring stick we saw in image 42 less necessary to keep Gary Cooper a certain distance from the camera.

129
Above: Although Renoir does not attempt to keep all his deep-staged action in focus, he encourages his audience to look at both the woman in the mid-foreground (left) and the man in the hat in the background (centre). *Le Crime de M. Lang*. 1935.

Toland did not shoot *Stagecoach*, but worked with Ford on other films such as *The Grapes of Wrath* (USA, 1940) and shot the landmark film, *Citizen Kane* (USA, 1941), which pushed the possibilities of staging action in depth so far that its visual style became famous.

Citizen Kane was the first feature film directed by Orson Welles, who apparently watched *Stagecoach* thirty times in preparation, to learn the craft of filmmaking. One scene shows Welles as the tragic newspaper magnate at his typewriter in the foreground, which must be less than a metre away from the camera; Joseph Cotten is in the middle ground about two metres behind him and Everett Sloane is so far away that, when measured, he is smaller than Welles' nose. This stylized or "expressionist" use of deep focus was comparable to the use of shadows in *Caligari*. Toland liked to tell how he would shoot with a lens with a focal length of just 24mm to get shots such as these, whereas the industry norm was 50mm and Garbo-esque soft close-ups were filmed with 100mm lenses or longer. 24mm lenses create visual distortions including the "ballooning" effect that expands the image's centre and forces the background away from the camera, miniaturizing it and exaggerating perspective to make it look further away than it is. (Many inexpensive or disposable stills cameras have lenses around 30mm. Anyone who has got too close to one of them in holiday snapshots and ended up with an elongated nose or expanded waistline, will know these distortions.) Toland also took advantage of new brighter arc lights which enabled him to close the aperture even further and achieve still deeper focus.

There is a sense here of Welles and Toland trying to shock the industry, their peers and the public with their extravagant spatial experiments, yet Toland's implication that this image of Welles at the typewriter was filmed in a new dynamic way is perhaps misleading. It has recently emerged that this dramatic sequence and some of the others in *Citizen Kane* were created using a more traditional process. For the typewriter scene, Cotten and Sloane were shot using Toland's short focal length lens technique, then projected onto a screen in front of which Welles-as-Kane sat. This was then re-photographed, creating a new image which appeared to have extraordinary depth of field. More than any other film, *Citizen Kane* reversed the visual schema of 1920s American cinema. Who was the personality behind such cinematic

130
Above: Like many scenes in *Citizen Kane*, this moment from a later Orson Welles film – *Chimes at Midnight* – stages action close to the camera's wide-angle lens. Spain–Switzerland, 1966.

game playing? Welles was born into a maverick family in Wisconsin in 1914. His father was an inventor and his mother was a concert pianist; both died young when he was eight and twelve years old respectively. He was staging Shakespeare aged four and was educated privately at a school that excelled in music. He was playing lead roles on the Dublin stage aged seventeen, debuted on Broadway at nineteen, formed the acclaimed Mercury Theatre at twenty-two, caused a sensation and national panic with a radio broadcast, *War of the Worlds* (1938), when he was twenty-three, directed some of the most acclaimed theatrical productions of the 1930s and made what many consider the best film of all time, *Citizen Kane*, aged twenty-six.

Those who knew Welles, and to whom I have spoken at length about him, use a word to describe him that has not yet appeared in this book – "genius". Certainly he seems to have had more talent than most directors and this talent developed and matured much earlier than in most cases. It has been well-argued elsewhere[35] that the genius label applied from an early age made the anti-intellectual Hollywood film world wary of him from the outset of his career. He should have been the D.W. Griffith of the sound era, extending cinema's parameters and taking others with him. In fact, in a career that lasted nearly fifty years, he did not direct a single foot of film for any of the four major Hollywood studios.

The perplexing achievements of, and motivations behind, Welles' work are extra-cinematic. His interest in playing with visual space is like that of an Italian Renaissance painter. His interest in people at the top of power structures – kings, business tycoons and inventors – is akin to Shakespeare's. Welles often looked to the past in his work, to times before democracy and liberalism, in order to find a template for the gigantic, power-crazed characters he would inhabit. *Citizen Kane*, Welles' first feature film, is about a newspaper magnate, Charles Foster Kane, who thinks of himself as a Medici at the time of the Italian Renaissance, a Mughal Emperor in India or a Turkish prince in Istanbul's Topkapi palace. Lustful for power but devoid of taste, he attempts to use his newspapers to influence world events and builds himself a monstrous, palatial house on an inhuman scale, buying and shipping works of art and installing whole rooms from classical Europe (131). The film was a powerful denunciation of the egomania and spiritual emptiness of a real tycoon, William Randolph Hearst, who had built a similarly extravagant house in California called

Hearst Castle a place akin to Griffith's *Intolerance* sets or Pastrone's *Cabiria* designs.

Hearst's regal aspirations were fuelled by the unchecked epic imagination of early 1920s Hollywood, and when he fulfilled them, Hollywood stars such as Chaplin flattered him, visited his palace and came to lounge at his gold swimming pools. Enter the boy-wonder Welles, who has travelled the world in his childhood, lived in Shanghai, visited the grand crumbling palaces of faded emperors, studied Shakespeare and knows the story of power. What does he do? He decides to apply cinema, the medium with its attendant social world that bloated Hearst's imagination in the first place and that now fires his ego, to the multi-layered construct that is Hearst. The parallel world of *Citizen Kane* was far removed from the more glamorous and perfect one of closed romantic realism. The rooms of Xanadu had to be vast and empty because Kane's ideas were colossal and vacuous. So Welles watched *Stagecoach* thirty times, was drawn to the deep-focus imagery and hired Toland, the best and most innovative Hollywood director of photography, and together they extended the dimension of the screen to its limits.

131
Above: Charles Foster Kane's storeroom of treasures – an image whose deep space is expressive of Orson Welles' aesthetic and his character's megalomania. *Citizen Kane*. USA, 1941.

The power of Welles' visual and human ideas cannot be ascribed only to his source material: Shakespeare and the Medicis, the Mughals, the Ottomans and *Stagecoach*. It also derives from his striking body and voice. His parents were both Anglo-Saxon, but Welles did not look it. His head was big, his eyes were far apart and deeper and older than expected. It was impossible for him to play a young person or a twentieth-century everyman. Repeatedly throughout his career, Welles would position himself close to a camera fitted with a 28mm lens to emphasize how gigantic he was and, correspondingly, the weightiness of the themes he was exploring, but he did so particularly in *Touch of Evil* (1958) and *Chimes at Midnight* (1966). He imported the idea of sonic space from radio, using whispers in close-up and distant echoes as well as sonic shocks, such as a squawking parrot in *Citizen Kane*. He extended the overlapping dialogue of Howard Hawks' comedies to fill a whole film.

The visual ideas of Toland and Welles started to influence directors such as John Huston and William Wyler. The image above (132 top) from *The Maltese Falcon* (John Huston, USA, 1941) was photographed in the same year as *Citizen Kane*.

Wyler, who had already worked with Toland in the late 1930s, made *The Little Foxes* (USA, 1941) and, like Welles, staged his actors at varying distances from the lens, but changed focus to emphasize the speaker. Toland was to photograph such deep-focus scenes for the same director in *The Best Years of our Lives* (USA, 1946) on a set that had to be flooded with light. For example, the image below (132 bottom) appears to be about the foregrounded people at the piano, if you do not know the story of the film. However, Dana Andrews' telephone conversation, which occurs in the tiny booth in the extreme background, is the important action. Welles' radical perspective distortions for dramatic emphasis and Eisenstein's conception of editing within a shot were here taken to still further extremes.

132
The visual style of deep staging and deep focus spread through Hollywood. John Huston had *The Maltese Falcon* (above) photographed in this way, as did William Wyler in this moment in *The Best Years of our Lives* (below): the key action is not the piano in the foreground but the telephone booth conversation in the background.

Citizen Kane, The Little Foxes and other deep-staged films (films in which action takes place close to and far from the camera, regardless of whether or not the action is in focus) had, after their post-war release in France, a significant effect on

French directors and gave birth to a new theory of the film image. Deep staging and deep-focus filmmaking would continue to be used, especially in dramatically and thematically intense movies: some of

world cinema's landmark films such as Ingmar Bergman's *Persona* (Sweden, 1966), Jacques Tati's later comedies, the Taiwanese films of Hou Hsiao Hsien, Michael Haneke's Austrian work, the films of Hungarian director Béla Tarr (133) and many more would build on these visual ideas. Deep staging would

become less fashionable again in 1950s American cinema because the new colour, widescreen film stocks were not usually fast enough to achieve this deep-focus effect. In the 1960s and 1970s, very long focal-length lenses, which flattened imagery and made focus shallow, were to open up formal possibilities at the opposite end of the visual spectrum. The newest types of such lenses, combined with the shooting style of music videos, created another period of ultra-shallow focus in the 1990s (134).[36] The depth of the film image is centrally important to the history of cinema, because it not only provides information about the lenses, lighting and sensitivity of film stock available to a director, but also points to the visual schema of the time.

The most innovative filmmakers who continued to work through and beyond the Second World War – Clair, Mamoulian, Eisenstein, Ozu, Mizoguchi, Lubitsch, Renoir, Ford, Hitchcock and Welles – had pushed out the boundaries of film sound and imagery and their achievements would affect post-war cinema. Others working at this time, such as Dorothy Arzner, P.C. Barua, Marcel Carné, George Cukor, Curtiz, Dovzhenko, Fleming, Alexander Korda, Mikio Naruse, Preston Sturges, James Whale and William Wyler had made their best films by the end of the war, and Minnelli, Siodmak and

Wilder were already directors. War became the backdrop for hugely entertaining Western films such as *Casablanca* (Michael Curtiz, USA, 1942), about an American café owner in Morocco who abandons his cynicism to help a former lover evade the Nazis. Musicals became so escapist and dramas so sentimental, that their glitzy, religious, patriotic or comforting stories can only be properly understood and excused against the backdrop of war, soldiers abroad and national uncertainty.

There were two other cases where innovation continued throughout the Second World War. Maya Deren, a Russian Jew whose parents had emigrated to New York in 1922, made such a powerful experimental film, *Meshes in the Afternoon* (USA, 1943), that it helped move the centre of avant-garde filmmaking from Europe to America. It is about a young woman having a dream. But unlike *The Wizard of Oz*, there are no certainties, nor a secure return to a familiar world. The dream is a lonely experience, her memories float through it. Deren said, "The protagonist does not suffer some subjective delusion of which the world outside remains independent ... she is, in actuality, destroyed by an imaginative action." The spatial dislocations of *Meshes in the Afternoon* prefigured the French films of Alain Resnais and Agnès Varda and her visual style influenced mainstream cinematographers such as Nestor Almendros.

On another continent, the Indian People's Theatre Project was also more experimental. It was launched in 1943 and was a deliberately radical theatre movement related to the Indian Communist Party, Working across the country, but particularly in Bengal in the north-east and Kerala in the south-west, it married traditional culture to modern ideas about political activism and experimentalism. It was not only widely influential in the theatre world, but also in literature and film and its impact, especially in Bengal, can be seen in the work of one of India's most important oppositional filmmakers, Ritwik Ghatak (see pages 208–09).

The first American film to be shown in newly liberated Paris in August 1944 was *Gone with the Wind*. In 1945, one of the film's actresses, Olivia de Havilland, won a three-year courtroom battle against Warner Bros. Her employer's habit of extending her contract if she refused a film part that did not interest her was disallowed. This precedent meant that actors could not be contracted for more than seven years and thereby gave performers more control over their careers. It was a setback for the studios, which had by this date also suffered other challenges to their production-distribution system, and heralded their unravelling in subsequent years.

One unique body of work married cinematic experimentation with gripping narrative during the Second World War in a way that

135

Above: The soft colour and the actors' horizon gaze in this image capture the optimism of *A Matter of Life and Death*, but the film also death, more adroitly than most, with the complexities of war. Kim Hunter and David Niven starred, the director was Michael Powell. UK, 1945.

defies description. The British company The Archers was formed in 1942 and combined the talents of English director Michael Powell and Hungarian screenwriter Emeric Pressburger, who had escaped the Nazis and then worked for Alexander Korda. They began their partnership as writers, producers and directors with *The Life and Death of Colonel Blimp* (UK, 1943) and continued with *A Canterbury Tale* (UK, 1944) and *A Matter of Life and Death* (UK, 1945) a series of films about the mythic qualities of Britain. They avoided outright propaganda and portrayed their perception of the

THE DEVASTATION OF WAR AND A NEW MOVIE LANGUAGE (1945—52)
The spread of realism in world cinema

5

How did filmmakers react to the devastation left by the Second World War? In Japan, Germany and Italy, they opened their doors in the morning and found that their city streets had turned to rubble. Some took up documentary cameras and filmed what they saw. Even those far removed from the battlegrounds read newspapers, and Hollywood was full of émigrés who would have seen newsreels about their broken homelands. Filmmakers were not detached from the historical events that were taking place around them. This chapter describes to what extent they engaged as artists with these events.

A NEW BEGINNING

During the war, 1,400 cinemas closed in Japan. Immediately after the Allied victory, all films were vetted by the new American authorities. Nationalistic and traditional themes were banned, but some directors, including the central figure in the previous chapter, Yasujiro Ozu, continued as before. His work was too intimate and domestic to offend the new American censors. His *Record of a Tenement Gentleman* (Japan, 1947) was written in only twelve days and told the story of a homeless boy, shunted between families unwilling to shelter him. Eventually a widow, Otane, reluctantly takes him in (137). Their relationship is bittersweet and the scenes in which she looks for him in the empty city streets are among the most beautifully realized by Ozu throughout his career. Only discreetly, at the end, does it engage with the contemporary realities of Japan, as the homeless boy gathers cigarette butts to sell and Otane makes a speech about the selfishness of people in modern society.

The situation was very different in Germany. Its most notorious directors, Riefenstahl and Harlan, had conformed so completely to Nazi ideology that a total break from them needed to be made. The Allies took complete control of the West German film industry for four years, as they did to a lesser degree in Japan, in order to enforce this separation. Some directors were prevented from producing work, while others made bland or merely inoffensive films. The most distinctive produced in the immediate post-war years came from the communist Eastern part of the newly divided Germany. Wolfgang Staudte had been an actor and appeared in *Jew Süss* (Germany, 1940). He had started directing during the war, but his film, *Die Mörder sind unter uns/The Murderers are Amongst Us* (German Democratic Republic, 1946), was strongly anti-Nazi. Rejecting Riefenstahl's bravura but aggrandizing style, he turned instead to one of the last credible German film idioms, 1920s expressionism, to tell his story. This became one of a small group of productions now known as *Trümmerfilm* or "rubble films".

In Italy, 1930s cinema had been more escapist than propagandist, but was still tainted by Mussolini's fascist ideals. Like the Germans, though not suffering the same censure and professional paralysis, Italian filmmakers had to look for new schemata. Searching for new themes and styles to reflect changing realities, they evolved a different language of cinema.

A series of films between *Roma città aperta/Rome, Open City* (Italy, 1945) and *Umberto D* (Italy, 1952) were central to this new language. They looked different and the experience of watching them was new. They broke open the parallel universe of closed romantic realism and changed cinema's sense of what constitutes time and the nature of drama. Responding to the shifting realities around them, they had a profound influence on cinema in Latin America and India, creating the possibility for post-colonial world cinema. Their approach was labelled "neo-realism", the new realism.

It was not only the realities of Mussolini's defeat that caused these Italians to rethink film-making. Some of the facilities that had been making glossy entertainments, such as the "white telephone" films and the work of Mario Camerini and Alessandro Blasetti, had been damaged in the war, and the main studio in Rome, Cinecittà, was being used as a barracks, which forced directors to shoot in part on the streets.

Filmmakers with a moral conscience addressed or expressed what was happening on those streets. The groundwork for their innovations had been laid in the previous decade. In 1935 an innovative film school, the Centro Sperimentale di Cinematografia, was opened, and three important film magazines were launched, including *Bianco i Nero*. These provided Italian cinema with a think tank and opened it up to Jean Renoir's 1930s realist work, Eisenstein's experiments and morally serious American films, such as those made by King Vidor. One of the major neo-realist directors, Luchino Visconti, worked as an assistant to Renoir in Rome on *Une Partie de campagne/A Day in the Country* (France, 1936) and another, Roberto Rossellini, was greatly influenced by the Frenchman.

The most significant of the neo-realist screenwriters was Cesare Zavattini, a novelist, theoretician and journalist who wrote three of the era's most influential films, *Sciuscia/Shoeshine* (Vittorio De Sica, Italy, 1946), *Ladri di biciclette/Bicycle Thieves* (Vittorio De Sica, Italy 1948) and *Umberto D* (Vittorio De Sica). In a 1953 interview Zavattini said, "Before this, if one was thinking over the idea of a film on, say, a strike, one would immediately invent a plot. And the strike itself became only the background to the film. Today … we would describe the strike itself … we have an unlimited trust in things, facts

137
Above: Ozu's first post-war film was *Record of A Tenement Gentleman*, a moving tale of an orphaned boy taken in by a widow. Japan, 1947.

and people."[1] Even allowing for some exaggeration on Zavattini's part, demolition of the plot was the revolutionary change the neo-realists effected. This is illustrated in *Bicycle Thieves*, about an unemployed man who has his bicycle, his only chance of getting casual work, stolen (138). Together with his son, he looks for it all over Rome. Eventually, worn out by the search and afraid of not finding even basic work without a bicycle, he tries to steal another for himself. His son witnesses this and the indignity of his father is exposed in this moment. The film's slide into despair is very moving, but it is not a story in the tradition of mainstream filmmaking, which outlines a tight chain of cause and effect, in which the action of each scene makes the following one inevitable. It is, rather, a string of incidents. At one point the man's son is nearly run over while crossing a street, an event his father does not see. In a mooted Hollywood remake, David O. Selznick suggested, at one point that Cary Grant might play the role of the father in the film. It is tempting to consider how Hollywood might have dealt with the story: the father would probably have seen the boy's near injury or found out about it later.

138
Below: The moment where the theft takes place in Vittorio De Sica's influential *Bicycle Thieves*. Italy, 1948.

He would then have realized how much he loved his son or how he was putting him at risk by taking him to look for the bike in such a busy and dangerous city. In *Bicycle Thieves*, the incident does not play back into the plot. It is a loose end in pure storytelling terms, but it is in the film because these things happen in real life. It belongs to the world of real people rather than the parallel world of cinema. Zavattini and De Sica were using the opposite of Hitchcock's condensed approach to story, instead they expanded their narratives to create space within them, a technique described by Thompson and Bordwell as "de-dramatizing" the film.[2]

This is the sea change that neo-realism brought about, and it is not always understood. Conventional film historians argue that the films of De Sica, Visconti and Rossellini (who all started their careers in the Fascist era) used natural lighting extensively and were visually gritty, but *Shoeshine*, and neo-realism's great precursor, *Osessione/Obsession* (Visconti, Italy, 1943), are full of stylized lighting. In addition, these films were not always shot on real streets or with non-professional actors as is sometimes claimed. However, the attitude at this moment in cinema was new. Zavattini said "when we have thought out a scene, we feel the need to 'remain' in it, because ... it can contain so many echoes and reverberations."[3] In a well-known sequence in *Umberto D* (139), a young housemaid (Maria Pia Casilio) lights a fire in the kitchen, sweeps the floor, relights the fire, looks outside, sprays some ants and starts to make coffee, all in silence. We watch her ordinary chores, of no consequence to the story, while she is alone with her thoughts and routines. The camera remains in the scene. In mainstream Hollywood cinema, such extraneous details would have been rigorously removed, creating "life with the dull bits cut out", as Hitchcock reputedly said. In many of these Italian films, the apparently dull bits remain and, consequently, time is expanded in them.

A thirty-nine-year-old Roman architect's son extended Zavattini's and De Sica's de-dramatizing ideas to express what he would term, "the pain of our times". In *Rome, Open City*, in *Paisà/Paisan* (Italy, 1946) and in *Germania anno zero/Germany Year Zero* (Italy–France–Germany, 1947) Roberto Rossellini told disturbing stories of what Zavattini called "today, today, today"[4] (136, see page 186). Resistance fighters are brutally killed by the German occupying forces in Rome; Italian civilians and American soldiers have difficulties living together in Italy after liberation; a young boy poisons himself and his father under the influence of the Nazis. Not only was the human drama shocking, but Rossellini challenged standards of taste in mainstream cinema by showing, almost for the first time, a shot of a toilet. He purposefully failed to show key dramatic moments of high emotion, which flattened the amplitude of his stories. He wrote, "If I mistakenly make a beautiful shot, I cut it out",[5] and by doing so, he removed the reasons, such as drama and visual gloss, why the public bought movie tickets. Rossellini turned 1920s dissident cinema into a national and political film movement although – perhaps unsurprisingly – the rigour of his techniques did not find favour at the box office. He would go on to marry the Swedish actress Ingrid Bergman in 1950, and make a series of influential films with her in the 1950s, such as *Viaggio in Italia/ Voyage to Italy* (Italy, 1953), then turn his attention to documentary and historical films.

139
Above: A housemaid in *Umberto D* performs everyday domestic tasks which are not strictly relevant to the plot of the film, but which add to its realism. Such de-dramatization found favour with other serious filmmakers, but was less popular with audiences. Director: Vittorio De Sica. Italy. 1952.

The achievements of Rossellini, De Sica, Visconti and Zavattini seemed like an exciting new start for cinema, but when they were reconsidered at the 1974 Pesaro conference in Italy more than twenty years afterward, their challenges to the mainstream looked less original. Critics such as Lino Micciche commented that Mussolini was not mentioned in their work and that the films' music was often operatic, as in 1930s Italian cinema. Some critics said that neo-realism continued fascist melodramatic cinema in a different guise and did not challenge popular beliefs or suggest how society could improve. Luis Buñuel, now working in Mexico, said that "neo-realist reality is partial, official, above all reasonable; but poetry and mystery are lacking in it."[6] Although some of these revaluations carry weight, they do not challenge the fact of neo-realism's profound worldwide influence, an influence that took several years to manifest itself.

The tone of post-war cinema becomes more varied as it moves further away from the vanquished countries. Many French films told stories of resistance: *La Bataille du rail/The Battle of the Rails* (France, 1945) was close in spirit to *Germany Year Zero*. Directed by documentary filmmaker René Clement, it was a detailed recreation of real events, in which resistance members derailed a German troop train. Clement was technical consultant on a stylistically very different film, *La Belle et la bête/Beauty and the Beast* (Jean Cocteau, France, 1946). Cocteau, who was notable among those tolerant of France's pro-Nazi Vichy regime, had made *Le Sang d'un poète/The Blood of a Poet* in 1930 and, despite the sixteen-year interval, his new film was as singular and Méliès-like as his first.

After four years with no film releases from Hollywood, Parisian audiences gorged on an influx of American movies. After *Gone with the Wind* (USA, 1939) there came, in July 1946 alone, Orson Welles' *Citizen Kane* (USA, 1941), John Huston's *The Maltese Falcon* (USA, 1941), Billy Wilder's *Double Indemnity* (USA, 1944), William Wyler's *The Little Foxes* (USA, 1941) and *The Best Years of our Lives* (USA, 1946). This feast of deep-staged films was a revelation, even in the homeland of Jean Renoir. The critic André Bazin argued that deep staging in such films enabled them to express the real world's complex realities. He detested what he perceived as naively stylized films such as *The Cabinet of Dr. Caligari* (Germany, 1919) and as a Christian and a profoundly moral critic, he likened deep space almost to an act of worship or a genuflection before a transcendentally designed universe. It seemed that Hollywood cinema had begun to gain intellectual credibility in Europe and certain French filmmakers soon used deep staging themselves. For example, a scene from director Jean Pierre Melville's *Le Silence de la mer/The Silence of the Sea* (France, 1949) was closely modelled on a scene in Welles' *The Magnificent Ambersons* (USA, 1942), which was released in Paris at this time.

Meanwhile in America, one of the implications of deep staging started to be explored – the long-duration shot or long take. This allowed a filmmaker to run shots long enough for the audience to understand the full dramatic geometry of the scene and to stage action at various distances from the lens. The earliest post-war long takes came from an unlikely source, *The Clock* (USA, 1945), which featured Judy Garland, the star of *The Wizard of Oz* (USA, 1939). She insisted that her lover (and, from 1945, husband), Vincente Minnelli, with whom she had made the nostalgic musical *Meet Me in St Louis,* the year before, direct her in this, her first film in which she did not sing. Minnelli, like Mamoulian, had begun his career staging musical theatre on Broadway and wanted the city to be a vivid backdrop to *The Clock*'s foreground story of a GI romance. He used wider shots, some deeper staging and most significantly, shots of an average duration of nineteen seconds.[7] There was more than a touch of Mizoguchi in Minnelli's flowing style, but it could not compete with Hitchcock's *Rope* (USA, 1948) and *Under Capricorn* (USA, 1949).

Hitchcock went to America in 1939 and made no less than ten films there between 1940 and 1948. He extended the tentative interest, which he had already shown in Britain, in the gulf between the looker and the looked at, the erotic power of objects and the unreliability of the visible world, in *Rebecca* (1940), *Suspicion* (1941), *Shadow of a Doubt* (1943) and *Spellbound* (1945). In this quartet, everyday things such as a painting, a glass of milk, black smoke and creases in a fabric become monsters from deep within the characters' minds. Parallel to his new psychological investigations, Hitchcock began exploring the formal limits of narrative filmmaking, and *Rope* was the extreme example of this. He extended Minnelli's shot durations to the limit of what was technically possible. *Rope* contained just eleven shots whereas an average film of the time would have had 600–800. Average shot durations were approximately ten seconds, but his lasted ten minutes, the length of a full roll of film, so were sixty times longer. He would later reject this radical approach, calling it "nonsensical"[8] as it violated his belief that editing together precisely chosen images is the core technique of empathic cinema. Hitchcock called *Rope* "pre-edited", by which he meant that by moving the camera around the film's single set, he was varying Eisenstein's idea of editing within the shot.[9] This not only satisfied Hitchcock's need to play with his medium's techniques, but it also raised the question of what the suspense effect of longer-held shots was. It is not always the case and most people do not notice it explicitly, but as a general rule, the longer a shot is held without a cut, the longer the actors are doing it "for real" without a break, the more absorbing it becomes. Like building a pyramid of playing cards, we can see accumulated achievement and drama in longer shots.

Hitchcock's profound interest in suspense made him a natural for such experiments, whereas subsequent filmmakers like Béla Tarr in Hungary and Alexandr Sokurov in Russia would use long takes for more philosophical purposes.

A second offshoot of deep staging were "films noirs", literally "dark films". The stylistic and thematic roots of these are particularly complex and their birth constitutes an intersection in film history – different filmmakers arriving at the same point at a similar time. At least 350 of them were made between 1941 and 1959, the majority produced in the ten years after the Second World War. The image below is from one of the earliest and most influential films noirs, *Double Indemnity* (USA, 1944).[10] The actress and the wall at the far end of the corridor are both in focus. The 1930s deep staging of Renoir, Mizoguchi, Ford, Toland and Welles is the antecedent of this image. The film's plot has Walter Neff (Fred MacMurray), an insurance man (centre), falling for Phyllis Dietrichson (Barbara Stanwyck), the attractive wife (left) of one of his clients. Gradually, she convinces

140
Below: A femme fatale, a weak insurance man and his suspicious boss: Billy Wilder's staging of a suspenseful moment in one of the first films noirs, *Double Indemnity*. USA, 1944.

him to help her murder her husband and share the life insurance pay-out with her. Meanwhile, MacMurray's boss, Barton Keys (Edward G. Robinson), starts to suspect that Stanwyck is the murderess and goes to MacMurray's apartment to pass on his hunch. If he witnesses Stanwyck in the apartment this would implicate MacMurray and clinch the case. So, in this highly suspenseful moment, Stanwyck hides behind MacMurray's outward-opening door.

At least six different schemas – including national film styles, literary and visual traditions and individual sensibilities – can be seen in a scene like this. The film's director, Billy Wilder, was an Austrian-Jewish former gigolo and screenwriter who spent his formative years in Berlin, fled the Nazis in 1933, co-wrote *Ninotchka* (USA, 1939) for Lubitsch and became one of the most celebrated American directors. Like many émigrés who made important films noirs, such as Fritz Lang, Robert Siodmak, Otto Preminger, Michael

141
Above: Off-horizontal shots, such as this one in Sam Fuller's *Pick-Up on South Street*, express the mental instability of many characters in films noirs. USA, 1953.

Curtiz and Jacques Tourneur, he loved the freedom and unpretentiousness of America, but was bitterly cynical about its worship of money, and his films expressed an astringent view of his host nation. One important critic calls the attitude of these directors "double estrangement",[11] implying that they are at home neither in Europe nor in the Californian sun. Most films noirs are about such estrangement. Whereas 1930s movies were often sunny in outlook, films noirs picture America as a troubled and ambiguous place. They feature men whose lust for money or women takes them beyond the borders of the so-called civilized world. *Double Indemnity* defines this classically. It begins with MacMurray, an American once holding down a regular job, now bloody and dying, describing his fall from grace with something akin to relish.

The majority of these émigrés who made films noirs lived through the period of German expressionism in the 1920s, or were subject to its influence. Before he died, Wilder denied any direct visual influence from Wiene or early Lang on *Double Indemnity*, but film-noir lighting is usually a lattice of expressionist directional beams and dark shadows and the actors in image 140 cast heavy ones. Earlier in *Double Indemnity* shadows are even more prominent. There was also an economic imperative behind such shadows as they meant sets could be more cheaply constructed.

However, it was not only expressionism's surface that was important, but also the characters. In the key Lang and Wiene films they were often deranged, with asylums being the setting or threat. Film noir's human tenor is similar, with frequent scenes of near hysteria in which life breaks open to reveal the passions and nightmares under the surface. The world view is so infected that even the imagery through which the story is told becomes unbalanced, in a similar way to *The Cabinet of Dr. Caligari*. The Great Unsaid in expressionist films was the idea of a happy, normal, balanced world. Film noir was the dissident response to the idea of such utopianism in Hollywood, where it was so far from being unsaid as to be positievly suffocating.

The influence of German aesthetics on these films is well known, but other fictions play their part. *Double Indemnity* was co-written by Raymond Chandler, the Chicago-born novelist whose fiction, along with that of Dashiel Hammett, created many of the character-types and situations to which noir filmmakers applied their shadows and sensibilities. Chandler's most famous character was Philip Marlowe, whose notoriously "hard-boiled" dialogue played so well on screen. Chandler had Marlowe narrate his novels, a clear prototype for film noir's frequent voice-overs. His first significant book, *The Big Sleep*, was published in 1939 and Howard Hawks filmed it in 1946, with Humphrey Bogart playing Marlowe (142), a role that many other actors would embody. It would become the most influential of films noirs since *Double Indemnity* for two reasons. Firstly, its plot was so complicated that it emboldened subsequent directors to take their work further in the direction of *Caligari*'s narrative insanity. Secondly, its script was co-written by Leigh Brackett, a fellow-novelist who wrote mystery books.

142
Below: Humphrey Bogart as Christopher Marlowe in Howard Hawks' labyrinthically plotted film noir, *The Big Sleep*. USA, 1946.

Brackett is an intriguing figure in film history because she co-wrote three of the most entertaining films in American cinema, *The Big Sleep*, *Rio Bravo* (Howard Hawks, USA, 1946, 1959) and *The Empire Strikes Back* (Irvin Kershner, USA, 1980). Her co-writing of *The Big Sleep* raises the question of how films noirs represent their female characters. Stanwyck in *Double Indemnity*, Lauren Bacall in *The Big Sleep*, Ava Gardner in *The Killers* (Robert Siodmak, USA, 1946) and Jane Greer in *Out of the Past* (Jacques Tourneur, USA, 1947) all haunt these films; they are constantly talked about by the men in the stories, toying with them and causing their downfall. These characters understand that their eroticism empowers them to manipulate men's minds and judgements, and what is original is that they achieve this with ease. The wartime emancipation of women is undoubtedly reflected in these films, but they are sexually fascinating because in tandem with assertive females there are men's weak, damaged or repressed erotic imaginations. Weakened men are blinded by strong women; in some cases, this can be literally so, where the woman is strongly back-lit and her face is in shadow (143).

143
Above: The use of facial shadows to suggest the mystery and moral darkness of women in film noir: Jane Greer in Jacques Tourneur's *Out of the Past*. USA, 1947.

144
Below: The only woman to direct a film noir: Ida Lupino (left) on location.

Only one film noir from the hundreds produced was directed by a woman, Ida Lupino (144). Born in London in 1918, she went to the US to follow an acting career. She was a rebel of sorts and in the spirit of Olivia de Havilland refused the lure of massive studio salaries if projects were not of a suitable standard. She started directing B-movies with tiny budgets in 1949, when a male director had a heart attack three days into a shoot. Her crews were impressed by the fact that a glamorous movie star knew enough about the craft of filmmaking to call the shots. Her most significant film, *The Hitch-Hiker* (USA, 1953), is a noir story about a brutal murderer who hitches a ride with two gentler characters, both fishermen. Even when the killer sleeps, he keeps one eye open like a reptile. Based on actual events and shot with economy, the film's portrayal of competing strains of masculinity was ahead of its time.

Wilder and his team on *Double Indemnity* were drawing on still other cultural threads. The presence of Edward G. Robinson was a reminder of how films noirs reawakened the early 1930s fascination with gangster films, in which Robinson had been a key player. The pessimism of noir directors, atypical in American cinema, was also an inheritance from the poetic realist films of France in the 1930s, such as those by Marcel Carné and Jacques Prévert. These were not seen widely by American audiences, as foreign-language pictures were not distributed conventionally, but film societies programmed them. If any proof of the influence were needed, Fritz Lang remade Renoir's *La Chienne* (1931) as the film noir *Scarlet Street* (USA, 1945) starring Edward G. Robinson.

145
Above: *Citizen Kane*'s faked newsreel sequence, complete with faked hidden camera shots (above), anticipated semi-documentary films such as *The House on 92nd Street* (below).

If *Citizen Kane*'s deep staging was one of the influences on films noirs, it was also a stepping-stone to other stylistic variations in American cinema. Welles' film started with an accurately faked newsreel, charting the life of its eponymous protagonist, the moguls, Charles Foster Kane (145 top). One of these newsreel's producers, Louis de Rochemont, in turn oversaw *The House on 92nd*

Street (Henry Hathaway, USA, 1945), a semi-documentary spy drama, which was filmed on real locations (145 bottom). There were antecedents for such filming – King Vidor and Dziga Vertov had used hidden cameras in the streets in the 1920s.[12] One year after *Double Indemnity*, Wilder had done the same with his film about an alcoholic, *The Lost Weekend* (USA, 1945), as had the Italian neo-realists, changing storytelling techniques by doing so. Jules Dassin's *The Naked City* (USA, 1948) became the most famous location-shot "semi-documentary" of its day. Its success led, twelve years later, to a television series of the same name.

Some of the most utopian American films of these years continued the debate about reality and fantasy which first surfaced

in *Ninotchka* and *The Wizard of Oz*, but even these found room for passages of pessimism and visual darkness. *It's a Wonderful Life* (Frank Capra, USA, 1946) is one of Western cinema's most emotive films and, like The Archers' *A Matter of Life and Death* (UK, 1946), it concerns a man hovering between the world of the living and that of the dead. Capra, a former gag writer turned director, had become one of the most powerful filmmakers in Hollywood during the 1930s. He made extremely effective works of rhetorical cinema about the nature of American populism, the flow of hope and despair running through the nation's soul. *It's a Wonderful Life* was not a great commercial success, but it is Capra's most significant work, not least because it was an independent production – of Liberty Films, the company Capra co-founded with William Wyler and George Stevens. In it, James Stewart plays George Bailey, an ordinary man in a small town, Bedford Falls, who is driven to the brink of suicide by financial hardships. As he is about to jump off a bridge, his guardian angel appears and shows him how much worse Bedford Falls would be if he had not been a part of the community. The film is one of the most affecting narrative films not based on a novel or stage play. The despair on Stewart's face when he realizes that money has gone missing from a co-operative savings company he runs is palpable. Earlier, Stewart's character has told his father that he wants to "design buildings and modern cities ... I just feel like if I didn't get away, I'd burst." At this stage of the film, he is a cosmopolitan, dreaming of going to Europe, but these touches of modernity in his personality are challenged by the angel's arrival. The latter shows him that without his influence, his homely town would be full of bars, a pawnshop (implied as Jewish), eroticized women, black people playing boogie-woogie piano and general aggression. In other words, it would be a film noir. Capra's moving tale is profoundly suspicious about such city life and teaches George a lesson about wanderlust and hating home. Its conclusion is very similar to that of *The Wizard of Oz*: "There's no place like home", an expression of relief that America is *not* a film noir.

John Ford's *My Darling Clementine* (USA, 1946), released in the same year as *It's a Wonderful Life*, is, in many ways, its cinematic sibling. In the film a legendary cowboy, Wyatt Earp (147), finds that the frontier town of Tombstone is in moral decline and full of bars and prostitutes. He restores order to it and establishes law and decency as its twin foundation stones. Capra allows us to imagine a town gone awry, whereas Ford looks back nostalgically to the time when a similar one stopped being so.

It is perhaps no surprise that American filmmakers were going through a period of narrative soul searching. Not only had war darkened their sunny view of life, but closer to home, their industry was changing. Ernst Lubitsch died in 1947. D.W. Griffith and Gregg Toland, American cinema's civilizer and its deep space experimenter, both died in 1948, as did Louis Lumière in France and Eisenstein in the Soviet Union. Victor Fleming, director of much of *The Wizard of Oz* and *Gone with the Wind,* died the following year. Structurally, the challenge to the studio system, initiated by Olivia de Havilland, continued. Ticket sales started to decline, people began to move to suburbs and spend their money on new consumer goods rather than movies. In 1947, fifty studio bosses and producers agreed to sack any of their employees who would not co-operate with the government's new anti-commu-

147
Above: Whereas Capra depicted what would happen if lawlessness was not challenged by decent men, in John Ford's *My Darling Clementine* order is restored by just such a man. USA, 1946.

nist House Un-American Activities Committee (HUAC). The five main studios were denounced by the US Supreme Court for their "conspiracy to monopoly" in 1948 and the first of them, Paramount, was forced by law to sell its 1,450 theatres in the following year. In 1949, the HUAC chairman, J. Parnell Thomas, was sentenced to a prison term for embezzlement.

Meanwhile in France, major actors led demonstrations against the influx of American films. The US industry, after a complex tussle, began to pay the UK to reduce its taxation on imported American movies and Mexico and Brazil set up anti-import policies. The wartime need for collective emotional experiences seemed to have peaked and new tiny, bug-eyed screens started to appear in people's living rooms. Gradually at first, but then with increasing strength,

148
Right: Director Zheng Junli's strong depiction of a landlord–tenant fight in *Crows and Sparrows* shows the influence of realism on Chinese cinema. China, 1949.

television, legislation and international opposition broke down American film's oligarchy.

The New York bankers who owned the American studios, had they been aware of the Far Eastern situation, would have taken cold comfort from what was concurrently beginning to happen in China. In 1949, when Mao finally ousted the nationalists, forty-seven million Chinese people went to the cinema. A decade later, after the introduction of government-built touring cinemas, based on the early Soviet Union's agitprop trains, annual attendances were up to four billion. China's massive expansion in movie-going was fostered by a communist government, an irony that would not have been lost on the US bankers and the studio executives who sided with the HUAC. Like his fellow dictators, Hitler and Stalin, Mao was interested in cinema as a tool of control and ideological indoctrination, rather than as an art. He appointed the Chinese actor and director, Yuan Muzhi, who had made *Street Angel* (China, 1937, see page 420), as head of the new Cinema Board. One of the first films to reflect the communist success was *Crows and Sparrows* (Zheng Junli, China 1949), often voted one of the best Chinese films of all time. It tells of the struggle in a Shanghai tenement building between its residents and their brutal nationalist landlord. It ends at Chinese New Year in 1949 with the celebration of Mao's victory, and its triumphalism now appears ironic in the light of China's future. However, the still forcefully realism of its scenes (148) is a reminder that China, as much as Italy, France or America, contributed to post-war cinematic naturalism.

The rise of communism was too much for many free-thinking filmmakers in Shanghai and many fled, as others had done before the Russian revolutions or the Nazis' rise to power. Their destination was Hong Kong, where Chinese filmmakers had first gone in the late 1930s, when Japan invaded. The wave that crossed over at the end of the 1940s and the early 1950s was more significant and some of the best mandarin-language films of all time were made by them. Wang Weiyi directed *Tears of the Pearl River* in Hong Kong at the end of the 1940s and Zhu Shilin, one of the best filmmakers of his era, made *The Secret History of the Imperial Palace* (Hong Kong, 1949) and *The Dividing Wall* (Hong Kong, 1952), which became classics. Zhu was a pioneer and continued to advance the 1930s tradition of realism in Chinese cinema (he had written screenplays for the great 1930s star Ruan Lingu). His work was the forerunner of 1950s Cantonese melodrama which, although less critical of society than his own work, was still splendidly emotional. The films of Zhu and Wang paved the way for the 1950s and 1970s filmmaking explosions in Hong Kong.

In other countries, decolonization established the possibility of local directors making more authentic work than had been allowed before. Within a year or two of the US withdrawal, the Philippinoe director Manuel Conde had made *Ghengis Khan* (Philippines, 1950) which was a hit at the 1952 Venice Film Festival and whose story was retold — badly — by Hollywood, with John Wayne in the lead. Philippinoe cinema would not come into its own until the 1950s and 1960s. Mexico may have had no colonizer to overthrow but its 1930s films had been popular re-treads of the 1911–18 revolutionary period's history. In 1931–32, Eisenstein had tried to make a film, *Que Viva Mexico!* in this country. It remained unfinished, but its symbolism influenced Mexican film style and ideas in this period. The Mexican government had set up film institutions in the early 1940s and, by the end of that decade, two main types of indigenous films had emerged: Eisenstein-influenced mythic works about life on the land, treated in an almost sacred way; and, by contrast, brothel and cabaret urban films. One of the earliest of the former was *Maria Candelaria* (Emilio Fernandez, Mexico, 1943) and one of the best of the latter, was *The Mother of the Port* (Emilio Gomez Muriel, Mexico, 1949). Native

Mexican filmmakers such as Emilio Fernandez used these two genres to debate the nature of their country's modernization, just as European directors had obsessed about the gulf between city and country life in the late 1920s. Mexican cinema's realist roots gave way to a tussle between piety and melodrama which continued for many decades. Together, these genres represented a quarter of the films shown in Mexico in the late 1940s, over 100 films in total. The majority of the rest were either American or Spanish.

British cinema was more in tune with Western cinematic trends and while stylistically it showed signs of expressionism and shadow play, it also did more than this. In 1949 it produced one of the most complex devastation-films of the

149
Above: Orson Welles as Harry Lime in Carol Reed's potent mix of film noir, expressionism and post-war themes, *The Third Man*. UK, 1949.

whole period. *The Third Man* (UK, 1949) is almost as pivotal to film history as the film noir cycle. It was one of the first British studio films to be shot entirely on location and was produced by a rare pairing, the ubiquitous Alexander Korda and *Gone with the Wind*'s David O. Selznick. It was written and directed by another extraordinary pair, the Catholic novelist Graham Greene and Carol Reed, the illegitimate son of an actor who had worked his way up through the British studio system.

The Third Man has an engaging scenario: an American in bombed-out Vienna, Holly Martins, attempts to find out whether his mysterious friend, Harry Lime, has died. In so doing, he becomes involved with Harry's girlfriend, Anna, and discovers that not only is Harry alive, but that he is an amoral penicillin trafficker. Greene invented a demonic character in Lime, played by Orson Welles (149), who benefits from this black-market trafficking at the expense of those children for whom the medicines are intended. Reed, who had just made the remarkable *Odd Man Out* (UK, 1947), liked the gravity of this idea. Its moody pessimism reminded him of the 1930s French films he admired. He had made a wartime documentary and, like the Italians and some of the Americans, felt that cinema had to engage more with reality. Post-war Vienna, with insistent zither music in the background, was a million miles away from the city of Strauss' light waltzes, besides being divided into French, British, Russian and US sectors. Using Hitchcock's string-of-set-pieces approach, Reed and his great cinematographer, Robert Krasker, shot the majority of the film with the camera angled off the horizontal axis. German filmmakers in the 1920s has used this technique to indicate mental imbalance. Their Vienna held as much madness as the asylums of Wiene and Kinugasa, Reed's expressionist precursors. Welles wrote his own scenes and some claim he was yet another influence on the visual style of the picture.

The film is driven by Holly's love for his friend Harry. The similarity of these names confuses several characters, allowing the filmmakers to point up the moral differences between them. However, Holly transfers this love to Anna. Greene envisaged a happy ending in which Anna takes Holly's arm, but Reed wasn't having this. In one of the most daring final moments in mainstream

150
Left: One of the most daring endings in mainstream cinema: a deep-staged shot of Alida Valli walking toward the camera in *The Third Man*. UK, 1949.

film history, he directed a deeply staged shot, with Anna walking from the distance toward Holly, who is placed near the camera position (150). When she finally reaches him, she simply walks out of shot, preferring the memory of the rogue Harry to the weak, decent man. This unromantic finale concluded a film that was as rich a conjunction of stylistic schemas as its setting was a conjunction of political systems.

Reed's insistence on filming Anna's final walk in real time, without truncating it, bore the marks of Italian neo-realism. This idea of capturing the texture of life by de-dramatizing it was spreading rapidly. The Brazilian director Nelson Pereira dos Santos was born in São Paulo in 1928 and he saw the films of Rossellini and De Sica while studying in Paris in the late 1940s. Their influence was seminal. His first feature, *Rio 40 Degrees* (Brazil, 1955) (151), combined neo-realist storytelling with slum locations and focused on working-class rather than middle-class people. It was also populist, portraying everyday events, such as football matches and samba classes. Pereira dos Santos can be seen as the father of the Cinema Nôvo or New Cinema movement in Brazil in the 1960s. He said later on in his career that neo-realism was a breakthrough for him because it allowed directors to bypass the main studio-based commercial industry in Brazil and make their own films, "without taking heed of the whole material and economic apparatus".[13] Brazilian New Cinema (see pages 311–13) would join movements in France, Italy, Japan, Eastern Europe, Sweden, Argentina, North Africa, America and India to mount the most profound challenge yet to the studio cinema's house style – closed romantic realism.

India was more prepared for storytelling's neo-realist revolution. Around its filmmakers lay a vast country, parts of it just as devastated as Italy. The British had withdrawn in 1947 and the country had split between a Hindu central section still named India and two separate Islamic territories to its north-east and north-west, known collectively as Pakistan. Ten million people migrated between the newly-formed countries and an estimated one million people died in the ensuing fighting and hardship. Anti-colonial peace campaigner, Mahatma Gandhi, was assassinated in 1948, landlord

151
Below: Pereira dos Santos' *Rio 40 Degrees* was a popularist film which featured everyday working-class scenarios. Brazil, 1955.

THE DEVASTATION OF WAR AND A NEW MOVIE LANGUAGE (1945–1952): REALISM IN WORLD CINEMA

exploitation was rife and the Indian government's modernizing aims were clashing with the traditional caste system.

The Indian Peoples' Theatre Association had galvanized political leftists and social reformers (see page 181) and its first film, *Dharti Ke Lal/Children of the Earth* (K.A. Abbas, 1946) was highly significant. It tells the story of a Bengali family forced from their land who migrate to Calcutta (152). The father, Ramu, tries and fails to find work and the mother resorts to prostitution. Finally, Ramu's father challenges the city's magnetic pull and the Bengali farmers collectivize.

Unsurprisingly, *Children of the Earth* was the first Indian film to attract a large audience in the Soviet Union. It was committed to social change and, in a similar way to contemporaneous Mexican cinema, married this to melodramatic storylines and potent symbols of hope and despair. It was, of course, a musical and was written and directed by Indian Peoples' Theatre Association founder member Khwaja Ahmad Abbas, India's equivalent of the Italian neo-realist writer, Zavattini. Five years later, Abbas wrote *Awara/The Tramp* (1951), which is one of the most famous Indian films of all time. The film's title is no accident: its director, lead actor and producer, Raj Kapoor, modelled himself on Chaplin's tramp and, like Chaplin, attempted to marry entertainment and social themes (153). The tramp is accused of murdering a wealthy and famous judge, but is

defended in court by the judge's ward, a young lawyer, Rita. She was played by the twenty-three-year-old Nargis, who would soon become the most famous actress in Indian cinema. *The Tramp*'s epic love story was nearly three hours long, which is the norm for Indian films. Its utopian musical numbers alternated with scenes that caustically contrasted the lives of rich and poor. Initially it was a modest success in India but, like *Children of the Earth*, it was extremely popular in the Soviet Union, which sent film prints to its troops stationed in the Arctic. Its social idealism even impressed Chairman Mao, whose favourite film it became.

Abbas was interested in the economics of inequality in India, but Kapoor "blended a Western-style romance with the theme of social

152
Above: Potent symbols of hope and despair in the leftist *Dharti Ke Lal*, which became Chairman Mao's favourite film. Director: K.A. Abbas. India, 1946.

revolt, and the result was that the unkempt inherited the Earth."[14] Chaplin had achieved this in muted form, but what makes Indian cinema of this period so complex and interesting is how Italian neo-realism further influenced an already potent mix of social and cinematic ideas. In 1952, the year of *The Tramp*'s release, De Sica's *Bicycle Thieves* and *Miracolo in Milano/Miracle in Milan* (Italy, 1950) were shown at the first International Film Festival of India in Bombay and many of the major directors such as Ritwik Ghatak, Satyajit Ray and Mrinal Sen saw them. Ray, India's most literary and most famous director, whose career will be considered in the next chapter, said that *Bicycle Thieves* "exercised a definitive influence" on his work. If Abbas' own films, as well as those he wrote for Kapoor and others, showed how affected he was by these, the work of India's most experimental director to date, Ritwik Ghatak, explicitly asserted their influence.

Ghatak, who came from the radical IPTA heartland of Bengal in north-east India, became the organization's playwright and then entered the film industry in 1950. Influenced by the neo-realists, he made his first film, *Nagarik/The Citizen* (1952), about a family forced to move to Calcutta after Bengal's partition (154). His use of wide-angle lenses was developed during his erratic, brilliant career. Ghatak left work unfinished, bartered film rights for alcohol, hated

works, such as *Hachigatsu No Rapusodi/Rhapsody in August* (Japan, 1991), seemed thematically exhausted. At the end of his career, Kurosawa turned to the question of the role and effects of colour, like the French impressionist painter Claude Monet in his last years. He had given up hope on social and human questions, so concentrated on purely aesthetic ones.

The story now takes us back to Hollywood where it is important to look at a counter-trend to films noirs and neo-realism, in some films that were not made by European émigrés. Three epitomize this trend: *The Paleface* (Norman Z. McLeod, 1948), *An American in Paris* (Vincente Minnelli, 1951) and *Singin' in the Rain* (Stanley Donen and Gene Kelly, 1952).

It is no surprise to discover that the Hollywood of *Double Indemnity* also made effervescent colour comedies with Bob Hope, nor that the same industry that produced the film noir cycle made two of its most escapist musicals, both starring Gene Kelly, at this time. The victors of the Second World War turned away from the rubble, poverty, division and uncertainties of the real world, as well as confronting them, and this was especially the case with its American-born, Anglo-Saxon filmmakers. Danny Kaye in *Wonder Man* (Bruce Humberstone, 1945) and Bob Hope in *The Paleface* (159) are hilariously funny. They are adult versions of Laurel and Hardy, similarly cowardly, unskilled with women and keen to look into the camera. Much of America had not been directly touched by war, so it could happily continue with the business of entertaining itself and, in the case of Hope and Kaye, laughing at the boyishness of men. The latter, who was as graceful and talented a performer as Chaplin, was politically to the left and ended up working for UNICEF. Hope's routines never took your breath away as Kaye's did. He was an ordinary Joe with great timing, on the right of the political spectrum.

An American in Paris and *Singin' in the Rain* were the sophisticated colour offspring of Mamoulian's pioneering early musical, *Love Me Tonight* (USA, 1932). Both starred an athletic modern dancer and choreographer, the Pittsburgh-born-and-educated Gene Kelly. Both

films were about earlier art forms, French impressionist painting in the former and silent cinema in the latter. Each one was overseen by Arthur Freed, a classy lyricist and producer who ran a semi-autonomous stable of talents within MGM, not unlike a painter's atelier. Although producer-led, the Freed Unit was unlike the production sub-sections of some Japanese studios of the 1930s and 1940s. Freed and his team were

159
Above: Bob Hope as the cowardly and inept dentist, "Painless" Potter, and Jane Russell as Calamity Jane in the comedy *The Paleface*. Director: Norman Z. McLeod. USA, 1948.

cosmopolitans and they knew not only Mamoulian's benchmark film, but also its debt to René Clair. They revolutionized the American musical, took it offstage, away from the gothic fantasy world of *Love Me Tonight*, and, in the case of *On The Town* (Stanley Donen and Gene Kelly, 1949), staged some scenes on actual streets in real cities. The huge success of The Archers' *The Red Shoes* (Michael Powell and Emeric Pressburger, UK, 1948) in the US, encouraged them to film a ballet finale for *An American in Paris* costing over half a million dollars[17]. *Singin' in the Rain* was less beholden to other art forms and European ideas. It was American, joyful and infectious.

These musicals and comedies are the most entertaining films in the years following the devastation of war, and both genres would continue to change and adjust to new ideas and technology. However, the bigger movie trend of this period was the maturing of mainstream cinema. Film noir, neo-realism and *Rashomon* were three advances in the seriousness of film and the story behind each is one of international influence. From now on, more than ever before, film style's complex evolution was the result of the cross-fertilization of aesthetic ideas from many continents. Yet filmmaking in Mexico, Brazil, Hong Kong and India certainly became distinctive and the prospects for world cinema seemed good. Sixty per cent of America's population still went to the cinema regularly, whereas only nine per cent do today. Early in the 1950s television had started to scare the world of film, but it responded by visually reinventing itself.

1. Zavattini, Cesare. Reprinted in *Sight and Sound*, Vol 23, No 2, Oct–Dec 1953.
2. Thompson and Bordwell, *Film History, An Introduction*, op. cit.
3. Ibid.
4. Ibid.
5. Quoted in *The Adventures of Roberto Rossellini* by Tag Gallagher, Da Capo Press, 1988.
6. Quoted in Kinder, Marsha, *Blood Cinema*, op. cit., p32
7. Salt, Barry, op. cit.
8. Truffaut–Hitchcock, op.cit.
9. The longer takes and more mobile camera work in *Ivan the Terrible Part 1* (1945) show that Eisenstein eventually rejected some of his pioneering montage techniques.
10. There is no clear agreement over which was the first film noir, though many cite *The Maltese Falcon* (1941). Its director, John Huston, is an example of a non-émigré whose war experience may have convinced him that Hollywood needed to make more serious, darker films. Others in this category are William Wyler, George Stevens and actor James Stewart.
11. Elsaesser, Thomas, *Weimer Cinema and After: Germany's Historical Imaginary*, Routledge, 2000. p374.
12. British wartime fiction films such as *Went the Day Well?* (Albert Cavalcanti, 1942) and *The Way Ahead* (Carol Reed, 1944) also had documentary qualities and would have been seen by Hollywood producers and directors at this time.
13. Quote in Roy Armes' *Third World Filmmaking and the West*, University of California Press.
14. Sankar, Kobita, *Indian Cinema Today*, Sterling Publishers Private, 1975.
15. Rajadhyaksha and Willemen, op. cit.
16. Quoted in *Luis Bunual: El Doble Arco de la Belleza y la Rebelda*, 2001, Downtown Book Center.
17. Although Kelly had been producing "dream ballets" since *Cover Girl* (1944) and *Anchors Aweigh* (1945).

160
Above: In the 1950s,
Western filmgoers finally
got a chance to see Asian
films. One of the first to
break through was Satyajit
Ray's *Pather Panchali*.
India, 1955.

THE SWOLLEN STORY (1953—59)
Rage and symbolism in 1950s filmmaking

6

Prime Minister Yoshida, a pro-West modernizer who had opposed the Second World War, was the key political figure in Japan in the early 1950s. US President Eisenhower was a Republican who had master-minded the Allies' European efforts in the Second World War and came to power in 1953. Nehru, a British-educated socialist, and was Indian Prime Minister between independence in 1947 and his death in 1964. Yoshida saw Japan as economically precocious, repentant about its disastrous years as an aggressor and able to stand on its own two feet. Eisenhower envisaged America as Christian, white, suburban and built around decent middle-class families. Many had spare money to spend on inessential things. Advertisers made objects desirable and people expressed their personalities according to what they acquired. Women could afford to dress a little like Janet Leigh and men could drive cars not unlike their movie idols'. Life in affluent countries was beginning to resemble the utopian world of escapist movies, at least on the surface. Nehru's India, on the other hand, was deeply religious and socially unequal and yet he had an atheistic and anti-caste political programme.

JAPAN'S SECOND GOLDEN AGE

Humiliated and ruined by the Second World War, Japan's national wealth rocketed throughout the 1950s. Advertising spend increased tenfold and the national ambition was for the "Bright Life", an America-influenced consumerist society. Politicians were to declare in 1955 that the "post-war period is over."

Kurosawa's internationally successful *Rashomon* (1950) boosted the country's international confidence. Soon, more than 500 indigenous films were being made every year. In 1959 classical master Yasujiro Ozu directed *Ohaya/Good Morning*,

which commented on the new consumerism through its story of two boys who attempt to force their parents to buy them a television by going on strike.

The period of Japanese filmmaking covered in this chapter began with a year, 1953, as outstanding as 1939 had been in the history of American cinema. Kenji Mizoguchi's *Ugetsu Monogatari/ Ugetsu*, Teinosuke Kinugasa's *Jigokumon/Gate of Hell* and Ozu's *Tokyo Monogatari/Tokyo Story* showed three directors, who have already figured in this story, in their very best form. When previously discussed (see pages 132–33), Mizoguchi was evolving a highly mobile camera style in *Osaka Elegy* (1936) and *Sisters of Gion* (1936) to tell emotionally underplayed period stories of women redeeming men with their love and stoicism. *Ugetsu* was his most acclaimed film and repeated *Rashomon*'s success at the Venice Film Festival. It is an understated tale of a sixteenth-century potter who dreams of being rich, but who is given spiritual guidance by his wife (161). The film was exquisitely shot by the great cinematographer Kazuo Miyagawa in long flowing takes coolly detached from the action. Miyagawa had also shot *Rashomon* and the two films shared producers and two actors. *Ugetsu*'s ending is one of the most serene in movie history, the disaffected potter returning home to find that his house has been destroyed and his wife has died. The lady he had met on his journeys had been her spirit. Her voice says, "Now at last you have become the man I wanted you to be."

The sadness of time passing, or "mano no aware" in Japanese, had also been central to Ozu's films, as discussed in earlier chapters. He made his most famous film, *Tokyo Story,* in 1953 by further refining his 1930s classical style. It was his most moving film on his trademark theme – the relationship between parent and child. The story is about an old couple who decide to visit their children. Distracted by their own lives, their offspring are too busy to spend much time with their parents. On the train home, the mother becomes ill and later dies. The film closes with the father sitting alone in his home, missing his wife, but resigned to the fact that this is how life is. All the techniques illustrated in *I Was Born, But ...* remain: the camera is almost always below eye level (162), camera moves are sparse, intermediate spaces or "pillow shots" create narratively neutral, poised images between sequences. However, there is less humour than in *I Was Born, But ...* . Ozu's classicism had become more sombre.

Kinugasa's return to form was an echo from an even more distant past. His *A Page of Madness* (1926) was

162
Below: Another Japanese master came belatedly to attention in 1953. Yasujiro Ozu's *Tokyo Story*, about an older couple visiting their busy offspring, was his forty-sixth film. Notice how, two decades after *I Was Born, But...*, Ozu was still placing the camera below eye level.

part of the 1920s insanity film cycle derived from *The Cabinet of Dr. Caligari* (see pages 96–98). In the 1930s and 1940s, his work became more conventional, but *Jogokumon/Gate of Hell* (1953) was a twelfth-century tale made in exquisite colour (163). In the pattern of *Rashomon* and *Ugetsu*, it was the toast of the Venice Film Festival and distinguished itself by occupying a screen that was wider than usual. Until 1953, the images of most international films were one-third wider than they were high, which was approximately the same shape as the canvases used by many Western landscape painters. Apart from the odd rare exception like Gance's *Napoleon* (see pages

163
Below: Japan's first widescreen film. Veteran director Teinosuke Kinugasa didn't direct all of *Gate of Hell*, but he and cinematographer Kohei Sugiyama created beautiful imagery.

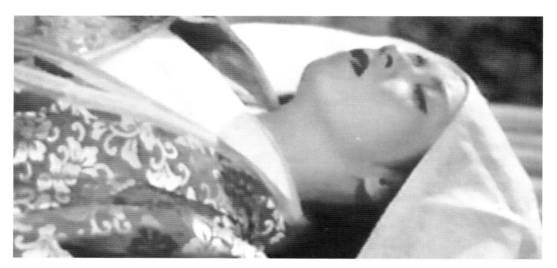

92–94) and Henri Chrétien's experiment described below, every other film image conformed to this shape, the "Academy" ratio. In the 1950s, Academy would be abandoned by filmmakers in the same way that silent cinema had been sidelined twenty-five years earlier and as a result film camera lenses, stock and even movie screens had to adapt. Industry bosses had been searching for ways to make cinema differ from television. Their solution was to make the screen bigger, more horizontal and "more epic".

WIDESCREEN IN JAPAN AND THE US

Widescreen was pioneered by the Frenchman, Henri Chrétien, in 1927. He wanted to achieve the ultra-widescreen effect of sections of Gance's *Napoleon*, without having to use three cameras. He added a lens onto a single camera, which would squeeze a very wide scene sideways onto a standard film strip. When the film was projected in the cinema, a polar opposite lens would de-squeeze it, to reveal the original widescreen scene. This effect was enthusiastically embraced by 1950s Japanese directors and cinematographers and, perhaps because their country had a long tradition of horizontal scroll painting and of triptych prints forming a single rectangular image, unlike the West, they dynamized the full width of the new wide screens.

A director new to this story, Kon Ichikawa, took Kinugasa's compositional schema further. Ichikawa had started his film career in comedy in the late 1940s and his first great film was *Mr Pu* (1953), a satire about Japan's modernization. When his *Yukinojo Henge/An Actor's Revenge* (1963) was re-screened successfully in the West decades after its release, his use of widescreen staging was a revelation. A character appears as a tiny point of light in the top left-hand corner of the image in one sequence, perhaps ninety-five per cent of which remains completely black. This cannot be illustrated in a book, but a comparable effect would be if this double page spread was entirely blank, except for the first letter on the left-hand page.

The first film in the B-movie cycle *Gojira/Godzilla* (Hondo Ishiro), about a Tyrannosaurus-like creature awakened by an atom bomb, was released in Japan in 1954. The country's most famous international director, Akira Kurosawa, had not yet taken to widescreen, but other innovations in *The Seven Samurai* (1954) made it his most successful film to date. Although this was not the first Japanese Samurai film, it was influenced by the Westerns that flooded Japan after its Second World War defeat. Particularly affected by *Stagecoach* (USA, 1939) and the other films of John Ford, Kurosawa mixed the Samurai and Westerns schema with his own interest in ennobling self-sacrifice and experiment. The story tells of a group of sixteenth-century villagers plagued by bandits. Ordinary samurai will not help them, except for a good-hearted one, Shimada. He gathers together six others including Kikuchiyo, who does not qualify as a samurai, but who is a great swordsman. In a series of battles, they defend the villagers and three of them, including Kikuchiyo, are killed. Eventually, the local people plant their rice for the new season and the remaining samurai pass their dead colleagues' graves as they leave.

The Seven Samurai was not only innovative in its mixture of Western and Eastern film narrative; for the first time in his career

Above: The most significant
conduit between Eastern
and Western cinema in the
1950s were the films of
Akira Kurosawa. His *The
Seven Samurai* worked the
Westerns of John Ford but
added more horizontal
compositions and
telephoto cinematography.
Japan, 1954.

Kurosawa used several cameras to film a battle scene. Doing so allowed it to be staged in longer sequences, which could then develop and evolve. It also afforded the director unparalleled freedom and continuity when cutting between the different camera angles in post-production. His use of lenses longer than 150mm flattened the space in key scenes, such as the one above (164).

Keen to emphasize the epic quality of their films, 20th Century-Fox produced America's first 1950s widescreen film, *The Robe* (Henry Koster, 1953) (165) using CinemaScope, a variation of Chrétien's pioneering process. In 1897, Enoch J. Rector had devised a widescreen method of shooting *The Corbett-Fitzsimmons Fight* (see pages 28–29), which helped popularize cinema. 20th Century-Fox marketed *The Robe* heavily, hoping to achieve a similar effect fifty-five years later. Other film studios followed suit.

Many American filmmakers were daunted by widescreen's creative implications. The screen no longer approximated human physiognomy. Western painting provided few models for such composition and audience members sitting close to the screen had to turn their heads to see its entire width. Afraid of disorienting the audiences with close-ups nearly twice their previous width, US directors at first positioned their cameras further from the actors, arranging their performers in frieze-like rows across the screen (166). This was repeated in the second CinemaScope film, *How to Marry a Millionaire* (Jean Negulesco, 1953) and is sometimes called "washing line" composition. These filmmakers were also afraid that cutting on such a big screen would be visually disruptive, so they staged more theatrical shots; as a result, average shot lengths increased from eleven to thirteen seconds. Recalling what happened in the 1940s when average shot lengths increased, the staging of these early widescreen films might be expected to be deeper. Yet everyone in images 165 and 166 is roughly the same distance from the camera. Part of the reason for this is that colour was now being used. (Television was black and white at this stage.) Colour film stocks were less sensitive to light, so the camera's apertures therefore had to be more open than in the previous decade's glistening films noirs. Wide apertures resulted in shallow focus, leading to shallow staging, which became the norm in the majority of widescreen films of the time.

The stereoscopic or "3–D" movie, which also emerged in the US during this period was a famous exception to this. It used a technique in which two adjacent cameras filmed a deep-staged scene from almost the same angle, approximately replicating how humans look at something with both eyes. The combination of these slightly different images, together with the use of special glasses, produced a startling sense of an advancing foreground and receding background. *Bwana Devil* (Arch Oboler, USA, 1952) was the first of these 3–D movies. The equipment was awkward and so camera movement was difficult. In order to close down the aperture somewhat, a very bright set was needed and, therefore, a large number of lights. This resulted in

165
Below: Not since silent times had film staging been so theatrical. Widescreen cinema became mainstream in the first CinemaScope film, *The Robe*. Director: Henry Koster. USA, 1953.

166
Above: Betty Hutton, Rory Calhoun, Lauren Bacall, Cameron Mitchell and Marilyn Monroe in one of the typical "washing line" compositions of *How to Marry a Millionaire*. Director: Jean Negulesco. USA, 1953.

extremely hot filming conditions. Directors felt frustrated by these constraints in the way that the earliest silent ones did, but no equivalent of René Clair or Rouben Mamoulian emerged to explore the intellectual and dramatic possibilities of this cumbersome new form. A few interesting films were made, such as *Taza, Son of Cochise* (Douglas Sirk, USA, 1954), Andre De Toth's *House of Wax* (1953, all the more remarkable because its one-eyed director could not see the three-dimensional effect) and Alfred Hitchcock's restrained, theatrical *Dial M for Murder* (1954), but the approach did not catch on. Audiences rejected it (because of the awkwardness of the glasses) and 3–D films stopped being produced in 1955, although they were revived sporadically in later years. Some vast Sony Imax 3–D cinemas were built in the 1990s and although few films were shot in this format, examples such as *Into The Deep* (Howard Hall, USA, 1994) and *Space Station* (Toni Myers, USA, 2002) proved very popular.

TENSION AND MELODRAMA IN AMERICA AND SOUTH ASIA

The most important difference between Japanese and American cinema during this period cannot be found in mere analysis of their respective film styles. Rather, the way those styles responded, in each country, to social change, must be examined. It is central to this chapter's argument that 1950s cinema reflected the tension of its times. Whereas Ozu and Mizoguchi registered the tremendous impact of war and Prime Minister Yoshida's modernization campaigns with caution and resignation,[1] American filmmaking was much marked by the strains of the Eisenhower era. Many US filmmakers were happy with the conventional, consumerist, optimistic picture of American life in the Eisenhower years and they created comparable filmic worlds. A nostalgic winter musical, *White Christmas* (Michael Curtiz, USA), was the top US box-office film of 1954, as was the feel-good island one, *South Pacific* (Joshua Logan, USA), four years later.

However, America's key filmmakers could not ignore that the emergence of the "teenager" and the paranoia of the new "cold" war with the Soviet Union made their country much less cohesive than it appeared. Secondly and more intriguingly, they could not fail to grasp that US cinema's tentative maturity of the late 1940s and early 1950s was opening up new schema and novel ways of writing and shooting scenes, which would not go away. Situations could be staged in depth with more dramatic complexity, acting could be rawer and edgier, lighting could be more natural and happy endings were not the only route to box-office success. Filmmakers tried to accommodate both philosophies. They attempted to embrace the Eisenhower vision and stem the flow of dwindling audiences by ensuring that their films were more entertaining and colourful than ever before. But at the same time, they wanted them to be psychologically and socially honest. As a result, their work was bursting at the seams during the seven years between 1953 and 1959.

Popular culture was undergoing a flurry of changes beneath the surface of 1950s conformity. In 1952, considering the case of Roberto Rossellini's *Il Miraculo/The Miracle* (Italy, 1948), the US Supreme court had ruled that films should enjoy the same freedom of speech as other art forms. The judgment had little immediate impact on films, but connected cinema to emerging ideas about self-expression. In 1954, Bill Haley and the Comets' song "Rock Around the Clock" injected new energy into popular music's current style and appealed to teenagers more than their parents. *The Moon is Blue* (1953), produced and directed by the independent filmmaker Otto Preminger, flouted the studios' crumbling production codes by using the words "virgin" and "mistress". In the same year, *The Wild One* (Laslo Benedek, 1953) showed a group of rebellious motorcyclists terrorizing a small town and escaping without punishment. Teenage delinquency and a lack of direction were more directly explored later in *Rebel without a Cause* (Nicholas Ray, 1955) (167) and *East of Eden* (Elia Kazan, 1955). The star of both films was a twenty-four-year-old James Dean, who had been an associate of New York's innovative Actors' Studio and who died in a car crash in the year of their release, ensuring his immediate iconic fame.

Drug addiction featured in Otto Preminger's second controversial film in two years, *The Man with the Golden Arm* (1955). The director Stanley Kubrick, who was more talented than Preminger, had a similarly adverse view of life. Kubrick was a former stills photographer who, from the start of his film career, controlled most aspects of his productions with exactitude. His third feature, *The Killing* (1956), was a tense account of a heist and *Paths of Glory* (1957) concerned the indifference of First World War officers. Soon it became clear that Kubrick was a major film artist,

167
Above: Nicholas Ray's widescreen film broke new ground by suggesting that teenage rage could not be blamed on social deprivation. James Dean in *Rebel Without a Cause*. USA, 1955.

Welles without the fluidity or liberalism, Keaton without the mirth. He was profoundly un-Eisenhowerian, brilliantly realizing physical worlds on screen, the very solidity of which pointed to the spiritual emptiness of his characters.

Television also nibbled at Eisenhower's vision. The drama *Marty* (1953) about a plain, fat butcher, was a sensation and was remade for the cinema by Delbert Mann in 1955, with its themes of loneliness, low self-esteem and despair being only slightly diluted. Television not only provided new, more realistic subjects, but also

THE SWOLLEN STORY (1953–59): RAGE AND SYMBOLISM IN 1950s FILMMAKING introduced fresh directors into the cautious film world: Sidney Lumet, Robert Aldrich and Robert Parrish, for example, as well as Mann. The following year, twenty-one-year-old Mississippi-born Elvis Presley sexualized Bill Haley's kinetic new music, mixed it with blues and jazz and became the most popular singer in the world, tantalizing teenagers and scandalizing parents. In 1956, the veteran Western director John Ford cast his iconic leading man, John Wayne, as a racist drifter in *The Searchers*. As in Japan, so in the US, cheap but popular and revealing sci-fi movies started to emerge. In these, the nation and even the bodies of ordinary Americans were threatened with alien invasion.

Director Elia Kazan co-founded New York's Actor's Studio based on the somewhat jumbled twin pillars of Sigmund Freud's psychoanalytic ideas and the acting theories of Moscow theatre director Constantine Stanislavski; in the latter actors were taught to access their inner fears and desires and then to suppress them. A new performance technique, the Method, resulted, in which actors no longer displayed their characters in the roles they played, but tried to hide them. *The Wild One*'s main protagonist, the Nebraskan-born Marlon Brando, had become a powerful star on the New York stage using such anti-Hollywood techniques and from *The Men* (Fred Zinnemann, 1950) onward, he imported his fragmented, unravelling approach to the craft of stage acting to film, whose triviality he despised. Modern, Western, inchoate, sexualized individualism was born. Brando acted in widescreen colour films and James Dean's two movies were also filmed using this technique; the visual schemas which had been created in opposition to television's everydayness, intended by industry bosses to increase the distance between the real world and their escapist parallel one, were used to film some of the most realistic performances in the history of cinema.

The list is long indeed and amounts to a fundamental shift in the themes, voices and targets of American popular art of the time. Some directors, like Preminger and Kazan, wanted to shift American cinema directly onto contemporary subject matter such as race, youth, sexuality and unionism. Kazan had made films about anti-Semitism (*Gentleman's Agreement*, 1947) and racism (*Pinky*, 1949) and in the semi-documentary tradition of Louis de Rochement. He had taken on mature US cinema's baton from Welles and the noir directors. In *On the Waterfront* (1954) he filmed Brando's character – a former boxer betrayed by his bosses, who stands up to union bullies – often on the streets, without any full light on his face (168). Kazan used his Method acting theories as a battering ram against closed romantic realism, Hollywood's idealized and emotional view of human life since the 1920s. The students of his Actors' Studio – Brando, Montgomery Clift, Shelley Winters, Karl Malden, Rod Steiger and many others – became the most influential performers in Western cinema.[2]

168
Above: Marlon Brando as a washed-up boxer who defies the powerful unions in *On The Waterfront*. The Method performances in the film influenced Robert De Niro and other New York actors of the next generation. Director: Elia Kazan. USA, 1954.

The Big Knife (Robert Aldrich, 1955) provides a microcosm of developments in US film and acting during this period. In it, Steiger plays a studio boss dealing with the film industry's uncertainties and questions about his sexuality in his own private life. Steiger decided that he could discover the layers of his character by going around a department store, asking himself what each item for sale, such as ties, shoes and kitchen hardware, would mean to his character. Having visited many of the store's departments, he noticed a tiepin in the shape of a question mark and he realized that that is what his character was, a "question mark" man. As a literal symbol of this, he bought the pin and wore it throughout the film. This kind of experimental, psychological archaeology greatly influenced the techniques of the most applauded actors in modern American cinema, Robert De Niro, Dustin Hoffman and Al Pacino.

Many film historians would now argue that the most interesting mid-1950s American directors were those who incorporated psychological and societal question marks into what were apparently conventional widescreen melodramas. Three in particular explored their characters' rage and near hysteria under the guise of mainstream entertainments. Their astonishing films were initially dismissed by reviewers, but were to become the most influential of the period. The first of these, Vincente Minnelli, has already been encountered. His flowing shots in *The Clock* (1945) paved the way for Alfred Hitchcock's ten-minute takes in *Rope* (1948), and he also directed *An American in Paris* (1951). Minnelli's artistic interests were broader than many other American directors. He lived for long periods in New York, saw European movies there, especially those of Max Ophüls, from which he learnt how to unify scenes into long sequence shots. He also read Freud's writings and was interested in surrealism. His film *The Cobweb* (1955) grew out of these intellectual concerns. The bizarre story of a wrangle between the staff and patients in a mental hospital over whether to buy a pair of curtains, it portrayed an almost comically neurotic microcosm. Robert Wiene's imagery in *The Cabinet of Dr. Caligari* had registered the mental distortions of its characters in 1919, but comparable shadows did not appear in *The Cobweb*'s apparently sane imagery. Instead, Minnelli and his cinematographer, George Folsey, exploited widescreen's new possibilities to overload their shots with visual connections and to design them to express their main characters' mental strain.

Director Nicholas Ray took this further. Socially conscious, troubled and bisexual, he was born in Wisconsin, studied architecture with Frank Lloyd Wright and made two of the most significant American films of the post-war years – *They Live by Night* (1948) and *In a Lonely Place* (1950). In 1954, he made *Johnny Guitar* (USA) a low-budget Western shot in a new CinemaScope film stock, Trucolor (169). He rewrote the script and introduced a fierce new political, anti-witch-hunt feel to the story of a saloon owner on the outskirts of Albuquerque, who is waiting for the railroad. Joan Crawford, the diminutive, self-styled "queen of Hollywood" in the 1930s and 1940s played the lead character, a principled individualist who stands up to the bullyboy tactics of local bankers and lawmen. This masculinization

169
Below: Joan Crawford as a saloon owner standing up against mob rule in Nicholas Ray's *Johnny Guitar*. Denounced by most American critics at the time, its passion and visual intensity make it regarded by some as among the greatest works of American Cinema. USA, 1954.

of her part gives the film some of its sense of fluid sexual identity and, as it grew, so the title character of Johnny Guitar (Sterling Hayden) was reduced in proportion. Effectively, they swapped roles, so it is Crawford and Mercedes McCambridge, a rival cattle queen, who have the shoot-out in the end.

Johnny Guitar was released in America to poor reviews. Crawford once said,

170

Right: Director Douglas Sirk
portrayed the stifling world
of Eisenhower's America in
All That Heaven Allows.
USA, 1956.

"there's no excuse for a picture being this bad." And yet it is one of the greatest Westerns, if not one the greatest films, ever made. The French director and critic François Truffaut wrote that anyone who rejects *Johnny Guitar* "should never go to see movies again ... such people will never recognize inspiration, a shot, an idea, a good film or even cinema itself." This is because of the maturity of the love story and the denunciation of mob rule; the psychotic intensity of Crawford and the other actors; the sense that this difficult movie star caused this beautiful thing to be made; Ray's placing of people like chessmen on a board and his architectural use of space; the film's fantastical and unusual use of colour and the hysteria about what constitutes a man and why men fear women. Seen today in its widescreen format, it is still full of repressed feeling.

Douglas Sirk's methods of disguising America's anxieties in the guise of mainstream entertainment films were just as interesting. Born in Denmark in 1900 and brought up in Germany, he became a theatre director in his twenties and then turned to film. After making nine features in Germany, he fled the Nazis and eventually went to Hollywood where, from 1943, he started building a new directing career. As an intellectual, he found the studio scripts limiting but, after the 3–D *Taza, Son of Cochise*, he made a string of hugely successful ultra-glossy melodramas about the sexual underside of middle-class America. The most influential of these films was *All That Heaven Allows* (1956), about a widow rejected by her society friends when she begins a relationship with her gardener. When he was thirteen or fourteen, Sirk had been given a copy by his father of Henry David Thoreau's pastoral book, *Walden*. He loved the book and wove it into his story of prejudice (170). Around the character of the gardener he created a series of images symbolizing nature, and contrasted these with the sterile lives of the widow's judgemental friends. Sirk lovingly portrayed the lush details of Eisenhower's middle-class America in an otherworldly light. Gradually, the widow becomes more and more constrained by this utopia, while Sirk exposes its conformity and viciousness. The community perceives the gardener as too young and too working class for her. They are scandalized by her continuing sexual desire and her wish to express it. They expect her to sublimate her inner life and translate it into a concern for curtains and manicured lawns. In a devastating late scene in the film, she is given a television set by her children. "Most of our ladies say that television gives them something to do with their time", says a salesperson and Sirk photographs her reflection imprisoned in its glass frame. *All that Heaven Allows* became one of the most quoted examples of subversive mainstream filmmaking, and the German

171
Below: Todd Haynes' Oscar-winning modernization of *All That Heaven Allows* borrowed heavily from Sirk's classic. Julianne Moore in *Far From Heaven*. USA, 2003.

director, Rainer Werner Fassbinder, updated its view of 1950s America to 1970s Germany and its own problems of denial and prejudice (see page 354). American independent director, Todd Haynes, recreated aspects of it in *Far From Heaven* (2003) (171) in which his lead character was married to a gay man and the gardener was African-American.

India was making about 270 films a year at this point, considerably fewer than Japan's annual production of 500. Less than half of those 270 films were in the national language of Hindi. By the mid-1970s, production would increase to over 500 and a decade later, it had more than doubled.

172
Above: An iconic poster of one of the most famous Indian films ever made: *Mother India*. It features the scene where actress Nargis, playing Radha, hauls a rock out of the soil. The camera was clocked off its horizontal axis to emphasize both her effort and the strong vertical of the composition. Director: Mehboob, 1957.

Indian films produced in the mid-1950s were still dominated by playback musical numbers but, stylistically, melodrama was even more important than in the US. Two directors in particular, Mehboob and Guru Dutt, were as central to the genre as Douglas Sirk and Vincente Minnelli were in America.

Mehboob was a legendary figure in Indian cinema between the late 1930s and his death in 1964. Born in a peasant village in Gujarat in the country's north west, he worked his way up the Indian studio ladder in Bombay, directing his first film in 1935 and establishing Mehboob productions in 1942. His early films were "socials" in the style of Painter, but in the 1950s he elaborated his passionate storylines and filmed them with new visual splendour, echoing the trends in American cinema of the time. The climax of this development was his *Bharat Mata/Mother India* (India, 1957), which has become a milestone in world film history and is appropriately called the *Gone With The Wind* of Indian cinema. Like *All That Heaven Allows* and many of the US melodramas of time, it charts a woman's suffering in order to explore the nature of society and social change. In this case the woman is Radha, an old lady looking back on her life. As she smells a garland of flowers, there is a flashback to her youth and wedding ceremony. We see how her family was exploited by a greedy landlord – a common theme in Indian cinema – and how one son accepts the persecution and another fights. Radha works hard tilling the fields, her gold-festooned face accented with a fluttering crimson veil, like one of those moving scenes from Dovzhenko's *Arsenal* (Soviet Union, 1929) (see pages 107–108), remade in fabulous colour, and with the camera angled to emphasize the effort required by her work. These images have the intensity of *Johnny Guitar*. It is not clear whether Mehboob, like Minnelli and Satyajit Ray, had read Freud, but his situations are bursting with primal psychoanalytic life, particularly so when Radha is forced to kill her son. The film's title suggests that its characters are not just individuals, but representatives of the struggling nation of India itself. At one point, Radha gets covered in mud and literally becomes part of the earth, while at another, peasants form India's geographical outline in a field (173). This film worships the land in a way similar to Dovzhenko, and as Sirk had done through Thoreau.

Mother India was produced by a more mystical and man-nered culture than America, but the themes of labour and modernity

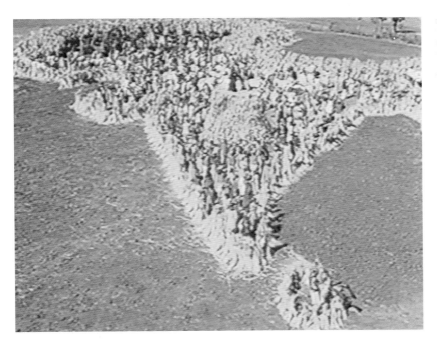

173
Left: Mehboob echoed Prime Minister Nehru's One India populism in images such as this one, where peasants working in fields formed the shape of their country.

flow beneath its surface. It contains both despair and exaltation like *Johnny Guitar* and *All That Heaven Allows*. "The world is full of magic" is a line from one of the songs, and its past is not distant nor is the future unreadable. When refused corn by their landlord, Radha cries with one of her sons – one of the least forced moments in cinema. This is largely due to the lead performance of India's most famous actress, Nargis, as Radha. She was just twenty-seven years old at the time and had been in movies since the age of five, having already scored a huge success in Raj Kapoor's *Awara* (India, 1951). Although there was no equivalent to Kazan's Actor's Studio in India, Nargis and others pioneered greater authenticity on screen. Image 172 shows her sweat as she and others are trying to raise a rock from the field. The film's power comes from how hard she works. Her make-up is like a mask that hides her suffering, just as it had done for Jane Wyman in *All That Heaven Allows*. In one scene she is framed so tightly that her hair cannot be seen. "If life is poison," according to one of lines in the most famous song in the film, "we must drink it." Martyrdom, stoicism and acceptance are the film's themes and this is where it departs from Sirk. It is more conservative than *All That Heaven Allows.* The latter film's message is "be true to yourself", Mehboob's is "be true to God and virtue".

    Mother India was a barometer measuring the accumulated pressure within India. Significantly, it broke box-office records not only there, but in most parts of the world where American cinema did not dominate, such as the Middle East, China, the Soviet Union and even Africa. Its social engagement – it opens with the construction of a new dam – combined with family melodrama became the new schema of non-Western cinema for at least a decade. One surprising point in this predominantly Hindu country's most famous film: both Mehboob and Nargis were Muslims.

    If *Mother India* was India's *Gone with the Wind*, Guru Dutt was its Vincente Minnelli. Like the neo-realist-inspired Ghatak, Dutt was born in 1925, educated in Calcutta and associated with the leftist intellectuals of the Indian People's Theatre Association. However, he was less radical than Ghatak, studying dance in the early 1940s and getting into filmmaking through choreography. He started directing in 1952, but his most significant film, *Kaagaz Ke Phool/Paper Flowers* (1959), was also the first Indian one filmed in widescreen. It is an intense experience because Dutt himself played the lead, an autobiographical role about a film director recalling the golden age of studio

combined the roles of director and actor, as his Indian counterpart, Dutt, had done in *Paper Flowers*. Born in Alexandria in 1926, he studied theatre in America for two years and fell in love with its musicals. Returning to Egypt, he started directing in 1950, aged just twenty-four. In 1954 he made the first film starring the young Egyptian actor Omar Sharif, who would later become an international movie star. Chahine's *Cairo Station* was his first stylistically original film. When the crippled newspaper seller realizes the object of his love is

178
Left: Director Youssef Chahine played the lead in his landmark melodrama *Cairo Station*. He would go on to become one of the greatest directors in African cinema. Eygpt, 1958.

having sex with her brutal fiancé, Chahine expresses his character's anguish semi-abstractly. The camera tracks into a Coca-Cola bottle from which he has been drinking and then obliquely away from him, passing a door behind which the sex occurs. This is intercut with a close-up of a train wheel bending a worn piece of track repeatedly. Chahine merged Eisenstein-ian, Egyptian and Hollywood melodrama in yet another 1950s scene about the human breaking point. His work would become more political in the 1960s as it became influenced by Egyptian president Nasser's Arab nationalist policies. By that decade's end, he had made the astonishing *La Terre/The Land* (Egypt–France, 1968). His 1970s films (discussed in Chapter Eight) would mix bracing accounts of his country's recent history, combined with musical numbers inspired by his hero Gene Kelly, subtle and daring depictions of homosexual desire and brilliant melodrama. Few world cinema careers mix the schemas of international film-making with such dynamic results.

Chahine was broadly free to explore his own complex ideas about society and filmmaking, but the same cannot be said of the communist bloc directors. The Lodz film school in Poland surpassed many similar Western institutions and produced at least four important international directors: Andrzej Wajda, Roman Polanski, Jerzy Skolimowski and Krzysztof Zanussi. The first of these was the most significant Eastern European director of the mid-1950s. Wajda (179) was born in 1926 in Poland. Aged sixteen, he fought the Germans in the Polish resistance movement. After the war he became a painter before studying at Lodz, then debuted with a film trilogy about Poland during the Second World War: *Pokolenie/A Generation* (1954), details the underground struggle; *Kanal/Canal* (1957) is about the Jewish uprising in the Warsaw ghetto in May 1943 and the best of the three; *Popiol i Diament/Ashes and Diamonds* (1958), starts with the first day of peace after the Second World War. This dialogue snippet captures the film's attitude:

POLICEMAN: How old are you?
BOY: 100 years old.
POLICEMAN (slapping him): How old are you?
BOY: 101.

"Every director in the world wants to do something original",[4] wrote Wajda, which could be the thesis of this book. His originality came partly from the way he disguised his films' meaning from the Polish authorities by encoding them in symbols. He later said, "After my first few films, the reviewers began to say that I was a 'symbol-oriented director'. Ever since then I have always been pursued by the white horse that appears in *Ashes and Diamonds*, the ineluctable sign of the Polishness of my films."[5]

Symbolism had been part of the way filmmakers expressed themselves, at least since Mario Caserini's *The Evil Plant* (Italy, 1912), whose opening shot featured a snake. Sergei Eisenstein's films were full of symbols of the destructive power of capitalism, whereas Dovzhenko had represented the Ukraine's pastoral qualities through them. Lubitsch in 1920s Germany and 1930s America used sexual symbols, as did the French surrealists

179

Left: The innovative Polish director Andrzej Wajda employed symbols in his films.

(in a different way) and Buñuel and Hitchcock. In Von Stroheim's *Greed* (USA, 1924) gold represented avarice. Certain frontier towns stood symbolically for the whole of modern America for Ford and objects represented the tranquillity beyond human experience for Ozu. Welles' *Citizen Kane* (USA, 1941) was full of metaphors for childhood and power. Leftist Chinese films used people and tenement buildings to symbolize the evils of nationalism. The train's arrival in *Pather Panchali* was the symbol of India's hopeful, industrialized future for Satyajit Ray and Kikuchiyo's shooting in Kurosawa's *The Seven Samurai* represented the passing from the age of the sword to that of the musket. The use of an image, an object or an event to represent something greater than itself already had a rich cinematic history.

Wajda's *A Generation* charted the waning idealism of young Polish anti-Nazis through the onset of communism and its failed promises. The third film's star, Zbigniew Cybulski (180),

Right: Unlike James Dean, whose image he adapted, Polish actor Zbigniew Cybulski's onscreen rage was not directed against himself. In *Ashes and Diamonds* he played a Second World War anti-Nazi resistance fighter who questions the reasons for killing. Director: Andrzej Wajda. Poland, 1958.

became a disoriented symbol of Poland's disillusioned youth, wearing blue jeans and sunglasses, just as James Dean had done in the US. Like Dean, his premature death (in a train accident in 1967, at the age of forty) increased his iconic power. The 1950s was not the only time Wajda would spearhead Polish film culture. In the 1970s, he was the inspiration for a movement of like-minded Polish directors, "The Cinema of Moral Unrest". He became a politician in the 1980s and returned to cinema in the 1990s.

The Czech animator and puppeteer Jirí Trnka was even more reliant on symbolism than Wajda. His fellow-countryman, J.E. Purkyne, had laid the foundation for the roots of cinema in 1818, arguing that if the human mind perceived still images in rapid succession, they would merge and create a sense of flow between them. Czech and Slovak film production started in 1910 and had some international success in 1919 and 1921. A handful of films were made in 1930 and, after the success of *Extase/Ecstasy* (Gustav Machaty, Czechoslovakia, 1932) and the construction of the Barrandov studio in 1933, production rose to about forty films by 1939. The Nazi occupation almost ruined the country's filmmaking, but its national film school, FAMU, was established in Prague after the Second World War and in the wake of the communist takeover in 1948, Czechoslovakia started to specialize in film animation and puppetry; Trnka was the figurehead of this development. He was born in 1912 and, descended from wood-carvers on his mother's side, started his career designing puppets and theatre sets. He made his first feature in 1947. By 1954, he had launched a series of shorts, based on the children's book *The Good Soldier of Schwiek* (1921–23) by Jaroslav Hasek (181). Sometimes, Trnka would simply film live puppet movements and at other times he would use the stop-frame methods of the Pole, Wladyslaw Starewicz, whose work contributed to the surrealism detailed in Chapter Three (see page 109). Trnka evolved a dignified way of continuing the Czech folk storytelling tradition when it was considered reactionary by the state. His film *Ruka/The Hand* (Czechoslovakia, 1965) became one of the most famous symbolic Eastern bloc films. In it, an appealing, unspeaking little puppet (Trnka did not use lip movements in his work) is terrorized by a disembodied hand (182), which clearly represents the oppressive communist state.

181
Above: Czechoslovakia's leading post-war animator was Jiří Trnka. Above is a scene from his *The Good Soldier of Schwiek*. 1954.

182
Below: Jiří Trnka's allegorical classic *The Hand*. Czechoslovakia, 1965.

FOUR ALTERNATIVES TO THE MAINSTREAM: DREYER, BERGMAN, FELLINI AND BRESSON

Most Eastern European directors discussed above used symbols in their films to get round political restrictions, just as their Western forebears, Lubitsch and Hitchcock, had to counteract sexual restrictions. Other 1950s filmmakers followed D.W. Griffith, Von Stroheim, Ozu, Ford, Welles and Kurosawa by using metaphor, not necessarily because of political or censorship restrictions, but simply to enrich their work. The Scandinavians Carl Theodor Dreyer and Ingmar Bergman were pre-eminent among these.

The Danish filmmaker Dreyer last appeared in our story in 1929, when his *The Passion of Joan of Arc* (France, 1927) represented the apogee of stylistic expansion at that time (see pages 111–112). This austere and religiously intense director made just four feature films in the intervening twenty-six years, but re-enters our narrative with *Ordet/The Word* (Denmark, 1955), one of the most daring films ever made. Based on a Kaj Munk play, which Dreyer immediately praised for its "astonishing courage", it tells a tale of a family whose mentally unstable middle son orders his brother's wife back from the dead and consequently regains his sanity (183). Cinema had seldom been so transcendental. Whereas closed romantic realism assumes its characters to be mundane human beings, similar to its audience but more glamorous, Dreyer's live in a universe in which a divine spirit is accessible to those with grace or insight. Mehboob's *Mother India* is another portrait of a godly world, but its exhilaratingly expressive and colourful qualities contrast with Dreyer's purity and minimalism. The latter's camera moves between characters and scenes in a way that implies that it can see the spiritual truth behind everyday events. Like *The Cabinet of Dr.*

183
Above: Twenty-six years after *The Passion of Joan of Arc*, Carl Theodor Dreyer depicted spirituality even more piously in *Ordet* (Denmark, 1955). In this scene the standing man orders his sister-in-law to come back from the dead. The subtle halo of white light around the seated man's head is typical of Dreyer.

Caligari, Dreyer's style is not reducible to an individual, humanistic point of view. But, unlike Wiene's film, it seems to represent an ideal consciousness, an overseer. This opposed the mid-1950s secular society trends, but influenced the Swedish director, Ingmar Bergman, and cinema's other great metaphysicians, Andrei Tarkovsky, Béla Tarr and Dreyer's fellow-Dane, Lars Von Trier. At the end of the latter's supposedly secular and modern film, *Breaking the Waves* (Denmark, 1999), heavenly bells appear just as *Ordet* sees a final incursion of the spirit. Von Trier's simple comment that such scenes are shot with a "God's-eye view" could be applied as easily to Dreyer's film. Examples of such pure expressions of Protestant Christian faith are rare in cinema and often dismissed by critics.

The seminal Swedish filmmaker, Ingmar Bergman, hit his stride in the mid-1950s. He was born in 1918 into a strict, Lutheran family and his father was pastor to Sweden's royal family. Like other masters of cinematic claustrophobia, such as Hitchcock and Polanski, the young Bergman was sometimes punished by being locked in a closet. Just as Orson Welles had been, he became entranced by theatre aged five, writing plays and mounting puppet shows. He doctored and wrote screenplays in the early 1940s, started directing in 1944, exploring themes of Sweden's post-war generation gap. *Gycklarnas Afton/Sawdust and Tinsel* (1953) was his first work to adopt the profound moral seriousness which was to become his signature. It was set in a circus and treated its characters as psychologically driven individuals, almost like marionettes manipulated from above, subject to superhuman forces of fate and spiritual destiny. It was a big hit at home, but it was the international success of his subsequent *Sommarnattens Leende/Smiles of a Summer Night* (1955) at the Cannes film festival, which established its director as an artist of world cinema.

Bergman's broader philosophical concerns will be discussed in the next chapter, but mention must be made of *Det Sjunde Inseglet/The Seventh Seal* (1957) and its place in the emergence of symbolism in 1950s cinema. The film's origins were unusual and stemmed from Bergman's boyhood memories of being taken by his father to small countryside churches. Left to explore, he would look at the churches' medieval paintings, saying later of *The Seventh Seal*, "My intention has been to portray in the manner of these frescoes. My characters laugh, weep, mourn, are afraid, speak, reply, question. They dread the Plague and Last Judgment. Our anguish

is of a different kind, but the words remain the same." The director conjured up this fearful mediaeval world by telling a story of a Swedish knight who returns from the crusades at the time of the Black Death, meets Death, plays chess with him and eventually succumbs (184). The film starts with shots of a cloudy sky and a quotation from the Book of Revelation, which talks of a time when God was silent for half an hour and when an

184
Above: Death (Bengt Ekerot) and the Knight Antonius Block (Max Von Sydow) play an allegorical game of chess as the Black Death rages around them in Ingmar Bergman's influential meditation on mortality, *The Seventh Seal*. Sweden, 1957.

angel "took the censer, filled it with fire from the altar and cast it into the Earth. And there were voices and thunderings and lightnings and an earthquake." These images symbolized the threat of nuclear war for Bergman and, like many intellectuals of the period, he had been influenced by the French existential writers of the late 1940s and early 1950s, who had argued that it was no longer possible to believe in God after the Nazi death camps and the bombs in Hiroshima and Nagasaki. What, *The Seventh Seal* argued, if God did not exist? Or what if he was "silent for half an hour"? What apocalypse would ensue? Neo-realism was cinema's sober moral response to the calamities of the Second World War, but a film had never before used extended metaphors to debate the philosophical implications of those calamities. Consequently Bergman, more than any other director since the 1920s, convinced intellectuals around the world that cinema was the equal of literature or theatre.[6]

Moving from Protestant Sweden to Catholic Italy, a near-contemporary of Bergman's was using filmmaking in an equally ambitious way. Federico Fellini was born in north-east Italy in 1920 and whereas Bergman's first symbolic world was the theatre, Fellini's inspiration was the circus, running away to one around the age of seven. Where Bergman found in puppetry his core thematic idea that human beings are worked by greater forces, Fellini found in the circus something more aesthetic – visual extravagance, display and larger-than-lifeness. He became a cartoonist and opened a shop in Rome, which was visited by Roberto Rossellini, who was planning a realist

a strange road I had to take to reach you." At the time of *Pickpocket*'s release Bresson explained this: "There must, at a certain point, be a transformation. If not, there is no art."[10]

So complete was Bresson's rejection of cinema norms that he has a tendency to fall outside film history. However, his uncompromising stance has been extremely influential in some quarters. His films were shown at the Film and Television Film Institute of India in Pune where his anti-expressiveness had a deep impact on the work of 1970s and 1980s Indian director Mani Kaul. The Lodz film school also screened Bresson films and the Polish director Krzysztof Kieslowski saw them. More recently, the

186
Left: Writer–director Paul Schrader used visual and thematic ideas from *Pickpocket* to end his film American Gigolo, in which Richard Gere is the imprisoned Julian Kaye and Lauren Hutton plays girlfriend Michelle Stratton. USA, 1980.

Scottish director Lynne Ramsay claimed that she had Bresson in mind while shooting *Ratcatcher* (UK, 1999) and *Morvern Callar* (UK, 2002). His approach is so profoundly contrary to US sensationalist cinema traditions that it is perhaps surprising to find that he has left his most direct mark on American critic turned director, Paul Schrader. He was so impressed by *Pickpocket*'s incursion of grace into the physical world that he ended two of his own films, *American Gigolo* (USA, 1980) and *Light Sleeper* (USA, 1991) in exactly the same way.

While Bresson was the period's most stylistically radical French filmmaker, other aspects of French film culture in the 1950s were equally extreme. A particular generation of film critics, writing

for the magazine *Cahiers du Cinéma*, advanced arguments that were almost as oppositional as Bresson's films and had considerably greater effect. In 1956, a protégé of André Bazin, the magazine's founder, the twenty-four-year-old François Truffaut, wrote, "*A Man Escaped* seems to me to reduce to nothing a certain number of accepted ideas that governed filmmaking, all the way from script writing to direction."[11] Truffaut (187) was born in Paris, had inattentive parents, left school at fifteen and became obsessed by cinema. He inherited some of the moral force of Bazin's criticism, but added a new 1950s anger to it. In the same year that France suffered defeat in Indochina, Truffaut wrote a now-famous article, "A Certain tendency in French Cinema" in *Cahiers*. A series of notes, the piece touched a nerve by denouncing the literary and script-driven prestige films made in his country at that time. Although it mostly focused on the adaptation of French novels to the screen, it pointed an accusing finger at the work of writers Jean Aurenche, Pierre Bost and directors Claude Autant-Lara and Jean Delannoy, whose impersonal films were technically glossy, lit in a cold, studio style and represented the cinematic equivalent of the perfectly ironed shirt. These films flew the French flag internationally, won awards, were popular with the middle-classes, but, failed to capture contemporary tension. Unlike Bergman, Fellini or Bresson, they did not ask questions about the nature of human life or cinematic symbolism. Truffaut argued that they had no reason to exist; they were dead.

BRITAIN IN THE 1950S

The same criticism could be applied to some of Britain's films. Out of the more innovative directors, Carol Reed's 1950s work failed to match the astringency of his earlier movie, *The Third Man* (1949). This film's executive producer, Alexander Korda, died in 1956, as had the poetic documentarist, Humphrey Jennings, six years earlier. Powell and Pressburger appeared to have exhausted ideas or subject matter in the late 1940s and dissolved their Archers partnership in 1956. Ealing comedies continued to capture the eccentricity of England and make jibes at the austerity measures of the Attlee government, and Gainsborough studios had scored successes with its

189
Left: David Lean, one of the most famous British directors. His work was the antithesis of Truffaut's.

melodramas aimed at women. Ealing's best director, the Scot Alexander Mackendrick, followed in the footsteps of Chaplin and Hitchcock and went to Hollywood, making *Sweet Smell of Success* (USA) in 1957.

David Lean's films were the closest Britain got to the type of filmmaking so detested by Truffaut. He was the dashing English son of an accountant, who climbed cinema's archetypal career ladder, from tea-boy in 1927 to co-directing his first film fifteen years later. Editing rather than cinematography or scriptwriting was his leg-up into the top job of directing and this may explain his movies' polish. His black-and-white films from wartime and immediately after, from *In Which We Serve* (co-directed with playwright, Noël Coward, UK, 1942) to *Oliver Twist* (UK, 1946) were popular portraits of Englishness on a human scale, uninflected by the expressionism of his colleague, Carol Reed. In 1955, his work began to take a more international perspective, firstly in the moving

190
Below: In the second phase of his career, David Lean's cinematic imagination was an epic one. The question remains, however, whether *Lawrence of Arabia* is as perceptive as his more intimate work. UK, 1962.

Summer Madness (USA), about a middle-aged American woman alone in Venice. In the three subsequent decades, his international-ism became something of a trade mark. He directed just five more films, each boldly extending the co-production scale and process which he pioneered: The quintet, *The Bridge on the River Kwai* (UK, 1957), *Lawrence of Arabia* (UK, 1962), *Doctor Zhivago* (USA, 1965), *Ryan's Daughter* (UK, 1970) and *A Passage to India* (UK, 1984), were grand, expensive productions, proudly upholding the "tradition of quality" in UK filmmaking. Lean was lauded and eventually given a knighthood. He had the most exacting production standards of any British director and inspired two of the most successful 1970s American filmmakers, Steven Spielberg and Francis Coppola.

However, a comparison with another director who influenced these American directors reveals Lean's shortcomings. Lean was Kurosawa's contemporary and was born two years before the Japanese director, in 1908. He started directing in 1942, Kurosawa the following year. Both were meticulous craftsmen and liked working on a grand scale, both adapted celebrated English writers, such as Dickens, Shakespeare and E.M. Forster and were considered great editors. Both went out of fashion in the 1970s. But from *The Bridge on the River Kwai* onward, Lean seemed to make landscape shots central to his schema, whereas Kurosawa's visual starting points were buildings or communities. Both directors were interested in loneliness, but in Lean's *Lawrence of Arabia*, his eponymous hero's inner life is dwarfed by the vastness of the imagery (190). Kurosawa connected his characters more to his time by broadening their isolation into the question of self-sacrifice. Though it has been cogently argued that Lean helped rescue widescreen from its "washing line" aesthetic, his imagery became depopulated,[12] more like a travelogue and although Kurosawa also retreated from his central humanism, even when he seemed to have nothing more to say about the human condition he remained interested in pushing cinematic boundaries, experimenting with colour in *Kagemusha* (Japan, 1980) (see pages 401–2) and in his latest works.

Among the critics who attacked the conformism of Lean's commercial revival of British cinema were the quartet behind the foundation of a UK film magazine, *Sequence* (1947–52), which predated *Cahiers* by four years. These were Lindsay Anderson, Gavin Lambert, Karel Reisz and Tony Richardson, who studied, unlike Truffaut, at the most famous universities in the land. They railed against middlebrow films such as Lean's *Brief Encounter* (UK, 1945) in the mode of Truffaut and the French critics, and found more worth in previously undervalued American filmmakers. Where Bazin, Truffaut and their film critic colleagues Eric Rohmer and Jacques Rivette celebrated Wyler, Welles, Hawks and Hitchcock, the caustic Anderson focused on the Western director John Ford. Ford was as laconic as Anderson was verbose and in contrast to the American, who was an outdoorsy man's man, the Englishman was bookish and gay. Yet Anderson understood Ford's poetics, his nostalgia and feeling for landscape, better than any other critic.

Truffaut, like Rivette and Rohmer, became one of the most significant directors of the 1960s (discussed in Chapter Seven). Anderson in the UK beat them to it by making fierce, socially penetrating documentaries, such as *O Dreamland* (UK, 1953) set in an English working-class amusement arcade, and reinventing Jean Vigo's *Zéro de conduite* (France, 1933) as a scathing attack on the English public school system in *If...* (UK, 1968). Lambert also blurred the lines between commentator and filmmaker, assisting and then becoming the lover of Nicholas Ray, director of *Johnny Guitar* and *Rebel Without a Cause*.

MATURE AMERICAN DIRECTORS

In America, Ford, Welles, Hitchcock and Hawks, the masters who had inspired the French and British critics' best writing, made their most mature films within a few years of each other. The industry these directors had known from the 1930s was changing fast. Humphrey Bogart, comedian Oliver Hardy and *Greed*'s director, Von Stroheim died in 1957. There were six thousand drive-in cinemas in the country in 1957, the staples of which were rather tame rock'n'roll, sci-fi and beach movies. No less than sixty-five per cent of US films made in 1958 were produced by independent companies and, with the turn of the decade, the subject matter of these became more daring. Drugs, sex and race became the hot new topics in respectable cinema as well as the exploitation pictures of Roger Corman and Russ Meyer. Television threatened cinema and at the same time provided it with new talents and styles. Minnelli, Nicholas Ray and Sirk were making melodramas that captured the rage and tension of these Eisenhower years.

Against this cultural background in which family life defined social norms, *The Searchers* (John Ford, 1956), *Touch of Evil* (Orson Welles, 1958), *Vertigo* (Alfred Hitchcock, 1958) and *Rio Bravo* (Howard Hawks, 1959) concerned isolated middle-aged men and their complex attachments to women. In this era of American history where families defined social norms, not one of these men belonged to one. Anderson did not consider *The Searchers* to be Ford's best

work, but this is countered by many other critics. The film's central character, Ethan Edwards, played by the director's iconic leading man, John Wayne, is so detached from society that he is more associated with the Western landscape or what the film calls "the turning of the earth" (191). He has been alone too long and has almost become inhuman. His search for his niece, kidnapped by Indians, is fired by rage and racism. Ford invented no new schema in *The Searchers*, but refined his classical style and, influenced by the more troubled psychology of director Anthony Mann's newer Westerns, deepened the characterization in his work.

Touch of Evil's lonely man, Hank Quinlan, was played by the now corpulent Welles himself. Quinlan is a lawman on the US–Mexican border but, like Edwards, he takes the law into his own hands, crossing ethnic boundaries. Whereas Ford had pared down his style, Welles, who was still only forty-three when he made *Touch of Evil*, elaborated his techniques, using innovative and unprecedented longer takes, hand-held cameras, depth staging, zoom lenses and extreme wide-angle filming, which distorted imagery (192). Both

191
Above: The great scene in John Ford's *The Searchers* where, after years of looking for his niece who has been kidnapped by the Comanches, and as snow starts to fall, John Wayne's character says that his search is like "the turning of the earth". USA, 1956.

directors were portraying civilized society, when things are past their best, the law is rotten and people have lost hope, but Welles chose to overwhelm his audience with a sonic and visual density, almost unique in American cinema. *The Searchers* ends with Edwards staring out into the timeless landscape, which has become a metaphor for his inner life. *Touch of Evil* closes with an abject Quinlan lying dead in a dirty canal, casually eulogized by the gypsy prostitute who recalls a time when he was alive.

Vertigo's main protagonist, Scottie, is as obsessed as Edwards and Quinlan and this leads him also to transgress. He falls in love with a woman who apparently dies, sees another who resembles her and cannot stop himself slowly remaking the second in the image of the first. As discussed in Chapter Five, Hitchcock had been influenced by Freud and surrealism since the 1940s and he based *Vertigo* on Freud's theory of socophilia, the sexual desire of looking. Scottie follows the second woman obsessively, the director's trademark

192
Below: Curls on the edges of the frame and expressionist lighting – an image as Baroque as those in Lubitsch's *The Mountain Cat*. Orson Welles plays Hank Quinlan in his film *Touch of Evil*. USA, 1958.

THE SWOLLEN STORY (1953–59): RAGE AND SYMBOLISM IN 1950s FILMMAKING

dreamy tracking shots move with him and reflect his snatched glimpses, wonderment and desire. The film is structurally similar to Keaton's *The General* (USA, 1926) with its repeated storyline, but whereas Keaton used this structure for comic effect, Hitchcock's strategy engenders dread. Will Scottie dare ask her to change her hair to look like the first woman's? Have a grey suit made like hers? Scottie, in effect, wants to sleep with a dead person. Hitchcock had his film designed in pastel colours. Even the make-up and the blue eyes of James Stewart (Scottie) are over-emphasized in a 1950s, artificial way. A dream sequence takes this connection between colour and desire about as far as it can go. In the film's climax Hitchcock tracked forward but zoomed back to ensure that the image stayed constant, so stretching the perspective to approximate Scottie's own vertigo. This was one of the first times this technique had been used (193) and thereafter it became a staple for depicting disoriented consciousness, in films like *Jaws* (Steven Spielberg, USA, 1975).

193
Above: The third of 1950s American cinema's isolated middle-aged men who are obsessed by women. James Stewart plays Scottie in Alfred Hitchcock's dreamlike *Vertigo*. USA, 1958.

John Wayne also played the main character, John Chance, in *Rio Bravo* – a rather different character from Ethan, Hank or Scottie. Chance is an aimless sheriff holding a town against bandits and, like Dorothy in *The Wizard of Oz*, he reluctantly assembles a motley crew to help him in his quest. This consists of a drunken sidekick, a toothless old man who fusses like a mother hen and a cocky young singer-gunslinger. The film endures because of the tenderness and good humour expressed between these men and the team's one woman, Angie Dickinson's bar-room girl. When his drunken sidekick's hands are too shaky to roll a cigarette, Chance does it for him. In the era that produced Sirk's melodramas, this bizarre collection of men in a frontier town at the end of the nineteenth century was the closest mature American cinema got to portraying a family. Hawks remained closed romantic realism's greatest exponent and although it is set in the West, the studio qualities of *Rio Bravo* are as intact as those of his screwball comedies such as *Bringing Up Baby* (USA, 1938) or

To Have and Have Not (USA, 1944). The world might have changed, but closed romantic realism remained. Hawks even had Dickinson repeat some of Lauren Bacall's lines from *To Have and Have Not*. In the Hawksian parallel universe, men and women always spar entertainingly and professionalism, decency and slowness to anger remain the law of the land.

TURBULENCE IN FRANCE

In France, critics continued to agitate at the gates of "tradition of quality" filmmaking. Truffaut wrote, "The film of tomorrow appears to me as even more personal than an individual and autobiographical novel, like a confession or a diary. The filmmakers will express themselves in the first person and will relate what happened to them: it may be the story of their first love or their most recent; of their political awakening ... The film of tomorrow will be an act of love."[13] It is a sign of how complex film culture had become in the 1950s that

194
Below: A former courtesan's tale is staged as a circus spectacle in Max Ophüls' dazzling *Lola Montes*. France–Germany, 1955.

these words conjure up Fellini perhaps, or Nicholas Ray or Dutt, but certainly not Truffaut's other heroes, Bresson or Dreyer. Not even Bergman fulfils this vision of cinema's future, which, taken literally, would be an impossible task for any filmmaker. French moviemaking reflected the multiplicity of emergent new trends, with its personal and philosophical cinema from outside the mainstream and melodramas swollen with tension from within. In addition to Bresson, Renoir, Cocteau and Carné, there were the thrillers of Henri-Georges Clouzot, such as *The Wages of Fear* (France, 1953), which would influence Hitchcock, and there were the comedies of Jacques Tati, whose increasing interest in architecture derived from Buster Keaton.

Max Ophüls, the German director who had pioneered sensuous tracking shots in a similar vein to Japan's Mizoguchi and who had influenced Vincente Minnelli in America, made his most significant film, *Lola Montes* (France–Germany), in 1955. It tells the story of a nineteenth-century courtesan's long liaison with King Ludwig I of Bavaria. Her story is recounted and orchestrated by a circus ringmaster. The film was shot in widescreen with colour as delicate as Kinugasa's *Gate of Hell* (Japan) of the previous year. *Lola Montes* is one of the greatest films in cinema's history because it adroitly avoids all the traps of vacuity and voyeurism inherent in its subject. It is a grand and sumptuous statement about heartlessness, morally detached from the pathetic life it encircles. Peter Ustinov, who played the film's circus ringmaster, compared Ophüls' approach to that of climbing the façade of a great cathedral on which a wristwatch is mounted to help spectators tell the time. The film's abstract quality impresses in the same way as Hitchcock's ten-minute takes in *Rope* (USA, 1948).

In the following year, France's complex film culture witnessed the arrival of the twenty-two-year-old ballet dancer and model, Brigitte Bardot, in *Et Dieu crée la femme/And God Created Woman* (Roger Vadim,

195
Below: Brigitte Bardot as a desirous eighteen-year-old woman who moves into the home of three young men in Roger Vadim's *And God Created Woman*. Bardot's open sexuality and every-day clothes challenged the norm of chic middle-class women in French cinema. France, 1956.

France, 1956) (195). She sexualized youth cinema and was rumoured to have become, with her haystack hair and refusal to dress like a middle-class Parisian woman, more commercially important to France than the Renault motorcar. That year, an innovative lens called "pan-cinor", which had the ability to zoom between 38mm and 150mm, appeared in France and, almost at once, changed the look of location

filming in this country. Two years earlier and within a few months of Truffaut's "A Certain Tendency" article, an eighty-nine-minute film, *La Point Courte/The Short End* was released by a Belgian, Sorbonne-educated, ex-stills photographer, Agnès Varda. Although she had seen few films, Varda structured *La Pointe Courte* around two stories based in the Mediterranean port where she grew up. One was a neo-realist tale about a fisherman and the other about a mismatched

196
Above: Agnès Varda (on one knee) shooting scenes of Mediterranean fishing life in *La Pointe Courte*. Her use of minimal crew and equipment both foresaw the revolution in filmmaking which is the subject of the next chapter. France, 1956

couple. Her editor, Alain Resnais, dexterously intercut between the two stories. Both director and editor were influenced in this by American novelist William Faulkner's book *The Wild Palms*. Their film was one of the first ripples of what would constitute the "New Wave", or Nouvelle Vague, a movement that would flood French and then world cinema in a matter of years.[14]

It is not difficult to see how the period between 1952 and 1958 heralded this New Wave, as Western culture became sexualized and fragmented and the non-Western world de-colonized itself. In a distinct echo of another post-war period – the 1920s – 1950s mainstream cinema was challenged by a whole series of dissidents, intellectuals and artists with personal visions. In the 1920s, these were made up of the German expressionists, the French impressionists, the Soviet montage directors, the naturalists from many countries and the French, German and Spanish avant-gardists. In the 1950s, the dissidents were Bresson, Bergman, Satyajit Ray, Fellini,

because it emphasized the flatness of the canvas. Godard had been part of the magazine *Cahiers du Cinéma's* "think tank". So immersed in cinema were Godard, Truffaut and others that they saw it not as something that captures real life, a mere medium, but as a part of life, like money or unemployment. So, when they became filmmakers themselves, movies were not just vehicles to carry stories and information or to portray feeling; they were also what those stories carried, part of the sensory experience of, say, sitting in a café watching the world go by. In the twentieth century, all the great art forms became self-aware in the same way. Truffaut once asked "Is life as important as the movies?"[2] and while the obvious answer is "no", the question clearly shows how passionate these young men were. Another of their number, Serge Daney, once said he was in cinema like a fish is in water. An Italian director, Bernardo Bertolucci, later added "In the sixties I was prepared to die for a shot of Jean-Luc Godard." Life and death feelings about shots and cuts.

Looking back it is clear that while Godard's explosive sequence was a revelation, it did not begin to explore the full implications of the new language of film. If a shot no longer had to be about getting a fireman into a burning building or getting a woman into or out of a car, then what was it? An expression of the filmmaker's attraction to his actress? Well, in part, yes. Indeed, most of the so-called "New Wave" films that followed on the heels of Godard's were in some way about men looking at women's faces. These younger filmmakers were bored with the high moral stance of neo-realism and the endless raking over the ashes of the Second World War. By taking their new lighter cameras loaded with faster film onto the streets, they could photograph everyday life, women of their own age, without make-up or fussy studio lighting. The subjects of their films were themselves, their erotic imagination, their fragility and alienation.

Godard and other New Wave directors began to explore further. If a shot is not just a slave to action, if once someone leaves the frame you do not have to cut, then a shot is a unit of time as much as action. It no longer said "Here is a scene of a woman sitting in a car which is relevant to the chain of events that make up our story", but "I think this moment in time in the back of this car is beautiful and of itself." In other words the shot said "I think". The fact that a shot is a thought was buried in Godard's innovation. In the explosive decade dealt with in this chapter, John Cassavetes in America, Nagisa Oshima and Shohei Imamura in Japan, Ritwik Ghatak in India, Michelangelo

Antonioni and Pier Paolo Pasolini in Italy, Roman Polanski in Poland, Ousmane Sembene in Senegal and Dennis Hopper in America in their very different ways cut cinema loose from its fifty years of accumulated style and methods. They thought with the camera. Intellectual and dissident filmmakers of the 1920s had paved the way in taking cinema seriously as an art form, 1950s filmmakers took this further. Never before had shots and cuts been so nakedly worshipped for themselves.

The impact of Godard's and Coutard's new liberating schema was first felt in France, before rapidly spreading elsewhere. In 1959 alone, eighteen new directors debuted; an astonishing 160 by 1962. Truffaut himself made his first feature film in 1959. *Les Quatres cents coups/The 400 Blows* did not use jump cuts like Godard's *A Bout de souffle* but was startlingly fresh and worshipped cinema just as much. The story of a twelve-year-old boy who escapes from a children's home, falls in love with film and goes on the run, was based on elements of the director's own life. Like Godard, Truffaut had his film shot with only natural light on real Parisian streets. His story was loosely constructed, in a similar way to the work of neo-realists. However, unlike them, he was not using these techniques to describe post-war problems or sociological trends. Truffaut was interested in the fleeting aspects of experience, life seen from the point of view of a passionate boy who was searching, like many of the New Wave characters, for something indefinable, a certain meaning or exhilaration or transcendence. His models were the humane naturalism of Jean Renoir and the poetic films of Jean Vigo. He even used the screen test of his young actor Jean Pierre Léaud in the final version of *The 400 Blows* because he preferred its spontaneity.

The 400 Blows was a success internationally and encouraged the French film industry to take risks with many other new directors. Louis Malle, Jacques Rivette, Eric Rohmer, Claude Chabrol and many more started directing in the late 1950s or early 1960s and, although their work diverged substantially in style, the contemporary search for meaning was central to them all. The question Truffaut, Godard and cinematographer Coutard were asking, in these first years of what became known as the New Wave in culture in general and film in particular, was a complex version of this simple one: How can we cut through the sobriety of cinema? When one asks this, anything can happen and new, disruptive, comic schema are discovered. In Truffaut's second film, *Tirez sur le pianiste/Shoot the Pianist*

199
Above: *Jules et Jim* used a range of stylistic jokes and devices including, in this scene, short freeze-frames of Jeanne Moreau's infectious laugh. Director: François Truffaut. France, 1961.

(1960), a character says, "May my mother drop dead if I tell a lie" and we cut to the mother falling dead. In his next film, *Jules et Jim/Jules and Jim* (1961), he freeze-frames on the face of actress Jeanne Moreau as she laughs, simply to extend the pleasure of looking at her (199). In the opening sequence in Godard's fourth feature *Vivre sa vie/My Life to Live* (1964), a conversation takes place between a woman and a man in a bar. They talk about love, and the camera takes close-ups of each character. So far everything is normal, except for one crucial detail: the camera is behind their heads throughout, as it was with Seberg in the car in *A Bout de souffle*. The actors are never shot from the front, so the audience never sees their faces. This is as radical a refusal of the most basic, apparently common-sense aspects of cinema and photography as Bresson's work had been. It is also absurd in the way that Buñuel and Dalí's *L'Age d'Or* (France, 1930) was. In *Vivre sa vie* the woman, a prostitute played by Anna Karina, goes to the cinema. She watches Dreyer's *The Passion of Joan of Arc* (France, 1928). Alone in the dark she looks up at the huge silent close-ups of Falconetti as Joan, and cries. Godard reveals to us how human this woman is, not through showing her reaction to a real-life event, but by showing how moved she is by one of the most delicate moments in the art of silent cinema. In yet another scene in the film, the character's joy is expressed in a spontaneous dance routine around a pool table, which is reminiscent of the lighter-than-air musical numbers in *Singin' in the Rain* (Gene Kelly and Stanley Donen, USA, 1952).

One crucial fact should be mentioned at this point: the New Wave was not a political movement. Some of its directors were, or became, left-wing, backing the students and union workers in the militant demonstrations in Paris a decade later. Others, like Truffaut, Chabrol and Coutard, were traditionalists, decrying the messy world of social engagement or actively disagreeing with it. Agnès Varda, whose *La Pointe Courte* (1954) partly heralded the New Wave, belonged to a different group of Parisian filmmakers. Her editor, Alain Resnais, had been drafted in the Second World War and subsequently made a sombre, poetic documentary about the Nazi concentration camps, *Nuit et brouillard/Night and Fog* (1955). Resnais and Varda were more politically committed than the *Cahiers* filmmakers and more interested in the new complex novels being written in France at the time, but his *L'Année dernière à Marienbad/Last Year in Marienbad* (1961) questioned the nature of film editing as much as Godard's *A Bout de souffle*. Set in a grand palace, it features a man thinking back to a year earlier when he may or may not have met a woman who may or may not have been with her husband. The first chapters of this book told how filmmakers, such as Ralph Ince (*His Last Fight*, USA, 1913) found a way of using reverse-angle editing and eye-line matching to clarify who was speaking to whom in a scene, or what they were looking at. *L'Année dernière à Marienbad* breaks all these rules. For example, on several occasions a character will talk passionately to another yet, when Resnais cuts, to what in Ince's system would be a reverse angle, to the listener, no one is there. This is disorientating, but is only the first step in the film's complete undermining of the spatial and temporal logic of editing. Throughout the film, the camera tracks through the grand mansion yet, just when a sense of geography is established, Resnais has rooms connect that surely could not. The same confusion occurs with time. The woman in the film is never sure whether she really met the man a year ago, but neither is it clear where he is, what he is remembering and what he is inventing. Based on a novel by Alain Robbe-Grillet, *L'Année dernière à Marienbad* questioned the very building blocks of narrative cinema as much as Bresson attacked its assumptions about truth and realism.

It was this determination to explode cinema, to shatter schema, that made French filmmakers the most interesting in the world in the early 1960s. Just as Resnais and Godard were re-evaluating editing, the Dane Carl Theodor Dreyer, now working in France, released his follow-up to *Ordet* (1955) in 1964. *Gertrud*, Dreyer's last film, an apparently stagy story about a woman in 1910 who leaves her husband to have an affair, then lives alone (200), was slaughtered by the trendy Parisian critics. In its closing moments, the woman, actress Nina Rode, says, "Look at me. Am I beautiful? No, but I have loved. Look at me. Am I young? No, but I have loved. Look at me. Do I live? No, but I have loved." These are among the most moving lines in cinema. To film them, Dreyer had his cameraman reflect light directly into the lens. When Dreyer died in 1969, Truffaut wrote "He has joined Griffith, Stroheim, Murnau, Eisenstein, Lubitsch, the kings of the first generation of cinema. We have much to learn from them and much from Dreyer's images of whiteness."[3]

This extraordinary passion for cinema felt by French filmmakers was not matched by the general public. Attendances dropped thirty-six per cent from 420 million in 1957 to 270 million just six years later. Principally it was middle-aged and older people who stopped buying tickets, in part because of television. For example, one channel, ORTF, showed no less than 320 feature films in one year. More commercially minded French directors than Godard, Truffaut or Dreyer tried to counteract this trend by filming in a visual style unlike television. Claude Lelouch, for example, had a huge international success with *Un Homme et une femme/ A Man and a Woman* (1966), a simple love story in itself but a landmark in movie history because it used very long focal length zoom lenses almost throughout. These had been around since the late 1940s and were used by Roberto Rossellini in 1960 but, by pushing them to their extremes and famously turning objects around his actors' heads into out-of-focus blobs, Lelouch set the visual style for

200
Below: Dreyer's *Gertrud* bucked the fashion for stylistic playfulness, using, instead, a sober visual style to explore a woman's lifelong search for love. France, 1964.

201

201
Right: The ultra-shallow
focus of Lelouch's *Un
homme et une femme*
influenced the photography
of films such as Robert
Altman's *McCabe and Mrs
Miller*. Notice how Julie
Christie is pin-sharp but
everything around her is
blurred, a look that was
fashionable throughout
much of the 1970s.
USA, 1971.

fashionable cinema of the late 1960s and 1970s. The films of Robert Altman, such as *McCabe and Mrs Miller* (USA, 1971) (201), clearly derive from *Un Homme et une femme*, as do many of the long-lens, widescreen ones of the 1990s, such as those by Michael Mann.

Despite the abrupt changes in 1959, some directors' innovations actually gained momentum as the decade wore on. Where Lelouch created a bold new visual and romantic style, Jean-Luc Godard's growing belief in Marxism and even Maoist communism led him to more radical techniques than even *A Bout de souffle* envisaged. In 1967, in an astonishing burst of productivity, he released no less than five films, including the collage-like *La Chinoise* (France) and *Deux ou trois choses que je sais d'elle/Two or Three Things I Know about Her* (France, 1966) with the shot of bubbles in a cup, which was mentioned in the introduction to this book (see page 10). Referring to Mao's Cultural Revolution and using some of the long-lens techniques popularized by Lelouch, *La Chinoise* is not so much fictional cinema as a daring mix of conversations, readings, arguments, printed words, captions and slogans. Two years earlier, in 1965, *Cahiers du Cinéma* had published key documents about Soviet cinema of the 1920s. Godard used some of their editing ideas and confrontational graphics, mixed them with 1960s sexual freedom and created a cine-manifesto. In 1968, young people, rather like those depicted in the film, staged a sit-down protest at the Sorbonne. By the end of

May, ten million French workers had joined them to demand better wages and working conditions. These events had international impact, especially in the world's most prolific filmmaking country at the time – America.

TECHNOLOGICAL CHANGE AND AMERICA'S NEW WAVE

America, like France, suffered from a decline in cinema attendance in the 1960s, but this did not greatly reduce the takings of the busiest films of the year. Before we get lost in a riot of 1960s innovation, let's not forget that the top box-office grossers throughout the period covered by this chapter were films like *Ben-Hur* (1959), *One Hundred and One Dalmatians* (1961), *Mary Poppins* (1964), and *The Sound of Music* (1965): epics, musicals and cartoons, as in previous decades, and not a jump cut among them. However, beneath this top line, there were signs of change and commitment as fervent as in France. Some of the key figures in the history of American entertainment cinema died in this decade – MGM's Louis B. Mayer in 1957, Columbia's Harry Cohn in 1958, Preston Sturges in 1959, Marilyn Monroe in 1962, Stan Laurel, Walt Disney and Buster Keaton in 1966. Technological advances increased the range of films being made. Cameras that shot 16mm film were made lighter and adapted so that they could be held on a cinematographer's shoulder. A new way of recording sound was invented which did not require the recording machine to be linked umbilically by a cable to the camera. Shoulder-mounted cameras raised the height at which shots were photographed and increased dramatically the range of places from which cameras could film. The sound-recording innovation increased mobility even more by not requiring the sound recordist to be next to the cinematographer while shooting.

Documentaries felt the first impact of these innovations. In 1959, four photographers and filmmakers convinced two US senators running for election that they should allow them to film everything they did in the candid manner of news magazine still photography. The result was the milestone *Primary* (1960). The filmmakers – Richard Leacock, Robert Drew, Don Pennebaker and Albert Maysles – became the key North American figures in what soon would be called "Direct Cinema". A parallel French movement – Cinema Vérité – predated Direct Cinema and had different aims. Whereas the North

Americans attempted to record events objectively, as if seen by an inconspicuous "fly on the wall", as Leacock called it, the French film-makers – primarily Jean Rouch, but also Michel Brault and Chris Marker – intervened more in what they were filming, sometimes provoking situations to reveal what they saw as the sociological truth – what Rouch called the "privileged moment" – contained within them.

Primary was new in a number of ways. It's filmmakers did not stage scenes as Robert Flaherty had in *Nanook of the North* (USA, 1921); they followed neither the low-key poetics of Humphrey Jennings nor the fascist operatics of Leni Riefenstahl; they did not do interviews as Harry Watt had done in *Housing Problems* (UK, 1935); nor did they hide their camera like John Huston in *Let There be Light* (USA, 1946). What was left? Take a famous scene from *Primary*, where one of the senators – John F. Kennedy, who would be President in a year – is in a car. Albert Maysles films him there with a new, light 16mm camera. Kennedy gets out, goes in to a meeting, shakes hands,

goes up a stairway and on to a stage. The camera follows him the entire way and does not cut. What's unusual in that, one might ask? Mizoguchi and Ophüls had both used long tracking shots and the opening scene in Orson Welles' *Touch of Evil* (1958) did the same thing. However, in these cases the scenes were staged, rehearsed, and filmed on dollies and tracks, in sets or cleared spaces. Maysles' long shot of Kennedy was filmed from the shoulder, in real-life, crowded spaces, following Kennedy wherever he went, regardless of focus or lighting. It would take nearly three decades and the invention of small video cameras before documentary filmmakers expanded further the freedoms exercised in *Primary*.[4]

At the same time as *Primary*, and even more daringly, a thirty-year-old New Yorker of Greek origin used the same technology for a fiction film. *Shadows* (John Cassavetes, 1959) followed the story of three African-American siblings living in a New York apartment (202). Director Cassavetes shot on 16mm, used few lights, natural sound

202
Above: 16mm film stock, minimal lighting and improvisation: John Cassavetes' distinctive style in *Shadows* anticipated later American independent filmmaking and was itself derived in part from Direct Cinema documentaries. USA, 1959.

and improvised scenes. He was influenced both by neo-realism and Brando–Steiger Method acting techniques. *Shadows* was one of the first films in what would be called "New American Cinema".

The next trendsetter in New American Cinema's pared down aesthetic is perhaps a surprising one. The country's most consistent mainstream innovator, Alfred Hitchcock, kept abreast of the fashions among film-makers two generations younger than him. At the beginning of the 1960s he abandoned his Freudian quest and colour films, for a black-and-white gothic study in loneliness and serial killing. Hitchcock was too meticulous to adopt the rough and improvisory style of Maysles or Cassavetes, but in *Psycho* (1960)

203
Above: Hitchcock's new visual minimalism and simplified production design resulted in his most successful film to date, *Psycho*. USA, 1960.

he did nothing less than reinvent his already complex career. The veteran director had, perhaps surprisingly, taken to television in 1955, producing, presenting and sometimes directing short macabre dramas. He liked the intimacy and faster working methods of the smaller TV crews, so decided to shoot *Psycho* in a similar manner. As he said to François Truffaut, "It was an experiment in this sense: Could I make a feature film under the same conditions as a television show?"⁵ Where conventional Hollywood was aggrandizing, making epics such as *Ben-Hur* (1959) and *Cleopatra* (1963), he stripped his work of its gloss, had his lead actress wear ordinary clothes and little make-up, and pared down dialogue so that whole sequences had no talking. *Psycho*'s opening scene, which introduces Marion Crane (Janet Leigh), who is having an affair with Sam Loomis (John Gavin) (203), was more sexually frank than any Hitchcock had filmed before. Again, he explained, "One of the reasons I wanted to do it that way was that the audiences are changing ... the straightforward kissing scenes would be looked down at by the younger viewers ... they behave as John Gavin and Janet Leigh did."⁶ No established director adjusted better to changing times.

Hitchcock correctly judged the public taste by shifting to more violent subject matter. A third of the way into *Pyscho*, Crane, who has stolen money to try to start a new life with her lover, stops at an isolated hotel, is checked in by a nervous young man and, having

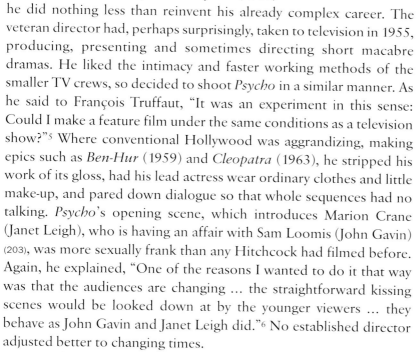

undergone a crisis of conscience and decided to return the stolen money, is brutally stabbed to death in the shower by what appears to be the young man's mother (204). In this infamous sequence, a spare and leisurely film suddenly splinters into Eisenstein-ian fragments. Instead of running long lengths of film through the camera, Hitchcock shot short strips, over seven days, from seventy different angles, resulting in just forty-five seconds of footage. Back in 1922, in *La Roue* (France), Abel Gance had edited film faster than the human eye could perceive it and everyone from Griffith onward had understood that increasing the rate of cutting in a chase sequence or high-drama scene quickens the pulse of the audience. No one before, however, except perhaps Eisenstein himself, had so completely structured a film with this in mind. The film terrified audiences, took twenty times its cost at the box office and established the schema for violent cinema thereafter. Hitchcock was somewhat influenced by the French films of Henri-Georges Clouzot. The former's mastery of film form in turn provided the model for Truffaut in *La Mariée était en noir/The Bride Wore Black* (France, 1968). Several whole careers, such as those of directors Claude Chabrol in France and Brian De Palma in America, have been amplifications of Hitchcock's methods. While the 1960s may in general have been a period when America

204
Below: One of the many trends in cinema in the 1960s was a tendency to increasing violence. The shower scene stabbing in *Psycho* was a landmark in this regard.

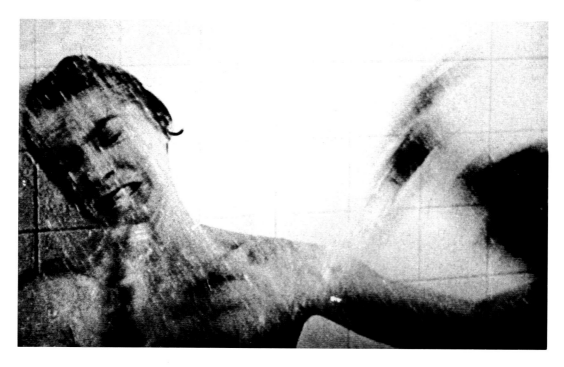

in 1960, a drop from 150 films to just fifteen. Their themes were considered too traditional, too patriotic, even racist and sexist, and only modern reworkings of them seemed to appeal, yet Leone revived them in Europe. He subtly altered their imagery, for example, and his typical building was an Hispanic mission churchbell tower rather than a ranch house. Out of the huge box-office success of *A Fistful of Dollars*, the so-called "spaghetti Western" cycle was born. Once again technological advancement played a part in Leone's success. Image 210 shows a frame enlargement from *A Fistful of Dollars*. At first glance it seems nothing more than a good example of the widescreen imagery that was familiar in Japan, America and

elsewhere from the mid-1950s. However, notice the staging of the image. The foreground and background are far apart, yet both are in focus. This was rare in widescreen photography, and the reason Leone could do this was because the Italians had invented Techniscope in 1960. Techniscope allowed two "unsquashed" widescreen images to be stored one above the other on a 35mm frame rather than one squashed frame. Although this made the result slightly grainier, it allowed shorter focal length lenses to be used.

210
Above: Sergio Leone and his cinematographers Massimo Dallamo and Frederico Larraya challenged the conventional "washing line" compositions of widescreen films in *A Fistful of Dollars*, whose massive success launched the spaghetti Western cycle. Italy–Germany–Spain, 1964.

As Gregg Toland's cinematography showed, short focal lengths lead to deeper space within the image. Leone was the first director to exploit this new technology to the full.

To this marriage of width and depth he added – thanks in part to Bertolucci – an almost mythic sense of the American film genres. His *C'era una volta il West/Once Upon a Time in the West* (Italy–America, 1968) featured grand crane shots, epic music, intense stand-offs, Edenic pastoral scenes, a brutal sense of retribution and an elemental feeling for the differences between men and women. It was about films themselves, the pleasure of watching them for their own sake and the beauty of their familiar scenes, exactly as *A Bout de souffle* had been. Like John Ford's *The Searchers* (USA, 1956), it was about how vengeance can become a man's reason to live. More daringly, Leone extended scenes, such as the opening one and another in a bar, so that the whole film became about waiting. Howard Hawks' *Rio Bravo* (USA, 1958) was about this too, in a way, but Leone's film was abstractly so: for retribution to come, for modernity to come, for the world to change. He had worked with the neo-realists at the beginning of his career and imported their sense of the timeless, de-dramatized moment into his operatic Westerns. In 1984, he made a sister film, *Once Upon a Time in America* (USA, 1984) (211), which mythologized and brutalized the gangster film as *Once upon a Time in the West* had the Western. In it Leone did not so much extend time as fragment it, telling his story out of sequence, with flashbacks within flashbacks, as confusingly at first as *L'Année Dernière à Marienbad*. The effect of these two films is unforgettable. A master Italian filmmaker had stolen America's two indigenous film genres, enlarged them stylistically, made explicit the masculine brutality of each, and filtered them through his pessimistic view of life. Leone's influence was great. The best Western director of the 1970s, Sam Peckinpah, said that he would have been nothing without Leone's example, and another, Stanley Kubrick, claimed that the Italian influenced his celebrated *A Clockwork Orange* (UK, 1971).

Leone was Italian cinema's most commercially successful 1960s director, but even more operatic than his films were those of Count Don Luchino Visconti di Modrone. Like Pasolini he was Marxist,

211
Above: Leone continued to emphasize the epic and brutal elements in American movie genres, for example in *Once Upon a Time in America*. USA, 1984.

Catholic and gay, yet his cinematic instincts were the opposite. Where Pasolini captured the brutal lives of impoverished people with the pared-down techniques of the late 1910s, Visconti was closer to Vincente Minnelli in decorating his frames and elaborating his camera moves to capture the decadence of the wealthy milieu in which he had been raised.

Or, at least, he was eventually, because in the 1930s he left Italy (fifteen years after Mussolini had come to power), designed costumes for Jean Renoir in France, and became a communist, before directing, in 1942, a forerunner of neo-realism, *Osessione* (Italy) (see page 191). In the 1950s he directed opera in Milan and it was only now that he evolved, in cinema, a style as sensuous as Mizoguchi or Minnelli, both of whom he admired. Of the filming of *Senso* (Italy, 1954), his sumptuous account of nineteenth-century Italian history, he said, "Sometimes I was dreaming of opera".[13] His *Rocco e i suoi fratelli/Rocco and his Brothers* (Italy, 1960) returned to that quintessential 1920s theme, a family migrating from the peasant countryside to a growing city. This film and his subsequent international box-office successes *Il gattopardo/The Leopard* (Italy, 1963) and *Morte a Venezia/Death in Venice* (Italy, 1971) extended the tensions of 1950s cinema –

212
Above: Elaborate production design and beautiful colour distinguished another operatic Italian film, Visconti's *The Leopard*. Italy, 1963.

glossy surfaces masking what Visconti called "the burden of being human" – into elaborate portraits of decay.

Swap aristocrats for prostitutes, fashionistas, filmmakers and orgiasts and you get a familiar figure in our story, who also started in neo-realism. Federico Fellini was an international directing star by 1959. *La strada* (Italy, 1954) and *Nights of Cabiria* (1957) had shown how effortlessly he could conjure up poignant cinematic dream states. *La Dolce Vita* (Italy, 1960) was a whole film as vicious as the religious scene in *Nights of Cabiria*, an influential but exhausting denunciation of fashionable people in Rome. *Otto e mezzo/8½*, (Italy, 1963) was rather more. In it a filmmaker, played by Fellini's alter-ego Marcello Mastroianni, struggles with his ideas for a new production and escapes into fantasies involving his wife, mistress and leading actress (213). Though often thought of as purely autobiographical, 8½ is better understood as a work of cinema, like the famous ballet in Minnelli's *American in Paris,* in which the theme is not courtship, but the creative process itself. This is a film about the agony or inadequacy of the conventions of schema plus variation. But not only so. Fellini used the language of fantasy cinema to describe a mid-life crisis – in this case an artistic one. This combination was entirely new.

8½'s storyline dipped in and out of Mastroianni's character's inner life but our final Italian director of the period rejected storytelling more radically than Fellini or any of his fellow countrymen. Michelangelo Antonioni started working in cinema by making documentaries, directed somewhat conventional features in the 1950s, became interested in the American abstract painting of the end of that decade and, in 1960, began a trilogy of films which are often thought of as the most modern of their time. *L'Avventura* (Italy, 1960), *La notte/The Night* (Italy, 1961) and *L'éclisse/Eclipse* (Italy, 1962) each try to express the anxiety of the modern age, as Fellini had latterly done, but use emptiness rather than fantasy as their central idea. This image from *La notte* helps explain (214). Jeanne Moreau plays the rich wife of a writer – Mastroianni again. They go to a party together, meet other people and, at dawn, she says to him, "I feel like dying because I no longer love you."

213
Above: A master director at the height of his powers during a great decade for Italian cinema: Federico Fellini's acclaimed account of creative indecison and mid-life crisis, *8½*. Italy, 1963.

214
Below: Although the film was shot in widescreen, this frame grab still reveals how Antonioni and his cinematographer Gianni di Venanzo framed their actors (here Jeanne Moreau), unconventionally in *La Notte.* Italy, 1961.

This is just a starting point, however. Where Pasolini photographed people square on and mostly in close-up, Antonioni's characters are often to the side of the frame or small in it, or half hidden. When they walk out of it entirely, the shot holds and we gaze at nothing, a concrete wall, the corner of a street, dying light in the sky. When he directs Moreau – the muse of the French filmmakers – he is very specific,

treating her like a chess piece on a board. Her character's feelings, her psychology, are not the centre of the film as were Brando's or Steiger's in America, for example. Space and dead time are as important. The imagery does not express what she feels but what the director feels about her isolation. As if to emphasize this point, the camera often films from way above eye level, looking down on the characters who wander through their lives like figures from Baudelaire. *L'Avventura, La notte,* and *l'éclisse* place their protagonists in a built landscape as Alain Resnais had done in *L'Année Dernière à Marienbad,* made at the same time (France, 1961). But where Resnais was interested in the ambiguities of memory and time, Antonioni looks at the despair and meaninglessness of modern life with the eye of an architect. He takes the themes of the dramatist Ibsen and films them with the uncluttered rigour of the buildings of Le Corbusier. Just a year or so after Godard's breakthrough, Antonioni reduced the action in his films – what the characters do – to just one of many other spatial and temporal elements. His long, slow, semi-abstract shots paved the way for three great European directors of the future: Hungary's Miklós Jancsó and Béla Tarr and Greece's Theo Angelopoulos.

Italy's fellow southern European country, Spain, was still governed by its right-wing dictator General Franco, so the cinematic celebration of lifestyle, freedom and ideas was somewhat curtailed. Nonetheless, powerful and original films emerged. The lightness of early Godard and Truffaut were unlikely to be

215
Above: Marco Ferreri's influential Spanish comedy *The Wheelchair.* 1959.

replicated in a society with such repressions, yet the first historically important work is a comedy. Marco Ferreri's *El cochecito/The Wheelchair* (Spain, 1959) is about Don Anselmo, a widower who, in trying to buy a motorized wheelchair, inadvertently ends up killing his whole family (215). Director Ferreri, an Italian working in Spain, took a social problem – the living conditions of old and disabled people – and mocked it. This unusual combination of realism and irony in

Spanish culture, derived from theatre, was called "esperpento". It is the wellspring of the approach of Spain's premier post-Franco filmmaker Pedro Almodóvar, to filmmaking. He said of *The Wheelchair*, "In the 50s and 60s, Spain experienced a kind of neo-realism which was far less sentimental than the Italian brand and far more ferocious and amusing. I'm talking about the films of Fernan Gomez ... and *The Wheelchair*." It is difficult to imagine his films *Mujeres al borde de un ataque de nervios/Women on the Verge of a Nervous Breakdown* (Spain, 1986) or *Todo sobre di madre/All About My Mother* (Spain, 1999) without the influence of Ferreri's work.

Though sixty years old at the beginning of the decade, Luis Buñuel's ability to unsettle authority was far from diminished. *Viridiana* (Spain, 1961) would become his most banned feature film. Franco himself had invited the director back to Spain from Mexico to make a film on any subject he chose, the first in his native land for

three decades. The result? A knee in the balls to everything the dictator held dear. The set-up seems a morally sincere one: a young trainee nun, whose uncle abused her, invites homeless and disabled people into his house for shelter. They trash the place during a profane meal reminiscent of the Christian Last Supper (216) – this is pure, anti-clerical Buñuel. Viridiana, "rotten with religion", serenely prays to a cross, nails and a hammer. Her uncle dresses in white high heels and a basque. Sexual images abound. He drugs her and lays her out on a bed. Hints of necrophilia, of Hitchcock's *Vertigo*. The uncle represents Franco, the niece is the naive or complicit church. Her gesture of goodwill to the beggars backfires spectacularly. She is patronizing and naive. Buñuel, who has no time for sentimental depictions of beggars, emphasizes their obscenity and deformity. They are just signs of how awful life is, indulging in an orgy to the strains of the Halleluiah Chorus. Pasolini's *The Gospel According to St. Matthew*, made just three years later, was as pro-Catholic as *Viridiana* was anti. Both were influential but it is questionable whether Buñuel's film retains its power today.

Carlos Saura was thirty years younger than Buñuel but his third feature, *La caza/The Hunt* (Spain, 1966), also took Franco as its target. Its story told of three friends who fought for the dictator during the Civil War. Together with a fourth they go rabbit hunting (217), a favourite pastime of Franco himself. The site of the hunt is the former battlefield where the three saw combat in the Civil War. They arrive and start drinking. The temperature rises and the men begin philosophizing. One man says, "The hunt is like life, the strong take out the weak." The shootings of the rabbits are staged like bullfights. Gradually the hunters begin to bicker and themselves become

hunted. One by one they die brutally. The Civil War is never mentioned – for reasons of censorship – but its savagery is attacked. Saura went on to become one of Spain's greatest directors. Sam Peckinpah said that *The Hunt* changed his life.

Finally, Sweden made an important contribution to the modernizing of film language and ideas in the 1960s. Mai Zetterling's *Nattlek/ Night Games* (1966), Vilgot Sjöman's *I am Curious,*

Yellow (1967) and Jan Troell's *Here's Your Life* (1968) were all significant but one made in 1966 by the country's towering director from the previous decade was in a class of its own. *Persona* (Ingmar Bergman, Sweden, 1966) was a real advance, as challenging to cinematic traditions as *A Bout de souffle*, *L'Année Dernière à Marienbad* or Antonioni's trilogy. Where Bergman in the 1950s had explored the relationship between social and Protestant truths, often using theatre as a metaphor, *Persona* was set in a world that was splintering, God was dead and human subjectivity was intangible. It opens with one of the most astonishing dream sequences in film history. Against a white background we see the death of a sheep, its guts; we see inside a projector, a nail going into a hand, a tap dripping, a phone ringing, a boy lying on a slab. Six minutes of this, then the flickering film titles, followed by the story: an actress (Liv Ullmann) dries up on stage, then goes comatose. She is filmed severely, like Falconetti in Dreyer's *The Passion of Joan of Arc* (France, 1927) or with the whiteness of the same director's *Gertrud* (France, 1964). She moves to a house on an island and is tended by a nurse (Bibi Andersson), who is herself troubled. The actress becomes a silent screen onto which the nurse projects her thoughts. Eventually their identities seem to overlap.

Then a shock. The film breaks down and in doing so seems to "release" a series of images which it has been repressing: Charlie Chaplin, the nail through the hand, an eye. Bergman has swapped theatre for a psychoanalytic metaphor for cinema. The ribbon of images is a pure surface of consciousness through which farcical, violent and disturbing sub-conscious images erupt. No director of the era more explicitly related the structure of cinema to the structure and workings of the human mind. By the end of the film there are hints that the actress's trauma is related to the Nazi extermination of Jews and to the Vietnam War. These link *Persona* back to *The Seventh Seal* (Sweden, 1957) which explored post-Hiroshima hopelessness, therefore

218
Above: One of the great works of its era, Ingmar Bergman's *Persona* opens with an astonishing montage of violent (bottom), sexual and mysterious imagery. Later, the film seems to stick in the gate and burn before our eyes. Sweden, 1966.

THE EXPLODED STORY (1959–69): BREAKDOWN OF ROMANTIC CINEMA/COMING OF MODERNISM

Bergman had not completely liberated himself from the idea that cinema is a response to world events. Not until his masterpiece *Viskningar och Rop/Cries and Whispers* (Sweden, 1972) would he abandon this entirely.

THE TURNING OF THE TIDE IN JAPAN

So we have another theme in 1960s cinema: the extent to which filmmakers rejected history or addressed its burdens in their work. Like Ingmar Bergman, some Japanese filmmakers continued to engage with the tragedies of their age. The country's economy took off in the 1960s. The 1950s "Bright Life" had become a roaring success. In 1959, the country renewed a political and trading pact with the US. This was opposed by leftist and student groups, as was consumerism in Europe and America.

Events in the film world paralleled those in France. Japanese cinema since the defeat in Second World War was seen as miserable, sociological, raking through the ashes of national defeat rather than personal and of the moment. An epic example of this was Masaki's Kobayashi *Ningen no Joken/Human Condition* (1959–61) a nine-hour-plus study of the Pacific War and its effects on Japan. Something had to change and radical wannabe directors pushed for that change. Compare Truffaut's demands for a more individualistic and autobiographical filmmaking with this quote from Nagisa Oshima, who would become Japan's most famous New Wave director, "[Cinema] since the beginning of sound ... held that the picture exists to tell a story."[14] Challenging this he argued that it was necessary instead to "create a cinematic method whereby picture and editing themselves would be the very essence of cinema." Such films should reject "the traditional methods of Japanese cinema such as naturalism, melodrama, recourse to the sense of victimization, politicism ... ." Their demands were essentially the same.

Oshima was born in 1932, just three weeks after Truffaut. Like the Frenchman, he started in the film world as a critic. From an intellectual background, he became a radical spokesman for Japan's younger generation. His second feature *Cruel Story of Youth* (1960) (219), contrasts an older sister whose generation demonstrated against America's involvement in her country with her younger sister who "indulges in every kind of pleasure" to express her rage. "We have no dreams so we'll never end up miserable like you", retorts the younger sister's boyfriend. The contrast is ambiguously explored. Oshima, who was only twenty-eight at the time, argues that the older sister's idealism is naive but that the younger's obsession with sex and empty passion is no alternative. The film ends viciously with her boyfriend murdered and her being trailed behind a car from which she has jumped. Oshima was against the conformism in Japanese society but his alternative was hardly a coherent critique, either of it or of the cinema it produced. Eventually he would define his terms, attacking the conservatism of Japan and exploring the disruptive power of sexuality in *Koshikei/Death by Hanging* (1968) and *Ai no Corrida/In the Realm of the Senses* (1976).

In 1961, two years before Yazujiro Ozu died, a former assistant of his made his first significant film. *Buta to Gunkan/Pigs and Warships* was a brilliant portrait of gangsters and prostitutes living around an American naval base in Japan. Its director, Shohei Imamura, was more focused than Oshima from the start. Born into a medical family in 1926, he came out from under the influence of Ozu like a

219
Below: Nagisa Oshima's bleak account of rebellion in contemporary Japan, *Cruel Story of Youth*, 1960.

bullet out of a gun. His subjects, he repeated, were the
lower part of the human body
and the lower part of the
social structure: sex and the
underclass. He shared the
former subject with Oshima
but his view of women was
far more distinctive. His
next masterpiece, *Nippon
Konchuki/Insect Woman*
(1963, 220), was again about
that most regular of international New Wave characters, a
prostitute, but unlike Lola

220
Above: Japanese
filmmakers often used
female protagonists to
explore questions of
modernity and conformism
in their country, but few
did so with more verve
and insolence than Shohei
Imamura in *Insect Woman*.
1963.

Montes or some of Godard's characters, she was wholly sensible, a
bit overweight, not an icon of beauty or a man's dream of what
a woman should be. The rudeness of Sachiko Hidari, who played the
prostitute, her survival instinct, her ability to understand dog-eat-dog
is still astonishing. Decades earlier, Mizoguchi's and Naruse's
women suffered for their men. Imamura's say forget that. His *Ningen
johatsu/A Man Vanishes* (1967) takes women's relations with men
into philosophically new areas. A documentary about a woman
whose husband has disappeared, it mutates into a story about her
lack of interest in him, her moving on and falling for the
filmmaker. In the ending Imamura demolishes the room in which
the filming is taking place, revealing everything as a set-up. *Kamigami
No Fukaki Yokubo/Tales from the Southern Islands* (1968) was
perhaps his best film of this period but in the 1970s, disappointed
by fiction cinema, he moved into documentary. His *Nippon sengo
shi: madamu omboro no seikatsu/History of Post-war Japan* (1970),
as told by a bar hostess, is about a real woman in the mould of Hidari
and the husbandless wife, looking at images of her so-called great
country and reacting to them nonchalantly. Imamura's was one of the
most coherent and original careers in international filmmaking at
this time. His radicalizing of documentary is still undervalued.

RENEWAL IN BRITISH CINEMA

Back in Europe, the new British filmmakers were as dissatisfied as those in Japan. As we have seen, traditional productions in the 1950s were challenged by well-educated, leftist critics-turned-directors like Lindsay Anderson and Karel Reisz. Their "Free Cinema" impetus did not follow the course of French filmmaking, however. British movies like *Look Back in Anger* (Tony Richardson, 1959), *Saturday Night and Sunday Morning* (Karel Reisz, 1960), *This Sporting Life* (Lindsay Anderson, 1963) and *The Loneliness of the Long Distance Runner* (Tony Richardson, 1962) were clearly new and inspired by political ideas and changes in society and art. But the realities they attempted to bring to the screen were not those of Godard, Truffaut, Antonioni, Oshima or Imamura.

For a start the British directors were more interested in male characters than female ones. In the above films, for example, we follow a troubled market stall owner (Richard Burton, 221), a factory worker (Albert Finney), a miner turned professional rugby player (Richard Harris, 222) and a young runner from a borstal (Tom Courtenay). Secondly, despite their own middle-class backgrounds, Richardson, Reisz and Anderson made films about working-class life, mostly out of London, in the north of England. Not for them Godard's capital city of Paris or the autobiography advocated by

221
Right: Claire Bloom and a fiery Richard Burton in one of Britain's first New Wave films, *Look Back in Anger*. Director: Tony Richardson. 1959.

Red and the White can be seen as a whole series of humiliating undressings, for example. At the end, the Red combatants march into a massive line of the enemy singing the "Marseillaise". This gigantic widescreen shot, which lasts well over four minutes, would nowadays be computer-generated but, like D.W. Griffith in *The Birth of a Nation* (USA, 1915), Jancsó dotted men across a vast plain (225 bottom). At the end, one of the soldiers looks directly into camera, saluting with his sword to his face as the bugle sounds. Humanity crashes into Jancsó's icy universe of control and despair. No one in the history of cinema used long takes better to evoke suffering and helplessness. The influence of Jancsó on the 1990s Hungarian director Béla Tarr was profound.

Despite the achievements of Polanski and Jancsó, Czechoslovakia was the most dynamic filmmaking culture in Eastern Europe in the 1960s. This is, in part, because politics in the country liberalized between 1963 and 1968, stimulating a New Wave in Czech cinema. Before this things were difficult and puppeteers and animators like Jiří Trnka were among the filmmakers to flourish. As in Britain, writing was central to the 1960s revival. The fable-like novels of the country's surreal satirist Franz Kafka were rediscovered at the beginning of the decade, while the contemporary novelist Milan Kundera and screenwriter Jaroslav Papousek inspired the new

225
Above: Humiliation and aesthetic rigour in Miklós Jancsó's *The Red And The White*. Below: The film's panoramic ending, filmed in a single shot, lasting more than four minutes. Hungary, 1967.

directors as much as Kafka. Three in particular emerged: Milos Forman, Vérá Chytilová and Jirí Menzel.

Forman's start in life was similar to Polanski's. They were the same age, Jewish, had parents killed by the Nazis and, like many other Eastern European directors in the 1960s, were film school graduates. Where the Pole was interested in the tense humiliations of intimacy, Forman represents another strand in Eastern bloc counter cinema – satire. Again like his British colleagues, whose Free Cinema he much admired, Forman's first films drew on documentary roots. *Cerny Petr/Peter and Pavla* (Czechoslovakia, 1964) (226) used the techniques of Cassavetes – improvisation, non-professional actors, etc. – to tell a

story about a young man who cannot manage his relationships with his father, his employers or his girl. Its observations about youth and love were as fresh as Truffaut's, more pointed than Oshima's. Forman's *Horí, má Panenko/The Fireman's Ball* (Czechoslovakia, 1967) did so well abroad that, disillusioned by the re-invasion of his country by the Russians in 1968, he, like Polanski, went to America, becoming, with *One Flew Over the Cuckoo's Nest* (USA, 1975), *Hair* (USA, 1979), *Amadeus* (USA, 1984) and *The People vs. Larry Flynt* (USA, 1996), one of that country's most prestigious directors.

The most innovative director in Czechoslovakia at the time was Vérá Chytilová. In the year that Forman made *Peter and Pavla*, she released a unique first feature; the appropriately titled *O necem jinem/Something New* (Czechoslovakia, 1963) intercut the lives of a housewife and a gymnast. Nothing unusual in that. Agnès Varda had intercut parallel storylines in *La pointe courte* (France, 1954). Chytilova's innovation was that while the housewife's story was fiction, the gymnast's was documentary. She wasn't merging non-acted film and fictional film style as so many previous directors had from the time of neo-realism and before. Instead she was pointing up the differences. Three years later she made *Sedmikrásky/Daisies* (Czechoslovakia, 1966) (227) which was again about two women, Marie 1 and Marie 2. This time each character occupied the same fictitious world, but Chytilová told the story of their rampage as an experimental montage with distortions and superimpositions. The authorities hated it and, after the Soviet re-invasion of 1968, Chytilová was banned from working for six years. Jean-Luc Godard detested *Daisies* too, calling it cartoonish and apolitical, misunderstanding how Eastern bloc filmmakers sought to subvert Socialist Realism. His own growing Marxism might have produced hollow laughter in Chytilová who took, instead of some political theory, the surrealism of Dalí and Buñuel as her model. *Daisies* became the most important Eastern European absurdist film of its time.

Jirí Menzel started as Chytilová's assistant and extended her comic tendencies in a less abrasive direction, making films that were the gentlest of these three Czech directors. The best known is *Ostre Sledovné Vlaky/Closely Observed Trains* (Czecholslovakia, 1966)

227
Below: Vérá Chytilová's experimental and absurdist *Daises*. Czechoslovakia, 1966.

which, like Forman's early films, looks at the delicacy of love as an escape from duty. In this case the situation was a young railwayman distracted from the rigours of the Nazi occupying force by his attempts to lose his virginity.

While the impetus behind the explosion of style in Western cinema in the 1960s was youth culture and anti-consumerism, the changes in film in Poland, Hungary and Czechoslovakia in these years represent an attempt to move away from a top-down, leftist view of society[15]. While this might sound like the respective filmmakers were moving in opposite political directions, what unified their outlook was an interest in autobiography and the vicissitudes of love. As we move further east into the Soviet Union itself, the socialist realist fortress, we find that there too filmmakers attempted to personalize what they put on screen. There were comedy directors in the Soviet Union in these years but the most distinctive filmmakers found limited freedom away from the authorities by exploring the inner lives of people or by looking to the past.

Take Andrei Tarkovsky, for example. The same age as Truffaut, Oshima and Polanski (twenty-six in 1959) he was, like Bertolucci, an intellectual and the son of a poet. He called the great Russian novel *War and Peace* by Leo Tolstoy his "art school". He studied Arabic and, like all the Eastern bloc directors, attended film school. His second film, *Andrei Rublev* (Soviet Union, 1971) so departed from the official style of film-making that it was banned for six years. Like Pasolini, he believed that "Modern mass culture, aimed at the 'consumer', the civilization of prosthetics, is crippling people's souls."[16] Like Douglas Sirk in the US in the 1950s, Tarkovsky was inspired by Thoreau's book *Walden,* and like Bergman in Sweden he was interested in theology and the role of god in human relations.

228
Above: "Through the image is sustained an awareness of the infinite": Andrei Tarkovsky's majestic *Andrei Rublev.* Soviet Union, 1971.

Despite all these connections, however, *Andrei Rublev* was startlingly, original. Set in the fifteenth century it depicts incidents in the life of a Russian monk who leaves the seclusion of his religious order and finds, beyond its walls, a chaotic world ruled by Tartars (228). His belief in love, community and brotherhood is shaken by this revelation but slowly, through experience, he accepts once more their transcendent importance. Stylistically, Tarkovsky, who knew the work of Bresson, Bergman and Buñuel, attempted in the film to create scenes that, in his own words, were "detector(s) of the absolute"[17]. Interested in Zen Buddhism he creates scenes that, like Ozu's intermediate spaces, are detached from the literal story time of his situations. In his later film *Zerkalo/Mirror* (Soviet Union, 1975) for example, a bird flies from the hand of a dying man in a split second and elsewhere gusts of wind animate landscapes. In the first of these Tarkovsky is depicting the flight of the human soul, while the wind stands for the pervasive Holy Ghost, in Christian belief the third person of the Trinity alongside Jesus and God. He was the first director in our story who could write, "Through the image is sustained an awareness of the infinite; the eternal within the infinite, the spiritual within matter, the limitless given form."[18] Dreyer and Bresson might have agreed with this but neither produced imagery like that of *Andrei Rublev* or *Mirror*.

Tarkovsky's work alone would have been enough to establish the Soviet Union as a major force in the evolution of 1960s film schema, but three other directors released key works. The best and least known of these was Kira Muratova. The first feature she directed alone was *Korotkie vstrechi/Short Encounters* (Soviet Union, 1967), a portrait of a love triangle as fresh as Truffaut's *Jules and Jim*. In this case two women, one a village girl and the other head of the water supply in Odessa (Muratova herself) are in love with a hippy, guitar-playing geologist. If there was a touch of Milos Forman in this, Muratova's next film *Dolgie provody/Long Goodbyes* (Soviet Union, 1971) saw her moving into her own distinctive style. Using repeated dialogue and an acute interest in speech and sound, she captured life in the Soviet Union and the way the state cheapened language and rendered human beings puppets. Their insights led to both these films being banned. When they were finally released in 1986, they were acclaimed around the world.

The Soviet director who suffered most at the hand of the authorities was, ironically, from a part of the Union far from Moscow. Sergei Paradjanov was born in Georgia in 1924, of Armenian descent, and worked in the Ukraine. Like the other Soviet directors he studied at the Moscow film school, VGIK. Where Tarkovsky's films were about spirituality and Muratova's about violations of speech and women's lives, Sergei Paradjanov was interested in the music, painting, poetry and folklore of his native land. His ninth film, *Shadows of our Forgotten Ancestors* (Soviet Union, 1964) was his first to benefit from these non-realist influences. In cinema he admired most the masterly Dovzhenko from the 1920s, who also worked in the Ukraine, and Pier Paolo Pasolini. "Pasolini is like a God to me", said Paradjanov, "a god of aesthetic, majestic style".[19] Although their interest in the roots of cultural traditions unites the two directors, Paradjanov in other ways departed radically from Pasolini's schema. *Shadows of Our Forgotten Ancestors* begins with a breathtaking point-of-view shot of

229

Right: Maverick Georgian director Sergei Paradjanov incorporated elements of folklore into richly visual films such as *Shadows of Our Forgotten Ancestors.* Soviet Union, 1964.

a falling tree, for example. His characters are framed like Russian icons (229). The theme is that of Romeo and Juliet; a love story set against the background of warring families in nineteenth-century Carpathia. The tensions in the culture of the time derive from the fact that the dominant religion is Christianity, yet pagan practices remain. Eleven minutes into the film, a shot is photographed from underneath a daisy looking up; Paradjanov's camera is seldom at eye level and no filmmaker since Welles uses foreground more. Images of deer, scarves and forests recur. After the girl dies we see her and her lover touch in a dream. Not since Fellini or perhaps even Jean Cocteau has such a magical and personal visual world been created in cinema.

"After I made this film, tragedy struck", said Paradjanov. *Shadows of Our Forgotten Ancestors* was everything the social realists hated: personal, regional, celebratory of pre-Soviet culture, sexual, in their word, "decadent". In this he was following, to some extent, the aesthetic ideas of Sergei Eisenstein. He supported political nationalists, made another beautiful film, *Sayat Nova/The Colour of Pomegranates* (Soviet Union, 1969), was arrested on charges of black marketeering, incitement to suicide and homosexuality and, in 1974, imprisoned. Filmmakers around the world protested and he was released four years later. He was imprisoned again in the early 1980s, made three more films, then died of cancer in 1990 aged sixty-six.

Another Georgian, Mikhail Kalatozov, had been making films since 1930. His *Letyat Zhuravli/The Cranes Are Flying* (Soviet Union, 1957) was a brilliantly performed lyrical story about a young girl who marries the man who rapes her but remains in love with her former fiancé, who goes to war. Six years later Kalatozov directed one of the most technically dazzling films of the era, a Soviet Union–Cuba co-production, *I am Cuba*. Using four stories to illustrate the inequalities of Cuba and the build-up to its revolution, Kalatazov and his cinematographer Sergei Urusevsky filmed in a style that rivalled Orson Welles and Greg Toland in Hollywood more than two decades earlier. After the opening widescreen landscape scenes on a barge, for example, they take us to a swinging middle-class pre-revolutionary party in Havana. In a single take the camera starts at the top of a building, descends in what must have been an open air lift, traverses sunbathers and then dives, without a cut, under the water of a swimming pool. The film was re-released in the 1990s to astonishment and acclaim.

230
Above: Paradjanov's *The Colour of Pomegranates* was even more arresting than *Shadows of our Forgotten Ancestors*. Soviet Union, 1969.

In the Soviet Union's communist neighbour, China, few filmmakers openly challenged the cinematic norms. Xie Jin, the most important director of the period, was born in 1923 into a family so wealthy that his mother's dowry was delivered on twenty boats. He left China in the 1930s when Japan invaded but went back after their defeat and became one of the Third Generation of directors to study at the Beijing Film Academy. In the 1960s, he directed classics such as *Hongse niangzi-jun/The Red Detachment of Women* (China, 1960) and *Wutai Jiemei/Two Stage Sisters* (China, 1964), sometimes called "revolutionary model operas". The latter is about two girls who join an opera troupe (231), go to Shanghai and become stars. One is seduced by the trappings of fame while the other becomes a revolutionary and forms a women's co-operative. These were studio films of the calibre of Douglas Sirk's, wedded to socialist ideas about fame and collectivity, with no hint of the New Wave. But *Two Stage Sisters* is a great, expansive melodrama and would make a wonderful double bill with Sirk's more hidden social critique.

231
Right: Xie Jin – the most
important Chinese director
working before the Cultural
Revolution – directed the
expansive melodrama *Two
Stage Sisters* in 1964.

Mao launched his Cultural Revolution in 1966, the year after the release of *Two Stage Sisters*. Really a counter-revolution, it clamped down on aesthetic freedom and the cinematic boldness of directors, such as Xie. Both Xie's parents killed themselves in the aftermath of 1966 and he was accused of "cinematic Confucianism", implying an interest in ancient Chinese philosophy which annoyed the authorities as much as Paradjanov's interest in Ukrainian folk traditions riled the Soviets. Xie was given a job cleaning the toilets of the film studio where he was once a leading director. After the leaders of the revolution were deposed he returned to filmmaking with *Furong Zhen/ Hibiscus Town* (China, 1986), a fierce attack on the inhumanity of the late 1960s. In 1997, he made a triumphant exposé of how the British flooded his country with opium, *The Opium War*.

In Hong Kong in the 1960s, producer Run Run Shaw and his filmmakers went from commercial strength to strength. Mixing the choreographed kinetics of Beijing opera with spaghetti Westerns, Kurosawa and Ian Fleming's *James Bond*, directors like King Hu formed a new infectious philosophical-action cinema. Hu's *Hsia Nu/A Touch of Zen* (Taiwan, 1969) will be considered in the next chapter.

NEW FILMMAKING IN CENTRAL AND SOUTH AMERICA

The roster of names of new 1960s filmmakers with fresh visions is already exhausting, but they keep coming. Unhampered by the realities of communism, Central and South American directors were invigorated by the spread of new leftist ideas. As we have seen, Cuba's revolution had taken place in 1959. Further south in Argentina, the father of Latin American new cinema, Leopold Torre Nilsson, made *La Casa del Angel/End of Innocence* in 1957. This was a self-consciously personal film in the manner of Luis Buñuel, whose anti-establishment stance Torre Nilsson much admired. But the gloss of his films was not typical of the work that followed from other directors. Add Italian neo-realism to his work and you get something like Nelson Pereira dos Santos' *Vidas Secas/Barren Lives* (Brazil, 1963). Torre Nilsson and he, together with the new ideas about culture and post-colonialism which flowed from the Bandung Conference, formed the building blocks of Cinema Nôvo, the socially engaged cinema of Brazil which would flourish in the 1960s.

Alongside *Barren Lives*, stimulating this burst of creativity was a sister film, *Dues e o diablo terra do sol/Black God, White Devil* (Brazil, 1964), directed by a twenty-five-year-old journalist and theoretician called Glauber Rocha. Born in the poor Bahia region of north-east Brazil, Rocha was deeply unhappy with the endless musical carnival films made by his country's industry. Brazil's indigenous Amerindian culture, unlike the much more developed ones of Egypt, India or Japan, had been almost completely wiped out by colonialism. The descendants of black imported slaves from Africa comprised two-thirds of the population by 1959. At the age of nineteen he wrote an essay, "The aesthetics of violence and hunger", very much in the spirit of Bandung, arguing that the complex realities of contemporary Brazil needed a cinema incorporating neo-realism's bracing shock tactics.

Black God, White Devil was Rocha practising what he preached. A political Western set in his Bahia peasant homelands, it was

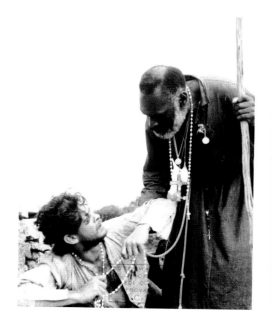

232
Below: One of the landmarks of new Brazilian cinema – Glauber Rocha's political Western *Black God, White Devil*. 1964.

photographed like one of John Ford's films and edited in an Eisenstein-ian manner. The story is about a cowboy who kills his greedy boss, becomes an outlaw and, together with his woman, follows a strange black Christian revolutionary preacher (232). En route he meets a wandering bounty hunter, Antonio Das Mortes, who will feature in later Rocha films. Forty minutes into the film a bravura scene reveals Rocha's approach. The cowboy, Manuel, heaves a rock onto his shoulders and agonizingly edges up a mystical mountain with it, accompanied by the preacher. Cut to an ecstatic scene. Someone shouts "the sun is made of gold". Manuel's wife writhes. Manuel is told to bring her to the preacher. "Tomorrow a golden rain will fall and the earth will turn into the sea." The preacher kills their child silently, making a sign of the cross on its head with its own blood. Then Antonio das Mortes shoots all the preacher's followers. He says he wants a world without gods or devils. At the end of the film a troubadour sings "A world badly divided cannot produce good ... the earth belongs to man, not god or devil." Rocha's complex message is that "violence is normal when people are starving"[20] and that religion will not address his country's problems.

234
Above: An intellectual ruminates on love, life and revolution in one of the great sixties essay-films, *Memoirs of Underdevelopment*. Director: Tomas Gutiérrez Alea. Cuba, 1968.

In 1964, a military coup in Brazil reduced freedom of expression. Five years later Rocha and another important director, Ruy Guerra, left the country and, in effect, ended the Brazilian New Cinema movement. Rocha died in Rio in 1981, aged just forty-three, but, together with Guerra and others, he had found a way of marrying innovative cinematic schemas to anti-colonialist ideas in a way that inspired cinema throughout the Third World.

Early Eisenstein, in particular, was an influence well beyond Glauber Rocha. Santiago Alvarez was a Cuban who studied in the US, joined the Cuban Communist Party and worked at the island's influential film school, ICAIC, which was started after the revolution. A documentarist, his eighth film, the short *Now* (Cuba, 1968), is a striking example of ICAIC's radicalism. Taking Lena Horne's title song as its only sound element, Alvarez edits it to images of black protest and police brutality in the USA. As Horne insists on equality "Now, Now, Now", events at civil rights demonstrations accelerate and American lawmen use more and more force (233). *Now* has real power and can be seen as a forerunner of music video techniques in the 1980s and since.

One of the first and most important feature films to come out of ICAIC was *Memorias del subdesarrollo/Memories of Underdevelopment* (Cuba, 1968). Perhaps surprisingly, this is a film as uncertain and dithery about revolution as *Now* was assured in its targeting of the civil rights atrocities of Cuba's enemy, America. Set in Havana in 1961 it tells of an intellectual whose woman leaves him and who is left alone listening to their taped conversations, thinking aloud, asking what is the meaning of life. Like Alvarez and Godard in France by this time, its director, Tomas Gutíerrez Alea, used authentic photographs of political events in his film[21]. Alea had studied in Italy in the 1950s, knew the lessons of neo-realism inside out but incorporated them into a more ambitious, personal essayistic style. The structure is the free-flow of the intellectual's thoughts, which roam between his personal life and that of the island. He considers the role priests and philosophers played in the subjugation of people before the revolution. The "underdevelopment" of the title seems to refer to his own "inability to relate to things, to progress". As we hear the character think, we see Antonioni-like slow pans through empty spaces at one moment, hand-held camera shots in crowd scenes the next. Eventually he is accused of raping a girl but is set free. *Memoirs of Underdevelopment* is one of the best examples of the 1960s film collage, the driving force of which was not narrative but the search for meaning. Nowhere in the world were these types of films as popular as the more traditional closed romantic realist ones, where story problems were encountered and solved in parallel universes with people like us but more glamorous, but for the first time in film history, they represented a significant alternative.

TRIUMPHANT BEGINNINGS IN IRAN AND SENEGAL.

The dominant art form in Iran in the twentieth century so far had been writing. In the first three decades of the century, during the silent period in Western cinema, an extraordinary range of Persian poets emerged. Then around the mid-1930s, modern Iranian fiction came to the fore. By contrast, no important indigenous films were made until the 1960s in the country which screened the first Lumière films, a year after they were made, in the Shah's palace in Tehran. The first, a short documentary directed by the female poet Farough Farrokhzad, was perhaps the single most

235
Below: Farough Farrokhzad's *The House is Black*, a documentary portrait of a leper colony, was the first indigenous Iranian film and is the only instance where a nation's first filmmaker was a woman. 1962.

auspicious initial step taken by any film culture. *Khaneh Siyah Ast/The House is Black* (Iran, 1962) was a film about a colony of people with leprosy (235), simply shot in black and white and given a poetic commentary by Farrokhzad herself. What really set the tone for much of Iranian cinema thereafter was this film's sincerity of tone, its deep humanity and its attempt to move beyond simple

description. There was a timelessness about these people's lives, and an economy which turned scene after scene into something like a hieroglyph.[22] *The House is Black* was a key influence on the spare Iranian poetic cinema of the 1990s and, in particular, on the director Samira Makhmalbaf whose *Sib/The Apple* (Iran, 1998) tells the story of two girls imprisoned at home for their own safety by their father. Two things were unique about this great film, which was written and edited by the director's father, Mohsen. The first was that most of the parts were played by the real people in question. The second was that its director was eighteen years old.

236
Above: Ousmane Sembene's *The Black Girl*, the first black African fiction feature made by a black person. It told of a young Senegalese woman (left) who is forced into service for a white French family, and eventually kills herself. Senegal, 1965.

Three years after *The House is Black*, another country entered the history of cinema. *La Noire de . . ./The Black Girl* (Senegal, 1965) was not only the first indigenous film made in Senegal in West Africa, it was the first black African film ever made by a black person. There had been Egyptian films for many years, of course, a film studio in Cairo and important directors like Youssif Chahine. Decolonialization in sub-Saharan Africa left Africans with the question, What sort of art – and film – do we want to make ourselves? In recent years there had been what was called "negritude" – blackness asserted with white, European intellectual ideas – but this itself was a kind of colonialism. *The Black Girl* was the first black African feature film to break with the tradition of negritude and begin to improvise an indigenous voice.

To say this implies that its director, Ousmane Sembene, started with a blank sheet, with no schema whatsoever, but this is not true. After nearly seventy years of filmmaking, this was conceptually impossible. Sembene was a Muslim, a former bricklayer, lived in the south of France for a while, and joined the French Communist Party. He had seen and absorbed many films. In the mid-1950s he published an autobiographical novel and became a major cultural figure. Dissatisfied with the small readership for his novels he went to Moscow in 1962, studied film with the same teachers as Muratova and others and returned to make *The Black Girl*. Using the simplest of camera techniques, touches of John Ford in his compositions, and very basic sound equipment, he told the story of a young Senegalese woman who becomes a servant in a white household (236), is forced to move to France with the family, becomes desperately lonely and eventually commits suicide. To internalize the film, he used an interior monologue by the girl. To separate this from the outside world so dominated by her bosses, the thoughts are spoken by a different actress. This was new and allowed the layers of her life to become central to the story. Sembene's pioneering work inspired other directors. The Tunisian critic and filmmaker Ferid Boughedir, for example, called *The Black Girl*, "Incredibly, powerfully moving, beautiful, dignified, humane and intelligent." Sembene would go on to make some of the most important African films of the 1970s.

INDIAN TRADITIONS AND NEWCOMERS

Black Africa was taking its first cinematic steps, but in India the situation was more complex. Established directors did some of their best work and new filmmakers emerged. The country's main film school, the Film and Theatre Institute of India (FTII) was established in 1960 and became a focal point and think tank for those who wanted to experiment with Indian film style. Radical Bengali director Ritwik Ghatak taught there from 1966, introducing the films of the neo-realists, Bresson, Renoir and Welles to the undergraduates. Ghatak himself had melded Indian melodramatic and mythic traditions with a rigorous interest in film language in 1960 in *Meghe Dhaka Tara/The Cloud-capped Star*.

The pupil of his who most extended the language of Indian cinema was Mani Kaul. His first feature *Uski Roti/A Day's Bread* (1969) took Ghatak's interest in how lenses create screen space to new heights. Using the story of the strained relationship between a bus driver and his wife as a starting point, Kaul filmed with great

237
Left: The most stylistically
innovative Indian film of
its period: Mani Kaul's
A Day's Bread. 1969.

forethought. Where Bresson always stuck to a 50mm lens, Kaul used a 28mm one to balloon the space around the driver and a 135mm one to flatten it to nothing, rendering almost everything fuzzy and ungraspable. *A Day's Bread* was India's *A Bout de souffle*, its *Black God, White Devil*, its *Andrei Rublev*. Like each of these it challenged a well-established film industry with new ideas about form.

Of course that industry was not homogeneous. Just as France in the 1940s and 1950s had modernist forerunners Bresson, Cocteau and Tati, as well as the tradition of quality films, so India had Ghatak and Satyajit Ray as well as Guru Dutt, Mehboob and its mainstream All India directors. Ray continued to be the only director from the country known and admired by the West. He remained firm in his dismissal of the escapism of All India films, but his 1960s work, far from following the fashion for experiment like Ghatak or the younger Kaul, became further absorbed by microcosms, unities of time and place, and psychological nuance. This is important because it explains his alienation from, and disappointment with, Indian film. Take this comment he made in 1982: "The concept of an art form existing in time is a Western concept, not an Indian one. So in order to understand cinema as a medium, it helps if one is familiar with the West and Western art forms. A Bengali folk artist, or a primitive artist, will not be able to understand cinema as an art form."[23] This is astonishing because Ray is saying that not only is the film camera a Western invention but its sense of what time is, is too. That he believed this in the early 1960s is clear from his films *Devi/The Goddess* (1960), *Teen kanya/Two Daughters* (1961) and, what many consider his best, *Charulata/The Lonely Wife* (1964). Just when Godard was fragmenting time, Warhol was numbing it, Alain Resnais was rendering it ambiguous, Jancsó was intensifying it and Tarkovsky was transcending it, Ray in each of these films was again emphasizing its real and classical properties against the grain of the films of his country. Like the novelist and songwriter Tagore he took enclosed worlds, describing them with minimalist detail. Tagore said that the whole world was reflected in the convexity of a dew drop and each of these films is just such a drop.

The Goddess (see page 491) is a beautiful film in which Sharmila Tagore – one of the greatest actresses in the world at this time – plays a woman whose father-in-law dreams that she is a Hindu goddess. People believe him and she is anointed in a fabulous ceremony. The imagery of the film, photographed by Subrata Mitra, is among the finest in world cinema. The theme is that of the clash between ancient Sanskrit culture and modern enlightenment values. In a manner similar to Fellini's *Nights of Cabiria* (Italy, 1957), it is an attack on religious fervour, but where the Italian film undergoes a series of stylistic transformations, *The Goddess* is consistent in its miniaturism. *Two Daughters* is, even more so, a mass of gripping details about a new postman from the city who comes to work in a tiny village. He gets to know his orphaned child assistant, reads Walter Scott novels, contracts malaria and leaves. *Charulata* is about the bored wife of an upper-class anglicized publisher. Ray's favourite among his films, and his most literary, it is also about how writing might free this woman's soul. It is perhaps appropriate that a film about repression is itself so contained physically and temporally.

THE NEW WAVE IN THE US AND THE DECLINE OF THE STUDIO SYSTEM

As we saw earlier in this chapter, at the start of the 1960s some American filmmakers began to beat new paths. The documentary *Primary* used up-to-the-minute equipment; John Cassavetes adapted the rough visual style that resulted; Alfred Hitchcock employed TV techniques in a story about ordinary people, and Andy Warhol turned gay desire into a static trance.

It wasn't until later in the country's momentous decade, however, that changes in world cinema in general, together with continuing social upheaval, began to influence more conventional filmmaking norms. By 1968, the Kennedy brothers were dead, Martin Luther King had made his famous civil rights speeches and the Vietnam protests had begun. In the world of cinema, no less than 1,500 film courses were now being taught throughout the country. European films were shown on campuses and in specialist cinemas.

A small but prodigious independent film company mopped up some of the social and stylistic ideas of the time and mixed them into its ultra-low-budget features. Influenced by Elvis, pop music, Marlon Brando in *The Wild One* (1954) and the emerging drug culture, American International Pictures (AIP) cornered the market in so-called "exploitation" teen pictures, cheap horror movies, sci-fi and biker films. Its most dynamic producer, Roger Corman, came from Los Angeles, studied literature for a while at Oxford in England, was obsessed by gothic writer Edgar Allan Poe, started producing in 1954, offered opportunities to untried directors, was strict about budget and keen on regular flashes of nudity in his films, but otherwise allowed his novice directors to smuggle leftist ideas and fancy European techniques into their films. This combination of generic formula and intellectual and stylistic openness was opportunistic on his part but historically important. Among the untried talents Corman worked with were Francis Coppola, John Sayles, Martin Scorsese, Dennis Hopper, Brian De Palma, Robert De Niro, Jack Nicholson, Jonathan Demme and Peter Bogdanovich (238) – the most important figures in US film of the 1970s and beyond. In his eagerness to latch onto something new, to flirt with edgy youngsters, Corman played a crucial role in modernizing American cinema.

Most of these will be discussed in the next chapter but to capture the flavour of invention on the hoof at AIP, to illustrate how its creative crassness helped plug America into the revolution sweeping through world cinema, let's take Peter Bogdanovich's first film. Finding that he had horror stalwart Boris Karloff on a contract for two days longer than

238
Below: Some American production companies started to combine the countercultural trends of the 1960s with ultra-cheap genre and exploitation techniques. Foremost among these was American International Pictures whose Roger Corman (left) became the doyen of rebellious B-movies for years to come.

he thought, Corman asked the young movie critic Bogdanovich to make up a story, film with Karloff for the two days, take twenty minutes from another Karloff picture Corman had made, shoot for another ten days without Karloff, and make a movie out of the result.

Bogdanovich had a better idea. He decided to make a film about a horror movie actor, Karloff, who notices that the world around him is changing and that the violence of real life makes his cheapie-style horror look stupid (239). Bogdanovich wrote a script. In it, Karloff says "I'm an anachronism ... the world belongs to the young." The director's inspiration was to interweave this story of the end of a movie era with a serial-killer narrative based on a real-life incident two years earlier when a Texan shot his wife, his mother and sixteen other people.

Released in 1968, after the Bobby Kennedy assassination, after the Martin Luther King assassination and at a time of social change, the resulting film, *Targets*, brilliantly explored the relationship between life, violence and cinema. Take one scene in the assassin's home, when he starts the killings. The 1960s pastel house, the knitting-pattern nuclear family, the way he calls his father "Sir" and the symmetry of the pictures, creates a stifling portrait of an authoritarian, anaemic, sexually repressive world which is bound to erupt. In the first shooting the camera moves in slowly, there is almost no sound, you hold your breath.

A year earlier Corman himself had directed *The Trip* (1967) which was written by Jack Nicholson and told of a TV director who takes the drug LSD. The TV man was played by Peter Fonda, the counter-cultural son of John Ford stalwart actor Henry Fonda. A drug pusher in the film was played by Dennis Hopper. The film included manic trip scenes, visual distortions, overlays and rapid editing: impressionism five decades after Germaine Dulac. It looks somewhat dated today, but the whole team shared the same world view and enjoyed shocking Middle America.

Hopper, Fonda and Nicholson ditched Corman to make one of the most famous, controversial and era-defining films of the late 1960s. Biker movies were nothing new but *Easy Rider* (1969) had its two protagonists, Fonda and Hopper, smuggle cocaine in their bikes before cocaine was a well-known drug. It showed the emotions experienced while tripping. Influenced by short avant-garde films by the director Bruce Conner,[24] the movie ends in tragedy — the two bikers are killed by conservative duck hunters. Hopper, who wrote and directed and had long had one foot in the art world, turned the film into an encyclopedia of modernist techniques. He used 17mm lenses to photograph the trip sequences; taunted his fellow actor Fonda about the death of his mother to elicit candid emotions from him; moved from one scene to the next by cutting to it, then back, then to it, then back again, before finally settling on it.

Yet these innovations didn't put audiences off. Why? Because young people were impatient with old-style filmmaking and its associations with the mainstream and conformism. Because Hopper and Nicholson had clearly smoked marijuana before doing scenes. More importantly, because *Easy Rider* was about endings. Fonda's character has a premonition that their road-movie-on-bikes life cannot go on for ever. When they are killed, Middle America gets its own back. Martin Luther King's death had had a sobering effect on young American radicals' dreams of utopia, but worse was to come. In the year of the film's release, the Polish director Roman Polanski got a call to say that his pregnant wife Sharon Tate and three of his friends had been murdered in their Los Angeles home. The news went around the world. Only one year later, in 1970, two of the era's musical heroes, Jimi Hendrix and Janis Joplin, would both die of drug overdoses aged just twenty-seven. A whole series of endings that *Easy Rider* somehow prefigured.

It wasn't only low-budget cinema that was portraying new lifestyles, exploding the old norms of closed romantic realism and anticipating the end of good times. In *The Graduate* (Mike Nichols, 1967), a well-off student played by Dustin Hoffman is as directionless, as paralyzed in the headlights of social change, as were Fonda and Hopper. The film was brilliantly written and photographed in ironic pastels, like the home scenes in Bogdanovich's *Targets*. And like the latter it had a curious reverence for the past. Yet its ending was as open as closed romantic realism is closed. The student and his girl depart on a bus, yet their facial expressions are far from happy. *The Jungle Book* was the most commercially successful film of the year in 1967, but the studios were in crisis. Most of their traditional films flopped, yet *The Graduate* took ten times its budget at the box office. Such returns speak to money men.

This includes those who were now running Warner Bros. Since the 1930s the studio had produced gangster films, flirting with the amorality of this American genre but usually denouncing the protagonists in the end. In 1967, they blew this balance apart with a movie that, like *The Graduate,* took ten times its cost. They hired a former TV director, Arthur Penn, to direct *Bonnie and Clyde,* [25] which told the story of two 1930s romantic bank and gas station

240
Right: *Bonnie and Clyde* was a new kind of gangster movie because its title characters were counter-cultural rebels and its style was influenced by the French New Wave. Director: Arthur Penn. USA, 1967.

THE EXPLODED STORY (1959–69): BREAKDOWN OF ROMANTIC CINEMA/COMING OF MODERNISM

robbers who became media stars and who died in a hail of bullets (240). Like Nichols, Penn mixed nostalgia for old gangster movies with modern devil-may-careness. He pushed stylistic questions further, however, borrowing ideas about pacing and freeze-framing from Truffaut. When *Bonnie and Clyde* die operatically, in slow motion, at the end, the tone is less of a come-uppance than it might have been with Cagney or Edward G. Robinson and his moll – although these were not straightforward deaths either. Instead, it is closer to the ending of *Easy Rider*, which it pre-dates by two years. The gangsters here were rebels and rebels get it in the neck.

The final ending of historical importance at this time took place in a science fiction film, a tried and trusted drive-in film genre. *2001: A Space Odyssey* (UK–USA 1968) was directed by Stanley Kubrick, whom we last met in the mid 1950s with *The Killing* (USA, 1956) and *Paths of Glory* (USA, 1957). After his box-office hit *Spartacus* (USA, 1960), which was not typical of his work, he moved to the UK in 1961 and, with the astringent satire *Dr Strangelove or How I Learned to Stop Worrying and Love the Bomb* (USA, 1964) achieved his bleakest, most fully realized film to date.

2001: A Space Odyssey, from a short story by Arthur C. Clarke, took things further, however. Starting with a dawn-of-man sequence in which apes play and fight, the film suddenly jumps to the year 2001 in perhaps the most audacious edit in film history. An ape throws a bone into the air (242 overleaf). It rises and rotates in slow motion. Then a soundless cut to a spaceship gliding similarly. From the earliest years in the evolution of editing, cuts have been used to shorten time. Only occasionally, in suspense cinema or in Sergei Eisenstein's Odessa steps sequence in *Battleship Potemkin* (Soviet Union, 1925), has the opposite been the case. Here Kubrick not only shortens time but elides the whole of human history. He uses the functional economy of a cut to remove from his film virtually everything that has ever been thought or done.

Thereafter, the future sequence is concerned with a black monolith that has been found on the moon. We saw a similar one in the dawn-of-man prologue. A year later two astronauts sent to investigate it are tyrannized by a psychologically sophisticated computer,

HAL 9000. One of them tries to get to the source of the mystery of the monolith but in doing so seems to travel through time and has mind-altering experiences. Kubrick's realization is astonishing throughout: the backgrounds in the ape sequences were still images projected onto a highly reflective new substance, Scotchlite; he moved the camera in grand rotations to create the sense that in space no particular direction is upward; to portray a pen floating through mid-air he and his special effects expert, Douglas Trumball, simply attached it to a pane of glass then gently rotated the glass. The ending

FREEDOM AND WANT SEE (1969—79)
Political cinema around the globe and the rise of the blockbuster in America

8

At first the momentum of 1960s innovation continued into the 1970s. The bandwagon of explicitly personal filmmaking, of sexual freedom, references to earlier cinema, of abstraction, of ambiguity, quest for meaning, open-endedness, self-consciousness, of the idea of a shot as a unit of time, all those giddy tropes of 1960s counter-cinema kept on rolling. Looking back now we can see that their days were numbered, but at the time, few could tell.

One film that captured the complexity of the New Wave's decline was *La Maman et la putain/The Mother and the Whore* (France, 1973). Directed by troubled young cinéaste Jean Eustache, it was a three-and-a-half-hour dissection of a love triangle between Truffaut's and Godard's iconic actor Jean-Pierre Léaud, his girlfriend (Bernadette Lafont) and a nurse (Françoise Lebrun) with whom he begins an affair. Its settings were the cafés and apartments where Godard's philosophical dreamers of a decade or more earlier had debated love. By now the debate has become an unstoppable torrent of words. The life of talk in cafés and drifting love affairs has become not only an addiction for young Parisians of the early 1970s, but almost a disease. Léaud's hyperactive performance and Eustache's bravura writing and directing turned *La Maman et la putain* into an epic of disquiet and regret.

Another French-language film that extended the ideas of the new wave was *Jeanne Dielman, 23 Quai du Commerce 1080 Bruxelles* (Belgium, 1975), the third feature of the Belgian director Chantal Akerman. Born in 1950 to Jewish parents, she studied in Paris, made her first film in 1968 and worked in a porn theatre in New York in the early 1970s, later incorporating elements of sexual abasement into her films. *Jeanne Dielman* was, like the dedramatized kitchen scene with the maid in *Umberto D* (Italy, 1952) (see page 192) extended to well over three hours in length. It recounted two days in the life of a divorcée who sleeps with men for money and finally kills one because she is beginning to enjoy the sexual experiences. Unlike Godard or Buñuel with their prostitutes, however, Akerman never eroticizes Dielman. Instead the scenes with the men are treated in the same way as those of making beds and peeling potatoes: they are shot rigorously frontally like the *Assassination of the Duc de Guise* (France, 1908) (see page 38) without reverse angles. Akerman was taking the stripped-down stylistic ideas of Bresson, Godard and Pasolini. The resulting tableau approach to staging a scene was radical and haunting.

SEXUALITY AND NEW CINEMA IN ITALY IN THE 1970S

La Maman et la putain and *Jeanne Dielman* both sounded notes of pessimism about the sexual revolution of the 1960s. It seemed that the new freedoms created their own problems. However, boundaries continued to be rolled back: France's president said on television that there should be an end to censorship; European, American and Japanese cinema became more sexually explicit than ever before; Indian film featured its first ever on-screen kiss in *Satyam Shivam Sundaram/Love Sublime* (Raj Kapoor, 1978); and in Italy, two of the country's most important directors each delivered a trilogy of films in which sexual freedom was a measure of national health. Where the religious rigour of Pier Paolo Pasolini's *The Gospel According to St. Matthew* (Italy, 1964) had impressed the

Catholic authorities in his country, his "Trilogy of Life" scandalized them. *Decamerone/The Decameron* (Italy, 1971), *Il Racconti di Canterbury/The Canterbury Tales* (Italy, 1972), and *Il Fiore delle Mille e Una Notta/The Arabian Nights* (Italy, 1974) are like three frescoes about the bawdy lives of peasants in pre-modern Europe and the Middle East. Full of sexual japes, scatological mishaps, nudity and phallic symbols (244) the films seemed to argue that only in the past, before consumerism and capitalism, were people genuinely uninhibited. Said Pasolini at the time, "Enjoying life and the body means precisely enjoying a life that historically no longer

exists."[1] His own attempt to live outside modern Italy's sexual and moral norms ended tragically when he was murdered by a male prostitute in 1975.

244
Above: The third in Pasolini's epic, joyous Trilogy of Life: *The Arabian Nights.* Italy, 1974.

Luchino Visconti also lived outside those norms. Where Pasolini focused on times and people who he felt were untouched by sexually repression, his aristocratic fellow-director did the opposite. *The Damned/Götterdämmerung* (Italy–Germany, 1969) (245) *Death in Venice/Morte a Venezia* (Italy, 1971) and *Ludwig* (Italy, 1972) each use a German theme or source material to find something fatal in repressed homosexuality. "To put the eyes on beauty", said Visconti in faltering English in a TV interview, "... is to put the eyes on death."[2] This could be his testament, the key to his pessimism. Visconti died just one year after Pasolini, in 1976.

A generation younger than either, Bernardo Bertolucci's view of human sexuality was less bleak. His first contributions to the story of film were his absorption of Godard in *Before the Revolution* (Italy, 1964) and his mythic screenplay for Leone's bravura *Once Upon a Time in the West* (Italy, 1968) (see page 288). In 1970, he released his greatest film yet, *The Conformist/Il Conformista* (Italy) (245). Set in 1943, during the decline of Italy's fascist regime, it told of a man trying to prove that he is normal and heterosexual. His way of doing so is to marry and join the fascist movement. Under their instruction he assassinates his former professor, a father figure and a decent man. Exploring the relationship between sexual and political repression, this film of ideas was shot like a Gene Kelly musical or a film by Max Ophüls. Cinematographer Vittorio Storaro, an intellectual with theories about the meaning of different colours, became as central a figure here as Raoul Coutard did with Godard and Truffaut a decade earlier. He took the choreographed style of the musicals and melodramas that Bertolucci so admired and applied them with rigour to the director's story. In one scene the camera sweeps upward on a crane as leaves blow in a whorl before it, just as it would on an MGM sound stage. In another, it dances with the actors. Bertolucci's central character, the repressed fascist, was psychologically as imprisoned as Bresson's characters. Bertolucci and Storaro's exhilaratingly liberated filming style was the embodiment of what he had lost.

245
Above: Visconti's trilogy was as grand as, but far more pessimistic than, Pasolini's. Beauty, decadence and despair in *The Damned*. Italy–Germany, 1969.

The Conformist was not only a major intellectual and aesthetic achievement, but one of the most influential works of the early part of the decade. Godard had used dance numbers in films before *The Conformist* but by introducing such visual pleasure into his work, Bertolucci made New Wave filmmaking seductive. The film was widely seen in America and became a touchstone for young directors like Francis Coppola who would later hire cinematographer Storaro for *Apocalypse Now* (USA, 1979). His fellow Italian-American Martin Scorsese saw its mix of thematic complexity and visual utopianism as a breakthrough, a double act of seduction and repulsion. This idea that the surface of a film, its form, could express the fascination we feel for brutality and self-destruction became central to his seminal film *Taxi Driver* (USA, 1976). That film's writer, Paul Schrader, would imitate *The Conformist* meticulously in *American Gigolo* (USA, 1980) (246). Two years after *The Conformist*, the two-way flow between US and European cinema resulted in Bertolucci's *Last Tango in Paris/Ultimo Tango a Parigi* (France, 1972) in which the director made what he called a "documentary" about Marlon Brando meeting Maria Schneider in a room and having anonymous sex with her (247). Once more, it was exquisitely photographed by Storaro, who this time took visual cues from the paintings of Francis Bacon.

246
Above: Bertolucci's stylized account of how repression leads to fascism, was his greatest film to date and widely admired by American directors. *The Conformist.* Italy, 1970. Paul Schrader hired *The Conformist*'s production designer Ferdinando Scarfiotti and had his cinematographer John Bailey emulate the film's lighting (by Vittorio Storaro) in *American Gigolo* (below). USA, 1980.

AMERICA IN THE 1970S

In America itself, the deaths of Malcolm X, Jimmi Hendrix, Janis Joplin and Polanski's wife, Sharon Tate, had a sobering effect on what some saw as the excesses of the 1960s. Four hundred colleges went on strike in 1970 in protest at the Vietnam War and at one, Kent State University, four were shot dead. The Watergate scandal of 1972–74 showed that the Republican Party and the CIA were involved in bugging the Democrat Party's offices. As a result, President Nixon was forced to resign. The artistic influence from Europe, the decline in attendance among older filmgoers, feminism and the debates about Vietnam together produced a film community more divided than at any time since perhaps the witch hunts of the House Un-American Activities Committee in the late 1940s. Even families were split. Actress Jane Fonda went on hunger strike to protest at, amongst other things, Western icon John Wayne's Vietnam film *The Green Berets* (John

Wayne, Ray Kellogg, (1968) in which the Vietcong were vilified and the Americans ennobled. Her father, Henry Fonda, took his friend Wayne's side against his daughter.

Cinemas at the end of the 1960s were closing at an unprecedented rate. Warner Bros. was bought by a company that owned car parks and funeral parlours. United Artists was acquired by a car rental and insurance business. In the early 1970s, 15.8 million movie tickets were sold per week in the US compared to 78.2 million in 1946. The movie industry was more "on its ass than any time in its history."[3] 20th Century-Fox lost $77 million in 1971 alone. MGM survived only because its string of Las Vegas hotels was profitable. Just one in ten films was making money. A sign of how insecure the studios were is that when two of the major television stations, CBS and ABC, started making what would soon be called "TV movies", industry leaders tried to sue them claiming that they were monopolizing by making and showing films, exactly what the moguls themselves had done until they were forced to sell their cinemas.

As far as what actually appeared on cinema screens goes, 1970s American cinema challenged some of the norms of traditional filmmaking. The new films had few heroes or romances, their endings were often ambiguous or left open. The insecurities, social upheavals and new creative influences produced three interwoven trends out of which emerged some of the best American films ever made. The first of these was the dissident trend: the direct continuation of the New Wave challenge to conventional cinema.

247
Right: Bertolucci's account of two people who meet in an apartment for anonymous sex took its visual inspiration from the paintings of Francis Bacon. Maria Schneider and Marlon Brando in *Last Tango in Paris*. France, 1972.

248
Left: *The Last Movie,*
Dennis Hopper's follow-up
to *Easy Rider,* was a
modernist Western in
which local people in Peru
fashion film equipment out
of bamboo (left) to emulate
a film shoot which has just
taken place in their
community. This most
Godardian of American
films flopped at the box
office and was critically
mauled. USA, 1971.

The second was assimilationist: many filmmakers found a way of applying new ambitious filmmaking schemas within traditional studio genres. The third was a revival of the pure entertainment of the 1930s and 1940s, and changed not only the American film industry, but much of Western production and exhibition.

The standard-bearer of the dissidents was Dennis Hopper. The success of *Easy Rider* (1969) convinced people that he had the Midas touch, that he more than anyone could judge what the new young audience wanted. Hopper lived the life of the dissident, growing his hair long, drinking all day, moving to the desert in New Mexico. His follow-up to *Easy Rider*, the prophetically entitled, *The Last Movie* (USA, 1971), was a hate letter to American film. It had a brilliant premise: after a Western is filmed in Peru, a stuntman stays on and gets involved with the local community (248). They, in turn, deal with the legacy of the filming by treating it almost as if it was a god that visited, making iconic models of the equipment out of bamboo and, eventually, emulating the staged violence that they witnessed. If it were not for the credits at the beginning of the film, one might have assumed that it was directed by Jean-Luc Godard. Hopper fragments his story, starting at the end, making scenes within scenes, even doing the most Godardian thing of splicing in a caption saying "Scene missing". The critics called the result "hateful", "a fiasco", "a disaster", "pitiful" and "an embarrassment". It went too far for them. They had to rearrange the film in their heads after seeing it. Hopper had blown it. One journalist claimed that as a result he – Hopper – cried every night.

Dissidence did not have to be box-office poison, however. *M*A*S*H* (Robert Altman, 1970) was as bitter about war films as *The Last Movie* was about Westerns, but was a huge box office success. Set during the Korean War, it tells of a group of front-line surgeons who perform grisly operations while behaving like aristocrats. Between bouts of bloody surgery they mix cocktails, play golf, converse wittily and avoid entirely any emotional engagement with the tragedies that surround them (249). It deflated the hauteur of real officers but also expressed the audience's more general disdain for the world of the military. Its irreverence derives from its screenwriter, Ring Lardner Jnr, who had been blacklisted for alleged communist sympathies. It was the first mainstream American film to ridicule religion and reputedly the first to use the word "fuck". Like Dennis Hopper, its forty-five-year-old director, Robert Altman, was born in the WASP (White Anglo-Saxon Protestant) mid-west of America. Having served in the Second World War, he worked on industrial films, made an exploitation movie and became interested in sound. What is striking about *M*A*S*H*, his first successful film, is how detached his style was from the influence of most other filmmakers. He may have used Claude Lelouch-style long lenses, but this was

249
Right: Robert Altman's view of American culture was as bleak as Hopper's but his comic-caustic *M*A*S*H*, adapted by Ring Lardner Jr, from Richard Hooker's novel about military surgeons during the Korean War, was sonically innovative, captured the public's imagination, and led to a TV series of the same name. USA, 1970.

FREEDOM AND WANT SEE (1969–79): POLITICAL CINEMA/RISE OF THE BLOCKBUSTER IN AMERICA

only a start. He give actors individual microphones, had them deliver lines randomly and talk over each other; he also allowed them to wander around the set or location, while he followed them surreptitiously with those long lenses as a zoologist might follow animals roaming around a cage. Weaving all these layers together in the editing suite, the result was like being far away from events yet eavesdropping on them. This aesthetic of voyeuristic irony was entirely new and established Altman as the most distinctive stylist in America at the time. He developed it further in a Western setting in *McCabe and Mrs Miller* (1971) and in the world of country music in *Nashville* (1975).

Francis Coppola, the third great Europe-influenced experimenter in American cinema of the early 1970s, was less oppositional than either Hopper or Altman. An Italian-American who was born in Detroit, he studied film at the influential University of California in Los Angeles (UCLA) and got his leg-up into the industry through maverick producer Roger Corman. From the start there was something of Orson Welles about him. He was prodigiously talented, interested in all the arts, not just film, flamboyant in his ambitions and, latterly, not averse to self-destruction. After his time with Corman he made mainstream but unsuccessful films for the Hollywood studios. His Wellesian interest in power and hubris won him an Oscar for his screenplay for *Patton* (1970), which led to him being hired to direct the film of a bestselling book about an Italian-American mafia family.

The Godfather (1972), a gangster picture shot like a Rembrandt painting, synthesized old and new techniques, so will be dealt with in the next section (see pages 348–50). Its massive international success won Coppola the freedom to direct a more experimental film, one he had written in the 1960s and which was clearly derived from European New Wave filmmaking. *The Conversation* (1974) took the long lenses of Lelouch and the implied voyeurism of Altman and stretched them to their logical conclusion. More than any film of the 1970s it enquires philosophically into the nature of such lenses by telling the story of a professional surveillance expert who accidentally captures on audio tape a conversation between apparent lovers (250). The expert, played by Gene Hackman, lives alone and interacts little with human beings, and so becomes obsessed with a mystery on the tape. In doing so he becomes more inward still and almost has a breakdown.

Alfred Hitchcock and Michelangelo Antonioni had addressed similar themes but new, highly directional microphones and ultra-long lenses made plausible Coppola's idea of getting so lost in the fragments of other people's behaviour that your own life dissolves. Only a filmmaker who has spent hundreds of hours in an editing suite would understand the dangers in such absorption, perhaps, so *The Conversation* did not initially engage large audiences and was at first a flop. But it was released just as the Watergate political surveillance scandals were coming to a head and soon was seen as an essay in the paranoia which ensued.

In 1970 Coppola had met a passionate, nervy young filmmaker at the Sorrento Film Festival in Italy. Martin Scorsese had studied at the film school in New York University, NYU, and had seen European films there and on television. In a single phrase, he expressed more clearly than anyone the aims of New Hollywood, "We were fighting to open up the form."[4] Nowhere nearly as radical as Hopper or Altman, nor as Wellesian as Coppola, Scorsese, our fourth 1970s dissident, would nonetheless become the most respected of them all.

It is not difficult to see why. He knew more about film than the other three, was more ardent, and used film to express more directly than any other US filmmaker of the time the rituals, violence and excitement of the world in which he grew up. Born in 1942 and brought up in New York City's Little Italy, frequent childhood illnesses detached Scorsese from participating fully in the life of the streets but increased his opportunities for observing it. His film school shorts registered these observations and, after a period working with Roger Corman, he made *Mean Streets* (1973) a layered anthropological work which transcribed onto the screen the behaviour of the men Scorsese knew. We saw in the last chapter how its Catholicism derived from Pasolini's *Accattone*. It starts with its main character, Charlie (Harvey Keitel), holding his finger in a flame in a church and confessing his sins, then follows this with a jump cut sequence of Keitel's head falling onto a pillow. Said Scorsese "The whole idea was to make a story of a modern saint in his own society, but his society happens to be gangsters."[5] At one point Charlie gets drunk. To represent his disorientation, Scorsese had a camera attached to the end of a board and braced to Keitel's chest. As he walks his head remains in the same position, but the room floats. He eases himself to the ground but it is the room that seems to tip over. Such impressionism had not been popular since Abel Gance in 1920s France.

A secondary character in *Mean Streets,* a nervy side-kick called Johnny Boy, was played by a young actor called Robert De Niro. De Niro and Scorsese had known each other as kids and met up in adult life in the house of a critic friend. In 1976, they would each become the most respected in their professions because of their collaboration on a screenplay about a Vietnam veteran driving around New York in a taxi – a metaphorical iron coffin. The screenplay was written by the author of a book on Ozu, Bresson and Dreyer, who was banned from seeing films in his youth, who drank heavily like his main character, Travis Bickle, who lived in his car, whose self-obsession was festering, like Bickle's. The screenplay leapt out of him, the writer, "like an

animal",[6] as he put it, and was completed in a matter of days. The film was *Taxi Driver,* the writer was Paul Schrader.

In the introduction to this book we saw how Scorsese borrowed from Carol Reed and Jean-Luc Godard the image of a character looking at bubbles in a drink (see page 10). This expression of Travis Bickle's loneliness and distortions is only one example of the rich schematic heritage of the film. Early on, Bickle walks along a New York street. Scorsese dissolves to a later part of the same walk. This is less disruptive than a jump cut, but is like a time lapse, a momentary loss of consciousness in his character. Later, as Bickle begins to unravel, an improvised scene with realistic sound has him talk to himself in a mirror. The technique is a standard one to indicate self-absorption and perhaps mental illness, but De Niro performs it with the intensity of Marlon Brando. At another point, when De Niro is making a phone call to a woman he has become infatuated with, but who does not reciprocate, Scorsese tracks his camera away from him to look down an empty corridor because, as he later explained, it was too painful to watch the scene. The horizontal move is again Godardian. Its emotional wisdom is closer to Mizoguchi's clear withdrawal from his characters' agony.

252
Above: Scorsese's ambition was to "open up the form" of American cinema. Few films did this more complexly than his underrated *New York, New York*. USA, 1977.

Taxi Driver was a huge success with critics and public alike. The new directors' storming of the Hollywood citadel seemed too easy. They were pushing at an open door. Never before had American filmmakers been taken so seriously as artists and, inevitably, fragile personalities like Scorsese's were somewhat damaged as a result. He started taking cocaine and his health deteriorated. Perhaps unsurprisingly, self-destructiveness became the keynote of his characters. Two more would follow, each played by Robert DeNiro. The first was an artist like Scorsese, having difficulties sustaining a stable relationship with a woman, like Scorsese. Led on by his love of Hollywood, however, the director attempted a near impossible task: to implant such a man into an MGM-style musical. He would "open up the form" to accommodate him. Would this work? There had been curmudgeons and violent men in musicals before, such as James Cagney in *Love Me or Leave Me* (Charles Vidor, 1955), but to take the most optimistic form of closed romantic realism and prise it open, to subject it to the repetitive and erosive style of De Niro's acting seemed daring indeed. To intensify the contrast, Scorsese cast Liza Minnelli, the daughter of MGM's star songstress Judy Garland and its most polished director Vincente Minnelli, opposite De Niro. The result was *New York, New York* (Martin Scorsese, 1977), one of the most schizophrenic films ever made (252). It was an expensive flop and many critics hated it. His next feature, *Raging Bull* (1980) was about a self-destructive Catholic boxer on a downward slope who reaches rock bottom before finding redemption. At the end of it he added a quotation: "I was blind, but now I see." Never before had there been such an explicit Italian Catholic theme in an American film. Ethnicity, it seemed, the specifics of ghetto life, had been disguised by closed romantic realism. Now they became one of the ways in which 1970s American cinema modernized.

These white university-educated filmmakers got to know each other and went to the same parties, sharing actors and even girl-friends, their professional rivalries in some way spurring each of their careers. The second, perhaps more important ethnicity which finally entered mainstream American cinema at this time was not socially related to them at all. It began when a fifty-seven-year-old former baseball player and photographer made *The Learning Tree* (1969). Gordon Parks, the youngest of fifteen children, was born in Kansas and wrote novels in France. One of them was about growing up on farms in 1920s Kansas. Nothing strange in that, except that both the lead character and the director of *The Learning Tree*, the film based on it, were black, and the 1920s idyll was plagued by racism. After years of protest, of Martin Luther King and Malcolm X, mainstream American cinema – in this case Warner Bros. – had finally opened up to black experience. Gordon Parks was the first black director to direct a studio film, eighty-four years after the birth of the movies.

There had been black directors before – Oscar Micheaux in the 1920s was one of the dissidents in Chapter Three. Black character actors appeared in *Gone with the Wind* and *Casablanca* (1942) and in films of the 1950s. Dorothy Dandridge, Harry Belafonte and then Sidney Poitier were distinguished exceptions to the whiteness of closed romantic realism. By the end of that decade liberal white directors addressed black themes in issue and problem pictures but only in 1969, four years after Ousmane Sembene's *The Black Girl* (Senegal, 1965) became the first film directed by a black person in Africa itself, did America follow suit. The gentleness of *The*

Learning Tree did not detract from its historical importance, a fact acknowledged in its registration in the National Film Registry of the US Library of Congress.

Parks went on to great commercial success with *Shaft* (1971) but *Sweet Sweetback's Baadasssss Song* of the same year broke more ground. Its director Melvin van Peebles was born in Chicago in 1932, served in the Second World War then, in a strange echo of Gordon Parks' route into the film industry, wrote novels in France – in English and French – before filming one of them as his second feature. Like Parks, Van Peebles was encouraged by the dynamic, low-budget autobiographical white films made in his adopted country and imported some of their techniques to the US. In order to film without union involvement, which was difficult in those days, he pretended that his third film *Sweet Sweetback* was a porn movie. Its central character, the ultra-cool Sweetback, sees white cops beating a black boy, attacks them, gets chased, meets women and escapes the law (254). The film's amorality and violence were echoes of *Bonnie and Clyde* and Roger Corman films, but what was new was how black the behaviour was. It glamorized ghetto life and simplified its gender politics in a way that would later be denounced by black intellectuals, but in exposing white corruption and racism and celebrating black male sexuality, it set new schemas for American filmmakers, which would be built upon and then rejected in decades to come by Spike Lee, Richard Pryor, Eddie Murphy, Whoopi Goldberg and the studios' first black woman director, EuzhanPalcy. *Sweetback* cost $500,000 and grossed $10 million.

Jewishness had not been so overlooked by American cinema. The first moguls were Jewish, there had been Yiddish comedies and dramas in the 1930s and 1940s, and directors such as Edgar G.

253
Below: The first film made by a black person for a US studio: Gordon Parks' *The Learning Tree*. USA, 1969.

253
Below: The first film made by a black person for a US studio: Gordon Parks' *The Learning Tree*. USA, 1969.

Ulmer, Ernst Lubitsch and Billy Wilder used Jewish situations and character types, often around the edges of their stories. Then, in the late 1960s, came Woody Allen, a New York-born, well-educated fan of jazz, baseball and Ingmar Bergman films, who did stand-up and had started in television. Where Scorsese "opened up" the forms of traditional American filmmaking like the musical and the boxing picture and Altman attacked America's values in his scathing reworking of

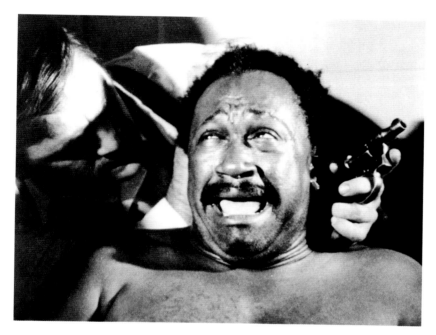

254
Left: Parks led the way for other black filmmakers such as Melvin van Peebles, whose grungy, low-budget *Sweetback's Baadasssss Song* was a real breakthrough. USA, 1971.

war movies and other genres, Allen inserted an explicitly Jewish comic character into the centre of genres and laughed at the result. The joke was that New York Jewishness is alien to just about anywhere except New York. This was inspired and made Allen one of the most famous directors in the world.

Like Chaplin, he played the lead character himself. *Take the Money and Run* (1969) spoofed crime pictures. *Sleeper* (1973) was a parody of sci-fi movies in which Allen's neurotic Manhattan musician is catapulted into the year 2174. *Annie Hall* (1977) was set in part in New York but Allen was an alien in it nonetheless because he fell in love with that most foreign of things, a mid-Western girl. In the first scene he shot he and Annie (Diane Keaton) are trying to cook lobsters (255). Allen, a typical New Yorker in that he seldom cooks and never boils lobsters, is terrified. The scene is a single take and the kitchen light is hit by mistake, but Keaton is laughing uncontrollably and the result is one of the funniest moments in American cinema. It began a period of less sketchy, more structured filmmaking for Allen. *Manhattan* (1979) would take nearly six months to shoot. Composition became central to his work (257). He became a filmmaker first and a comedian second. For a while he approached the rigour of Chaplin and the exactitudes of Buster Keaton or Jacques Tati. Then, in the late 1980s, he started to abandon this architectural approach. Despite his love of Bergman and Fellini, he started to film his screenplays almost in the way Maysles and his colleagues shot the Kennedy documentary *Primary* back in 1960, in long takes, with a camera following the action, using almost no rehearsal or reverse angles. As a result, his edits took just a few weeks.

Hopper, Altman, Coppola, Scorsese, Parks, Van Peebles and Allen each in their way, and influenced to various degrees by European filmmaking, opened up the form and ethnic range of American cinema. They did not envisage an entirely clean break with the past, however, and at the same time that they were making their ground-breaking films, janus-faced movies were produced which were aesthetically ambitious but rooted in Hollywood traditions. The first of these, *The Last Picture Show* (1971) was like a funeral service

255
Right: Filmed in one shot this hilarious scene from *Annie Hall* is Woody Allen at his best. USA, 1977

for old Hollywood, a tale about graduating high school seniors set in a small southern town whose cinema was closing (256). It was not a New Wave film like those of Hopper or Scorsese; its most decent character was Sam the Lion, played by Ben Johnson, a regular

actor for John Ford. The *New Yorker* magazine's comment that "our recent films have been about self hatred ... there has been no room for decency or nobility" captures its flavour. It is no surprise, then, to hear that it was directed by Peter Bogdanovich, who had made *Targets* for Corman, which was also about the decline of movies (see pages 320–21), and who had befriended John Ford and Orson Welles. To add to the elegiac tone, the film was shot in black and white.

The Last Picture Show was seen by veteran director John Huston, who cast its leading actor, Jeff Bridges, in a boxing film to be released the next year. *Fat City* (1972) is set in one of the poorest towns in the US, where the proportion of black people is so high that white fighters are novelty acts. Bridges plays such a fighter (258), dreaming of success but never achieving it. The film was politically far more radical than those of Coppola or Scorsese, and, just to show that New Hollywood directors weren't the only ones to be stylistically innovative, Huston had it shot in a new way.[7] He hired cinematographer Conrad Hall, who filmed dark interiors and bright exteriors without changing the aperture of the lens. As a result the barrooms were gloomy and the streets blindingly white, just as in real life. He was influenced in this by French cinematography. *Fat City* broke down taboos of good lighting in the US.

Also in 1972, a musical assimilated traditional panache with new sobriety beyond anything achieved by Scorsese's later *New York, New York*. Its director Bob Fosse was born of musical theatre parents, steeped in Broadway and an athletic choreographer and dancer in the 1950s. Also like Huston and Orson Welles, he kicked his heels while film caught up with his ideas, so it was no great surprise that *Cabaret*, his bold film of a musical about Christopher Isherwood's character Sally Bowles in decadent Berlin at the time of

the rise of Nazism, seemed so modern (259). As performed by Liza Minnelli and choreographed by Fosse, the songs were exhilaratingly amoral celebrations of money, living for the moment and non-conformist sexuality, post-1960s in a way that Scorsese's ideas about sex seldom were. The real coups in the piece – its intercutting of Sally's underworld life amongst bisexuals with Nazi atrocities, the gear changes between fun and sobering numbers like the Nazi anthem "Tomorrow Belongs to Me" – were in the original stage musical, but Fosse brought them to the screen with panache.

The decade's most successful upgrading of another 1930s American genre also appeared in 1972. Francis Coppola at first looked down on *The Godfather* because it was an adaptation of a violent, popular novel. As his interest grew, he clashed with his producer over casting and hired cinematographer Gordon Willis, explaining that he wanted a simple style like an old movie, no 1970s long lenses, no helicopter shots. "It was tableau filmmaking", said Willis, "where the actors move in and out of frame, very straightforward."[8] The film extended the range of the gangster film in several ways. Its story comprised five sections or acts rather than the usual three. It was based around a family – the Corleones – rather than a few individuals. Its

258
Right: Young directors were not the only ones pushing the boundaries in US cinema of the seventies. Veteran filmmaker John Huston saw Jeff Bridges in *The Last Picture Show* and cast him in his innovative boxing film *Fat City*. USA, 1972.

259
Left: Another veteran,
Bob Fosse, married vividly
realized musical sequences
with modern depictions
of sexuality in *Cabaret*.
USA, 1972.

profile was the rise and rise of the Corleones and the transfer of power
from the Don (Marlon Brando) to his son Michael (Al Pacino) rather
than the morally more acceptable rise-and-fall form of most gangster
pictures. This failure to denounce, this accumulation of power, left the
film open to charges of amorality – even fascism – in later years.
Visually, Willis underexposed the imagery, rendering it darker than was
the norm (260). He lit Brando from overhead to create shadows in his
eye sockets like those in Franco Citti's in Pasolini's *Accattone* (see page
282). This was considered unsophisticated but prevented audiences
from seeing the eyes of the Don. The low lighting levels also meant that
focus was shallow, constraining actors to certain minimal movements,
internalizing their performance. Though Coppola thought it would
flop, the film was a vast success, the most influential gangster picture of
the 1970s, if not of the entire post-war era.

Over dinner one day during its shooting, *The Godfather's*
powerful producer Robert Evans commissioned another film about
the lust for power. This time it would focus on the way that Los
Angeles developers stole water from farmers in the valley to the north
of the city. The film, *Chinatown*, one of the most important works of
its era and a scathing attack on the American Dream, would be
directed by Roman Polanski.

It was nearly three years since Polanski's wife had been
murdered. He returned to the US and stripped down the screenplay

260
Above: A third genre modernization was Francis Coppola's brooding and amoral *The Godfather*. USA, 1972.

of *Chinatown*, which had been written by Robert Towne, to a manageable length, adding a tragic ending. The result enriched the film noir tradition of Old Hollywood as much as *The Godfather* enriched the gangster tradition. The story weaves the land grab theme into a complex family drama about a detective who discovers that the woman he is investigating was raped by her own father who in turn metaphorically raped the farmers by engineering the theft of their water. Polanski was never attracted by the stylistic freedoms of the New Wave filmmakers and here, as in *Rosemary's Baby*, he filmed with wide-angle lenses, bright lights and precise framing, the opposite of both Willis' approach on *The Godfather* and the whole of the film noir cycle (261). Morally, however, this was noir: the world was corrupt, law was suspended, people were evil. So much so that in the end the father shoots his own daughter through the eye. "Most people never face the fact that at the right time, in the right place, they capable of anything," says the father, played by John Huston. Polanksi had taken a key genre in closed romantic realism to its logical conclusion. *Chinatown*'s cynicism and despair was profoundly un-American. After the success of the film, Polanski fled the US havig been charged with unlawful sexual intercourse with a minor. The case was unresolved so he continued his filmmaking career in France with the *The Tenant/Le Locotaire* (1976), in which he plays a paranoid, claustrophobic and transvestite tenement dweller. Its excesses were booed on release but it can now be seen as another masterpiece in one of the most singular of film careers.

Our final straddler of Old and New Hollywood in these days is also its most reclusive figure. Terrence Malick was more academic than any of the other new American directors. Born in 1943 into an oil family, he studied philosophy and worked on screenplays before debuting with the *Bonnie and Clyde*-like *Badlands* (1973). His follow up was *Days of Heaven* (1978), a story about a migrant worker (Richard Gere), his sister and soul mate who flee industrialization and end up on the estate of a wealthy Texan landowner

(Sam Shepard). Malick saw this landowner as a pharaoh-figure and the ensuing passions as versions of biblical stories. He hired cinematographer Nestor Almendros, who had worked with Truffaut and the great French directors, to shoot it. They did so in Canada, taking the films of D.W. Griffiths as their visual model, using sideways window light for interiors and, like Conrad Hall in *Fat City*, overexposing exteriors. This went against the "professionalism" of the day and Almendros had to convince his crew that it was okay to have the sky too bright but faces in shade. Here was the clash between Old and New Hollywood in microcosm. Some crew members resigned in protest.

To achieve a flowing sense of movement Almendros sometimes filmed with the camera attached to his own body in an elaborate cantilevered brace called a Panaglide. This was the first time this was done; Panaglides would soon evolve into the rather similar Steadicams which have given a floating feeling to much of cinema of the 1980s and since. Malick insisted that key scenes were shot at the

261
Below: Whereas the crimes in forties films noirs were usually committed under cover of darkness, many of the offences in Roman Polanski's *Chinatown* – including the sale and flooding of Owens Valley farm land – take place in blinding Californian sunlight. USA, 1974.

so-called magic hour – after the sun has dipped below the horizon but before its glowing light has died from the sky. This hour lasts in fact about twenty minutes, so there is always a panic to capture it, but Malick and Almendros managed to and the images have a unique delicacy. To simulate a locust swarm they dropped peanut shells from a helicopter whose rotor blades made them into a whorl. This had been done before – their innovation was to shoot these scenes normally but have the actors walk backwards then reverse the footage so that the actors were moving forward and the whorls appeared to swarm upward. The climax of the film occurs when wheat fields are set on fire. These were shot for two weeks at night-time, using only the light from the sometimes distant flames as illumination. The resulting images have the shallowest focus of almost any filmed for cinema. The delicacy of this cave-like darkness worked brilliantly with the film's mythic ambitions.

NEW GERMAN CINEMA

More than any film *Days of Heaven* reveals the central role that cinematography – especially European cinematography – played in America's cinematic modernization in the 1970s. With the exception of the new ethnicities that came to the fore, much of this modernization involved taking traditional subject matter but expanding it with new ideas about shooting, acting and editing. To switch from Hollywood in the 1970s to Munich, is to find the opposite. For the first time since the 1920s, German filmmaking was reviving artistically. As in the earlier decade, public subsidy played a key part in the revival. A new liberal political regime had come to power and filmmaking became its public confessional. But where America took old content and applied new form, West German directors took some of the form of the American cinema they had grown up with and applied it to new psychological, national and formal questions of daunting complexity.

This had its roots in the 1960s. Under the influence of the European New Waves, a group of filmmakers at a 1962 short film festival in Oberhausen launched a manifesto which rejected "the conventional German film" which, under the threat of TV, was in free fall. "We declare our intention to create the new German film", they wrote, "This new film needs new freedoms." A generation gap had opened up between German baby boomers and their parents who had either voted for Adolf Hitler or had endured him. An economic boom in West Germany began to numb the guilt felt by the country over the atrocities of the Holocaust. New right-wing tabloid newspapers pasted contentment over everything. There was a TV news black-out about left-wing terrorism. Mainstream cinema continued to churn out "heimat" films, homey regional stories which dodged the big issues in German life and reinforced nationalism. The feel-good factor was everywhere. It disgusted many young creative people on the left. So was born a national cinema of unease. This comprised a network of filmmakers whose astonishing body of work over a twelve-year period would come to be known as the New German Cinema. Alexander Kluge, Jean-Marie Straub, Daniele Huillet, Werner Herzog, Rainer Werner Fassbinder, Margarethe Von Trotta, Volker Schlöndorff, Wim Wenders, Helma Sanders-Brahms, Hans Jurgen Syberberg, Edgar Reitz and others together made films "about a world of false images and real emotions, public failures and private fantasies".[9] No national cinema in this chapter was more driven than Germany's. None answered the question "Why make movies?" with more passion.

This national cinema needled at the false optimism of the times. Its leading members were a disparate band of formal, political, sexual and feminist outsiders who took issue with their country's ostrich-like behaviour about its own past. Like filmmakers in Japan, they saw their history being written all around them, by the Americans who occupied both countries after their defeats at the end of the Second World War, by the conservative politicians of their parents' generation, by the fogey filmmakers who went before them. Fassbinder, Wenders, Kluge and Sanders-Brahms had, like Imamura and Oshima in Japan, been lectured too much about the past, but told too little. They wanted to be free to get on the road, to have sex with whomever they desired, to play loud music, as their occupiers did, but also to push all that away and inspect what it was to be modern and German and thoughtful in the 1970s, but not tainted by the Nazis.

It was one of the youngest and the most prolific of the New German Cinema directors who best captured this ambiguous relationship with the US. "The ideal is to make films as beautiful as America's," said the self-destructive, gay theatre and film obsessive Fassbinder, "but to move the content to other areas."[10] While Kluge and Sanders-Brahms did not play this game, Fassbinder, Wenders and

Right: A love affair across the divides of race and age: *Fear Eats the Soul.* Director: Rainer Werner Fassbinder. Germany, 1973.

Schlöndorff did so almost obsessively. In 1970 and 1971, Fassbinder saw six films by the German master of the swollen cinema of the Eisenhower era, Douglas Sirk. A leftist German anti-Nazi in Hollywood, he used melodramatic stories to deal with the questions that absorbed the then twenty-five-year-old Fassbinder about his own country – repression and despair. This discovery changed Fassbinder's life.[11] He travelled to Switzerland where Sirk was then living in retirement and remade his gleaming, impotent, melodrama *All that Heaven Allows* (USA, 1956) as *Angst essen Seele auf/Fear Eats the Soul* (West Germany, 1974). Jane Wyman suffered because of the complacency and intolerance of her friends and family when she began an affair with her gardener, Rock Hudson, in *All that Heaven Allows*. In the remake, Wyman's character is now an ageing cleaner who falls in love with a Moroccan immigrant. In the first film a television set is the only companion that Wyman's disapproving friends will accept her having (see pages 231–32); in Fassbinder's version it is kicked to pieces in an expression of racist rage. It was the thirteenth cinema film he had directed in five years, some derived from US models, others influenced by Godard, radical theatre and German literature. Throughout his career Fassbinder's pessimism and Marxist political beliefs led him, like Visconti, to portray closed worlds from which people could not escape. Trapped by capitalism and mired in desire, they self-destruct.

Two years older than Fassbinder, the Düsseldorf-born and Munich-educated Wim Wenders also found a starting point for his home, but was much more rooted in social realities. Loach filmed with few lights, made the acting process as true-to-life as possible for the boy, and filmed on real locations. The boy learns to train a kestrel but his background prevents him from making a decent life for himself. The result was heartbreaking. Loach developed his techniques, telling his often unprofessional actors less and less about the script and story so they would react naturally as events unfolded. His techniques have changed little over the years, and some have criticized this, but he was one of the 1970s' great realist directors and was particularly influential in France.

Ken Russell also evolved his style at the BBC, but that style was more Federico Fellini than Roberto Rossellini. Born in the south of England in 1927, Russell served in the Royal Air Force, became a ballet dancer – a rare segue in itself – then made extravagant television films about composers. His third feature, *Women in Love* (UK, 1969) continued his interest in artistic and bohemian milieu by adapting a novel by D.H. Lawrence. The film's portrayal of decadence and bisexuality pre-dated *Cabaret*. It was visually innovative in a number of ways, for example in the scene where Russell turned his camera on its side to film actors Alan Bates and Jennie Linden walking naked through a field (268). Two years later the director trumped Fellini in sexual display at least in his orgiastic *The Devils* (UK, 1971). Based on a novel by Aldous Huxley about the demonic possession of nuns in a convent in the 1600s in France, it was as irreligious as Satyajit Ray's *Devi* (India, 1960), Fellini's *The Nights of Cabiria* (Italy, 1957) and Buñuel's *Viridiana* (Spain, 1961), which it resembles most closely. The masturbatory and burning scenes in *The Devils* scandalized polite opinion as much as Buñuel's sacrilegious ending in *Viridiana* had, so much so that the film was cut and even banned in some quarters.

The sets in the *The Devils* were designed by Derek Jarman, a twenty-nine-year-old experimental painter and filmmaker who was influenced by Pasolini, Jean Cocteau, Powell and Pressburger and the paintings of Caravaggio. In 1976, the year of the death of Carol Reed, the year in which the anarchist punks erupted in youth culture, he co-directed *Sebastiane*, about a Roman soldier who becomes a Catholic martyr. Made with almost no money and written and performed in the Latin language, its frank homoeroticism made it a milestone in the history of gay cinema (269). Jarman and his collaborators later devised a way of filming on amateur film stock, slowing it down, transferring it to video, and combining in with other footage to produce trance-like feature films. His themes were Englishness, Shakespeare, homosexuality, the barbarity of contemporary life and, eventually – in the revolutionary *Blue* (UK, 1993), one of the most abstract films ever made, in which the screen remained a single colour throughout – the director's own blindness and AIDS-related illness.

269
Above: Painter and avant-gardist Derek Jarman's *Sebastiane*, a landmark work in gay cinema which was by turns vicious and intimate. Co-director: Paul Humfress. UK, 1976.

Cinematographers played a key role in modernizing American cinema of the 1970s, and in Britain one of them became the finest director of the period. Nicolas Roeg worked his way up through commercial cinema as a distinguished cameraman. His first feature was a gangster picture like no other, as radical in form and meaning as *The Godfather* was conservative. Co-directed with the Scottish avant-gardist Donald Cammel, *Performance* (UK, 1970) tells the story of a clean-cut petty gangster (James Fox) who goes into hiding in the London home of a rock star (Mick Jagger) and his two female companions. In getting drawn into their world of drug-taking and promiscuity, the gangster confronts his own sexual ambiguities; the rock star sees in his innate violence something feral that he himself has lost. Using mirrors, wigs, make-up and spatial ambiguities, Roeg and Cammell portrayed the merging of these two identities (270) just as the actress and the nurse merge in Bergman's *Persona* (Sweden, 1966). *Performance* is even more concerned with what it is to be an artist than the Swedish film, however. The gangster introduces himself as one. Scenes from his past life were sometimes shot with

12mm "fish eye" lenses, distorting everything. After a gunshot, the camera appears to travel in the path of the bullet through a skull, into a head, crashing through a picture of the Argentine fabulist Jorge Luis Borges, then moving deeper. The film as a whole does this too, starting in the showy world of London gangsters then moving into the subconscious lives of its characters, the place where sexualities and whole identities are ill-defined.

Rather than returning to the theme of adults in a closed world, Roeg's next film looked at children in an open one, the Australian outback. *Walkabout* (UK, 1971) is a mythic tale of a white fourteen-year-old English girl and her six-year-old brother who are forced to trek across Australia after their father shoots himself at a family picnic. As the gangster fluids in *Performance*, the experience seems

270
Left: A gangster (James Fox, left) and a rock star who has lost his muse (Mick Jagger, right) merge identities in Nicolas Roeg and Donald Cammell's remarkable *Performance*. UK, 1970.

to allow them to shed their rational twentieth-century selves and become reborn into what aboriginals would call "the dream time", to live a more mythic, primitive experience which is closer to the cosmos, animals and sexual instincts. At one point the girl swims naked with an aboriginal youth (271). Years later, back in the white world of tower blocks, fitted kitchens, make-up and nine-to-five husbands, she thinks of this free, erotic moment and the sense of loss is overwhelming. Like Pasolini and Herzog, Roeg believed in a paradise lost where people were not ruled by their conscious thoughts and moral assumptions. Unlike them, and under the influence of the anthropologist Carl Jung, he seemed to suggest that this paradise ultimately resided not in pre-industrial lands but deep inside the structure of the human mind. *Walkabout* and subsequent films like *Don't Look Now* (UK–France–Italy, 1973), in which he fragmented into shards of memory, superstition and fear a Daphne du Maurier story set in wintertime Venice, were cinematic attempts to expose the workings of this structure. It became clear that for him, time was not linear there. Past and future crowded into the present, never more so

271
Below: Roeg's wide-ranging use of lenses and non-linear cutting (in collaboration with editors like Antony Gibbs and Graeme Clifford) established him as the most stylistically innovative director of his generation. *Walkabout*. UK, 1971.

FREEDOM AND WANT SEE (1969–79): POLITICAL CINEMA/RISE OF THE BLOCKBUSTER IN AMERICA

cinematic minimalism, Hu's dazzling editing and art direction – both of which he undertook himself – dramatized the metaphysical expansion of his characters and their world. *A Touch of Zen* was hugely influential, directly inspiring the international box office hit *Wo Hu Zang Long/Crouching Tiger, Hidden Dragon* (Ang Lee, Hong Kong–Taiwan–US, 2000) and the kinetic-philosophical 1990s films of Hong Kong director Tsui Hark. The Hong Kong-US action director John Woo called Hu "a cinematic poet, a cinematic painter and a cinematic philosopher."

The Indian film industry grew at such a pace in the 1960s that by 1971 – when it produced 433 films – it was the biggest in the world. Amitabh Bachchan, a cross between the Western actors Sean Connery and Robert De Niro, became its biggest star. Born in 1942, Bachchan became an Indian national obsession in his early thirties, fortifying the Hindi film industry in Bombay. The comparison to Western actors captures the degree of his fame but not the complexity of his masculinity. His screen persona was often that of a troubled working-class rebel who was avenging a crime committed against him or his kin. Yet, this being mainstream Indian cinema, Bachchan also danced. His method of doing so, of combining reserve with grace, was influential and, according to some, helped determine how Indian people "move in the streets, at wed-dings and at religious pro-cessions."[14] In the classic *Sholay* (Ramesh Sippy, 1975), the most popular of his mid-1970s films, he plays one of two bandits hired to retaliate for the killing of an ex-policeman's family. The film derived as many of its ideas from American Westerns as did Sergio Leone's *A Fistful of Dollars*. If anything, its visual grandeur, flashback structure and set pieces made it even more operatic than that film.

275
Below: The most popular of actor Amitabh Bachchan's mid-seventies films, the epic vengeance Western *Sholay*. Director Ramesh Sippy. India, 1975.

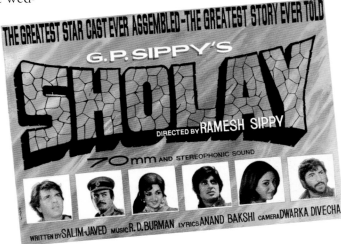

Outside the vivid but conformist mainstream, Mani Kaul's stylistic innovations in *Uski Roti/A Day's Bread* (India, 1969) helped create the New Indian Cinema movement. As in Germany and

Australia, public subsidy nurtured this. The films of Kaul, Mrinal Sen and Kumar Shahani helped stimulate debates about low-budget alternatives to the spectacular films made in Bombay. Shahani in particular was a link between the French and Indian New Wave movements, having worked with Bresson and participated in the demonstrations in Paris in 1968. Like other film movements, New Indian Cinema had its preferred actors such as the forceful and iconic Shabana Azmi and the understated Naseeruddin Shah. Again, as in Germany, state subsidy was short-lived. As early as 1976, the Indian Committee on Public Undertakings announced, in a sideswipe at the intellectual cinema of Kaul and Sen, that "films are primarily a means of entertainment."[15]

BEYOND THE NEW WAVES: POLITICAL MODERNISM

Most of the films that have been considered so far in this chapter either addressed traditional subject matter with new schemas or used traditional filmic techniques to explore new ethnicities and historical problems. But some countries in the 1970s underwent a more radical renewal in their approach to cinema, abandoning not only old forms but old content as well. Chapter Six showed how the Bandung Conference in Indonesia in 1959 began the process in which the non-Western world would cope with decolonialization. These ideas filtered into and sometimes grew out of the world of the arts in the 1960s; Brazilian Cinema Nôvo in the 1960s was the most prominent result of this in the film world. By the end of that decade the politicization of non-Western film was gathering pace.

Take India for example. Inspired by an uprising in the village of Naxalbari, the left of that country's Communist Party created a political movement called the Naxalites which radicalized the ideas of documentary filmmakers in India in the 1970s and filtered into the approach of masters like Ritwik Ghatak (see page 316) and Mrinal Sen. Building on such ideas and in particular the radical work of Brazilian and Cuban directors of the 1960s, two Argentine filmmakers wrote a manifesto for non-Western filmmaking which was highly influential. "Towards a Third Cinema: Notes and Experiences for the Development of a Cinema of Liberation in the Third World" by Fernando Solanas and Octavio Getino argued that throughout most of the history of the medium, film had been a commodity. Filmmakers in the developing world should reject this history and start again, they argued, treating cinema as a weapon to fight oppression, a revolutionary tool. Their approach was Marxist, they wrote like V.I. Pudovkin in the Soviet Union in the 1920s. Their ideas were built on by others and a new categorization of the stages of film history emerged: First Cinema was industrial and commercial, lasting from the earliest days of narrative film until around 1958; Second Cinema was the modernist art movies of individual creative directors like Godard, Antonioni, Bergman and Fellini and had its heyday between 1959 and 1969; Third Cinema was political modernism, opposed to both industrial and autobiographical art cinema, and would come to the fore in non-Western countries after 1969. The simplifications of this model are clear to anyone who has looked at the subtleties of closed romantic realism and its interplay with its alternatives. Nonetheless the idea of Third Cinema influenced the course of African, South American and Middle-Eastern cinema of the 1970s.[16]

The most popular images of Africa in cinema until the late 1960s were those of Tarzan movies, where blacks are usually mysterious figures in the background, or John Huston's *The African Queen* (USA, 1951), which is told from the point of view of white people and missionaries. In the north of Africa, Egypt's master director Youssef Chahine had, for more than a decade, been challenging this mainstream formula. Long before German filmmakers in the 1970s did so, in films like *Cairo Station* (Egypt, 1958) he used the form of American melodrama but moved to other areas of content. At the first Carthage Film Festival in Tunisia in 1966 he said "Freedom of Expression is not given, it is taken".[17] After Israel defeated his country 1967 and claimed large sections of its land, his semi-detachment from Western cinema became politicized. "For me the Third World is England, France, the USA", he later said, "I'm the first world, I've been here for 7,000 years."[18] *The Sparrow/Al'usfour* (Egypt, 1973) was a stunning expression of this stance. It follows the stories of a young policeman and a journalist whose lives interweave and overlap in the house of local hostess, Bahiyya, and culminates with Egypt's premier, Nasser, announcing on television that Israel has won the Six-Day War and that Egyptian territory has been lost. Chahine captures the shock effect of this on the lives of ordinary Egyptians with astonishing vividness. His ending — tracking shots of Bahiyya running through the streets shouting "We won't accept defeat" – sounds crudely propagandistic but is one of the greatest moments in the whole of Third Cinema.

Right: Satirizing the wealth and dress sense of colonizers: Djibril Diop Mambety's playful *Touki Bouki* presented "fantasies of African modernity never before seen in film". Senegal, 1973.

Also in northern and Arab Africa, important documentary directors started to make their mark, amongst them Abellatif Ben Ammar who studied in Paris and worked with Roberto Rossellini. His Tunisian film *Sejnane* (1973), about how poor people shouldered the brunt of the burden of the independence struggle, was very moving. The former French colony of Senegal began to emerge as a major filmmaking country in the 1970s. Ousmane Sembene had made the first black African feature *The Black Girl* (1965) there (see page 315) and despite a population of just eight million, several key figures followed in his footsteps. Djibril Diop Mambety was born in the country's capital, Dakar, in 1945 and raised by a strict father who taught him to look beyond the material things in life. At the age of twenty-eight he released *Touki Bouki/Journey of the Hyenas* (Senegal, 1973), a kind of African *A Bout de Souffle* or even *Easy Rider*, about two ironic young drop-outs who swank around and swindle money in order to try to go to Paris to live the high life. The man, Mouri, works in a slaughterhouse but drives a motorbike with oxen horns on his handlebars. Anta, his somewhat mystical partner, is a political worker. They ride around and meet villagers who say that the only things to come from France were "white women and the clap", drifting between mystical scenes of ritual lovemaking intercut with the blood sacrifice of a goat, and open mockery of locals, village life and colonialism (276). They stitch up a rich fat man who fancies Mouri. Later he strips and rides naked in the fat man's car, fist held high, making a mock political speech which is intercut with a cavalcade of black Citroëns, the car of choice of the colonialists. Celebrated dancer Josephine Baker's song "Paris, Paris, Paris" plays ironically throughout.

Touki Bouki has the energy of *Easy Rider*, of Imamura, of all those films that say "fuck you" to the previous generation. The historian of African cinema Manthia Diawara wrote that it "tears up the screen with fantasies of African modernity never before seen in film or literature".[19] Its assertion of youthfulness and cinematic irreverence was a door-opener for new African filmmakers. Its title means "journey of the hyenas" in Mambety's local language, Wolof, and throughout his career he would use hyenas to symbolize the viciousness of human beings, in one instance pulling out a stuffed one to illustrate his point. It would be twenty years before he made his next feature, itself called *Hyènes/Hyenas* (Switzerland–France–Senegal, 1993), by which time the vision of this innovative director had darkened considerably.

Still in Senegal, Safi Faye, Africa's first important female director, made *Kaddu Beykat/Peasant Letter* (1975) the first black African film to focus on the cultural details of village life. A documentary about the impact on farmers of the fall in the market value of their peanut crop, it is told in the form of a letter about a day in the life of villagers. At one point the letter-writer says "I have often wondered why we live and die without any pleasure." European anthropologists like Jean Rouche had long made documentary films about Africa; Faye's went further than any of these.

Nine years after *The Black Girl*, Ousmane Sembene made *Impotence/Xala* (Senegal, 1974), which was almost as caustic as *Touki Bouki*. The former Citroën factory worker and celebrated novelist chose as his next subject the temporary sexual impotence of a black business man in an unnamed African country who so co-operates with the colonizers that he washes his limousine with their expensive imported mineral water. Where *Xala* (pronounced "hala") was funny and popular, Sembene's next film, *Ceddo/The People*

(Senegal, 1976), used a simple style to tell a symbolic and controversial tale about the impact of Islam in Africa. Featuring horrific slave branding scenes, it argued that the future of Africa relies on its refusal to have imposed on it any monotheistic religion. Its ending, in which a princess slays a Muslim imam, was considered scandalous, and the films was banned in its own country for eight years. Souleymane Cissé, another great African director emerged in the 1970s. Born in 1940 in Mali, Senegal's eastern neighbour, and trained in Moscow, he had his first success with *Baara/Work* (Mali, 1978). *Finyé/The Wind* (Mali, 1982) and *Yeelen/Brightness* (Mali, 1987) would establish him as the most important African director of the 1980s.

In 1967 a young Ethiopian, Haile Gerima, left Africa to study

in America. He returned in the early 1970s to make a film as stylistically bold as *Touki Bouki*, another step forward for Third Cinema and, a drama with one of the longest time lines in movie history. *Mirt sost shi amit/Harvest: 3,000 Years* (Ethiopia, 1975) told the story of three millennia of colonization in East Africa. Shot in low-contrast black and white (279), it starts at dawn with the words

278
Above: Still in Senegal, the father of black African cinema, Ousmane Sembene, addressed the theme of the arrival of Islam onto the continent in *Ceddo*. 1976.

"Almighty God, give us a nice day." Throughout, Gerima uses the long lenses favoured by Robert Altman to create a distance from the situations in his film about which he feels so passionate: a family of farmers appallingly treated by a black, trilby-hatted armchair tyrant. The farmer sings a song about a 3,000-year-old wedding dress as his wife walks endlessly across the fields until she is a pinprick in the landscape. The size and timelessness of the land is the first concern of the film but then Gerima weaves in details of the exploitation it is host to, and then a process of politicization begins. Where Sembene worked in parables, Gerima, who became a Harvard University film professor, is more intellectual in his approach to form. He rejects the reverse angles and establishing shots of Western cinema, using chanting and breathing on the soundtrack, always pointing his camera downward. Like Glauber Rocha in *Black God, White Devil* (Brazil,

1964), he introduces mythic characters like a mad political visionary, an old man called Kebebe whose land was stolen years before. The 3,000-year-old dress becomes a metaphor for the old ideas the locals clothe themselves in. They have been the same people for three millennia and now, with help from the madman, they rebel. Kebebe tells how the farmers were herded into concentration camps because the Queen of England didn't want to see them on a visit to the country. "If you'd witnessed that, you'd have lost your sanity like me", he says. Two hours into the film, Kebebe calls the black trilby-hatted landlord a bloodsucker and batters him with a stick. "Help, help, he killed the lord", the people shout. The farmer says "The landlord is dead – the state might give us the harvest." Voices begin to flood the sound track. People are beginning to talk to each other.

The rejection of the norms of Western cinema in Africa was echoed in the Middle East. In Iran, Farough Farrokhzad's landmark epilepsy documentary *The House is Black* (1963) inspired other filmmakers. Around ninety features were made in the country each year in the early 1970s, some supported by the Ministry of Culture. The best of these was *Gav/The Cow* (1969) by Daryush

279
Below: Haile Gerima's long, symbolic account of exploitation of peasants, the stylistically rigorous *Harvest 3000 Years*. Ethiopia, 1975.

280
Above: The rise of Iranian cinema continued with Daryush Mehrjui's *The Cow*. 1969.

Mehrjui, who studied film at UCLA at what appears to have been the same time as Francis Coppola and who was very influenced by Farrokhzad. *The Cow* was the fictional bedrock of Iranian cinema, it "transform(ed) the very definition" of it.[20] Told with great simplicity, it concerns Hassan, the devoted owner of the only cow in a village (280). When it dies the locals concoct a story that it has wandered off. Hassan is inconsolable and slips into despair, then something closer to insanity. Like many subsequent Iranian films, a physical element in the real world – a cow – is gradually transformed into something poetic and metaphysical. Ambitious directors in other countries usually begin with a human problem which their film explores or, less often, a spatial situation. It is striking how often objects are at the centre of the poetics of filmmaking in Iran. The resulting balance between tangible and abstract elements is as satisfying as the classic equilibrium in the work of Yasujiro Ozu.

In 1972 the Arab neighbours of Iranians like Mehrjui published a New Arab Cinema manifesto at the Damascus Film Festival in Syria. This called for a new political commitment in Middle-Eastern film and led to several landmark films. The first of these was by the most talented Lebanese director of the 1970s, Borhan Alawiye, who trained in Belgium and who, in 1974, released the outstanding documentary *Kafr Kassem* (Lebanon, 1974) about an Israeli massacre of Palestinians in the years 1947–51. Omar Amiralay's *Al-hayat al-yawmiyya fi qaria suriyya/Daily Life in a Syrian Village* (Syria, 1974) received even better reviews.

The most notorious Middle-Eastern filmmaker of the period was the Kurd Yilmaz Güney. Born into a peasant family in southern Turkey 1937, he became a writer and actor in the late 1950s. Thereafter, Güney's career was unique. He was jailed in 1960 for writing communist fiction, the first of many imprisonments. By the end of that decade he had become a star in Turkey, a scruffy, gruff hero figure, sometimes called the "Ugly King" (281), in wildly commercial movies mixing Hollywood with neo-realism. His stardom prefigured Amitabh Bachchan's in India in that he was less an object of sexual desire and romantic fantasy as are celebrities in the Western star system, than an on-screen spokesman for ordinary people. The authorities disliked him not only for his leftism but exactly because of this closeness to the people.

In 1968, he started directing his own movies but in 1975, during a fight with an anti-communist judge in a restaurant, a gun was pulled – by Güney's nephew, it seems – the judge was killed, and the director was imprisoned for eighteen years. During this time he scripted his most important films *Sürü/The Herd* (Zeki Otken, Turkey, 1978),

281
Left: Kurdish actor-writer-director Yilmaz Güney who became a huge star in Turkey and who, while in prison, wrote his most important films.

Dusman/The Enemy (Zeki Otken, Turkey, 1979) and *Yol/The Way* (Serif Goren, 1982), each of which was filmed by other directors under his precise instructions. The first was his history of the Kurdish people told through the metaphor of a flock of sheep taken by train to Turkey's capital, Ankara. "I could not use the Kurdish language in it," he explained, "or all my actors would be arrested." Ironically, given that *Yol* was about five prisoners released from prison for a week to see their families, Güney himself escaped from prison in 1981 to complete its post-production. He died of cancer in France in 1984.

Across the border from Turkey a near-contemporary of Güney became Greece's most significant filmmaker to date. Theo Angelopoulos was born in Athens in 1935, studied at Paris's famous film school, IDHEC, in the 1960s, and debuted as a feature director in 1970. *O Thiassos/The Travelling Players* (Greece, 1975) brought him to international attention and exemplifies the themes and style of his body of work. 230 minutes long and composed of around 80 shots – 1,500 would be more typical for a film at the time – it used the journey of group of intinerant actors staging *Golfo and the Shepherdess* in bleak, wintry villages as the means to explore the politics of Greece in the years 1939–52. The performers are like refugees in their own country, their work reflecting some of the iniquities of the Nazi invasion as well as the ensuing civil war between communists and royalists. Angelopoulos' grand tracking shots are in the spirit of Mizoguchi, their complexity capturing the country's complicated history. Most of his subsequent films would also be allegorical journeys modelled on Homer's *Odyssey*, redolent in particular of that work's oar and winnowing fan sequence, in which a borderline between cultures is found when locals stop recognizing an oar as a maritime instrument and start identifying it as an agricultural one. Greece's borderline position between Europe, Asia and the Balkans seems to have made the idea of contested space a central political and historical one in Angelopoulos' great films – for example *Topio stiu omichli/Landscape of the Mist* (1988), *To Vlemma tou Odyssea/Ulysses' Gaze* (1997) and *Mia anioniotita kai mia mera/Eternity and a Day* (1998). His consistent use of the sequence shot has made the nature of time a parallel concern.

Finally, it comes as no surprise to discover that the continent of Torre Nilsson, of Glauber Rocha and Santiago Alvarez itself contributed much to Third Cinema in the 1970s. In the first year of the decade a former doctor called Salvador Allende won an election in Chile on a socialist ticket. His government gave Miguel Littin, a twenty-eight-year-old TV director, the job of running its new national film body, Chile Films. In 1973, Littin made *The Promised Land/La Tierra prometida*. Just as he was about to release it, Allende's government with overthrown in a military coup led by General Augusto Pinochet and supported by the US government. Littin was forced to leave the country but returned in disguise, risking his life to attempt to make a filmic account of the history of his country from the stock market crash to the coup. The Chilean novelist Gabriel

García Márquez documented Littín's experiences in *Clandestine in Chile: The Adventures of Miguel Littín*. The months leading up to the coup itself were brilliantly documented in Patricio Guzmán's four-and-three-quarter-hour non-fiction film *The Battle of Chile/La Batalla de Chile* (Cuba–Chile, 1975–79), which was edited in Cuba over a period of nearly four years. Guzmán presented in detail a heated debate at a trade union rally about whether or not the new leftist government should expropriate factories, incorporated newsreel of the aerial bombing of La Moneda palace where Allende was killed and used footage filmed by an Argentine cameraman as he was shot dead. The latter was a troubling first in non-fiction cinema. *The Battle for Chile* was one of the most influential of Third Cinema films.

WANT SEE AND THE SEISMIC CHANGE IN AMERICAN CINEMA

Looking back on the fourteen years between the release of Jean-Luc Godard's *A Bout de souffle* (France, 1959) and the anti-Allende coup in Chile, it is difficult not to be astonished by the ambitions of film-makers around the world. The European directors put their own lives on screen with such passion that they made us care. They rethought cinema as modern art, took it seriously and drew moral conclusions about its form. Americans followed suit, looting their own cinematic traditions for situations that they could modernize and problematize. South Americans used film as a political tool, Australians, Africans and Middle Easterners began to picture themselves on screen with originality and imagination.

But all was not well. The artistic renewal of cinema charted in this chapter and the previous one may have played well in cinemas in Paris, London, Rome, New York, Berlin, Sydney, Dakar, Tehran, Beirut, Mumbai and Santiago, but beyond the modern cities, it did not capture the imagination of moviegoers. Then something happened. In the year of the Chilean coup, an American horror film about demonic possession was the first film ever to take more than $200 million in the US. Two years later, a movie about a shark topped it by $60 million. Both, like *The Godfather*, were adaptations of best-selling novels. Two years after that, a sci-fi movie about the battle between good and evil forces in space demolished all records by taking over $500 million. There had never been figures like these, even in the days of *Gone with the Wind* (1939). Some kind of seismic change was taking place. The industry didn't understand it and had to run to catch up, but catch up it did. The success of *The Exorcist* (1973), *Jaws* (1975) and *Star Wars* (1977) changed American and then world cinema. The reason for making a film became that the audience would want to see it, not that a director wanted to make it. The interests of young people became more prioritized. To make things exciting, to conjure new escapist worlds, more and flashier special effects were used. As a result, the typical cost of a film increased by a factor of five. Because of this, far fewer were made. Since that meant that more was riding on the success of each, more money was spent on selling them to the public. In order to streamline this process, rough cuts were shown to average movie-goers whose responses were used to modify the film before its final release. Test screenings had been used before in Hollywood, but not on this scale. This system worked because by the end of the decade three out of seven films were making money. New movie theatres called multiplexes were built with a suite of small screens rather than one big one. In 1973, Columbia pictures was worth $6 million and carried $223 million of debts. Five years later it was worth $140 million and was just $35 million in the red. The era of the blockbuster had begun.

How did *The Exorcist*, *Jaws* and *Star Wars* revive the fortunes of the dying American industry? Some argue that they were just brilliantly crafted stories astutely marketed, but this is not the whole truth. Each built itself around something buried deep in the minds of audiences, something apparently unfilmable that they wanted to see – the devil, a monstrous shark, space ships. For nearly sixty years, from about 1915 to 1973, with exceptions like *King Kong* and the 1950s sci-fi pictures, American movies had been about people and what they do – fall in love, explore the mid-west, commit crimes, drive cars, dance, sing, etc. Many of the new blockbuster films also had strong characters but they drew more from comic books, the ideas of psychoanalyst Sigmund Freud, and from myth. Like very early, pre-psychological cinema, they used the promise of sensation, thrill and fear to lure people back to the cinema. These films were like Roger Corman B-movies but produced on a massive scale. One of the many ironies of the period is that unlike those making the more artistically ambitious films of the time, none of the men behind these three films had actually started out with Corman.

Take William Friedkin, the director of *The Exorcist*. Rather than going to film school or worshipping European films in art cinemas, he got a foot in the door by working in the mail office of a TV station, then worked his way up to documentary directing. In 1971 he had a big hit with the gritty detective film *The French Connection*. His next movie, *The Exorcist*, was about a white, middle-class, pubescent girl who becomes possessed by the devil and who battles with priests who attempt to exorcise her (282). As Polanski had done with *Rosemary's Baby* (1968), Friedkin took this story seriously, filmed it with technical brilliance, turning its apparently innocent girl into an abject creature,

her body battered, her features porcine, her mind and speech poisoned by evil. What if we treated a supernatural tale as if it was a documentary? he seemed to ask himself. He fired guns on the set to scare people, slapped an actor hard on the face then immediately filmed his trembling response. Such techniques created tensions on the set which ended up on screen. His constant aim was to suggest the ferocity of the devil's power rooted in an absolutely credible middle-class American setting. *The Exorcist* caroused through delicate sensibilities. Reviews were mixed but audiences flocked. People lined around the block to see the film, to test their

282
Above: The beginning of a new era in commercial cinema: event movies such as *The Exorcist* emphasized sensation rather than contemplation, and broke box office records. Director: William Friedkin. USA, 1973.

stamina as they would on a roller coaster. Some fainted, others were sick, many had nightmares for years to come.

Although *The Exorcist* would demolish many taboos about religion, profanity and childhood, Friedkin's approach to telling its story was traditional. His attitude to the more ambitious filmmaking of the time is neatly captured in his reaction to the first draft of *The Exorcist* screenplay, which was more tricksy than the bestselling novel on which it was based. After reading it he told its writer, William Peter Blatty, "I just want to tell a straight story from beginning to end, with no craperoo."[22] Friedkin got this no-nonsense approach to storytelling from veteran director Howard Hawks. He had been going out with Hawks' daughter Kitty and when she introduced him to her father he told Friedkin that audiences don't want "that psychological shit."[23] Friedkin was shaken by this blast from Old Hollywood's past. "I had this epiphany that what we were doing wasn't making fucking films to hang in the Louvre", he said.[24] He would begin to make films which used the straight storytelling techniques of closed romantic realism, rejecting anything too subjective, autobiographical, experimental or philosophical. By heeding Hawks, by ditching what he called the craperoo, by equating New Hollywood with pictures hanging in an old art gallery, he did nothing less than sound the first cry of the counter-revolution. "I have my finger on the pulse of America"[25] was his rationale. These nine words killed New Hollywood.

283
Right: Like Friedkin, Steven Spielberg emphasized the thrill of American cinema, re-exciting audiences in traditional storytelling. *Jaws*. USA, 1975.

They could also have been spoken by the director whom *Time* magazine eventually called the most influential in cinema history. Like Friedkin, he was a lower middle-class Jewish American. Two years after *The Exorcist*, he made a film which similarly tapped into the nervous systems of baby boomers, the new generation of young Americans who were conceived in the years of post-war optimism.

Steven Spielberg had been making amateur films since boyhood. He was more influenced by directors like Victor Fleming, who had made *The Wizard of Oz* (1939) and the sentimental *A Guy Named Joe* (1944) than the new crop of Europeans. "I was more truly a child of the establishment," he said later, "than I was a product of USC or NYU or the Francis Coppola protégé clique."[26] He tricked his way into the Universal studio and soon directed the strikingly intense chase TV movie *Duel* (1971) there. It was clear that he was a master storyteller, a graceful reinvigorator of closed romantic realism. *Jaws* (1975) was about a small holiday community terrorized by what seems to be a homicidal Great White shark. In order not to dent business the local mayor refuses to close the beaches. Eventually a Hawksian band of professionals – a salty fisherman, a nerdy shark scientist and a police chief – go out in a small boat and hunt and kill the beast.

At first Spielberg felt that a film about a killer shark was beneath him. He was more interested in modernism than Friedkin. Eventually he took the job of directing it. Traditionally this would have involved casting movie stars and shooting in a tank but Spielberg, in the manner of Friedkin's aggressive realism, wanted to film on the open sea with less well-known actors. To make the material more personal he re-fashioned a nerdy scientist character, to be played by Richard Dreyfuss, into a version of himself, having his actor at one point crush a polystyrene cup in his hand in mockery of the macho way of crushing a beer can. This was comically Hawksian. Dreyfuss' character was an ordinary, slightly childish, not very heroic or handsome man. This became Spielberg's signature character, and the actor would play him again in Spielberg's next film *Close Encounters of the Third Kind* (1977).

The shoot of *Jaws* went badly; there was seasickness and argument, and the production overspent by a factor of three. The twenty-seven-year-old director almost reached breaking point. As the mechanized shark failed to work for much of the shoot and was unconvincing when it did, it was decided not to reveal it until the final section of the film, when the men are in the boat. When Dreyfuss first sees the full size of the shark, his face goes blank, he's choked, he backs away (283). This would be one of Spielberg's first awe-and-revelation scenes. Key moments in many of his films thereafter, they were masterpieces of camera positioning and acting. The one in *Jaws* was effortless storytelling and turned the film into an epic.

At *Jaws'* first previews, a man ran from the cinema. Spielberg thought he hated the film but in fact he was scared. The film electrified audiences. Studios had started to advertise their films on television in 1973, but Columbia made a quantum leap, spending $700,000 on thirty-second TV promotions, and they opened it on over 400 screens at once, far more than usual. Not only was the visceral effect of *Jaws* immediate, so too was its selling. The market was immediately saturated by it. There was no time for reviews or word of mouth to affect its box office. Everybody knew about it, everywhere, at once. Since it's a good and nuanced film, *Jaws* would probably have performed very well under the old system of releasing films but that is irrelevant now. Its huge success made film storytelling and film marketing alike a science of the momentary big impact. This approach more than anything, weakened the practice of releasing smaller, more complex films in a more limited way at first, so that word of mouth about them could build slowly.

The themes that were touched on in *Jaws* – the decency of ordinary men, troubled father figures, the security of family life, the awe felt about something sublime or terrifying – would become central to Spielberg's career thereafter. The new multiplexes were where that career developed. That they are often in the suburbs, on the edges of towns, is appropriate, because it is there that Spielberg's imagination was most fertile.

It seemed that the success of *Jaws* would be the benchmark for commercial American cinema for years to come but less than thirty months later another film almost doubled its box-office take. Unlike Spielberg, George Lucas did go to film school and was a protégé of Francis Coppola. A native Californian and former racing driver, he was artistically somewhat ambitious and made prize-winning films. After the success of his second feature, *American Graffiti* (USA, 1973), he thought "Maybe I should make a film for even younger kids. *Graffiti* was for sixteen-year-olds; this [*Star Wars*] is for ten-and twelve-year-olds".[27] This film for ten-year-olds turned out to be the most influential film in post-Second World War cinema. Critic and director Paul Schrader said that it "ate the heart and soul of Hollywood."[28] It cost $11 million and took $460 million.

The film starts like a fairy-tale – "A long time ago, in a galaxy far, far away." The sound-track, which was immensely powerful and engulfing, was recorded in the relatively new format of Dolby six-track stereo. Few cinemas were able to reproduce the full richness of this system but those that could were so successful with *Star Wars* than most of the others followed suit. After the credits, spaceships as big as cities loom into shot (284). These were detailed models filmed with motion control cameras called DykstraFlexes after John Dykstra, the special-effects expert who designed them for this film.Similar ones had been used in television but not much in cinema. Instead of dollying on a machine moved by grips, their desired moves were programmed by computers. Such moves could then be replicated precisely so that separate shots of models moving in different directions through space could be superimposed onto a single image. The fight scenes later in the film revealed the new dynamism possible with this technique. Most of the production's 400 special effects shots were undertaken by a subsidiary company,

284
Below: The third film which adrenalized American cinema at this time was *Star Wars*. Like *The Exorcist* and *Jaws* it reversed the modern and mature themes of New American Cinema, replacing them with the pleasures of escapism and shock. Director: George Lucas. USA, 1977.

285
Above: Many of *Star Wars'* story elements were drawn from Kurosawa's *The Hidden Fortress*. Japan, 1958.

Industrial Light and Magic, which would become central to American special effects cinema in the years to come.

Then the film introduces us to an apparent orphan, Luke, who lives on a farm with his aunt and uncle and who yearns for adventure. Lucas, who had spent more than two years writing the script, saw Lucas in literary or even mythic terms, as a knight who would eventually save the universe. He does so by assisting a princess who has programmed into a small robot – the famous R2D2 – the plans of the Death Star, the vast spaceship vessel of the evil emperor who has temporarily taken over the planet. The director later claimed that he had the recently shamed American president Richard Nixon in mind when he wrote this part. R2D2 goes in search of the greatest knight of them all whose wisdom has allowed him to master the force of the universe. Luke follows the robot, meets the great knight and learns from him the mystical techniques of will to conquer evil.

This is the most absurd scenario of any detailed so far in this book. Yet even its outline suggests the breadth of its schema. The business about knights and their self-discipline came from Kurosawa's samurai films. *Kakushi Toride No San-Akunin/*

The Hidden Fortress (Akira Kurosawa, Japan, 1958) in particular – about a princess, a master warrior and an R2D2–C3PO pairing of characters Tahei and Matashichi – seems to have provided Lucas with elements of his story (285). The evil characters in the tale were filmed in a way that was reminiscent of German director Leni Riefenstahl's *The Triumph of the Will* (1935). The quest narrative structure, with its series of defeats and recoveries, derived from shor adventure serials shown before feature films in earlier decades. These were certainly not obvious starting points for the most commercially successful American film of all time but Lucas used them to enrich what was in fact a fable for boys. Shot with bright flat lighting and edited in part using "wipes" moving horizontally across the screen, it had the moral clarity of a 1930s B-movie Western, cutting between goodies and baddies, building excitement through action, offsetting it with romance and humour.

Star Wars had no sex and little graphic violence, it was the story of a young man becoming a hero, achieving his destiny, awaking to the mystery of life and saving the universe along the way. He was masculine, had an inner life of sorts, and got the girl. Watching it felt like no other film experience. It was louder, it seemed to make the cinema shake, it moved through space with more dynamism than any previous film. It was also less about adult human beings than most films of its time. It made no attempt to "open up the form" of sci fi, as *2001: A Space Odyssey* (1968) had done. Twice as many people saw it as *Jaws*. It got more young people and families into cinemas than previous films. Lucas doubled his already huge profits by having models made of Luke, the princess and the spaceships and selling them to children. Not since Mickey Mouse had merchandizing been so successful. Also, it came along just as yet another invention extended film even further into people's lives: a little rectangular box containing video tape.

The Exorcist, *Jaws* and *Star Wars* were a phenomenon that would probably have been enough to re-orient American cinema away from the personal visions of serious directors toward the pulse of sub-urban teenagers, but this grand three-point-turn was confirmed by the box-office failure of two expensive personal films. Martin Scorsese's reimagining of an MGM musical as a brilliant but deadlocked piece of creative pessimism, *New York, New York*, cost a fortune, lost most of it, nearly ruined the director and was taken by many as New Hollywood's bridge too far. Three years later his fellow Italian-

American Michael Cimino made a bleak, dreamlike and personal Marxist Western *Heaven's Gate* (1980), which lost so much money that it crippled its studio, United Artists (286). No matter that it was serene and magnificent. Both films were seen as monstrous works of ego, disdainful of audience pleasure, self-indulgent and even self-destructive. They were the final nails in the coffin of New Hollywood.

The 1970s saw the extension and then reversal of the 1960s idea of cinema. African, Middle-Eastern and South American filmmakers made political films about their own countries, rejecting the form and content of traditional Western cinema. Over in Germany, a series of bold new films frequently adopted this traditional form to address new historical, sexual and national content. American directors in the early part of the decade did something like the opposite of this, taking the war, gangster, musical and Western genres of their nation's past and, influenced by European directors and great cinematographers, applied new formal approaches to them to explore complex human and philosophical ideas. In an echo of the 1920s, all these things extended the art of cinema.

But perhaps it was at the expense of thrill and spectacle. Baby boomers seemed to tire of change, of activism, of new types of art, and wanted to switch off for a bit. They joined the younger ones in

286
Right: One of the final nails in the coffin of personal American filmmaking was the Michael Cimino's epic, glacially paced Western *Heaven's Gate*. Its box office failure was blamed on the indulgence and hubris of its director and, thereafter, filmmakers were kept on a tighter leash. USA, 1980.

the front row of the new multiplex cinemas, blasted away by light sabres, the Force and the Millennium Falcon. It was back to the thrills of the earliest years. Humanism, for better and worse, leeched out of American cinema and by the end of the 1970s, its movies were no longer a means of personal self-expression for the directors.

1. Pier Paolo Pasolini in *A Future Life*, op. cit., p159.
2. Interview used in Luchino Visconti, *Arena*, BBC Television, 2002.
3. Former Paramount executive Peter Bart, quoted in *Easy Riders, Raging Bulls*, Simon and Schuster, p.20.
4. Martin Scorsese in an interview with Peter Biskind in *Easy Riders, Raging Bulls*, op. cit., p.152.
5. Martin Scorsese in *Martin Scorsese, A Journey*, Kelly, Mary Pat, Secker and Warburg, p71.
6. Paul Schrader in an interview with the author, *Scene by Scene*, BBC Television.
7. *Fat City* was among the first fiction films not to compensate for exterior overexposure and interior underexposure, but the Direct Cinema documentarians of more than a decade earlier pioneered this disregard for the conventions of balanced lighting.
8. Gordon Willis in *Easy Riders, Raging Bulls*, op. cit., p154.
9. Thomas Elsaesser, quoted in author's essay on New German Cinema, unpublished.
10. Quoted in "Forms of Address", Tony Rayns, *Sight and Sound* 44, vol. 1, pp2–7.
11. Thomsen, Christian Braad, *Fassbinder*.
12. Richard Dyer, op. cit.
13. Werner Herzog in *Time* magazine, 20 March 1978, p57.
14. Rajadhyaksha and Willemen, op. cit.
15. Quoted in Rajadhyaksha and Willemen, op. cit.
16. The Philippines' most political filmmaker of the period was former TV writer Lino Brocka. Brocka debuted in cinema in 1970, but it is his 1980s work that is most significant. *Bayan ko: Kapit sa patalim/My Country: Gripping the Knife's Edge* (1984) is a powerful social drama about a print worker who robs his bosses to pay for his child's medical bills. *Macho Dancer* (1988) looked at the country's teenage sex industry but was criticized for what some considered its ambivalence about the sexual activity portrayed.
17. Youssef Chahine in the documentary *Camera Arabe*, BFI.
18. Ibid.
19. Manthia Diawara.
20. Hamid Dabash, *Close Up: Iranian Cinema Past, Present and Future*.
21. Quoted in Armes, Roy, *Third World Filmmaking and the West*, op. cit.
22. William Friedkin, ibid., p203.
23. Howard Hawks, ibid., p203.
24. William Friedkin, ibid., p203.
25. William Friedkin, ibid., p203.
26. Steven Spielberg, ibid., p278.
27. George Lucas, ibid., p318.
28. Paul Schrader, ibid., p316.

MEGA-ENTERTAINMENTS AND PHILOSOPHY (1979–90): THE EXTREMES OF WORLD CINEMA

MEGA-ENTERTAINMENTS AND PHILOSOPHY (1979—90)
The extremes of world cinema

9

By the end of the 1970s, the New Wave directors had been routed by Darth Vader and the multiplexes, and also by a shift in the country's self-image. A right-wing former actor, Ronald Reagan, was inaugurated as president in January 1980. His message that America had indulged in enough self-criticism, that the country was noble and that the 1960s generation had been mistaken, was an explicit rejection of their troubled conception of modern American life. America wanted to think of itself as heroic once more and along came Reagan to say that it was.

1970s American cinema had certainly been skewed in the direction of downbeat male themes. Of the US films detailed in the last chapter, only *Cabaret* (1972) was substantially about a woman. The anti-heroism, open-endedness, ambiguity, abstraction, irony and self-doubt of New American directors like Scorsese and Coppola were hung around male characters, and even the traditionalist Sam Peckinpah had pictured his violent men – James Coburn in *Pat Garrett and Billy the Kid* (1973), Warren Oates in *Bring me the*

287
Far Left: Challenging images of masculinity and nationhood in Derek Jarman's avant-garde film *The Last of England*. UK, 1988.

Head of Alfredo Garcia (1974), Coburn again in *Cross of Iron* (UK–Germany, 1977) – as if they were caught in a slow-motion cycle of pessimism and self-destruction. This bleak view of masculinity died in Ronald Reagan's triumphant consensus. Instead, the number-one films at the world box office for each of the years of the new optimistic decade of the 1980s were: *The Empire Strikes Back* (1980), *Raiders of the Lost Ark* (1981), *E.T. The Extra-Terrestrial* (1982), *Return of the Jedi* (1983), *Ghostbusters* (1984), *Back to the Future* (1985), *Top Gun* (1986), *Three Men and a Baby* (1987), *Rain Man* (1988), *Batman* (1989) and *Home Alone* (1990). With the exception of *Rain Man*, all were about fantasy and adventure, the fun of regressing to boyhood or the adrenalin rush of masculine power.

INITIAL PROMISE IN 1980S AMERICAN CINEMA

The counter-revolution that this involved did not happen all at once. In fact, the beginning of the 1980s was a great time for complexity in US cinema. In the first year of the decade alone *Raging Bull*, *American Gigolo*, *The Elephant Man*, *The Shining*, *Heaven's Gate* and *Return of the Secaucus 7* seemed to promise a maturity in US cinema. But the uncertainty and pessimism of these films would soon become untenable in the bright light of the new era. Even *The Empire Strikes Back* (Irvin Kershner, 1980) was an improvement on its prequel *Star Wars*. Its lighting style was noticeably lower key, its trainee Jedi knight Luke Skywalker was having doubts about his ability to use the Force, his band of coalition friends were facing defeat, he discovered that the evil Darth Vader was in fact his father. Martin Scorsese's *Raging Bull* was his most painful story yet about spiritual fall and redemption. The asthmatic, artistic, physically delicate Scorsese perhaps surprisingly found a metaphor for himself in the bullish, inarticulate boxer Jake La Motta. There were little psychic connections between the two men, like both being somewhat embarrassed by the fact that they had small hands. Such details allowed the author to read himself into the fictional character. Jake could take a beating but many thought he was worth nothing on any higher level, a point that La Motta finally realized when, abject and imprisoned, he punches the cell walls moaning, "I am not an animal, I am not an animal." Scorsese knew everything about this rage. It was hyper-real for him and, in the boxing scenes in the film, he showed what it felt like, how it floated through space, how it went mute then snapped into fear again (288). Crane shots captured the disorientation of a beaten body, switches between slow-motion and speeded-up filming caught the lurches in La Motta's mental state. The meticulous sound-track layered organic noises as if they were recorded inside a reeling head. This was magic filming, as good as Méliès, Cocteau or Welles. But after such moments the director would nail his camera to the floor.

To capture Jake's home life – arguing with his wife (289), trying to fix the TV – Scorsese filmed in the kind of tableau scenes he'd used when he made the documentary about his parents, *Italianamerican* (1974). No one had combined expressionism and non-fiction shooting styles in this way.

Although *Raging Bull* is sometimes called the best film of the 1980s, it had

nothing to do with that decade. Its screenwriter Paul Schrader was the first to capture the tinny narcissism of 1980s masculinity in his third film as director. *American Gigolo* (1980) was about a prostitute – a very New Wave subject – except this one was a man, an appropriate inversion to launch a decade of cinematic male-worship. Played by Richard Gere, he enjoys being both the seller and the commodity and delights in the shallow pop music, designer clothes and fast cars that were the 1980s' symbols of power and success. Like the decade itself,

Schrader seemed to be saying, this man has no inner life or, rather, no spiritual life. His sex scene with Lauren Hutton is a series of abstract body parts, an almost shot-for-shot replica of one in Jean-Luc Godard's *Une Femme mariée/A Married Woman* (France, 1959). Directly copying Bresson's ending in *Pickpocket* (France, 1959) he imprisons his main character then, through the visit of a woman, has him

290
Above: John Sayles' novelistic portrait of the social and political connections in a medium-sized town went against the simplifying trend in eighties cinema. *City of Hope*. USA, 1991.

finally break out of his emotional isolation (see page 251–3). Schrader's exploration of bodies and surfaces, combined with his interest in the transcendence of bodily experience, make him one of the most ambiguous figures in modern American cinema.

The critic in Schrader was able to articulate the intellectual and formal achievement of his films, as was another writer-turned-director, the prolific John Sayles. After starting with Roger Corman, working on small budgets and going against the Reaganite drift of his times, Sayles soon became America's State-of-the-Nation filmmaker and one of the key independents of his day. Rather than make movies about himself, as Martin Scorsese, David Lynch and Woody Allen did, Sayles' subjects were marginal and complex communities. His first film, *Return of the Secaucus 7* (1979), was a timely look at a group of 1960s political protesters, twenty years on. *City of Hope* (1991) was the greatest anti-Reagan film of the decade. About the compromises of small-city business and politics, it featured a mesh of no less than fifty-two speaking parts, with characters from one storyline walking into the ending of another, which Sayles in the screenplay called "trading" (290). The complex interaction between characters and story points was difficult to follow at first but slowly the references to developments and deals made sense.

The period's other radical director, Spike Lee, was less of a sociologist. His feature debut *She's Gotta Have It* (1986) turned on its head the sexual bravado of films like Melvin Van Peebles' *Sweet Sweetback's Baadasssss Song* (1971) by telling the story of a young black woman's erotic successes. Like Martin Scorsese, Lee studied at New York University and, although his budgets were as low as Sayles', his imagery – photographed by the outstanding Ernest Dickerson – was considerably more stylized. His *Do the Right Thing* (1989) was a great advance in this regard. Set on a single, sweltering day in Brooklyn, New York, its tensions between local blacks and Latinos are sparked by events at a pizzeria. Like *City of Hope*, it features a cross-section of characters. The intensity of Dickerson's colours

291
Below: Spike Lee as pizza delivery man Mookie in his brilliant disquisition on inter-ethnic violence in New York, *Do The Right Thing*. USA, 1989.

match the film's boiling themes (291). Lee used the tilted camera angles of one of his favourite films, *The Third Man* (UK, 1949, see page 204) to render everything off kilter. He himself played the character Mookie, who eventually throws a trash can through the window of the pizzeria, shouting "Howard Beach", a reference to a real white-on-black racist attack, as he does so. At the end Lee paired a quotation from Martin Luther King denouncing violence with one from Malcolm X advocating it in self-defence. It was this that enraged some critics. One New York magazine wrote "The end of the film is a shambles, and if some audiences go wild, [Lee] is partly responsible."[1]

David Lynch, another serious American filmmaker of the period, came from the opposite end of the political spectrum. He was the most original director in 1980s cinema, its only surrealist. He studied painting in, amongst other places, Philadelphia, a city he hated so much that monstrous versions of it would recur throughout his work. His nightmarish debut feature, *Eraserhead* (1977), drew its expressionism from the city, but layered it with numerous intangible fears – of fatherhood, dark corners of rooms, the unknown at the edge of everyday experience. These manifested themselves as grub-like animals, fleeced infant creatures and extended hairdos. Lynch's follow-up, *The Elephant Man* (1980), was again about deformity and the fear of cities but he added an unexpected tenderness to its central character, the disfigured John Merrick who lived in Victorian London. The scene where a sympathetic doctor finally comes across Merrick hidden away in the shadowy underworld of the city is intensely moving – Lynch tracks in just as a tear falls down the doctor's cheek, yet the originality of Lynch's schema prevents the film ever becoming a conventional one.

292
Below: Deformity and tenderness in David Lynch's the *Elephant Man*. USA, 1980.

In his mind the director connected the bulbous growths on Merrick's skull (292), for example, both to the explosions of smoke from a recently erupted volcano, Mount St. Helens, and to the cloud-like forms that paint makes when it is poured into water.[2]

This intuitively abstract approach to the imagery of a film found its greatest outlet in Lynch's astonishing *Blue Velvet* (1986). This was a fable about a teenager who grows up in a small town like the young Lynch, hides in a mysterious woman's wardrobe and spies on her as Lynch had dreamt of doing, then gets drawn into the

Sudheshwar Anand who started in promotional films for television, and became one of the most powerful directors of escapist cinema.

There was much to escape from. In 1983 the country's army stormed a sacred Sikh temple at Amritsar. Over 800 people died. The following October, the country's prime minister, Indira Gandhi, was assassinated in a revenge killing by two of her Sikh bodyguards. Two months later, a toxic gas leak from a pesticide factory owned by the American company Union Carbide killed over 2,000 people in a single day in the city of Bhopal in the centre of the country. Hundreds of thousands have since gone blind or have suffered liver or kidney failure.

India's more intellectual filmmakers continued to produce non-mainstream work, but the success of masculine action films further marginalized them. The most experimental of them, Mani Kaul, who made *Uski Roti* (see pages 316–17), managed to direct *Siddheshwari* (India, 1989), a poetic documentary evocation of the life and music of the legendary thumri musician of the film's title. The film is glacially slow and influenced by Robert Bresson, but among the most haunting and beautiful ever made (298).

The case of Akira Kurosawa reveals how cruel are the reversals of fortune in the film industry. In 1950, he was the toast of the film world, the keeper of the flame of art cinema. Two decades later, he could not get funding and, in 1971, attempted suicide. Meanwhile, across the globe, George Lucas borrowed from his *The Hidden Fortress*, set it in outer space, called it *Star Wars*, and rang the world box-office bell.

In some kind of acknowledgement of that debt, Lucas and his friend Francis Coppola helped produce Kurosawa's *Kagemusha* (1980) (299), his first film in five years. So much time had the out-of-work director on his hands (like Welles, he made a crust doing drinks commercials) that he did hundreds of drawings and paintings for the film. It became the most pre-designed of his movies and the most expensive in Japanese film

298
Below: Mani Kaul continued to be one of India's most contemplative directors. *Siddheshwari*, his semi-documentary about the life of a great female musician, was his most beautifully photographed work. Its cinematographer was Piyush Shah. 1989.

Right: The story of
Kagemusha told of a thief
who resembles a warlord,
but what is striking about
these two images is how
much director Akira
Kurosawa's shot scene
resembles his design (far
right). Camera angle and
height, figure and
prop placement are
almost identical; only
the wallpaper design has
substantially changed.
Japan, 1980.

history. This painting of the seated lead character (299, bottom right),
a thief who so resembles a dead warlord that he becomes his "stand-in"
("Kagemusha" in Japanese), is much more finished than any
storyboard needs to be. As well as stipulating the exact square-on,
low-camera level, full seated-height framing, Kurosawa anticipates
precisely the composition of the action: Tatsaya Kakadai centred,
symmetrically flanked by the two women. The painting also details
questions of make-up, hair, costume and set design. Kurosawa was
acting as director, cinematographer and production designer. It is as
if, fearful of the possibility that the film might not be made and
nostalgic for a classical time in filmmaking when such details were
meticulously addressed, he poured all his creative energy into its

his own, original sense of gender, feeling, coincidence and the absurd. This former telephone company worker rocketed out of the uncertain period in Spanish history between the death of dictator Franco in 1975 and the election of socialist prime minister Felipe Gonzáles in 1982. Madrid felt like the centre of the world to its newly liberated youth and, in *Laberinto de pasiones/Labyrinth of Passion* (Spain, 1980), Almodóvar splashed the capital city's freneticism onto the screen. He loved the swinging 1960s London films of Richard Lester (see page 300) blending their anarchism with the *esperpento* tradition of absurdist humour (see page 292). Bucking the trend in America to celebrate traditional gender roles, he peopled his film with fifty characters of every sexual persuasion including Sexi, a nymphomaniac who is afraid of sunlight, Riza, the gay heir to a fictitious Arab throne, whom student terrorists are trying to kidnap, Toraya, an aristocrat who tries to seduce him, and Sexi's father, a famous fertility doctor. Against all odds, Sexi and Riza meet in a disco and fall in love. *Esperpento* was always about the gap between Spain's fascist image of itself and the grim realities of the country. In this film and his subsequent 1980s films such as *Qué he hecho you para merecer esto!/What Have I Done to Deserve This?* (Spain, 1984), *La Ley del deseo/Law of Desire* (Spain, 1987) and *Women on the Verge of a Nervous Breakdown* (Spain, 1988) he turned that fascist image on its

305
Below: In Spain, new director Pedro Almodóvar also used bright colours and garish production designs in his films, but his heightened characterization and absurdist plotting made his work more subversive – though less popular – than that of his French contemporaries. *Labyrinth of Passion.* Spain, 1980.

306

Above: *Law of Desire* continued Almodóvar's interest in narrative and gender reversal. Spain, 1987.

head. The father figures are lusted after; the mothers are sources of power and symbols of the law. Years of sexual rigidity are blown away by these films, which were often photographed by Angel Fernandez in the bright primary hues of American cartoons. Almodóvar, who had once written a memoir of invented porn star Patti Diphusa in the form of a comic strip-like photo-novel, wallowed in the absurdist emotions of such forms. The humour and irreverence of his films, their pop-art brightness, their sexual explicitness and discovery that, for their women characters at least, subjugation is the first step on the road to recovery and dignity, made his work strikingly popular. Even conservative Spanish newspapers supported his explicitly homosexual *Law of Desire* when it was a hit at the 1987 Berlin Film Festival and no less than six of the top thirteen Spanish films released in the US were directed by him.

Where the new leftist-liberal political climate in Spain created a creative boom in cinema, a shift to the neo-liberal political right had a similar effect in the UK. Like Ronald Reagan, Margaret Thatcher, who was elected prime minister in 1979, felt that business should be vigorous and even iconoclastic but that art and culture should reassure and bolster a traditional sense of national pride. Many agreed with her, as the success at home and abroad of the nuanced literary adaptations *The Bostonians* (UK, 1984, novel Henry James), *A Room with a View* (UK, 1985, novel E.M. Forster), and *Howards End* (UK, 1992, novel E.M. Forster) showed. Each was directed by an American James Ivory, written by a German-Polish-Jewish novelist married to an Indian, Ruth Prawer Jhabvala, and produced by the Indian Ismail Merchant. Merchant Ivory films found in Britain's past, whether in its colonies or in its stately homes, an ambition to be a tolerant and civilized nation which it did not always live up to. Their films were dignified and intelligent in the manner of Claude Autant-Lara or David Lean and were a showcase for actors like Daniel Day-Lewis, Maggie Smith, Helena Bonham Carter, Anthony

NEW TALENTS IN AUSTRALIA AND CANADA

Right at the end of Australia's first decade of indigenous filmmaking, the 1970s, a New South Wales-born former doctor, George Miller, poured his emergency ward experiences[9] into an apocalyptic low-budget sci-fi film, edited it in his bedroom, and rang the box-office bell so much with it that in Australia more people saw it than *Star Wars*.

Mad Max (Australia, 1979) and its sequel *Mad Max 2 The Road Warrior* (Australia, 1981) told of a good cop, Max Rockatansky (Mel Gibson), in a future world where the rule of law has deteriorated and road rats and somewhat effeminate druggies terrorize people then walk free from the courts on technicalities. This staple B-movie scenario proceeds, predictably enough, with the cop's wife and child being viciously

murdered by a psychotic gang and Gibson, as a result, turning into a mad avenger. Miller's vision of society had the simplicity of Reaganite Republicanism, while his vision of masculinity was pure *Rambo: First Blood Part II*, both films, while square in line with the new Western video-influenced cinema, were dazzlingly made. When Gibson's child is murdered, we see only his (or her – it's very impersonal) shoes flying through the air. In the sequel Miller mounted some of the most thrilling chase sequences ever filmed. Gibson is by now a drifting loner, petrol is scarce, he and a group of good people protect a refinery, but various desert rats in complexly designed high-speed vehicles (312) and in desperate need of fuel, attack. The schema of cinematic chase, first established in the 1900s, was enlivened by such sequences but, despite Miller's attempts to dignify his film with references to the *Iliad*, his ideas remained those of 1980s conservatism: simplistic moralism, fear of outsiders, endorsement of the nuclear family, and a sense that the judicial system has failed society. The first film by an Aboriginal director, Brian Syron, *Jindalee Lady* (Australia, 1992), would not appear for another decade.

312
Above: The use of wide-angle lenses and baroque vehicle design made *Mad Max 2 The Road Warrior* a vivid, if dystopic, experience. Director: George Miller. Australia, 1981.

311
Far left: Davies used the rosy familial optimism of Hollywood and the dreamlike mood of tracking shots such as this one as a counterpoint to the bleakness of the events he depicted. *Young at Heart*. Director: Gordon Douglas. USA, 1954.

It is perhaps unsurprising that Canadian cinema took a more dissident attitude to 1980s conservatism. In fact, for the first time in film history, that country produced cinematic voices that gained international recognition. The most distinctive, David Cronenberg, a mild-mannered Toronto intellectual who studied literature, released a series of metaphorical films about the nature of the grotesque. Like Britain's Peter Greenaway, he was fascinated by what happens to the human body when it decays or is invaded, and became the centre of a group of directors exploring Western society's anxieties about this. Commentators at the time called this tendency "body horror" and connected it to the fears about illness and physical contact resulting from increased awareness of AIDS. "See the movies from the point of view of the disease", was his radical inversion of the anthropomorphic norm. "You can see why they would resist all attempts to destroy them. These are all cerebral games, but they have emotional correlatives as well."[10] His tenth movie, *The Fly* (USA, 1986) demonstrates this approach most clearly. A remake of a 1958 sci-fi movie of the same title, it reverses the values of the original, finding liberating positives in its story of a scientist (Jeff Goldblum) whose biochemistry becomes combined with that of a fly when it accidentally flies into a telepod, which Goldblum has invented to transport his body through space. The new adjunct creature is more sexually able and more powerful than mere man. Cronenberg's best films have been chamber works set in small microcosms with few actors and, despite being an American studio film, this one is too (313). It is basically two characters in a room, that looks like a cellar, with dust constantly in the air. Only the music is epic. The claustrophobia is reminiscent of the films of Roman Polanski, but Cronenberg's portrait of a man losing his humanity and gaining fly-like qualities is an unexpected work of optimism.

Released in the mid-1980s, it was widely taken to be a film about AIDS. In fact, what attracted the director was the way that Goldblum, in love with a woman who is repelled by his looks, ages

313
Below: Jeff Goldblum's grotesque metamorphosis in David Cronenberg's moving satire on ageing, *The Fly*. USA, 1986.

remained Japanese until 1945, was taken in 1949 by the Chinese nationalists, and has remained independent of mainland China ever since. Filmmaking in Taiwan had been sporadic and action-oriented in the 1970s but, as on the mainland, it blossomed in the 1980s. A film festival and archive were founded in 1982 and, stimulated by these, a more philosophical and less commercial approach to filmmaking emerged. Edward Yang and Hou Hsiao-Hsien were its standard-bearers, with Hou the more distinctive of the two.

Of the ten films he made in the 1980s, *Beiqin Chengshi/City of Sadness* (Taiwan, 1989) is perhaps the most revealing. Set in those crucial four years between 1945 and 1949, it uses the Lin family as the lens through which to picture the complexity of life on the island and the birth of the modern Taiwanese nation. The oldest of the four brothers, for example, turns a Japanese bar into one called Little Shanghai. Hou's family had emigrated to Taiwan in 1948 and this film, like most of his others, is autobiographical.

What is immediately striking about it is that, like Terence Davies' *Distant Voices, Still Lives*, it uses long-held shots to enact this remembering. Unlike Davies, these shots are usually static. The film lasts 158 minutes and contains only 222 cuts, meaning that the average shot length is an astonishing forty-three seconds, longer even than those of Mizoguchi in Japan in the 1930s. The effect is almost a repudiation of the kinetic cinematic style of the island's neighbour Hong Kong. Where Tsui Hark imported American shooting and editing techniques, Hou's film is a meditative longing for the past and,

as he said, "A screen holding a long-shot [i.e. long take] has a certain kind of tension".[11] Although the Hitchcock of *Rope* (USA, 1948, see page 194) would certainly have agreed with these words, Hou does not refer to the issue of narrative suspense or dread. Instead, the tension in his films lies in their ability to contain such complex portraits of rural Taiwan in the 1950s and 1960s in such rigorous, minimal formal structures. The dread is that the structure will collapse. An

316
Above: The story of the birth of modern Taiwan, *City of Sadness'* static shots were influenced by Ozu. Director: Hou Hsiao-Hsien. Taiwan, 1989.

example of such rigour is how consistently Hou films certain locations in *City of Sadness*. After the second oldest brother in the film returns from a tour of duty in the war and has mental health problems, he is treated in a local hospital. As has been pointed out by other critics,[12] each time he returns to that hospital Hou shoots from exactly the same camera angle, there is no variety, there are no reverses or alternatives. In Hou's spare conception of cinema, there is only one way to film a place. Or, rather, since these are films about remembering, places and visual memories of them are the same thing.

The one body of work which profoundly influenced Hou in choosing to film in such an understated way is Yasujiro Ozu's. Hou admired not only the formal rigour of the Japanese master, but also the philosophical repose of his work. Like Ozu, Hou seldom uses close-ups and limits camera moves. Space for Hou – the filming of the hospital in *City of Sadness* again works as an example – is not something to move through at speed, to activate, as it was for most 1980s directors. Instead, again like Ozu, it was something to contemplate and balance.[13] This makes Hou the great classicist of cinema's modern era. In tribute to his master, the Taiwanese director uses an excerpt from Ozu's *Late Spring* (Japan, 1949) on a television set in his later film, *Haonan haonu/Good Men, Good Women* (Taiwan, 1995).

In the Soviet Union the appointment of the modernizer Mikhail Gorbachev as general secretary of the Communist Party in 1985 led to a new spirit of openness. In the same year, a fifty-one-year-old former engineering student, Elem Klimov, who had seen many of his previous

films shelved by the authorities, released *Idi i Smotri/Come and See* (Soviet Union, 1985), a masterpiece about a teenage boy in Belorussia in 1943 who witnesses the Nazi atrocities committed on his country and its villages. In its use of deadening sound to represent tinnitus, its glimpses of piles of naked corpses as the boy traverses bleak landscapes, its portrayal of his attempts to kill himself by forcing his head into the sodden earth (317), and the accumulation of horrors so appalling that his hair turns grey, *Come and See* distinguishes itself as one of the greatest war movies ever made. The tragedies of real life within the Soviet Union matched those depicted in the film. The following year, a nuclear reactor in Chernobyl exploded, sending radiation around the world. Two years later, in 1988, over 100,000 people were killed in an earthquake in Armenia. When Elem Klimov was appointed first secretary of the Union of Filmmakers of the Soviet Union he almost immediately –

on the back of Gorbachev's reform programme – initiated the rehabilitation of banned films. In the years that followed, a treasure trove was opened. The film with the most direct effect, *Pokjanide/ Repentance* (Soviet Union, 1984, released 1987), heralded huge changes. Directed by the Georgian Tengiz Abuladze, it depicts how, after the mayor of a small town dies and is buried, a local woman angry about the crimes he committed in the name of Stalin, continually digs

up his body (318). Abuladze based his film on a true story: "A man who had been unjustly sent to prison was finally released ..." he said later, "... when he came home he found the grave of the man who had sent him to jail. He opened the coffin, took out the corpse, and leaned it against the wall. He would not let the dead man rest. This awful fact showed us that we could show the tragedy of an entire epoch by using this device."[14] The film made thought-provoking viewing for Gorbachev who was encouraged to see it by Edvard Shevardnadze, the future President of Georgia. Gorbachev approved its release and millions saw it. Never before had a single film so contributed to a country's debate about its own horrific past. Films that had been on the shelf much longer than *Repentance* were also finally released. For example, Kira Muratova's *Short Meetings* (1967) and *Long Goodbyes* (1971) (see page 307) finally established her as one of the great directors of the 1970s. And new films addressed taboo subjects such as environmental pollution, drugs and AIDS.

318
Above: Tengiz Abuladze's *Repentance* daringly used the dead body of a brutal mayor as a symbol of the iniquities of Stalinism. Soviet Union, 1984.

Back in the communist countries of Eastern Europe, these events were watched closely. In Hungary Istvàn Szabò had been marrying French New Wave stylistic elements to political themes since the mid-1960s. In *Mephisto* (Hungary, 1981) he turned his attention to Germany during the war and the character of an acclaimed leftist actor who compromises with the Nazis. The film was an international success. Also in Hungary, Márta Mészáros, the ex-wife of director Miklós Jancsó (see pages 302–03) made a trilogy of films – *Náplo*

319
Above: The physical brutality of murder was unwatchably vivid in Krzysztof Kieslowski's *A Short Film About Killing*, which contained elements of Hitchcock and Klimov. Poland, 1988.

gyermekeimnek/Diary for my Children (1982), *Náplo szerelmeimnet/Diary for my Loves* (1987) and *Naplo apámnak, anyámnak/Diary for my Father and my Mother* (1990) – which represent not only the country's greatest films of the decade but the best ever about women living in the shadow of Stalin.

It's very seldom that a filmmaker comes along who uses the medium as originally as Dovzhenko or Jean Vigo, but in Poland in the 1970s that's exactly what happened. Krzysztof Kieslowski was born in Warsaw in 1941, studied in the famous film school of Lodz just as Roman Polanski had done, made documentaries in the early 1970s and became the most distinguished figure in the movement called "Cinema of Moral Unrest" which had been initiated in 1976 by Andrzej Wajda's *Man of Marble*. After several fiction features he cemented his reputation with *The Dekalog* (1998), ten one-hour films on the theme of the Ten Commandments, justifying this by saying that "millions of people have died for these ideals".[15] All are set around the same apartment block, "it is the most beautiful housing estate in Warsaw ... It looks pretty awful so you can imagine what the others are like", said the director,[16] and each explores one of the biblical injunctions. None literally so, however. Instead the films are like parables, using reversals of fate, family taboos, social unease and the recurring appearances of a young man who perhaps symbolizes death, to explore human values in modern Polish life.

Two of the ten were expanded into features and one of these, *Krótki Film O Zabijaniu/A Short Film about Killing* (Poland, 1988), became Kieslowski's best work to date. In it a depressive teenager kills a sleazy taxi driver, is represented in court by an optimistic new lawyer and is hanged for his crime. The two death scenes are amongst the most excruciating ever filmed. As the still opposite shows (319), cinematographer Slawomir Idziak underexposes them and uses puce green filters as if the light of God has abandoned the earth. The death of the taxi-driver is awkward and brutal; as he is hanged by the neck the student defecates.

In the early 1990s, Kieslowski undertook a new film series, the trilogy *Trois Couleurs: Bleu/Three Colours: Blue*, *Trois Couleurs: Blanc/Three Colours: White* and *Trois Couleurs: Rouge/Three Colours: Red*, based on the colours of the French tricolor and the three elements of the French revolutionary ideal "Liberté, Egalité, Fraternité". *Blue* (France–Poland–Switzerland, 1992) explored the theme of liberty obliquely by telling the story of a young wife widowed when her composer husband dies in a car crash. So great is her grief that she literally blanks out at times, at others she – and the movie screen – is misted with blue light (320), again by Slawomir Idziak. Red filters have occasionally been introduced into film imagery in the past to represent anger or fever, for example in Powell and Pressburger's *Black Narcissus* (UK, 1948). Here, in the decade in which American cinematographers started using coloured light derived from music videos simply to make their imagery trendier, the effect powerfully represents the widow's losses of consciousness. Throughout the film, and in the final triumphant montage, extreme close-up and wide-angle lenses distort intimate moments in the lives of the widow and the other characters. We hear the widow's husband's music, which she co-wrote, and a voice sings:

Right: In his *Three Colours: Blue*, Kieslowski found a new filmic way to show his character Julie Vignon (Juliet Binoche) dipping out of, then back into, consciousness. France-Poland-Switzerland, 1992.

CAN SEE (1990–PRESENT): COMPUTERIZATION TAKES CINEMA BEYOND PHOTOGRAPHY

CAN SEE (1990—Present)
Computerization takes cinema beyond photography

10

By the end of the 1980s the target audience of much of Western commercial cinema was teenage, male and hooked on MTV. Other parts of global film culture were reviving but the multiplexes changed the pace and conditions of film consumption in the West, seriously reducing the diversity of cinematic voices that had existed a decade before. It was a gloomy time for those who cared for the breadth and ambitions of cinema and only the most quixotic cultural commentator would have predicted a cinematic renaissance.

Yet that is exactly what happened. The 1990s and the beginning of the new millennium were the single most interesting period yet for international cinema, the centres of innovation constantly moving. It has not been understood that the vibrancy of filmmaking around the globe in the last fifteen years has become a more significant phenomenon than the world expansion of style in the 1920s, or the succession of energetic new waves of the 1960s. This is not an argument about which periods in world film history have produced the greatest number of outstanding films, merely a

325
Far left: Victor Erice's documentary portrait of artist Antonio Lopez painting a tree in his garden, *The Quince Tree Sun*. The grain in this image, its sepia-ness and scratches, its ghostly shadow of a traditional camera carrying old film magazines and mounted on a wooden tripod – all these things capture the delicate pleasures of photographic cinema. This chapter describes what happened when cinema started to go beyond photography. Spain, 1992.

statement of the simple fact that only in the 1990s did every continent undergo a revival of cinematic confidence. Iranian directors made astonishingly original films, the Australians and New Zealanders had a heyday; Eastern and Northern Europe produced great new work and, in Dogme, an important new aesthetic movement; in Western Europe, French-language movies at least explored new philosophical ideas; South Korea, Thailand and Vietnam made the most distinctive films in the later part of the decade; African and particularly North African filmmakers continued to innovate; Central and Latin America came to the fore with work like *Amores perros/Love's a Bitch* (Mexico, 2000) and *Y tu mama tambien/And Your Mother Too* (Mexico, 2002); and the increasing postmodernization of American cinema began to be rethought in the light of the possibilities opened up by digital production.

LEADING LIGHTS IN IRAN

Iran became a centre of cinematic innovation in these years. The pioneering poet and filmmaker Farough Farrokhzad had died in 1967, Daryush Mehrjui, who made *The Cow* in 1970, was still working, the influential Institute for the Intellectual Development of Children and Young Adults (Kanun-e Parveresh-e Fekri Kudakan va Noja-vanan), known as Kunan, began in the 1970s to fund films about young

people, oil revenues increased greatly as a result of OPEC price rises in the same decade, and Abbas Kiarostami, a Tehrani born in 1940, started making short Kunan-funded films. One of the first indicators of his greatness was a modest-sounding work about a boy called Ahmad (326) who by mistake takes home his friend Nematzadeh's school homework book. Ahmad knows that Nematzadeh has been threatened by his teacher that if he fails to do his homework this time he will be expelled from school, so he sets out to try to find Nematzadeh's house to return the book.

As the outline suggests, *Doost kojast/Where is My Friend's House?* (1987) was about the decency of a strong-willed little boy.

Its approach would be Kiarostami's hallmark thereafter. Together with the simplicity of the stories in his films there was usually a focus on apparently trivial events – here the mistake about a school book – the story would be told in a patient, unrushed manner, there would be no attempt to create fear, panic or excitement in the viewer; moral and emotional clichés would be rejected so that, for example, in *Where is My Friend's House?*, Ahmad is never cute and is often quite stubborn; a child's logic would often represent the main point of view. Most importantly, individual scenes would strive for the kind of originality of tone that the poets whom Kiarostami read as a young man achieved through looking for an unspoken layer of meaning between two self-evident ones.

Commercial Western cinema by the 1990s frequently remade and added sequels to successful films but could never have conceived of one of the next turns of events in Kiarostami's career. Three years after he completed *Where is My Friend's House?*, the village in the Rostam-abad region where he filmed it was hit by a terrible earthquake. Kiarostami went back with his crew and made *Zendegi Va Digar Hich/And Life Goes on* (1992), a glorious film about the

327
Above: In Kiarostami's conceptually stimulating sequel, an earthquake has taken place near the village where Ahmed lived, so an actor playing the filmmaker who made *Where is My Friend's House?* goes to see if Babek Ahmed Poor is still alive. This shot, like many in the film, is photographed from the car of the director as he drives through destroyed villages. *And Life Goes On.* Abbas Kiarostami. Iran, 1992.

unstoppability of the everyday, and the rapturous disorder of human life. In it, people from the first film plan weddings, talk about sport and rebuild as best they can (327). Kids play in the streets. The delicate questions of life – like the importance of returning a friend's school book – remain entirely undamaged by the disruptive force of a natural disaster.

In the light of the second film – sometimes called a "paradocumentary" – the simplicity and focus of the first seemed like a premonition. Together they were reminders of the timelessness that Pasolini aimed for in his films and established Kiarostami as one of the great directors of his age. But he had not finished. Two years after *And Life Goes On*, the director returned for a third time to

328
Right: The third film in the trilogy – *Through the Olive Trees* – depicts the fictionalized process of filming the second film and includes characters from the second, including the wife of a couple who were about to get married. Iran, 1994.

Rostam-abad to complete what has become known as the Rostam-abad trilogy. *Zir-e darakhtan-e zeytun/Through the Olive Trees* (1994) is about the making of *And Life Goes On*. A crew is in a village devastated by an earthquake. People are living in temporary housing. The director finds two young people to act in the story of a couple who are to be married – an incident from the second film (328). He is a bricklayer; she comes from a wealthier family which disapproves of him. In real life, just as in the director's story, he has been pursuing her. The film ends in a series of long-held shots of the two of then walking through olive trees, talking about the possibility of their relationship, him trying to convince her of its worth.

CAN SEE (1990–PRESENT): COMPUTERIZATION TAKES CINEMA BEYOND PHOTOGRAPHY

The third film was the excavation of the philosophical implications of moments from the second. Here was the last element in Kiarostami's wholly distinctive approach to cinema: the examination of the relationship between the unpredictable flow of real life on one hand and the artworks that try to construct a shape out of it on the other. At other times and in other countries filmmakers like Ozu and Satyajit Ray had instinctively been minimalists, but neither more experimentally so than Kiarostami. As if to prove the point, in 2002 he directed *Ten*, a cinematic work more minimalist than any but the avant-garde films of Andy Warhol (see pages 281–82). Fixing two small video cameras to the dashboard of a car, one pointed at the passenger seat, the other at the driver's, he filmed ten conversations between the young Tehrani at the wheel and the people – her son, her mother, local people and a prostitute – whom she picks up (329). In only one instance does the camera leave the interior of the car. While most of the people in the film are actors, the performances are among the most naturalistic ever to have appeared on a film screen. *Ten* pared down cinema way below even the level envisaged by Bresson. It was one of the first great films of the new millennium.

Twelve years earlier, in a move that is inconceivable in Western cinema, Kiarostami made a film about a small event in the life of one of the other major Iranian filmmakers of the time. Seventeen years younger than Kiarostami, Mohsen Makhmalbaf was also born in Tehran. A teenager in the 1970s, he formed an underground Islamic militia, and was imprisoned for more than four years for stabbing a policeman.[1] During the time of his incarceration he taught himself sociology and aesthetics. This led him to abandon his political extremism and to start making feature films. From 1982 on ward he met with success and even fame, which is where Kiarostami's project becomes relevant. At the end of the 1980s a man called Ali Sabzian pretended to be the celebrated director Makhmalbaf and convinced an elderly couple and their children that he would make a film about them. He was exposed and imprisoned but the story intrigued Kiarostami who convinced the family and Sabzian, after his release

329
Below: Eight years later and Kiarostami was still innovating: *Ten* was shot, almost in its entirety, with two locked-off video cameras, one photographing the driver of a car (Mania Akbari) and the other her passengers. Iran, 2002.

from prison, to re-enact the events. This process of re-entering reality rather than ventriloquizing it with professional actors and dramatic enhancement, was familiar from Kiarostami's other films but was, if such a thing is imaginable, taken even further by Makhmalbaf. His fourteenth film, *Noon va Goldoon/A Moment of Innocence* (Iran–France–Switzerland, 1995), which was shown at an astonishing forty-six film festivals around the world, is the ultimate example of this.

A few years earlier Makhmalbaf put an advertisement in a newspaper asking for non-professionals to come to a casting call. One who did so was the policeman he had stabbed nearly twenty years before. Why was he there? asked Makhmalbaf. Because he was out of work and the film world seemed more interesting, replied the ex-policeman. Seeing at once the rich ironies of this situation, Makhmalbaf did what no planned industrial film production could easily do. He scrapped the film he was casting and decided instead to make one about the stabbing incident. He proposed that the policeman, who of course had never made a film before, recreate the events on camera from his point of view, and that in parallel the director – who was also his stabber – would do so from his point of view. Immediately we have a scenario that is engaged with the relativity of truth. What made the resulting intercut film so rich and moving was, among other things, the role of a girl in the story. In the intervening years the policeman had thought often of a girl who had been talking to him in the moments immediately before his stabbing. In his version of events, she is a romantic figure; his theme is the loss of her possible love. In Makhmalbaf's version it is revealed that she was in fact acting with the plotters, distracting the policeman and certainly not motivated by love. When the ex-policeman realizes this, he storms off, twenty years of dreams dashed. Makhmalbaf could not have known that something as rich as this might emerge out of the disparities of the two versions of the tale. He ends his film with the fictional girl asking the fictional policeman the time. She does so again; then again. Then he offers her flowers "for Africa" and bread "for the poor". Then a freeze frame. The unpredictability of Iranian paradocumentary was again doing justice to the unpredictability of lived experience. *A Moment of Innocence* is one of the most original accounts of an aspect of a filmmaker's life in the whole of cinema, a comedy about the absurdity of the years before the 1979 revolution and as philosophically complex as Shohei Imamura's somewhat similar *A Man Vanishes*.

Using his own self-education as a model, Makhmalbaf took time off from filmmaking to form Makhmalbaf Filmhouse, an immersive experience for teenagers who would be taught philosophy, film, aesthetics, poetics and sociology. One of the most distinguished graduates of this was his daughter, Samira, who made her award-winning debut feature *Sib/The Apple* (1998) at the age of eighteen. Again it was a paradocumentary and, like her father, she showed a feel for unforced symbolism and moral richness, which established her in the front rank of world filmmakers. Her third feature film *Panj é Asr/At Five O'Clock in the Afternoon* (2003) focuses on a young woman studying at an Islamic college in Afghanistan, immediately after the end of the Taliban regime. Although apparently pious, after class she secretly pulls back her burkha and puts on feminine shoes, walking

about, thinking what it would be like to become president of her country. Moving around because of the crowds of refugees entering her home town, she and her father and sister come across a grand, bombed building (330) which, as she thinks aloud about the presidency, begins to look like her palace. Her shoes add regality as well as femininity but she takes them off often, liking the feel of the earth on her soles. Samira Makhmalbaf's maxim – don't preach, don't judge – and her belief that in Western culture imagination is wedded to escapism rather than the transformation of reality – serves her splendidly.

REVIVAL IN AUSTRALASIA

No other film culture in the last section of this book quite meets the high standards of Iran, but Australasia had its best period since the mid-1970s. The most innovative figures in its revival were Jane Campion, Baz Luhrmann and Peter Jackson. Born in Wellington, New Zealand, in 1954, Campion moved to Australia and studied in the same film school – AFTRS – as filmmakers of the previous generation such as Gillian Armstrong (see page 364). After several shorts and an award-winning feature, *Sweetie* (New Zealand, 1989), she delivered

An Angel at my Table (New Zealand, 1990), based on the three-part autobiography of the same name by Jane Frame, New Zealand's most distinguished novelist. Campion evokes Frame's life – her impoverished childhood, hen growing interest in language, her shyness, a diagnosis of schizophrenia, more than 200 electric shock treatments and battles with the mental health world – in a frontal, patient and highly coloured way. Actress Kerry Fox, who plays Frame for much of the film, stares at the camera in a way that is sometimes penetrating, sometimes on the verge of a panic attack (331). Campion and her cinematographer, Stuart Dryburgh, used wide-angle lenses to exaggerate spaces in the film, placing actresses in the bulging foreground of the image and having New Zealand's magical landscapes in the background. One of the things that is moving about Campion's films is that her lonely women are often aware of how other people see them. As with Fox as Frame, they live so intensely and sometimes appear startled because of this double burden of simply being themselves but also being what the world wants them to be.

331
Above: The edgy stare of Kerry Fox as Janet Frame as well as Jane Campion and Stuart Dryburgh's square-on framings made *An Angel at My Table* an unusually intense portrait of mental illness and creativity. New Zealand, 1990.

Campion followed *An Angel at my Table* with a lushly metaphorical film about the sexual repression of just such a woman in *The Piano* (Australia, 1993) and then, revisiting the theme of female masochism, the icy *Portrait of a Lady* (UK–USA, 1996). Like many directors, Campion pays particular attention to how her characters use words to express and conceal themselves.

Eight years younger than Campion, the New South Wales-born Baz Luhrmann was a flamboyant Vincente Minnelli to Campion's analytical Ingmar Bergman. In the early 1980s, the *Mad Max* films brought exuberance to Australian filmmaking, but Luhrmann's *Strictly Ballroom* (Australia, 1992), *William Shakespeare's Romeo + Juliet* (USA–Australia, 1996) and *Moulin Rouge* (USA–Australia, 2001) were the mirror image of Miller's films. Each was a musical of sorts where everything would stop for extended, exalted dance routines. Where Miller confirmed the key elements of

332
Left: Baz Luhrmann's heightened mix of pop promos, Sergio Leone, Bollywood and Hollywood musicals made his hybrid films exhilarating and unpredictable. *William Shakespeare's Romeo + Juliet*. USA–Australia, 1996.

Australian masculinity, Luhrmann, like Campion, challenged the country's gender stereotypes.

Strictly Ballroom was overrated camp but the schemas for *Romeo + Juliet* and *Moulin Rouge* were fascinating. In the first, Luhrmann took Shakespeare's play about teenage lovers from warring families and re-imagined it in the explosive contemporary US setting of a border between Hispanic and Anglo enclaves (332). It opens with a petrol station stand-off between rival gangs, filmed with Sergio Leone-type close-ups and gun play, and with the rapid editing techniques and speeded-up shots of MTV, a decade after the channel's inception. In other sequences he uses the sensuous intercut tracking shots of Hong Kong directors such as Tsui Hark and John Woo.

Moulin Rouge augments the influence of Asian cinema. Similar to *Romeo + Juliet* in that it is a parable about idealized lovers tragically separated by death, it is a full-blown musical in the Bollywood tradition, where set and costume design maximize colour and glitter, where dancing suddenly becomes ensemble. One musical scene uses explicitly Indian costumes and choreography (333). As in his previous two films, in what Luhrmann started calling his "red curtain trilogy" about the nature of performance, the songs themselves are Anglo-American pop of the MTV era. At one point in *Moulin Rouge* the female characters sing, "Voulez-vous couchez avec moi?" from LaBelle's "Lady Marmalade", while the men crash into the chorus of Nirvana's "Smells Like Teen Spirit". Where Campion's interest in grown-up women went against the tide of her cinematic times, Luhrmann's themes were those of the multiplex: teenage love and rebellion. Yet his aesthetic recipe – elements of stage

333
Below: The influence of Bollywood musicals is clearly visible in this image from Luhrmann's *Moulin Rouge*. The film was designed by Catherine Martin and shot by Donald McAlpine. USA–Australia, 2001.

opera, Mamoulian's *Love Me Tonight* (see page 214), Hong Kong action movies, Hindi musicals, pop videos, 1970s disco, gay costume and performance style – radicalized his themes, winningly insisting on a new cinema where the frontiers between Asia and the West, men and women, gay and straight, do not exist. Together with Pedro Almodóvar he was the most exhilarating Western director of the period.

Nine years younger than Luhrmann, the New Zealander Peter Jackson made his first feature, *Bad Taste* (New Zealand, 1988), between the ages of twenty-two and twenty-five. His *Braindead* (New Zealand, 1992) combined low-budget horror with comedy, but special effects remained his passion. He got to indulge this passion extravagantly in his trilogy of J.R.R. Tolkien's *Lord of the Rings*, (USA–New Zealand co-productions made between 2001–03). Although they added nothing to the schemas of the movies, these sword-and-sorcery adventures became the most profitable films of the new millennium.

THE PAST AND THE FUTURE IN AMERICAN CINEMA IN THE 1990S TO PRESENT

No American filmmaker dynamized the language of film as Luhrmann did, nor did any conceive their work as philosophically as Kiarostami or the Makhmalbafs. That the industry continued its reorganization begun in the 1980s is partly to blame for this. The corporatization of mainstream production increased in the 1990s; leisure goods were increasingly introduced into scenes in films in what became known as "product placement"; the cross-fertilization that the Time-Warner conglomerate achieved with *Batman* (see pages 432–33) was repeated across the industry, with Time-Warner leading the way once more when it in turn merged with internet giant America Online (AOL); and the most powerful of the agencies that represented talent in the industry continued to package whole productions with their actors, directors and writers behaving, in effect, as studio bosses once had.

Despite the corporate dominance, the 1990s and since have seen a broadening of the art of American cinema. Traditional, quality genre films such as *The Silence of the Lambs* (Jonathan Demme,

1991), *Schindler's List* (Steven Spielberg, 1993), *Heat* (Michael Mann, 1995), *L.A. Confidential* (Curtis Hanson, 1997) and *The Sixth Sense* (M. Night Shyamalan, 1999) were a return to the solid narratives and adult psychological grounding of the closed romantic realism of, for example, the 1940s. More significantly, films across the spectrum attempted to marry such nostalgia for pre-1980s humanism with some of the formalism of the video age. Martin Scorsese's *GoodFellas* (1990), the work of the Coen brothers, *Reservoir Dogs* (1992), by a precocious new talent, Quentin Tarantino, and the movies of Oliver Stone were each recognizably of their age yet obsessed with cinema's past. Together they represented movie postmodernism in early 1990s cinema, the last years in the run up to the digital revolution.

334
Above: Joe Pesci's character – although long dead in the story – shoots straight into the lens in *GoodFellas*. USA, 1990.

After making some of the best films of the mid-1970s, Martin Scorsese's cinematic soul-searching took its toll. His *New York, New York* (1977) was an epic, disastrous, beautiful, schizophrenic musical that dragged him down so much that *Raging Bull* (1980) was about his recovery. Scorsese had been hospitalized, his private life was in a mess and he was a cocaine addict. It was only in 1990, however, after efficient but less deeply-felt films such as *The Color of Money* (1986), with 1980s icon Tom Cruise, that Scorsese managed to capture the complexity of what was happening in the movie world. In that year he made a film that was as fast as Hollywood's video-edited mega-entertainments, but that also looked back to the most primitive era in cinema.

"You want it fast?", he said about *GoodFellas*, "OK, I'll give it to you fast, really fast."[2] The film was about the rags-to-riches-to-spiritual-ruin of a bunch of "wiseguys", no-hopers from Brooklyn. It followed their lives and schemes from 1955 to the 1980s. The title referred to gangsters who never talked to the police. They deal in food, clothes, liquor, anything to get money and control, but unlike most of Scorsese's characters who go through hell but see the light, for them there is no redemption.

GoodFellas had shorter scenes, and more of them, than any other Scorsese movie. The director had recently made a promotional video for Michael Jackson's song "Bad" and brought some of the energy of this to the new film. Unlike many of the Jerry Bruckheimerproduced films of the period, however, the pace of *GoodFellas* did not feel imposed, as, if it were simply the shallow patina of the times. Nicholas Pileggi, the writer of the book on which the film is based, says about the mafia characters portrayed, "I used to know a lot of them and one thing they all have is an unbelievably high metabolic rate. They are, almost every one of them, highly manic, highly energized ... They were 'spielkas' – that's Yiddish for 'ants in the pants'."

This was not only the era of high metabolic rate films, however. As if in response to the amnesia of the times, film history had become fashionable. Abel Gance's *Napoleon* (France, 1927) had been masterfully restored in the 1970s. In 1986 David Lean's *Lawrence of Arabia* underwent a similar process. In 1996, Alfred Hitchcock's *Vertigo* did too, as did Orson Welles' *Touch of Evil* in 2000. The search for new thrills sent the film world looking in the most unusual of places – the past. At the very end of *GoodFellas*, reformed gangster Henry Hill (Ray Liotta) is living in bland suburbia. As he finishes a voice-over, Scorsese and his long-time editor Thelma Schoonmake suddenly cut to his long-

335
Left: Scorsese's inspiration for the unusual Pesci shot was an example of schema without any variation: George Barnes' emblematic scene in *The Great Train Robbery*. Director: Edwin S. Porter. USA, 1903.

dead partner in crime, Tommy (Joe Pesci), who points a gun straight at the camera and shoots. Boom. The end (334). This was a direct reference to Edwin S. Porter's *The Great Train Robbery* (1903), in which a gunman (George Barnes) is framed in head and shoulders, square on, and fires straight into camera (335); Pesci was shot in exactly the same way.

Cinema was still about pure spectacle then; it still had the power to shock moviegoers, to jolt them in their seats. Mainstream American cinema of the 1980s wanted nothing more than to jolt people in the multiplexes. Martin Scorsese was wise enough to know this and reached back to the earliest period in the movies when this had been done.

One last point about the emblematic shot. It is hard to imagine now, but at the time such images as Barnes shooting into the barrel of

336
Right: Luhrmann and Scorsese both used film in a post-modern way, but Quentin Tarantino's *Pulp Fiction* played so completely with the norms of, for example, assassin scenes in gangster movies, that the performers were able, knowingly, to slip out of character to talk about foot massages. Tarantino regularly photographs, or refers to, feet in his films, a case, perhaps, of work expressing the fetishism of its director. USA, 1994.

the lens were designed to be shown either at the beginning or the end of the movie. They floated free of the story. They were not part of it. In *GoodFellas*, Pesci meets his demise by being shot in the back. No piece of the story fits with the last image of him shooting. It is not a flash-back. It floats free.

Pulp Fiction (Tarantino, 1994), another gangster film of the 1990s, took Scorsese's experiments with postmodernism so much further that it became one of the most influential films of the decade. Its innovations are among the most striking examples in modern cinema of Gombrich's idea of varying schemas. Take this situation from the third section of the film, for example, where two hired killers are going to do a hit (336). Such scenes are familiar from hundreds of crime B-movies and films noirs from the USA in the late 1940s and 1950s. The killers typically talk tersely, if at all. They are functions of the plot. Here, however – and this reveals how 1990s post modern cinema transformed the movies that inspired it – they converse as follows:

VINCENT: Have you ever given a foot massage?

JULES: Don't be telling me about foot massages. I'm the foot massage master.

VINCENT: Given a lot of them?

JULES: Shit yeah. I got my technique down an' everything. I don't be ticklin' an nothing.

VINCENT: Would you give a guy a foot massage?

JULES: Fuck you.

VINCENT: You give' em a lot.

JULES: Fuck you.

VINCENT: I'm kinda tired. I could use a foot massage myself ...

JULES: You, yo, yo man. You best back off. I'm getting a little pissed here. Now, this is the door ...

And with that they revert to generic killers again, Jules is saying, "let's get in character" as they do. *Pulp Fiction*, was full of such digressions and atypical discussions of minutiae. Borrowing a phrase from Scorsese about the 1970s, it "opened up" the world of US genre cinema to feminized disquisition. One critic commented that in films such as *Pulp Fiction* the "verbal set-piece takes precedent over the action set-piece".[3] This effect became known as "Tarantinoesque", after the writer–director of *Pulp Fiction* Quentin Tarantino, who was just thirty-one-years-old at the time. His second feature, *Reservoir Dogs* (USA, 1992), a reworking of Ringo Lam's *Long hu feng yun/City on Fire* (Hong Kong, 1987), was such a success at the Sundance Film Festival of independent cinema, that his co-written screenplays for *True Romance* (Tony Scott, 1993) and *Natural Born Killers* (Oliver Stone, 1994) quickly got made. He had breathed new life into the cardboard characterization of American genre cinema and, for years afterward, ardent young male directors copied his approach.

While Tarantino influenced the structure and dialogue of American screenwriting in the 1990s, he was less innovative when it came to camera placement and visual style. Oliver Stone's *Natural Born Killers*, taken from Tarantino's screenplay, illustrates this point. Where Tarantino wrote innovatively and shot classically, former US infantryman and screenwriter Stone, who was born in New York City in 1946, went a great deal further, experimenting with visual texture in several of his 1990s films. Collaborating with cinematographer

337
Right: While many
questioned the morality
of *Natural Born Killers*'
content, its variety of film
stocks and visual textures
was highly influential.
Cinematographer: Robert
Richardson. Director:
Oliver Stone. USA, 1994.

Robert Richardson on most of his work from the mid-1980s onward,
he shot on amateur 8mm film, the black-and-white 16mm stock that
used to be employed for TV news, and various video formats, and
combined these with pristine 35mm widescreen imagery (337). More
traditional filmmakers, such as Steven Spielberg, had long accepted the
maxim that the grain of film imagery should not be visible to audiences
because it would remove the illusion that they are actually experiencing

the events on-screen, reminding them that they are only watching moving imagery. Richardson and Stone smashed this conceit, portraying the violent rampage of a young couple as a mosaic of media and film footage. As a result, mainstream American cinema was cautiously separated from a single, unified photographic style throughout the course of a film.

A fourth strain of 1990s postmodernism was to be found in the kooky, technically brilliant films of Minnesota-born brothers Joel and Ethan Coen. Starting in 1984 with *Blood Simple*, Joel directed, Ethan produced and both of them wrote. The success of *Raising Arizona* (it cost $5 million and took $25 million) in 1987 afforded them, by the beginning of the 1990s, a rare position as semi-mainstream filmmakers working for Hollywood studios who retained right of final cut for their films and who created, in each, a highly distinctive world. *Miller's Crossing* (1990) was typical: it was set in the past, reworked a movie genre (here, a gangster picture in the spirit of Dashiell Hammett), revealed a fascination for iconic imagery (in this case a trilby hat of the type worn by Humphrey Bogart), and was laced with black humour and explosive violence.

As a respite from writers' block while they worked on its screenplay (whose plot they claim not quite to have understood) they wrote and later directed *Barton Fink* (1991), a striking mood piece about a worthy screenwriter who wants "to do something for one's fellow-man" but who is, himself, suffering from writer's block. Photographed by the Coen's regular DP Roger Deakins in shades of putrifying green and yellow, it featured hilarious scenes such as that where Fink's producer responds to his intellectual script for a boxing movie with "We don't put Wallace Beery in some fruity movie about suffering".

In the second half of the 1990s the Coens honed their comic-discrepant world-view further by focusing on what used to be called in Frank Capra films the "little man" caught up in events and social changes in modern society which he barely understands. In *The Hudsucker Proxy* (1994) a novice mailroom worker, Norville Barnes, is installed as the chief executive of Hudsucker Industries. Together with the lead characters in *The Big Lebowski* (1998) and *O Brother, Where art Thou?* (2000), Barnes can now be seen as a Coen archetype: a gormless, rather asexual man who has strayed into the closed romantic realist world of Hawks, Capra or Preston Sturges, who doesn't understand its strangeness and who is all at sea.

The lackadaisical Dude in *The Big Lebowski* in particular captured the slacker mood of his times, but the Coens' affection for these men – together with their instinctive surrealism – made their films among the most singular of their times.

Beyond traditional films like *L.A. Confidential* and *The Silence of the Lambs*, and the innovators of the post-modern mainstream such as Scorsese, Tarantino and Stone, and the Coens, American cinema of the 1990s developed a lively independent production sector. Stimulated in part by actor Robert Redford's Sundance Film Festival and Institute (found in 1981) and the Miramax distribution and production company (launched in 1979), which together helped create an American cinematic middle-brow in reaction to 1980s, low-brow teen cinema, key directors such as Gus Van Sant, Steven Soderbergh, Hal Hartley and Jim Jarmusch emerged. Harley's breakthrough film *The Unbelievable Truth* (1989), funded by a series of bank loans, set the pattern for his work in emphasizing rich dialogue over innovative shooting techniques. Jarmusch came to attention as early as 1983 with his beautiful pre-slacker study in boredom and friendship, *Stranger Than Paradise*. His infrequent 1990s work continued to find intrigue in inactivity. Soderbergh's *sex, lies and videotape* (1989), a landmark reworking of *La Ronde* for the video age, launched its director in an astonishingly diverse career, ranging from experimentation in *Kafka* (1991) to mainstream success in *Erin Brockovich* (2000) and *Ocean's Eleven* (2001), a remake of a 1960 heist movie of the same name.

Just as diverse and equally interested in remakes was Gus Van Sant, the Kentucky-born son of a travelling salesman who was inspired by the work of Andy Warhol while studying at Rhode Island School of Design in the early 1970s. In 1985, Van Sant released his first film *Mala Noche*, about the love affair between a Mexican immigrant and a gay liquor-store salesman. The success of this led to *Drugstore Cowboy* (1989) and then his most innovative film, *My Own Private Idaho* (1991). This is the story of the relationship between two male hustlers, one of whom (River Phoenix) has narcolepsy, the other (Keanu Reeves) of whom will inherit a fortune on his twenty-first birthday. The first fifteen minutes of *My Own Private Idaho* are among the most original American filmmaking of the decade. Using Phoenix's character's sleeping sickness as a starting point (338), Van Sant films the landscapes through which his characters drift with time-lapse photography, as if a gear had been suddenly thrown and real time had become dream time. Van Sant's career developed into one of the most curious in modern American cinema, veering between sentimental mainstream films about the education of young men, such as *Good Will Hunting* (1997) and strangely conceptual works such as his act of worship of *Psycho* (1960), where he remade Alfred Hitchcock's film scene by scene, departing from the original in only a few, tiny, but surreal, details.

The career of Matthew Barney was just as unconventional. He made a series of five films between 1994 and 2003, each of which was named after the cremaster muscle in the human body which makes the testicles rise and fall. Barney, like Salvador Dalí, Andy Warhol and Jean Cocteau, was an artist first and a filmmaker second, and conceived his Cremaster cycle as an innovative elaboration of the idea of male bio-determinism, presenting them, eccentrically, in the order *4* (1995), *1* (1996), *5* (1997), *2* (1999), *3* (2003). The last of these further flouts the norms of mainstream film sequels by being 182 minutes long, featuring the lower legless actress Aimee wearing glass stiletto prostheses, a phallic Chrysler Building and a vaginal Guggenheim Centre. David Lynch's *Eraserhead* (1977) and David Cronenberg's *Videodrome* (1982) were reference points for Barney's elaborate biological symbolism; *The New York Times* called him "the most crucial artist of his generation".

338
Above: In *My Own Private Idaho* director Gus Van Sant reflected the narcolepsy of the character played by River Phoenix (right) in the form of his film. USA, 1991.

THE DIGITAL REVOLUTION BEGINS IN AMERICA

In the year of the release of *My Own Private Idaho*, *Silence of the Lambs* and *Barton Fink* (1991), *Terminator 2: Judgment Day* (1991) demonstrated, more dramatically than ever before, the startling potential of imagery which was created digitally. As the image overleaf shows (339), a photographed image of an actor changed into a "liquid metal" version of him and that version continued to move through space. The filmmaker, James Cameron, had his design and technical teams scan the photographed image into the computer, transforming photochemical information into the digits – an immensely complex

339
Below: The combination of live-action (background fire) and computer-generated imagery (the 3-D, photographically-real "liquid metal" assassin) in *Terminator 2* demonstrated the possibilities of CGI and began a process where photographed and "drawn" imagery in mainstream cinema would become difficult to distinguish.

340
Above: It had long been possible to combine live-action and animation but until the early nineties, the latter seldom had the same visual detail, volume, or complexity of movement as the former, as this moment from *Anchors Aweigh* demonstrates. Director: George Sidney. USA, 1945.

pattern of zeros and ones – which computers understand. Thereafter they manipulated those digital patterns, drawing in shiny surfaces, movements and reflections to simulate the effect of a human being turning into a mercury-type substance. Live action and animation had been combined before, as far back as Gene Kelly dancing with Jerry mouse in *Anchors Aweigh* (340) and Ray Harryhausen's stop-motion work in *Jason and the Argonauts* (Don Chaffey, USA, 1963), but this was crucially different. Whereas in the latter the animated figures were models that were made to look as if they were alive, the liquid metal men were drawn figures with the same degree of volume, movement and menace. The technique became known as Computer-Generated Imagery, CGI. For the first time in movie history, animated imagery did not need to appear cartoon-like or artificial. Live and drawn action could converge. Any conceivable image could be rendered in photographic reality. In films like *Titanic* (James Cameron, 1997), *Jurassic Park* (Steven Spielberg, 1993), *The Matrix* (Andy and Larry Wachowski, 1999), *Gladiator* (Ridley Scott, 2000) and *Toy Story* (John Lasseter, 1995) the main elements of the film (the ship, the dinosaur, the trace of a bullet, ancient Rome, the living toys) looked real, or, in the case of the latter, wholly three-dimensional and mobile. Want See became Can See.

Despite the impact of *Terminator 2's* liquid metal sequences, they represented only a minor aspect of the revolutionary potential of digital filmmaking. The movie was still shot on film, for example, at a time when it was becoming possible to shoot entirely on digital video-tape, bypassing film altogether. And *Terminator 2* was still sent out to cinemas as reels of 35mm film and projected onto a screen, when some had already talked of eschewing film prints and beaming digital films directly into cinemas.

Inventors had foreseen the revolutionary impact of some kind of electronic cinema decades earlier. As early as 1921 a young electrician called Philo Farnsworth was ploughing a field when he realized that an image could be captured by fast-moving electrons scanning in rows. Other inventors had used more cumbersome methods of generating the earliest electronic imagery, such as spinning discs. Farnsworth demonstrated in 1927 that his ploughed field-inspired approach worked but it was not until 1949 that independent Hollywood producer Samuel Goldwyn suggested that the film industry should install large-screen televisions in cinemas, so that films could be sent down cables electronically, directly onto those screens.

In the 1990s, the production and transmission of digital cinema advanced neck and neck. In the year following *Terminator 2* Goldwyn's dream of transmitting films electronically was realized when *Bugsy* (Barry Levinson, 1992) was sent by Sony Pictures Entertainment from Culver City to a Convention Centre at Anaheim, not far away. Three years after that, *Toy Story* was the world's first entirely computer-generated feature film. In 1999, George Lucas' *Star Wars* prequel, *Episode 1: The Phantom Menace*, was shown digitally in four cinemas, and in the same year a low-budget horror film, *The Blair Witch Project* (1999) was not only shot on low-tech digital video, but was marketed on the internet. In the same year digital cinemas opened in Korea, Spain, Germany and Mexico and in 2001–02, George Lucas shot *Star Wars Episode 2: Attack of the Clones* entirely digitally.

The question for a history of the creativity of cinema is how such innovations would affect the aesthetics of the medium. In mainstream American cinema new types of shots emerged. Directors used CGI to simulate a camera floating over the recreated Colosseum in Rome in *Gladiator* (341), and around the *Titanic* in mid-ocean.

341
Left: CGI recreated the drama of Rome's Colosseum in *Gladiator*, but did the technique capture the physical mass of the building, and from what point of view? Director: Ridley Scott. USA, 2000.

These magic carpet rides, or "fly arounds", were crane shots for the digital age, the Can See logical conclusion of the innovations of R.W. Paul and Pastrone. Yet these were weightless and point-of-view-less moves, exhilarated by the possibility of CGI but devoid of feeling. America had again raced into the future of cinema technology but, as before, others such as Abbas Kiarostami in his film *Ten* (see page 441) thought through the implications of the new technology more rigorously.

The most influential use of CGI married the new digital fluidity of "fly arounds" to a technique from Asian cinema called "wire fu". Woo-ping Yuen was born in China in 1945, and became an action director in stunt films in Hong Kong in the 1970s. He helped evolve the graceful style of the Shaw Brothers' fight scenes and, when the equipment became available, started attaching fine wires to the waists of his actors, the wires being suspended from a pivoting circular head on a crane. When the crane head was raised, the actor would seem to levitate, when it moved, they seemed to fly, when the head rotated, they seemed to spin. Thus a form of actor puppetry was born which, when rigorously practised and mastered, afforded a kind of on-screen movement that Gene Kelly could only dream of.

Yuen's wire fu masterpiece from the 1990s is *Iron Monkey* (1993), a simple story set in China in 1858 about a folk hero who robs warlords to feed peasants. In its loveliest sequence, Dr Yang and Miss Orchid glide through space to catch papers snatched by a gust of wind. Soon after the film was released in the East, two young California-based filmmakers, Andy and Larry Wachowski, took an idea for a movie to big budget producer Joel Silver. Since childhood the brothers had been interested in both comic-strip fiction and myth and their script, called *The Matrix*, melded both. Silver loved their story of a computer programmer who is told by an underground figure, Morpheus, that the world around him is merely a simulation – the matrix of the title. The Wachowskis wanted Yuen to choreograph the fight sequences, and Silver had him tracked down in China. He trained Keanu Reeves and the other actors for five months in Kung Fu techniques, then taught them the craft of the wire. Gradually they learnt to jump, spin, kick, somersault and glide through space. These movements were so striking to Western mainstream audiences who had never seen them before that, as with morphing, wire fu quickly became fashionable in films like *Charlie's Angels* (McQ, 2000), and pastiched in Dimension Films' teen horror movie spoofs.

Yuen's work in *The Matrix* was indeed one of the key staging advances in computer-era cinema, but there was another innovative component in the Wachowskis' designs for the film, and it too came from the East. Japanese animation had, as we have seen, been hugely popular since the 1950s but, in its Original Anime Video (OAV) work of the 1980s, it had portrayed violent and sexual imagery in increasingly dynamic and explicit ways. In fight scenes in particular OAV had evolved fly-around shots which seemed to freeze the action so that you could see it from every direction, and video games followed suit. The idea of recreating this god's-eye view of a fight appealed to the Wachowskis and the sensation-chasing Silver. What if they used Yuen's staging techniques with OAV camera techniques? Was there any way that they could have actors leap into the air, have the camera swish right around them in a moment, then continue the movement? The fastest high-speed cameras could certainly film so many frames per second that the action would seem to have stopped, but what they wanted was for the camera to move as it was doing this. This could not be done. No camera dolly could track at the thirty or so metres per second – a tenth of the speed of sound – required.

As has often been the case in the evolution of movie style, the question "How can we do this differently?" led to a breakthrough. First they filmed Yuen's action with ordinary cameras in relatively fixed positions. Then they scanned the shot footage into a computer and from this worked out exactly where a camera would need to be at any moment in order to do the *Anime*-influenced fly-around. Then they went back to the set and installed sophisticated stills cameras all along the length of the curving camera movement that they wanted to create (342 top). Way back in the 1870s, the English photographer Eadweard Muybridge had used a similar line

of cameras to photograph the galloping of horses and the movements of people as they ran. His strips of images became immensely popular and greatly affected how painters portrayed movement thereafter.

Things had moved on a lot by the mid-1990s. The Wachowski brothers didn't want to fragment the action to see what was really happening, so much as stop time so they could gracefully fly around it. The next stage in achieving this was to have the actors redo Yuen's fight movement within the arc of the stills cameras. The resulting still images created a series of snapshots of the overall effect, but without movement. These were then scanned into another computer that created the "missing stages" of the action. The computer was given moments A, D and G of the action, and created images to represent what happened at moments B, C, E and F. When the result was projected, the implied speed of the camera move was so fast that the result became known as "bullet time" (343).

Never before in movie history had mainstream Eastern cinema had more influence on mainstream Western cinema than in its headlong dash for new sensations. The influence continued in the film's sequel, *The Matrix Reloaded* (Andy and Larry Wachowski, 2003). In terms of the language of film, not much new was added, but details such as the following revealed the grander conception that Warner Bros. had for the Matrix over what is called "multiple media platforms": When Keanu Reeves' character Neo arrives in the underground city of Zion, an ardent young man runs up to him saying how glad he is to see him again. What is this "again"? The character did not appear in the first film. Instead he was introduced in one of a series of short animated spin-offs together called *The Animatrix*. The various manifestations of *The Matrix* were themselves becoming a matrix.

343
Above: A moment from the scene filmed in the images on the previous page: *The Matrix*. Directors: Andy and Larry Wachowski. USA, 1999.

DOGME AND EUROPEAN CINEMA SINCE THE 1980S

While the Wachowskis and Cameron manipulated digital imagery to show audiences things they had never seen before, a group of film-makers in Denmark in 1995 took a leaf out of the books of Bresson and Pasolini in arguing that far from becoming more technical and all-seeing, cinema had to become primitive again. Part marketing ploy part "rescue action", their "Dogme" manifesto knowingly echoed François Truffaut's words (see page 254) in countering "certain tendencies' in cinema today".[4] They argued that the 1960s New Wave inspired by Truffaut's article "proved to be a ripple that washed ashore and turned to muck."[5] Commenting on the present, they said, "Today a technological storm is raging, the result of which will be the ultimate democratization of cinema." To steer this democratization, the signatories of the manifesto – Lars Von Trier and Thomas Vinterberg – pledged a "Vow of Chastity" by adhering to the following daunting rules: no sets should be built, real locations should be used, no props should be brought to those locations, music should not be added, the camera must be hand held, no lighting should be added, no "superficial action" (such as murder) would be allowed, no flashbacks or genre elements would be permissible, the shape of the screen should be the old 4:3 one, and the director must not take credit.

By 2003, thirty-three directors in Europe, America, Asia and South America had bound themselves to these rules, the best of the resulting films being: Thomas Vinterberg's *Festen/The Celebration* (Denmark, 1998), Søren Kragh Jacobsen's *Mifunes sidste sang/Mifune* (Denmark, 1999), and Harmony Korine's *Julien Donkey-Boy* (USA, 1999). *Festen* in particular was a visual revelation. Shot with a domestic video camera in low or candle light, its fuzzy, yellow imagery by Anthony Dod Mantle broke all the rules of crisp cinematography, yet was remarkably readable and sensuous. Many of the *Dogme* films were weak and conventional but the comic-moral disruption they created in the world of cinema aesthetics had an even greater liberating effect on 1990s cinema than Oliver Stone's textural experiments with *Natural Born Killers*. The diametrically opposed approaches of *The Matrix* and *Festen* illustrate the diverging possibilities of digital cinema.

Although a signatory of the Vow of Chastity, Lars Von Trier himself waited three years before he made his first *Dogme* film

Idioterne/The Idiots (Denmark, 1998). Two years earlier he directed *Breaking the Waves* (UK–Denmark, 1996), a widescreen, hand-held, digitally-shot film about a naive young Scottish woman who prays to God to have her Danish lover return from his work on an oil rig. He does, but with his neck broken. He then encourages her to take lovers and describe her sexual activities to him. At a time when most Western cinema was liberal and secular, *Breaking the Waves* was an endurance-testing work of Christian piety, directly inspired, as we have seen, by

344
Right: Lars Von Trier, the co-instigator of the Danish film movement *Dogme*, experimented with the idea of minimalism at the movement's core. In *Dogville* he shot the whole movie on a sound stage, used almost no sets, instead symbolically marking out the position of walls and doors with white lines. The effect could have been very un-filmic but the intensity of the film's performance and direction made it triumphantly so. Denmark, 2003.

Carl Theodor Dreyer (see pages 112 and 246–47). Von Trier's conception of his central character, Bess, took the simplest of catechistic forms, yet his moral implausibility was rooted in an astonishing, *Dogme*-inspired, filming authenticity. The actors were free to move anywhere within the rooms in which the filming took place. Trier did take after take, then edited together – using jump cuts as bold as Godard's in *A Bout de souffle* (France, 1959) – those moments of each take which seemed to him most true. In *Breaking the Waves* and *Dogville* (Denmark, 2003), he operated the camera himself, often touching Nicole Kidman, the leading actress in the latter, during takes of her frequent close-ups. This is unheard of in film history and again contributed to the moment-to-moment intimacy of her performance. As with Trier's previous films, critics questioned his broader theme – in this case the tendency to violence in American society – but there was no doubting the radicalism of his aesthetic: *Dogville* was filmed entirely in a studio, with almost no sets or props (344).

While Von Trier was the most innovative European director of the period, others had a far richer conception of human beings. The "cinéma du look" in France continued with films as diverse as *Les Amants du Pont-Neuf* (Leos Carax, 1991) and *Doberman* (Jean Kounen, 1997), but other French-language directors such as Claire Denis, Mathieu Kassovitz, Gaspar Noé, Bruno Dumont and the Dardennes brothers turned to working-class and disenfranchised characters to produce a powerfully innovative reaction against glossy 1980s cinema. Released in 1995, at the time of the election of a new right-wing government in France and two years after France negotiated a "cultural exception" to the free flow of commerce because "creations of the mind cannot be assimilated to simple products", actor Kassovitz's *La Haine/Hate* (1995) was a forerunner in this, taking as its starting point the real-life shooting while in police custody of the sixteen-year-old Zairean Makome Bowole in 1993. In a calculated provocation of the tripartite blue, white and red of the French flag, Kassovitz told the story of a day in the life of three youths, one Jewish, one Beur (Islamic) and one black African. They come from Paris's impoverished peripheral housing estates, commit petty crimes, and one of their friends has recently been assaulted by the racist police. At the time, Kassovitz was compared to Quentin Tarantino, but his film was much more rooted in social realities.

Bruno Dumont was ten years older and far more philosophical than Kassovitz. His debut was *La Vie de Jésus/ The Life of Jesus* (1996) about the wasted lives of teenagers in run-down northern France. His follow-up, *L'Humanité/Humanity* (1999), was also filmed in static CinemaScope shots in northern France. It takes as its starting point a police investigation about the rape of a young woman. Far from being story driven, however, the film's stare at its landscape and its people is ice-cold, like marble. The policeman, Pharoan (Emmanuel Schotté), is unblinking, nearly autistic and strikingly unusual to look at (345), like a character from a Pasolini film, his inexpressive acting inspired by Bresson. Whereas in *La Vie de Jésus*, young people with real faces and real bodies have sex in fields and express racist attitudes, the magnificent and spare first few minutes of

345
Below: Bruno Dumont's *L'Humanité* was not widely seen, but the intensity of its stare and the blankness of its performances were as striking as Bresson or Pasolini. France, 1999.

L'Humanité make Dumont's first film seem almost conventional. Shots are held for so long that we see the action and continue to look after it has finished, as if it will recur. Pharoan is locked in his own numb inactivity and loneliness. We see a mid-shot of the raped girl's naked genitals. Later, in a direct echo of Pasolini's film *Teorema/Theorem* (Italy, 1968), Pharoan actually levitates in a garden. Such scenes established Dumont as a master almost the equal of the Iranians.

The Belgian former documentarists Jean-Pierre and Luc Dardenne were as devoted to a transcendent view of everyday life. Like Kassovitz and Dumont, they took as their subject disenfranchisement in contemporary Europe.

Rosetta (Belgium, 1999) is about a feral teenage girl who is desperate to get a job. The brothers' brilliantly simple stylistic innovation was to have her run throughout the film and follow her with a hand-held camera. Like Dumont they rejected the closed romantic realist grammar of shot/reverse-shot, achieving instead a purity of screen direction – nearly always moving forward – and a unique sense of being at the shoulder of the girl during her quests. Their follow-up, *Le Fils/The Son* (Belgium, 2002), used the same unidirectional style to equally powerful effect.

Moving eastward to Austria we find another filmmaker who uses a static camera to explore social malaise. Michael Haneke studied philosophy at Vienna University and started making films in 1989. Their story outlines speak volumes: his *Benny's Video* (Australia–Switzerland,1992) is about the boy of the title who, having watched a pig being slaughtered, videos himself committing murder. In *Funny Games* (Austria-Switzerland, 1997), two youths visit their neighbours to borrow eggs but end up brutally terrorizing them (346). At one point they address the audience directly and rewind the film. *Code Inconnu: Recit Incomplet De Divers Voyages/Code Unknown* (France, 2001) is a series of virtuoso long takes of

346
Above: The startling moment when one of the characters in *Funny Games* rewinds the film and we see its horrific violence in reverse (bottom) is as conceptually provocative as the moment in Bergman's *Persona* where the film burns. Director: Michael Haneke. Austria–Switzerland, 1997.

Parisian actor Juliette Binoche, attempting to avoid the violence of the city in which she lives. In *La Pianiste/The Piano Teacher* (France, 2002), an exacting teacher of Schubert's exquisite music cuts her inner thighs with a razor blade and sniffs the used tissues in porn cubicles (Austria–France, 2002). Each is set in a sophisticated, middle-class, highly industrialized society out of which the possibility of love has leached. Other filmmakers share Haneke's pessimism but few find such rigorous formal analogues. In *Code Inconnu*, for example, the total lack of human connection in big Western cities is brilliantly echoed in the fact that each long take fades to black before the next emerges out of black onto the screen. Even the shots don't touch. This was revolutionary. Haneke famously wishes audiences "a disturbing evening" when he introduces his films and talks about their portrayal of "reality losing its realness" ("Entwirklichung" in German). If there was a theme to ambitious 1990s cinema it was the extent to which this was happening. The American postmodernists thought so, and played with the implications of it; by contrast Kiarostami and Makhmalbaf in Iran were finding ways in their films to add realness to reality.

347
Below: Haneke's *La Pianiste* in which Isabelle Huppert's character is both sensitively tuned in to beauty and numbly desperate for sexual gratification and physical contact. France, 2002.

As we travel further east still, we encounter filmmakers grappling with the same question of the degree to which cinema can penetrate the nature of reality, but in the light of the collapse of communism. In Hungary, Béla Tarr applied Miklós Jancsó's experiments with long tracking shots to the question of what the real world was like once Marxism ebbed. His massive *Satantango* (Hungary, 1993) is set on a failed collective farm. Its first shot, which lasts seven-and-a-half minutes, one-sixtieth of this seven-hour film's total duration, attunes us to his world and shows how he extended Jancsó's aesthetic. The farm is barely visible in the morning gloom. Menacing music underscores. We track left past a building to cows that are being slowly herded. In the background there is the sound of bells from a Byzantine church. *Satantango* is a film in twelve sections; like Pudovkin in the 1920s (see page 106), Tarr used a musical structure. In a tango, the dancers take six steps forward, then six steps back. Cultural critic Susan Sontag called the film "Devastating, enthralling for every minute of its seven hours", adding, "I'd be glad to see it every year for the rest of my life."[6] Sontag also admired a young German filmmaker Fred Kelemen, who had previously photographed Tarr's *Utazas az alfoldon/Journey on the Plain* (Hungary, 1995). Kelemen's *Verhängnis/Fate* (Germany, 1994) followed a Russian accordion player and then his girlfriend during one bleak endless night in Berlin. Filming on Hi-8 video, Kelemen used takes of ten minutes or more, sometimes static and brooding, other times serpentine, to tail his characters along dark streets, into bars, around public fountains, etc. The film's smudged and under-lit visuals pre-figured *Festen* by several years and managed to make the bright new medium of videotape appear ancient. Kelemen's follow-up, the three-hour film *Frost* (Germany, 1998), about a woman and child on a journey across bleak winter landscapes, lacked some of the social rage of *Fate*, but was mythic and clearly derived from German Romanticism.

Unlike Western Europe, in the former communist countries women directors continued to set standards. In Poland Dorota Kedzierzawska's *Wrony/Crows* (1994) about a brusque nine-year-old girl who kidnaps a three-year-old boy and attempts to leave Poland by sea was as great a film about childhood as Kiarostami's *Where Is My Friend's House?* In the former Soviet Union itself, master director Kira Muratova made what is perhaps her best film *Uvlecheniya/ Enthusiasm* (1994). Set in the racing world, its Fellini-esque story of a jockey, Sacha, and a circus performer Violetta, is treated with great sonic subtlety. On Wednesday 19 July 1961, 101 people – fifty-one girls, fifty boys – were born in Leningrad. One of them was documentary filmmaker Viktor Kossakovsky. Thirty-four years later he undertook the momentous task of finding them all and making a ninety-three minute film – *Sreda/Wednesday 19.7.1961* – to explore their lives, allocating less than one minute per person. One man stole a packet of cigarettes from his mother and was imprisoned, two died in the war in Afghanistan, many wanted no part in the film. Instead of being a hectic jumble, the tide of humanity portrayed, the economy with which Kossakovsky conjured these disparate lives was deeply moving.

Like the US directors, Russians were also looking to their cinematic past. Critic and theorist Oleg Kovalov's *Sergei Eisenstein: Autobiography* (Russia, 1995) used images from Eisenstein's films, plus footage from the worlds he moved in to attempt to reveal the thought processes of the man in 1929 when he left the Soviet Union for the West, but also what the seminal director means to us today. Referring to Eisenstein's bisexuality and using no commentary or captions, the film tried to apply the montage ideas of the 1920s in a modern context.

The most popular films in Britain in the 1990s were comedies

348
Below: Alison Steadman (right) as Wendy, the dancercise teacher, and Timothy Spall (left) as Aubrey, the owner of Regret Rien, in Mike Leigh's incisive portrait of contemporary Britain, *Life is Sweet*. UK, 1991.

such as *Four Weddings and a Funeral* (1994) penned by Richard Curtis and produced by Working Title Films. The country's most distinctive director was Mike Leigh who, like the French film-makers of the period, focused on disenfranchised protagonists, mostly suburbanites. Using improvization to develop characters, he went beyond the French in finding the often comic nuances in the British class system. In *Life is Sweet* (1991), for example, the mother teaches dancercise classes for tiny children, the father's big scheme to make money is a new hot-dog trailer, one daughter is a plumber and a grotesque family friend opens a hopeless French restaurant called "Regret Rien" (348). Most of Leigh's films are full of such tragi-comic detail. Former jazz musician Mike Figgis was more formally experimental. After the atmospheric debut *Stormy Monday* (1988) he went to the US to make *Internal Affairs* (USA, 1990), an unusually bleak portrait of a Los Angeles policeman. Neither, however, was as original as *Time Code* (UK, 2000), a remarkable film in which four unedited takes following characters whose stories intersect, are presented simultaneously on four quadrants of a split screen. At some screenings Figgis himself varied the sound levels of each take to emphasize different sections of dialogue and, therefore, action. Four continuous takes would not have been possible on film, of course, and *Time Code* was the most innovative digital film to date.

The polar opposite of this, but equally innovative, was the latest meticulous film from the Spaniard Victor Erice, whose *The Spirit of The Beehive* (Spain, 1973) had so beautifully taken the film *Frankenstein* as its starting point. *El sol del membrillo/The Quince Tree Sun* (Spain, 1992) was a documentary of sorts about a famous Spanish painter, Antonio López, doing nothing more than painting the fruit of the tree of the title, measuring how it drops slightly as the tree's branches sag and listening to news about the Gulf War on the radio (see page 436, 325). As he paints the fruit begins to decay and his work is an attempt to defer that decay. Erice's approach was as detailed and loving as López', each artist mirroring the other. The film's patience and spirituality make it almost as great as the 1990s benchmark for such things, Iranian film.

CONTEMPLATION AND HORROR IN NEW ASIAN CINEMA

While the most significant European films of the last fifteen years – those by Von Trier, Dumont, the Dardenne brothers, Haneke, Tarr, Muratova, Kossakovsky, Leigh and Erice – were sober and rigorous, the best work from Asia was often far more sensuous. In South Korea, there had long been a populist mainstream tradition of martial arts films and melodrama. In May 1980, an anti-government uprising at Kwangju, though violently suppressed, catalyzed a new spirit in the arts. By 1986, an independent film movement had emerged and its directors collaborated on a documentary about peasant farmers, *Parangsae/The Bluebird*. Some of the filmmakers involved were prosecuted but another oppositional film *O Gumenara/O Dreamland* (South Korea, 1989) went further, portraying the events at Kwangju and being shown at universities across the country.

The stage was set for Korean filmmaking to mature and the career of its most distinguished director shows how it did so. Im Kwon-taek had been making popular films from 1962 but in 1981, with *Mandala* (1981), his approach became more serious. Thereafter he became the Kurosawa of Korean cinema, addressing the increasingly humanist themes of enlightenment and sexuality, as well as shamanism. His *Seo-Pyon-Jae/Sopyonje* (South Korea, 1993) did well internationally and splendidly at home. Set in the crucial decade of the 1950s, after Japan's thirty-five-year occupation of the country, its division into North and South Korea and the subsequent Korean War, it follows three travelling singers of the country's remarkably melancholic narrative music, Pansori. One Pansori singer who found fame after *Sopyonje* was Cho Seung-Hyun, who dominates Im's even more splendid *Chunhyang* (South Korea, 2000).

349
Above: The beauty of cinematographer Christopher Doyle's work for director Wong Kar-Wai was evident in their first collaboration, *Days of Being Wild*, a sensual updating of Nick Ray's *Rebel Without a Cause* (page 226). Hong Kong, 1990.

From an established mainstream Korean director whose work became more artistically ambitious, to a Hong Kong innovator, twenty-two years his junior: Wong Kar-Wai was born in China, moved to Hong Kong in 1963, and trained as a graphic designer. Finding the martial arts films of the Shaw Brothers too detached from the realities of young people there, he began improvising scriptless films about drifters and existential loners, the sort of characters that had dominated the French "cinéma du look" in the 1980s. Together with Australian-born cinematographer Christopher Doyle, who would become central to his rambling and anarchic way of working, he replicated some of the gloss of those films. *Ai-Fei Zhengchuan/Days of Being Wild* (Hong Kong, 1990) was his first distinctive film, the first shot by Doyle, and a landmark in Hong Kong non-martial arts cinema. An updating of Nicholas Ray's *Rebel without a Cause* (USA, 1955), it established Wong's central theme of loss. Doyle's imagery (349) creates fleeting moments of beauty in the lives of the characters, the memory of which leads to

350
Above: The Wong–Doyle collaboration continued in their semi-improvised *In the Mood for Love,* about a man (Tony Leung) and a woman (Maggie Cheung) who move into adjacent apartments in Hong Kong in 1962 and fall in love. Hong Kong–France, 2000.

longing and unfulfilled desire. At one point a character in *Days of Being Wild* says, "I always thought that one minute flies by. But sometimes it really lingers on. Once a person pointed at his watch and said to me that because of that minute, he'd always remember me. It was so charming listening to that. But now I look at my watch and tell myself I have to forget this man."

This sums up Wong's vision. He and Doyle sometimes became so carried away with alcohol-fuelled invention that what they had to say was barely discernible, making their films little more than post modern mood pieces, but when they cohered, as in the downbeat gay love story *Chunguang Zhaxie/Happy Together* (Hong Kong, 1997) and a rapturous heterosexual one, *Huayang Nianhua/In the Mood for Love* (Hong Kong–France, 2000), the depiction of the transient beauty of young life was heartbreaking. In both, Latin American music represents passion from another world. As in the films of Rainer Werner Fassbinder, hope has been so squeezed out of the human elements of the film that it has emigrated into form – photographic beauty (350). As with the Italian neo-realists, Wong Kar-Wai weaves "dead time" into the incidents in the lives of his characters; and, as with François Truffaut, he sometimes freeze-frames moments of poignancy, somewhat indulgently so.

single frame images – the technique of Abel Gance way back in *La Roue* in 1923 – to represent the flickering decay on his cellular life. This series of over 1,000 pictures of molecules, planets, pornography, textures and torture becomes purely abstract and hypnotic. Eventually, in a flashback to his childhood, we discover the root of his anxiety and rage: he and his brother watched his father force his mother to fellate a phallic gun.

The Tetsuo films were clearly metaphorical. The Godzilla series of the 1950s onward had demonstrated how deeply ingrained was Japanese culture's interest in monstrous destruction. Here it was again, and critics once more related it to the national shock of the atom bombs dropped on Hiroshima and Nagasaki. Whatever the roots of these anxieties, they found expression once more in the terrifying films of Hideo Nakata and Takashi Miike.

Nakata saw, and was impressed by, Friedkin's *The Exorcist* (USA, 1973) while at university, and admired in particular the dreamlike way in which Mizoguchi represents the ghost in *Ugetsu Monogatari* (Japan, 1953, see page 219). Combining the grace of the latter with the demonic theme of the former he adapted a bestselling novel, *Ring*, by Koji Suzuki, to make the most talked-about Japanese horror film of the decade, and the most commercially successful ever released in that country. The story of a cursed video which, when watched, brings about the viewer's death within a week, *Ringu/Ring* (Japan, 1998) built upon a popular urban myth and itself

354
Below: Hideo Nakata combined elements of *The Exorcist* with Mizoguchi's portrayal of ghosts in one of the best Japanese horror films of the nineties to have women as central characters, *Ring*. 1998.

spread like one. Using the slow and suggestive methods that the Pangs would later adopt for *The Eye*, Nakata changed the gender of the protagonist in the novel so that it becomes the story of a woman's persecution and wrath (354). The video scenes themselves were filmed with no clues to location or light source, denying the viewer all reference points and perspectives. The sound in the same scenes combined a remarkable fifty tracks of effects; the noise of a ringing phone in the film was constituted from four different types of telephones as Nakata didn't want it to sound anything like a Hollywood phone. While it borrowed some elements from American teen horror cinema, the scenes of the dead walking among us, and its avoidance of the Christian idea of the human soul, made it distinctly Asian. Nakata made a sequel, *Ring 2* (Japan, 1999), and Hollywood bought the remake rights.

His *Honogurai mizu no soko kara/Dark Water* (Japan, 2002) was an equally slow and creepy combination of Western and Asian horror traditions. Once again, like the work of 1930s directors Mizoguchi and Naruse, his story was about female suffering. This time the single mother's psyche is damaged by guilt about neglecting her daughter (355). Ruined by an inelegant coda, the film nonetheless demonstrated how lacking in spirituality contemporary Western horror cinema was in comparison.

Takashi Miike's *Oodishon/Audition* (Japan, 2000) was an altogether more brutal bloodbath but again, remarkably, took an outwardly polite and withdrawn young woman as an emblem of the loneliness and rage beneath the surface of Japanese society. Takashi

355
Below: A single mother's anxiety about neglecting her daughter is the wellspring of the horrific events in Nakata's *Dark Water*. Japan, 2002.

CAN SEE (1990–PRESENT): COMPUTERIZATION TAKES CINEMA BEYOND PHOTOGRAPHY

entered the film industry as
assistant director to the master
portraitist of impolite women,
Shohei Imamura. Like his men-
tor he was interested in the disruptive power of raw sexuality,
but his situations are drawn
from the punk underground.
As such his career runs in tandem with Shinya Tsukamoto's.
Like every other distinctive
Japanese director of the
period, including Tsukamoto,

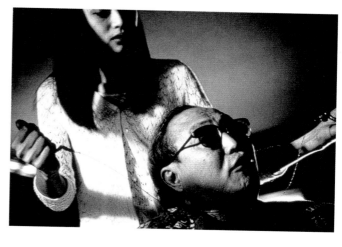

Miike's starting point in *Audition* is the apparently graceful stasis of
contemporary Japan, the "floating world". His story is that of a shy,
modest young woman who attends the auditions of a film producer
who pretends that he is casting for a new film but is really looking for
a wife (356). Throughout these sequences, the camera is as stable as that
of Ozu but after the young woman disappears in the night, it is hand
held. Like the work of Michael Haneke, Takashi prepares for terror
with blankness and minimalism. About fifty minutes in we visit the
woman's apartment. In the background of a shot is a sack. Later we
will discover that a mutilated man is in that sack. Like Nakata,
Takashi's hints at what lies ahead are often sonic. Here animal noises
like roaring dinosaurs are heard long before we discover, for example,
that the woman feeds the amputee in the sack with her own vomit.

The fantastic in Japanese cinema in the last fifteen years has
not always been wedded to the violent, however. *Anime* continued
creatively to dwarf American animation, never more so than in Hayao
Miyazaki's *Mononoke Hime/Princess Mononoke* (Japan, 1997),
which extended awareness of his work internationally. Set in ancient
times in forests where spirits of the gods dwelt (357), its story of Prince
Ashitaka, who must go west to search for the source of hatred, was so
imaginatively told that the film became the second-biggest box-office
hit in the history of Japanese cinema. En route Ashitaka meets the
ingenious wolf, Princess Mononoke, hears of the night walker, a
forest spirit who looks like a giraffe, conjured from the Milky Way.
He has an astonishing dream of a multi-antlered beast, of a fish whose
kisses heal, of another animal at whose feet flowers blossom.
Miyazaki's film was a masterpiece, a mythological reading of the

ecosystem, a metaphorical account of anger as stupidity. Its scenes of guns becoming studded with flowers are the antithesis of Tetsuo. Miyazaki and Tsukamoto represent the hopes and fears of the most deeply anxious film culture of the age.

THE CONTINUING ACHIEVEMENTS IN AFRICA AND CENTRAL AND SOUTH AMERICAN REVIVALS

Completing the unique situation for film history where every continent in one era was doing original work, we come to Africa and Central and South America. In Africa, the established filmmakers continued to work, and new directors joined them. The Tunisian Moufida Tlatli studied filmmaking in France in the late 1960s. After a stint as an editor on Arab-themed documentaries and dramas, she directed *Saint el Qusur/Silences of the Palaces* (France–Tunisia, 1994), in which the death of Tunisian Prince Sid Ali inspires Alia, the daughter of one of his female servants, to return to his palace where her mother worked and where she spent her childhood (358). A series of slow and painfully revealing flashbacks ensues. The period remembered is that of the end of colonialism when the Arab system of female semi-servitude remained unaltered by the French. Tlatli delicately interweaves her story's present and past tenses, beautifully comparing the loneliness of each. Alia hopes that her singing will allow her to overcome the traditions of servitude but her conclusion is bleak: "My life has been a series of abortions. I could never express myself. My songs were stillborn."

In the same year as Tlatli's debut, Dani Kouyaté also made his first film, the splendid *Këita, L'Heritage du Griot/Këita! Voice of the Griot*. Born into a family of traditional storytelling griots, in the same town in Burkina Faso as Gaston Kaboré, who directed 1982's landmark *Wend kuuni*, Kouyaté, who was nine years younger, also studied in France. His *Këita* told of a thirteen-year-old boy, Mabo Këita, who lives in a middle-class urban African family. He goes to a good school and learns how Christopher Columbus discovered America. One day, Djeliba, a folk teacher from way outside the city boundaries, visits Mabo's family and tells him another type of history. Djeliba's stories are mythical, about the origins of life. Mabo hears how his own family is descended from buffaloes, how the blackbirds will look after him, how people – like trees – have roots that go deep into the ground. *Keita's* brilliant screenplay – also by the thirty-four-year-old Kouyaté – deals with the relative nature of truth and the metaphorical aspect of history, in the most engaging way. Its realist flashbacks to ancient times are in turn amusing and revealing.

358
Left: Memories of Arab servitude in Moufida Tlatli's *The Silences of the Palaces*. France–Tunisia, 1994.

In Egypt, nearly forty years after his landmark *Cairo Station* (see pages 240–41), seventy-year-old Youssef Chahine made *Al Massir/Destiny* (Eygpt–France, 1997), a vivid attack on Islamic fundamentalism. Set in Andalucia in the twelfth century, it tells of Abu ibn Rushd (known as Averroës in Europe) who teaches Greek philosophy and is therefore accused of undermining religious orthodoxy.

Averroës fights back, calling the clerics "merchants of faith", arguing that divine law combines revelation and reason, challenging his persecutors by saying "do you know enough about love, about truth, about justice to be able to proclaim God's word?" Stylistically the film is an epic in the mode of Hollywood in the 1950s (359) but this being Chahine there are again Gene Kelly-like dance sequences, and the opening bathing scene in moonlit waters shows the influence of Hindi cinema.

359
Above: *Destiny*, Youssef Chahine's prescient attack on Islamic fundamentalism, emphasized the religion's moderate and tolerant roots. Egypt–France, 1997.

Filmmaking in Brazil had done little that was distinctive since the end of the Cinema Nôvo movement in the mid-1970s. The political ambitions of the Bandung Conference which gave rise to the radical film movements in Brazil and then elsewhere, which collectively became known as "Third Cinema" (see pages 368–69), waned in the decade of the blockbuster.[8] Of its Brazilian standard-bearers Glauber Rocha died in 1981 and Nelson Pereira dos Santos lost his bite. Twenty years later, after years of formulaic melodramas and musicals, the son of a banker from Rio de Janeiro, who was too young to have seen the work of Rocha and dos Santos on its initial release, turned a documentary he made called *Socorro Nobre/Life Somewhere Else* (Brazil, 1995) into a fiction film *Central do Brasil/Central Station* (Brazil, 1998) and revived the spirit of the 1960s. Echoing in some ways the microcosm of Chahine's *Cairo Station*, Walter Salles' film focuses on a cynical former school teacher, Dora, who makes money by writing letters for the illiterate people who crowd Rio's main railway station. She cares little about those for whom she writes, even nine-year-old Josue. Then Josue's mother dies and Dora takes him to find his father in the country's north east (where Rocha's *Black God, White Devil*, 1964, was set). During the journey she undergoes a transformation. The authenticity of Salles' film derives from its roots in a documentary, but the actors – the boy, the bitter schoolteacher – improvise substantial sections of dialogue, with splendid results.

The success of *Central Station* gave Salles the clout that enabled him to help other Brazilian filmmakers. He co-produced Katia Lund's and Fernando Meirelles' *Citade de Deus/City of God* (Brazil, 2002), which was even more successful internationally than his own film. The city of the title is an ironic name for a 1960s Rio housing project that in the 1980s became one of the most violent places in the country. Narrated by a young, black peasant photographer, Busca-Pe, the film used the schemas of Scorsese's *GoodFellas* and Oliver Stone's *Natural Born Killers* to hurtle through its story of brutal killings of children. Meirelles trained in advertising and his style could not be further away from neo-realism. He uses multiple-tilted, speeded-up tracking shots, deep focus and fast cutting to dynamize space (see page 435, 324), loads his sound-track with layers of effects and kinetic music, has his shots processed so as to saturate their colour, stages scenes in order to eradicate the possibility of momentary stasis. His co-director, Katia Lund, the daughter of middle-class American parents, ran community video projects designed to help young drug addicts, through which she found some of the actors who appeared in the film.

The spectre of Luis Buñuel continued to hang over Mexican cinema – which continued to make low-budget genre movies – through good times and bad. The country produced some distinctive films in the late 1960s. The most original, since Buñuel made his twenty there between 1947 and 1965, were by Arturo Ripstein, who had been Bunuel's assistant on *El ángel exterminador/The Exterminating Angel* (Mexico, 1962). Ripstein's first film, which he made when he was just twenty-one, was *Tiempo de Morir/A Time to Die* (Mexico, 1962), written by Gabriel García Márquez and Carlos Fuentes. His best was *Cadena Perpétua/Life Term* (Mexico, 1978), an innovative film noir which explored the relationship between a petty thief and the Mexican authorities. Jaime Humberto Hermosillo also did interesting work in the 1970s, gradually moving the theme of homosexuality to the centre of cinema, and breaking through to international audiences with *Doña Herlinda y su hijo/Doña Herlinda and Her Son* (Mexico, 1985). His interest in long takes made him the most formally inventive Mexican director of the 1980s. In 1999, however, a film more significant than anything by Ripstein or Hermosillo came along – *Amores Perros/Love's a Bitch*. Directed by Alejandro González Iñárritu, it takes the three-part structure of Tarantino's *Pulp Fiction*, as well as that film's mix of reverie and brutality, and adds to them the social commentary of Buñuel. Great filmmakers are often fuelled by rage. González Iñárritu drives every gory, Goya-esque sequence with it. His opening scene, a car crash, links his three stories. He films the first as if there's a rip-cord engine attached to his camera which propels it through the grotesqueries of Mexico City. The second is the most Buñuel-like, a caustic story about a fashion model and her lover suffering in their middle-class apartment. In the third, an old, cynical ex-revolutionary tries to discover what happened to his daughter. González Iñárritu and cinematographer Rodrigo Prieto judiciously took as their main visual reference the stills of American photographer Nan Goldin. The unflattering honesty with which she films people and her habit of not colour-correcting sodium lighting, reaps rich rewards in their film. The director also cited 1990s directors Wong Kar-Wai and Lars Von Trier as influences. The charged visuals of the former and the pessimism of the latter are clearly visible. At the centre of the film is a metaphor: People as dogs

(360). In deserted swimming pools, dogs fight each other to the death. Von Trier would soon adopt this metaphor for his own film *Dogville* (France, 2003). González Iñárritu later told journalists that his grand film was a comment on the seventy years of one-party rule in Mexico.

Gael Garcia Bernal, one of the actors in *Amores Perros*, starred in another innovative, internationally successful Mexican film which was released the following year. Taken together they were seen as the start of a Mexican new wave. *Y tu mamá también/And Your Mother Too* (Mexico, 2001) was co-written and directed by Alfonso Cuaron, Mexico's most commercially successful director in years. After a stylish sex comedy feature debut, *Sólo con tu pareja/Love in the Time of Hysteria* (Mexico, 1991), shot in widescreen by Emmanual Lubezki, who would become his long-term collaborator, he went to Hollywood and made a delicate film of the classic children's novel *A Little Princess* (USA, 1995). This received rave reviews, and he and Lubetzki became known as

360
Above: Fighting dogs are metaphors for human aggression in Alejandro González Iñárritu's boldly visual triptych film *Amores Perros*. Mexico, 1999.

sophisticated visual stylists. They collaborated next on a glossy adaptation of Charles Dickens' *Great Expectations* (USA, 1997), which was interested in focus and design but which lacked substance, so the filmmakers returned to Mexico to make Y *tu mamá también*. Cuarón and his screenwriter brother Carlos took as their starting point one familiar from American teen pics: two hormonal seventeen-year-olds whose girlfriends have gone away for the summer. They make far more out of this than a multiplex film would, however. The boys come from rich families – the Cuaróns regularly stop the soundtrack of their adventures to introduce a sobering commentary about the sociology and deprivations of Mexico – we hear of drug busts and road accidents and see shanty towns. Where US teen sex romps are somewhat coy, director Cuarón has his two characters lying on the diving board of their family's swimming pool masturbating in full view. At a society wedding

they meet a sexy twenty-eight-year-old woman and persuade her to drive with them to an idyllic beach, which they are not sure exists. Again a commentary undercuts the reverie, telling us that the beach will be purchased for a tourist hotel. The drive and their bawdy adventures en route comprise the body of the film, Cuarón alternating their sexual banter with his intermittently political sound-track. Each boy has a frank sexual experience with the woman, the Cuaróns subtly using the geometry of this triangle to suggest that the boys will eventually kiss each other (361). In an erotic situation encouraged by her, they eventually do, but recoil. Their friendship cannot sustain the implication of this. They meet some years later, regretful of the loss. The shifts in tone of these new Latin films, their visual richness and the incorporation of elements of tragedy into their storylines represent a new aesthetic in South American cinema.

It is appropriate that in the final section of a book that charts the history of filmmakers asking "How can I do this differently?", we find a chorus of answers. In the last fifteen years, more than in any previous period in film history, filmmakers around the world have explored the quality of their medium. The Iranian para-documentaries set the benchmark in this regard by finding new ways to elevate the details of life. In Australasia, Jane Campion and Baz Luhrmann took on the question of genre with more aplomb than any antipodean filmmakers had shown before. American cinema began to recover after having abandoned many of its artistic ambitions in the 1980s. Its self-improvement took two forms: Looking back to earlier achievements in cinema, leading to 1990s postmodernism, and planting the seed of digital production, post-production and exhibition. These two trends came together in the films of Oliver Stone, whose ebullience was derided at the time but whose visual experiments in *Natural Born Killers* can be seen to have influenced multi-textural cinema thereafter.

The computer-generated fly-around was probably the most distinctive shot to emerge from big-budget CGI. The European mainstream contributed little in the last fifteen years but, almost certainly in reaction to CGI fly-arounds and the lowering of standards in filmmaking, the greatest filmmakers emphasized aesthetic rigour. Like Bresson, Pasolini and Warhol in an earlier generation, Lars Von Trier, Bruno Dumont, the Dardenne brothers, Michael Haneke, Béla Tarr and Victor Erice each seemed to respond to the excessive possibilities of CGI by narrowing their stylistic palette or emphasizing the low-tech extreme of the digital spectrum.

There was no such formal consistent among the best Asian filmmakers, however. All the important ones touched on the theme of loneliness, and many suggested that sexuality was at the root of that loneliness, but their portrayals of it were wildly different. Wong Kar-Wai and Tsai Ming-Liang used dead time within their films to express it, whereas the Japanese directors Tsukamoto, Nakata and Miike were interested in the fact that when it is not expressed, it can explode into violence and rage. This gave Japanese horror cinema a richness not seen in genre cinema elsewhere in the 1990s and since.

In Africa and Central and South America, new filmmakers emerged who selectively engaged with the Third Cinema themes of their forebears: Tlatli in Tunisia, Kouyaté in Burkina Faso, Salles and Meirelles in Brazil, Gonzáles Iñárritu and Cuarón in Mexico. Because of the vagaries of film financing, the first two in particular have not been prolific, but each pushed the boundaries of what to say and how to say it.

1. In the year of 1974, three major filmmakers were in prison: Yilmaz Güney in Turkey (1972–74), Sergei Paradjanov in the Soviet Union (1974–78) and Mohsen Makhmalbaf in Iran (1974–78).

2. Martin Scorsese in *Scene by Scene*, BBC Television. Conversation with the author.

3. Gavin Smith, "When You Know You're in Good Hands", Film Comment, July–August 1994.

4. www.dogme95.dk/menu/menuset.htm

5. Ibid.

6. *New York Times*.

7. The country's most distinguished filmmaker before Vithanage was Lester James Peries who debuted in 1956 with *Rekava* and directed *Wekand Walauwa/Mansion by the Lake* (2003) at the age of eighty-four.

8. Hector Babenco's *Pixote* (1981) was an exception to this trend.

362
Above: One moment from
the longest shot in film
history: the ballroom
scene toward the end
of Alexander Sokurov's
landmark exploration of
the nineteenth-century
history of his country,
Russian Ark. Russia, 2002.

CONCLUSION

I said at the start of this book that it was a story of innovation, because innovation fuels cinema. I also mentioned that it was written for an intelligent general audience. I hope that in it you have discovered films that you really want to see and parts of the history of film to explore further, because there is no doubt that intelligent audiences fuel innovative cinema.

In my introduction I promised three adjustments to conventional movie histories. The first was that this would be a story of world cinema, not just Western filmmaking. The second was that I would describe – somewhere between the emotionally excessive films of Hollywood and Bollywood and the minimalist films of Bresson and the like – a uniquely balanced body of classical work, that of Ozu. My third challenge to conventional wisdom has been to argue that since 1990, the films of directors such as Kiarostami, Luhrmann, Sokurov, González Iñárritu, Von Trier and David Lynch have shown the global film world to be in better health at any time in its history.

The medium of film crashed into the lives of Western people at the end of the nineteenth century like a precocious, attention-grabbing, quickly exhausted child. It had the heartbreakingly beautiful confidence of something without history. Then, as the late 1910s, the 1920s and the 1930s passed, as filmmakers tried and failed and had insights and saw those insights enter the medium or being forgotten by it, so cinema began to be aware that it had a history of its own, the stuff of this book. When it looked back it discovered that it already had pioneers, legendary figures, and rightly became ambivalent about that past. Some filmmakers became too fond of the old ways of doing things, the tried and trusted methods. Others – in the 1960s and 1990s – felt that the medium that was running through their cameras at twenty-four frames per second was beginning to feel old. It needed to be renewed. This explains Bresson, Godard and Von Trier, but not Mambety, Ghatak, Rocha and Kiarostami. Film history has more than one line of narrative. African, Asian, South American and Middle-Eastern cinema simply do not relate to that precious nineteenth-century child in any direct way. They began later and, like younger, alienated siblings, had consciously to find their own voices. Then these younger cinemas in turn influenced the old. Southern and Eastern ideas about form flowed into the West, and vice versa.

There are other ways in which the story of film has not been a slow, steady progression along a single road. Take the invisibility of Ozu and Muratova, for example. A filmmaker in Japan conceived film as aesthetically and philosophically balanced in a way not to be found in Western cinema, yet his classicism had no influence on most film cultures until the mid-1950s, when he belatedly found recognition. Imagine how Western closed romantic realism might have developed had his example been followed earlier. As for Muratova, her work was first shelved by the Soviet regime and, even after its belated release, she remained underrated. The absence of female filmmakers for much of film history has damaged the artistic claims of the medium.

Alongside this history of deferred starts, absences and oversights is the real substance of this book, the grass roots: lying in bed at night, pacing the sound stage floor, sitting at a keyboard, talking with other filmmakers, watching films for inspiration – the nature of invention in cinema itself. This is where E.H. Gombrich's schema plus correction, which I modified to schema plus variation, came in. The proof that Gombrich was right, that ideas about form zigzag through a medium, building on or keeping their distance from what went before, can be seen in those rare times in film history where creativity seems to go up a gear. Look at what I have called the Soviet think tank of the 1920s. Under the tutelage of Lev Kuleshov, a group of ardent young people who were new to the medium got their heads together, bounced ideas off each other, determined to reject what went before, and accelerated the rate at which film form was invented – yes invented – in their country, beyond anything that happened there before or since. A similar process took place in the offices of *Cahiers du Cinéma* in the mid- and late 1950s. Through talking and writing about and eventually making films, critics who became directors accelerated formal growth and introduced the medium to a set of new stylistic ideas which would sweep across the world. Likewise, to a lesser extent, in Copenhagen in the mid-1990s, when a group of filmmakers prohibited certain stylistic techniques for ethical reasons. They varied the schema, created a whole new set of possibilities and became the most influential filmmakers of their day. In each of these three situations, the young men were acting out of self-interest; their manifestos propelled them into film production. When will conventional filmmakers and public-sector film bodies around the world realize that in order to get themselves noticed, to refresh cinema, they must ask the question with which this book started, "How can I do this differently?"

To do so is to engage in risk. The best line in Preston Sturges' very funny book about his career underlines the point: "It was the enormous risks I took with pictures, skating right up to the edge of non-acceptance, that paid off so handsomely."[1] These weren't the words of a maverick newcomer but a filmmaker at the end of his life. Kuleshov's soup and freedom editing experiments risked professional disapproval (see page 104). Paradjanov's challenging of ideological conformism by filming folk tales in a baroque style was so risky that they led to his imprisonment. Scorsese's idea of "opening up the form" risked alienating audiences, Fassbinder's use of the American form but moving "the content onto other areas" ran the risk of making a dog's breakfast. The sustained stasis in the films of Akerman, Tarr and Kelemen must have tried the patience of producers and distributors. In each case they did something new and splendid.

So many films in this book are good because of thought and courage. But as David Lynch's talk about ideas "just popping" (see page 396) suggests, invention in cinema, as in other art forms, also relies on pure, unthought-out, unheralded inspiration. The purest – and funniest – example I know is American novelist and critic James Agee's detailed essay "Comedy's Greatest Era", where he's talking about the silent comedy producer Mack Sennett:

"Sennett used to a hire a 'wild man' to sit in on his gag conferences, whose whole job was to think up 'wildies'. Usually he was an all but brainless, speechless man, scarcely able to communicate his idea; but he had a totally uninhibited imagination. He might say nothing for an hour; then he'd mutter 'You take ...' and all the relatively rational others would shut up and wait. 'You take this cloud ... .' Thanks to some kind of thought-transference, saner men would take this cloud and make something of it. The wild man seems in fact to have functioned as the group's subconscious mind ... ."

The example Agee gives of a contribution by the wild man concerns Laurel and Hardy moving a piano across a very narrow bridge

363
Right: An opportunity for wild comic invention: what would be the funniest thing that could happen to Laurel and Hardy as they carry a piano across a bridge over a ravine?

over a plunging ravine. What could happen that was really funny? The wild man suggests that halfway along they meet a gorilla (363).

Rational invention, determined invention, surreal invention. These are the traits that drive great cinema. They exist between two poles: on the one hand what could be called the difficulty of film, Kuleshov's proof that a shot couldn't even say a simple thing like "this man is feeling hunger" or "this man is feeling freedom"; on the other, the ease of cinema, its innate, effortless, precocious (back to that child again) ability to capture the splendour of the real world. Look at these two images, one of Jean Pierre Léaud (364 top) and one of Sharmila Tagore (364 bottom), two of the greatest actors in the world. Look at the intelligence in their eyes, the keenness of mind of each. Cinema can show this in a heartbeat, and then enlarge it onto a big screen.

The earliest histories of film argued, understandably, that the greatest films were those that pushed to the fullest possible extent the editing, focus, composition, lighting and tracking possibilities of the medium. After the Second World War critics such as André Bazin dismissed this, arguing instead that realist films, compelled by history or filmmaking instinct to be morally serious, were the most valuable and cinematic. Then in the 1950s came Alexandre Astruc's argument that the worth of a film should be measured according to how closely it expresses its director's vision of life. Astruc emphasized this by comparing the camera to a novelist's pen. Finally, in the 1960s and 1970s, more philosophically-inclined film writers began to see in Dreyer, Ozu, Bresson and Antonioni the essence of a more metaphysical or abstract aspect of cinema. It is difficult at first to square these four mutually exclusive visions of cinema: formalism, realism, expressionism and transcendentalism. Until, that is, it is realized that all films can be placed within the square that they form. Very few contain only one of these qualities and so exist outside the square; most can be plotted in relation to its corners.

It is commonplace to be pessimistic about the medium of film. Certainly cultural globalization, while in theory opening up major film markets to a trickle of films from minor ones, exacerbates the standardization of film form and movie-going. Hollywood's totems of release, freedom, achievement, competition, self-actualization and expansion are winning on screen at the expense of co-operation, balance, anti-materialism and contraction. Yet, as the last chapter argued, creativity in film is more equally distributed around the planet than ever before.

If this is indeed so, the timing could not be better. The digitization of the film process, which began properly in the early 1990s, is more than a trickle now. The most striking comments about this come from film editor, director and sound designer Walter Murch in a *New York Times* article, "Digital Cinema of the Mind". He compared film at the beginning of the twenty-first century to painting in the Renaissance and early modern periods. In moving from painting frescoes using pigment in wet plaster to painting in oils on canvas, artists went from an expensive, collaborative process requiring patronage and dedicated to "public" subjects, to a cheap, individual process depicting more personal situations and themes. So it is with film, Murch argued. The slow digital revolution opens the doors to what *Dogme* called "the ultimate democratization of cinema", in ways that Scorsese could only dream of. The need for crews of forty people, budgets of millions of dollars, and the qualified, restricting approval of the providers of that money, is removed.

364
Above: Cinema's greatness derives in part from the way it can capture the thoughts and beauty of great performers such as Jean Pierre Léaud (top) and Sharmila Tagore (bottom). *Domicile Conjugal*. Director: François Truffaut. France, 1970. *Devi*. Director: Satyajit Ray. India, 1960.

While a period of modest cinema, made possible by this, would perhaps have a detoxifying effect, it cannot be argued that digitization would mean the end of grandeur in films. As if to prove this point and also to refute those who argue that cinema is inevitably in creative decline, in 2002 a Russian director made a film as revolutionary as *The Jazz Singer* or *A Bout de souffle*. Alexander Sokurov was born in Irkutsk in 1950 and was taught by Andrei Tarkovsky, who called him "a cinematic genius". He first came to my attention in 1995 at the Berlin Film Festival, where his five-hour, trance-like documentary *Spiritual Voices* played to an almost empty cinema. A year later he released an even better film, *Mother and Son* (Russia, 1996), an overwhelming study of the relationship between a dying mother and her attentive son. Featuring the visual equivalent of what mathematicians call shearings (the distortions of a fixed shape as if it was elastic), shrouded exposures, photography through glass and lenses painted with Chinese brushes, the visual originality of the film was matched by the sober intensity of the love it portrayed. The mother looks up to a sky of thunderclouds and says, "Is there anyone up there?" When she dies, a butterfly lands on her hands. Paul Schrader called it "seventy-three heart-aching, luminescent minutes of pure cinema". Sokurov had made a work as great as Dovzhenko's *Arsenal*.

Then he surpassed even that. After films on Hitler and Stalin he made *Russian Ark* (362). On the day that it premièred at the Cannes Film Festival in 2002, there were rumours that it contained not a single edit. In a ninety-minute film? That is impossible. No digital video tapes run that long. The lights went down. The film started. Whispered voices of actors backstage at a theatre. Compositions like Von Sternberg's. Then the film broke. Lights went up. The projectionist rewound the film and we began again. What played on the screen in the next hour and a half was the single most dramatic variation of the schema of cinema that I have witnessed in my lifetime. As we have seen in this book, the question of the long-held take – its suspense, beauty and intensity – has engaged filmmakers from Mizoguchi to Minnelli, Hitchcock, Jancsó, Tarr and Kelemen. In *Russian Ark*, Sokurov outdid any of them. Shooting neither on film nor on tape but directly onto a computer hard disk, he invented a film in which a civilized nineteenth-century European travels through the Hermitage art gallery in St. Petersburg, debating the nature of nineteenth-century Russian culture, arguing with the drowsy, dreaming, off-screen voice of Russia itself. His minstrel-like journey covers 1,300 metres of ground, through thirty-three galleries of Rembrandts, da Vincis, and the like. And Sokurov had indeed filmed it in a single unbroken shot.

Sokurov's single shot, achieved on the second take, took place on 23 December 2001 and it shows that, far from being at an end, the history of this great art form is only beginning.

❊❊❊❊❊❊❊❊❊❊❊❊❊❊❊

The purpose of this book was to chart the creative highlights of cinema, a singular and selective focus, and in some ways an old-fashioned one, which will have alienated some, but so be it. The simplest reason why this book is valuable is that it distills between its covers more great films than most chronological accounts of the medium. If you have followed me to the end you will have learned how ambiguous the filmmaker's relationship with the real world has been, how fraught the role of personal expression in such a public medium has been, how there has been a tug-of-war between those who love the medium and those who love the industry. Like Lauren Bacall, I am on the side of the former, yet am immensely proud of the great flickering art form of film when it gets onto the front pages and enters what Hélène Cixous called "the arena of contradiction, where pleasure and reality embrace". I may have missed important films along the way, or overstated a work or a director that excites me, but in the end this book has been about how cinema, more than any art form, is capable of portraying that embrace: in other words, despite her glaring absence, about Shirley Maclaine running down that street.

1. *Preston Sturges on Preston Sturges*, ed: Sandy Sturges, Faber and Faber, 1991, p. 294.

GLOSSARY

Academy Ratio: The standard shape of movie screens before the mid-1950s: one-third wider than it is high.

Avant-garde: Individual artists, movements or ideas which are ahead of the mainstream.

Blimp: Any kind of insulating box or jacket which is mounted around the camera to reduce the whirring noise it makes.

Boom: The pole on which sound recordists' microphones are mounted in order that they can be away from the action.

Cinema Nòvo: A new, politically informed and stylistically ambitious trend in Brazilian cinema of the 1960s in which Glauber Rocha was the most significant figure.

Cinema Verité: A parallel French trend to Direct Cinema which did not try to be as "invisible" as its American counterpart and laid more emphasis on interviewing and the way in which the presence of a film crew can help extract the truth from a situation.

CinemaScope: The first commercially successful, copyrighted widescreen filming process in which a panoramic scene was squashed horizontally to fit onto a 35mm negative then stretched again on the projector in cinemas.

Cinematographer: The craftsperson who – on instruction from the director – plans the lighting and exposure of a scene and oversees the camera moves.

Classicism: The period of, or tendency to, balance and order in an art-form. Work that is neither highly decorated nor stylistically spare, neither emotionally excessive nor minimalist.

Close-up: An image which enlarges the thing it photographs in order to emphasize or reveal more detail about it.

Closed Romantic Realism: The dominant style of mainstream cinema in Hollywood and elsewhere. The films are "closed" in that the actors seem to inhabit a parallel universe and don't look at the camera, and the stories are seldom open-ended. "Romantic" because emotions in such films tend to be heightened and the protagonists are in some way heroic. "Realism" because, despite these artifices, the people in such movies are recognizably human and the societies depicted have problems similar to our own.

Continuity Editing: The convention in mainstream filmmaking which allows action to appear to flow from one shot to the next, particularly in relation to the direction.

Cutting: see **Editing**

Deep Focus: A technique, often involving very bright lights and sensitive film stock, which allows filmmakers to keep things close to and far away from the camera in focus.

Deep Staging: A technique in which the action in a scene takes place on planes at a wide range of distances from the lens. these actions need not be in focus.

Direct Cinema: American and Canadian documentary films shot in the late 1950s and 1960s which largely eschewed conventional lighting and interviewing. Its main exponents were Robert Drew, the Maysles brothers and D. A. Pennebaker.

Dolly Shot: A move created by mounting the camera's tripod on a specially designed trolley.

Edit/Cut: A single join between two shots.

Editing: The joining of shots to establish pace, rhythm and, where appropriate, narrative flow.

Establishing Shot: An image used at the beginning of a sequence to show the location of the ensuing action. Often an exterior, it seldom involves dialogue and often shows little more than a location.

Expressionism: A technique of exaggerating acting, make-up, lighting and production design in cinema to express the dreams, nightmares and psychoses which lie beneath the surface of human behaviour. The German film *The Cabinet of Doctor Caligari* (1920) was the first to employ the technique. It was most consistently used by filmmakers in that country in the ensuing decade.

Film Noir: Visually and morally dark crime films first made in America in the 1940s, often directed by European emigrés, and influenced by crime fiction and German Expressionism.

Focus Pull: A change of focus within a shot, often used to keep a moving object or person sharp, or to direct the audience's attention.

Gaffer: The chief electrician on a film.

Gombrich, E.H.: The art historian who argued that technique in art evolved through "schema plus correction".

Grip: The technician who positions film lights, pushes or pulls the dolly, or mounts "flags" in front of lights to control what they illuminate.

Impressionism: The use of shots, cuts and photography to capture the fleeting aspects of human perception, mostly associated with French filmmakers like Abel Gance and Germaine Dulac but employed sporadically by directors before and since.

Jump Cut: An unconventional join between two pieces of usually similar action which does not obey the convention of "invisible" and continuity editing.

Kinetoscope: A machine into which individuals looked to see moving images in the days before cinemas and projection.

Master Shot: A wide view of a situation, revealing all the main elements in a scene.

Method Acting: A raw performance style inspired by the theories of Konstantin Stanislavski and developed by the Actors Studio in New York.

Montage: This French term for editing has come to mean either a discreet sequence in mainstream cinema which summarizes – or captures the flavour of – a series of events or, alternatively, a more theoretical way of looking at how the editing has structured a film.

Naturalism: A general term used to describe a style of cinematography which approximates everyday lighting and storytelling and which does not overdramatize real events. Some writers argue that naturalism is a surface quality whereas realism captures a deeper truth about lived experience.

New American Cinema: The 1970s films of Martin Scorsese, Francis Coppola, and others which were more personal and stylistically ambitious than the mainstream, often family oriented, studio pictures.

New Wave/Nouvelle Vague: In general this self-explanatory term refers to the emergence of a group of new – sometimes dissident – artists. In film history it is usually applied to those directors in the 1960s in many countries around the world who tried to refresh film language or make movies more relevant to the political imperatives of their time.

Pillow Shot: A phrase used by some commentators on Japanese cinema to describe images in Ozu films whose spaces do not necessarily relate to the incidents around them and which function more like meditative pauses in the action.

Reverse-Angle Shooting: Cutting between a person and what he or she is looking at or talking to. Also sometimes used when people are not in a scene – for example when an inflammable liquid is flowing towards a naked flame, an editor is likely to cut between the liquid and the flame.

Schemata/Schema: A unit of technique.

Schema Plus Variation: How a filmmaker takes an existing technique and modifies it to his or her own purpose.

Shot: A single piece of exposed film, without joins.

Soviet Montage/Editing: A theoretical, dynamic and polemical cutting style devised by Lev Kuleshov, Sergei Eisenstein and others in the USSR in the 1920s. Challenging the conventional idea that the purpose of editing is invisibly to create narrative coherence, they suggested instead that the ideas in each of two shots, when brought together, produced a third.

Surrealism: Ideas in, and styles of, cinema which portray the irrational aspects of life – particularly associated with the work of Luis Buñuel.

Tableau Shot: A wide, static and frontal image which looks as if it was created by photographing a stage play from the front row of the stalls. Widely used in cinema's first decade, its distancing and compositional possibilities interested later Avant-garde directors such as Peter Greenaway, Hou Hsiao-Hsien and Bruno Dumont.

Tradition of Quality: A term used by French critics in the 1950s to disparage the technically proficient but impersonal films which they so disliked.

Y

PICTURE CREDITS

T = Top B= Bottom L= Left R= Right
C = Centre; BFI: British Film Institute

We would like to thank all the film production and distribution companies and photographers whose publicity photographs appear in this book. We apologize in advance for any unintentional omission or neglect and will be pleased to insert the appropriate acknowledgement for any companies or individuals in any subsequent edition of this work.

Endpapers: Getty Images/Hulton; **2** Ronald Grant Archive; **4** 1 Ronald Grant Archive; **4**, 2 Ronald Grant Archive; **4** 3 BFI/Dulac/Vandal/Aubert; **4**, 4 Kobal Collection/MGM; **4** 5 Joel Finler Collection; **5**, 6 Moviestore Collection/Columbia; **5**, 7 BFI/Paramount Pictures; **5**, 8 Ronald Grant Archive/Kestrel Films; **5**, 9 Ronald Grant Archive/Guangxi Film Studios; **5**, 10 Moviestore Collection/Carolco; **6** Moviestore Collection/Amblin/DreamWorks /Paramount Pictures; **10**T *Odd Man Out*, Carol Reed, UK, 1946; **10**C *Deux au trois choses que je sais d'elle*, Jean-Luc Godard, France, 1967; **10**B *Taxi Driver*, Martin Scorsese, USA, 1976; **12** BFI; **13**T Joel Finler Collection; **13**B BFI; **14** Moviestore Collection/Mehboob Eros; **17** Science & Society Picture Library/National Museum of Photography, Film & Television; **19** Ronald Grant Archive/Mosfilm; **20** Ronald Grant Archive; **22** Joel Finler Collection; **24** Ronald Grant Archive/Lumière Brothers; **25**T Barry Salt Collection; **25**B Kevin Brownlow Collection; **26**T Joel Finler Collection; **26**B Ronald Grant Archive/Méliès; **27** Kevin Brownlow Collection; **28** George Eastman House/Stills Collection-Motion Picture Department; **30** Ronald Grant Archive; **31**T BFI; **31**B Ronald Grant Archive; **32** Ronald Grant Archive/Mosfilm; **33** Ronald Grant Archive/Dino De Laurentiis; **34** Joel Finler Collection; **35** BFI; **36-37** BFI/Edison Company; **38** Barry Salt Collection; **40** National Film Center/Courtesy of National Film Center, The National Museum of Modern Art, Tokyo; **43** BFI; **44** Barry Salt Collection; **46** Danish Film Institute /Stills & Posters Archive; **47** BFI/Phalke Films; **48** Kobal Collection/Itala Film Torino; **49** BFI/Associated British; **50**T Barry Salt Collection; **50**B Barry Salt Collection; **51** Ronald Grant Archive; **52** Ronald Grant Archive; **53**T Kobal Collection/Itala Film Torino; **53**B Joel Finler Collection; **54** Ronald Grant Archive; **55** Mary Evans Picture Library; **56** BFI/Shochiku Films Ltd.; **57**T Barry Salt Collection; **57**B Barry Salt Collection; **58** Kevin Brownlow Collection; **60** Ronald Grant Archive/UFA; **63** Ronald Grant Archive; **64** Joel Finler Collection; **65** Kobal Collection /Paramount; **66** Ronald Grant Archive /MGM; **68** Ronald Grant Archive/MGM; **70** Kevin Brownlow Collection; **72** Motion Picture & Television Photo Archive /MPTV.net; **73** Kobal Collection/Ponti-De Laurentiis; **74** Kobal Collection/Roach /Pathé Exchange; **75** BFI/First National Pictures Inc.; **77** Ronald Grant Archive /Buster Keaton Productions; **78** Joel Finler Collection; **80** *The Girl with the Hat Box*, Boris Barnet, Soviet Union, 1927; **81** Kobal Collection; **82**T BFI/Pathé Exchange Inc.; **82**B Robert Flaherty Paper Collection, © The International Film Seminars, The Flaherty /Columbia University Rare Book & Manuscript Library; **84**B Kobal Collection, The/Svensk Filmindustri; **84**T © 1924 AB Svensk Filmindustri; **85**T Lebrecht Collection/Rue des Archives/Lebrecht Music & Arts; **85**B BFI; **87** Joel Finler Collection; **88**T BFI/MGM; **88**C Moviestore Collection/Mirisch/MGM; **88**B Joel Finler Collection; **90** BFI/Dulac /Vandal/Aubert; **92-93** BFI/Films Abel Gance; **94** Kevin Brownlow Collection; **95** Kobal Collection/UFA; **96** Ronald Grant Archive/Decla-Bioscop AG.; **98** BFI /Gainsborough Pictures; **99** Joel Finler Collection; **100** Moviestore Collection /Universum; **102** Ronald Grant Archive /Fox Film; **103** Novosti (London, UK); **104**T BFI/Goskino; **104**B BFI/Goskino; **105**T Ronald Grant Archive/Mosfilm; **105**C Joel Finler Collection; **105**B Joel Finler Collection; **106** *Mother*, Vsevolod I Pudovkin, Soviet Union, 1926; **107** *Arsenal*, Alexander Dovzhenko, USSR, 1930; **108** Eva Riehl/Walter Ruttman; **109** Joel Finler Collection; **110** Ronald Grant Archive; **111** Ronald Grant Archive/Dino De Laurentiis; **112** Joel Finler Collection; **115** Kobal Collection/ Paramount; **116** Kobal Collection/Warner Bros.; **119** George Eastman House/Stills Collection-Motion Picture Department; **121** Kobal Collection/Paramount; **122** BFI/Paramount Publix Corporation; **124** BFI/New Theatres Ltd.; **127** Barry Salt Collection; **128** BFI/Shochiku Films Ltd.; **129** Corbis/Bettmann; **130** *I Was Born, But...*, Yasujiro Ozu, Japan, 1932; **131** BFI/Paradise Films/Unite Trois; **132** BFI/P.C.L. Co. Ltd.; **133** *Osaka Elegy*, Kenji Mizoguchi, Japan, 1936.; **134** Photofest; **135** Joel Finler Collection; **136** Kobal Collection/Universal; **139**T Kobal Collection/Warner Bros./First National; **139**B Ronald Grant Archive/Universal Pictures; **140**T *Scarface Shame of the Nation*, Howard Hawks, USA, 1932; **140**C *Scarface*, Brian De Palma, USA, 1983; **140**B *Scarface*, Brian De Palma, USA, 1983; **141** Ronald Grant Archive/Dog Eat Dog; **142** Joel Finler Collection; **144** Motion Picture & Television Photo Archive/photo by MacJulian/MPTV.net; **145**T Joel Finler Collection; **145**B Ronald Grant Archive /RKO; **146** Ronald Grant Archive/Saticoy Productions; **147** Ronald Grant Archive/ Hal Roach Studios; **148** BFI/MGM; **149** Ronald Grant Archive/Orion Pictures; **150** Ronald Grant Archive/Paramount Pictures; **151** Joel Finler Collection; **152**T BFI /Cinedia; **152**B BFI/Themerson; **153** BFI **154** BFI; **156** BFI/Gaumont British Picture Corporation Ltd.; **157** Chrysalis Image Library/London Film Productions; **158** Ronald Grant Archive/GPO Film Unit; **160** Ronald Grant Archive/Mosfilm; **161** Joel Finler Collection; **163** Ronald Grant Archive/Cine-Alliance; **164** BFI/Paris Film; **165** © Disney Enterprises, Inc.; **166** Photofest/© Disney Enterprises, Inc.; **167** © Disney Enterprises, Inc.; **168**T Moviestore Collection/MGM; **168**C Kobal Collection/MGM; **168**B Moviestore Collection/MGM; **169** *The Wizard of Oz*, Victor Fleming et al, USA, 1939; **171** *Gone with the Wind*, Victor Fleming et Al, USA, 1939; **172** Joel Finler Collection; **173** Joel Finler Collection; **174**BFI /Copacabana Filmes; **175**T *Naniwa Elegy*, Kenji Mizoguchi, Japan, 1936; **175**B *Le Crime de Monsieur Lange*, Jean Renoir, France, 1935; **176** BFI/Alpine Films; **178** *Citizen Kane*, Orson Welles, USA, 1941; **179**T *The Maltese Falcon*, John Huston, USA, 1941; **179**B Joel Finler Collection; **180**T Ronald Grant Archive/Mafilm; **180**B Ronald Grant Archive, The/Warner Bros.; **182** Ronald Grant Archive/Rank/Carlton International; **186** Ronald Grant Archive/DEFA; **189** BFI/Shochiku Films Ltd.; **190** Joel Finler Collection; **192** Joel Finler Collection; **195** Joel Finler Collection; **196** BFI/20th Century-Fox; **197** Kobal Collection/Warner Bros.; **198**T Kobal Collection/RKO; **198**B Ronald Grant Archive/RKO; **199**T *Citizen Kane*, Orson Welles, USA, 1941; **199**B Ronald Grant Archive/20th Century-Fox; **200** *It's a Wonderful Life*, Frank Capra, USA, 1946; **201** Ronald Grant Archive /20th Century Fox; **202** BFI/International Film Circuit; **204** Joel Finler Collection; **205** Joel Finler Collection; **206** BFI /Equipe Moacyr Fenelon; **207** BFI/IPTA Pictures; **208** Photofest; **209**T BFI /Ritwick; **209**B BFI/Atenea Films S.L; **211** Kobal Collection/Ultramar Films; **212** BFI/Daiei Motion Picture Co. Ltd.; **213** BFI/Daiei Motion Picture Co. Ltd.; **214** Ronald Grant Archive /Paramount Pictures; **216** Photofest; **218** Moviestore Collection/Daiei; **219** Ronald Grant Archive/Shochiku Films; **220** *Gate of Hell*, Teinosuke Kinugasa, Japan, 1953; **222** Ronald Grant Archive/Toho Co.; **223** BFI/20th Century Fox; **224** Ronald Grant Archive/20th Century Fox; **226** Kobal Collection/Warner Bros.; **228** Chrysalis Image Library/Columbia Pictures

Corporation/Horizon Pictures; **229** Kobal Collection/Republic Pictures Corporation; **230** BFI/Universal International Pictures; **231** BFI/Clear Blue Sky Productions/John Wells Productions; **232** Moviestore Collection/Mehboob/Eros; **233** *Mother India*, Mehboob, India, 1957; **235** *Paper Flowers*, Guru Dutt, India, 1959; **236** Ronald Grant Archive/Run Run Shaw; **238** Joel Finler Collection/The Satyajit Ray Society/The Ray Family; **239**T The Satyajit Ray Society/The Ray Family; **239**B The Satyajit Ray Society/The Ray Family; **239**C BFI/The Satyajit Ray Society/The Ray Family; **241** BFI/Studios Al Ahram; **243** BFI; **244** Joel Finler Collection; **245**T BFI; **245**B BFI; **246** BFI/Palladium Film; **248** Kobal Collection/Svensk Filmindustri; **249** Joel Finler Collection; **253** Lebrecht Collection/Rue des Archives/Lebrecht Music & Arts; **254**T Ronald Grant Archive /Les Films du Carrosse; **254**B BFI /Documento; **255** BFI; **256** Moviestore Collection/Columbia; **259** Moviestore Collection/Warner Bros.; **260** Ronald Grant Archive/Universal International; **261** Moviestore Collection /Hitchcock/ Paramount; **262** BFI/Florida Films/Oska-Film GmbH; **263** Ronald Grant Archive/Cocinor; **264** BFI/Cini-Tamaris; **266** BFI/Paramount Pictures; **270** Ronald Grant Archive/Imperia; **273** Image France/Raymond Cauchetier; **275** Ronald Grant Archive/Palladium Film; **276** Photofest; **278** Ronald Grant Archive/Lion International; **279** Kobal Collection /Paramount; **280** Ronald Grant Archive /Universal Pictures; **281** Andy Warhol Foundation/© The Andy Warhol Museum, Pittsburgh, A museum of Carnegie Institute. All rights reserved; **282** BFI /Arco Film S.r.l.; **283** Art Archive /Dagli Orti; **285** Ronald Grant Archive /Arco Film; **286** Ronald Grant Archive /Cineriz; **287** Photofest; **288** Ronald Grant Archive/Warner Bros.; **289** Ronald Grant Archive/Titanus; **290**T Ronald Grant Archive/Cineriz; **290**B *La Notte*, Michelangelo Antonioni, Italy, 1961; **291** Kobal Collection/Film 59; **292** Ronald Grant Archive/Film 59; **293** Ronald Grant Archive/Elias Querejeta Producciones; **294** *Persona*, Ingmar Bergman, Sweden, 1966; **296** Photofest; 297 Photofest; **298** Kobal Collection/Woodfall /Associated British; **299** Ronald Grant Archive/Rank/Carlton International; **301** Kobal Collection/Film Polski; **302** Ronald Grant Archive/Paramount Pictures; **303**T Photofest; **303**B Kobal Collection/Mafilm /Mosfilm; **304** Kobal Collection /Ceskoslovensky Film; **305** Kobal Collection/Filmove Studio Barrandov; **306** Ronald Grant Archive/Mosfilm; **308** Kobal Collection/Dovzhenko Films; **309** Ronald Grant Archive/Armenfilm; **310** Ronald Grant Archive/Tianma Film; **311**Photofest; **312** BFI; **313** Kobal Collection/Cuban

State Film; **314** BFI/Studio Golestan; **315** BFI; **317** Kobal Collection/Infrakino Film; **319** Kobal Collection; **320** Ronald Grant Archive/Saticoy Productions; **322** Ronald Grant Archive/Warner Bros.; **323** Ronald Grant Archive/Warner Bros.; **324-5** Photofest; **328** Ronald Grant Archive /Columbia Pictures; **331** Kobal Collection /PEA/Artistes Associes; **332** Kobal Collection/Pegaso/Italnoleggio /Praesidens/Eichberg; **333**T Kobal Collection/Mars/Marianne/Maran; **333**B Kobal Collection/Paramount; **334** Kobal Collection/Prod Europee Asso/Prods Artistes Association; **335** Kobal Collection /Universal; **336** Ronald Grant Archive /20th Century Fox; **338** Ronald Grant Archive/Paramount Pictures; **339** Ronald Grant Archive/Warner Bros.; **340** Kobal Collection/United Artists; **342** Ronald Grant Archive/Winger; **343** Kobal Collection/YEAH; **344** Kobal Collection /United Artists; **345** Photofest; **346-7** Kobal Collection/United Artists; **348** Kobal Collection/Columbia; **349** Kobal Collection/ABC/Allied Artists; **350** Photofest; **351**Ronald Grant Archive /Paramount Pictures; **354** Ronald Grant Archive/Tango Film; **355**T Kobal Collection /Universal; **355**B Kobal Collection /Filmverlag der Autoren; **356** Ronald Grant Archive/Helma Sanders-Brahms Filmproduktion; **357** Ronald Grant Archive /Werner Herzog Filmproduktion; **358** Ronald Grant Archive/Kestrel Films; **359** *Women in Love*, Ken Russell, UK, 1969; **360** Ronald Grant Archive/Cinegate; **361** Ronald Grant Archive/Warner Bros.; **362** Ronald Grant Archive/20th Century Fox; **363** Ronald Grant Archive, The/Picnic Productions Pty.; **365** Ronald Grant Archive/Golden Harvest Company; **366** BFI/International Film Company; **367** Ronald Grant Archive/G P Sippy; **370** BFI/Cinegrit; **371** BFI; **372** Ronald Grant Archive/Films Domireew; **373** BFI/Halle Gerima; **374** Photofest; **375** Ronald Grant Archive; **379** Ronald Grant Archive/Warner Bros.; **380** Ronald Grant Archive/Universal Pictures; **383** Kobal Collection/Lucas Film/20th Century Fox; **384** Ronald Grant Archive/Toho; **386** Kobal Collection/United Artists; **388** BFI/Anglo International Films; **390** Kobal Collection/United Artists; **391** Moviestore Collection/Chartoff-Winkler/UA; **392** Photofest; **393** Kobal Collection /Universal; **394** Kobal Collection /Paramount; **395**T Kobal Collection/De Laurentiis; **395**B Ronald Grant Archive/De Laurentiis; **396** BFI/CIBY 2000/New Line Cinema; **398** Kobal Collection /Warner Bros.; **399** Ronald Grant Archive /Paramount Pictures; **400** BFI/Anabasis N.V./Carolco Entertainment; **401** BFI; **402-3** Ronald Grant Archive/Toho; **403** HoriPro Inc./© Kurosawa Production Inc. Licensed exclusively by HoriPro Inc.; **404**

BFI/Higashi Productions; **405** Ronald Grant Archive/Imamura Productions; **406** BFI; **407** Ronald Grant Archive/Les Films Galaxie/Studio Canal +; **408** Corbis /Camboulive Patrick; **409** Photofest; **410** Ronald Grant Archive/El Deseo S.A.; **411**T Ronald Grant Archive/STV/NFFC; **411**B Ronald Grant Archive/Goldcrest Films; **412** Kobal Collection/Working Title/ Channel 4; **413** Ronald Grant Archive/BFI /C4; **414** *Young at Heart*, Gordon Douglas, USA, 1954; **415** Ronald Grant Archive/Kennedy Miller Productions; **416** Ronald Grant Archive/Brooksfilms; **417** Photofest; **420** Ronald Grant Archive /Guangxi Film Studio; **421** Ronald Grant Archive/Artificial Eye; **422** Ronald Grant Archive/Mosfilm; **423** Ronald Grant Archive/Mosfilm; **424** Kobal Collection /Film Polski; **426-7** Ronald Grant Archive /MK2; **429** BFI/Baobab Films; **430** BFI/ California Newsreel; **432** Ronald Grant Archive/Les Films Soleil; **435** Kobal Collection/Globo Films; **436** Ronald Grant Archive/Maria Moreno P.C.; **438** BFI/The Institute for the Intellectual Development of Children and Young Adults; **439** Ronald Grant Archive/IIDCYA; **440** Kobal Collection/Farabi Cinema/Kiarostami; **441**Kobal Collection/MK2/ Abbas Kiarostami Prod; **443** Moviestore Collection/Bac/Wildbunch/Makhmalbaf; **444** Photofest; **445** Photofest; **446** Photofest; **448** Goodfellas, Martin Scorsese, USA, 1990; **449** Ronald Grant Archive; **450** Moviestore Collection/A Band Apart/Jersey /Miramax; **452**T Ronald Grant Archive/Warner Bros.; **452**B Ronald Grant Archive/Warner Bros.; **455** Ronald Grant Archive/New Line Cinema; **456**T Moviestore Collection/Carolco; **456**B Kobal Collection/MGM; **457** Kobal Collection/Dreamworks/Universal; **459** *The Matrix*, Andy Wachowski Larry Wachowski, USA, 1999; **460** Moviestore Collection/Groucho/Silver Pictures/Village /Warner Bros.; **462** Kobal Collection /Zentropa Ents.**463** Ronald Grant Archive /Le Studio Canal +; **464** *Funny Games*, Michael Haneke, Austria/Switzerland, 1997; **465** Photofest; **467** Ronald Grant Archive/C4; **469** Ronald Grant Archive/In-Gear Film/Golden Network; **470** Photofest; **471** BFI/Central Motions Picture Corporation; **472** BFI; **474** Ronald Grant Archive/Kaijyu Theatre/Toshiba-EMI K.K.; **475** Moviestore Collection /Kadokawa Shoten/Omega; **476** Kobal Collection/Kadokawa Shoten; **477** Photofest; **478** Photofest; **479** Moviestore Collection/Cinetelefilms/Mat Films/Capitol Films; **480** Photofest; **482** Photofest; **483** Photofest; **486** Moviestore Collection/Egoli Tossell Film /Fora Film/Hermitage Films/Artificial Eye; **490** Ronald Grant Archive, The/Hal Roach; **491**T Photofest; **491**B Kobal Collection/Satyajit Ray Films.

ACKNOWLEDGMENTS

The Story of Film
© Pavilion Books, 2004
Design © Pavilion Books, 2004
Text © Mark Cousins, 2004

Published in the United States by
Thunder's Mouth Press
An Imprint of Avalon Publishing Group
Incorporated
245 W. 17th Street
11th Floor
New York, NY 10011

Library of Congress Control Number:
2004107524

ISBN: 1-56025-612-5

9 8 7 6 5 4 3 2 1

Design: Jason Godfrey @ Godfrey Design
Colour reproduction: Anorax Imaging Ltd,
England
Printer: Imago, Singapore
Distributed by Publishers Group West

The Story of Film has its origins in an article about my TV series *Scene by Scene*, commissioned by Ruth Metzstein for London's *Independent on Sunday*. In it, I wrote that there is no accessible, single-volume history of world cinema for intelligent general readers. Vivien James at Pavilion asked me twice to write such a book, so what you have before you was as much her idea as mine.

Thereafter, many people were involved. My peerless agent Caroline Chignell at PBJ management taught me so much about the world of books. Lizzy Gray, my editor, was central to the project, her dedication driving it throughout. Picture researcher Zoë Holtermann presented us with a treasure trove of images and found her way through the labyrinth of their permissions. She was adeptly helped by Jamie Dikomite and Tim Wright. When the exact picture was not available, Andrew Borthwick expertly sourced and burnt screen grabs. Tony Rayns generously provided tapes for the latter. Alexander Ballinger helped standardize the film titles and iron out inconsistencies.

After I delivered the manuscript, Pavilion's Kate Oldfield imaginatively squired it to its present state. Her overview was invaluable and I benefited from it. Designer Jason Godfrey presented the material with clarity and grace. Roger Hudson was a lucid, talented and tough editorial eye. David Parkinson was tougher still and his detailed comments improved this book. I appreciate, too, the wise responses of Kevin Macdonald, Walter Donohoe and Professor Grahame Smith. I would also like to thank the publishing team behind the scenes: Richard Quinn and Marcus Leaver. Thank you, also, Stuart Cooper. Phil at The Kobal Collection and Martin at The Ronald Grant Archive provided many of the wonderful images in the book.

GLM was with me throughout this project. Her vitality fuels mine.

Mark Cousins, Edinburgh, 2004